D1302566

COURTAULDS

AN ECONOMIC AND SOCIAL HISTORY

SAMUEL COURTAULD III (1793–1881), in old age

D. C. COLEMAN

COURTAULDS

AN ECONOMIC AND
SOCIAL HISTORY

I

THE NINETEENTH CENTURY
SILK AND CRAPE

THE ANGUS L. MacDONALD LIBRARY
ST. FRANCIS XAVIER UNIVERSITY
ANTIGONISH, N. S.

OXFORD
AT THE CLARENDON PRESS
1969

HD
9929
.2
G74
C68
v. 1

Oxford University Press, Ely House, London W. 1

GLASGOW NEW YORK TORONTO MELBOURNE WELLINGTON
CAPE TOWN SALISBURY IBADAN NAIROBI LUSAKA ADDIS ABABA
BOMBAY CALCUTTA MADRAS KARACHI LAHORE DACCA
KUALA LUMPUR SINGAPORE HONG KONG TOKYO

© COURTAULDS LTD. 1969

PRINTED IN GREAT BRITAIN

114639

For A., more . . .

PREFACE

'Resolved: that all such letter books of the predecessors of this Company anterior to the formation of this Company and all such account, sales and other books up to and inclusive of the year 1914 as Mr. Bell may select, be destroyed.'

Courtaulds Ltd.: Board minute, 10 March 1921

CERTAIN facts about this work must be made clear at the outset. First, it is the result of a commission. Second, it is a history of the firm up to 1941 and not thereafter. Third, it was conceived as an academic study and is intended to be a contribution not to popular mythology but to economic history. Fourth, the responsibility for the published text is mine: Courtaulds Ltd., as the commissioners of the work, have censored neither the arguments which I have used nor the criticisms which I have made.

This is not the first history of the company. *A History of Courtaulds* by C. H. Ward-Jackson was published, for private circulation, in 1941. Mr. Ward-Jackson—who kindly passed on to me many useful notes which he had made at that time—was, however, given only very restricted access to the company's records. This was particularly true in respect of the voluminous records which exist for the years after the date of the cheerless Board minute quoted above. Shortly after the end of the Second World War efforts were made to commission a more detailed history but these proved abortive. In 1956 there was set up in the company a committee—called the History Working Committee—under the chairmanship of Mr. A. H. (now Sir Alan) Wilson. Its task was to examine certain economic and technical aspects of the company's development. Information was collected on various questions; and eventually Sir Alan drafted some chapters on the early years of the rayon industry and Samuel Courtauld & Co.'s participation therein. Ultimately, it was decided that the task of writing the company's history should be entrusted to a professional historian. I would like here to record my gratitude to Sir Alan Wilson for having handed on to me the draft chapters which he wrote as well as a variety of useful information assembled in connexion therewith. After discussions in the latter part of 1961, my own work on this history formally started on 1 January 1962.

The destruction sanctioned by the 1921 resolution, quoted above, and the normal inroads of damp, rats, and fire have ensured a patchy survival of records from the period with which Volume I is largely concerned. Some accounts but very little head office correspondence have survived from the nineteenth century; until 1893 there is no detailed or statistical information on sales and markets. On the other hand, a substantial amount of material, including production data, was found at the company's older textile mills. Much of this has been deposited at the Essex County Record Office (see note on Sources, p. xxi) and is now available for further research. During the period of Volume I the company was very much a family business, and thus susceptible to historical investigation through the medium of family correspondence. Here I am very grateful to Mr. George Courtauld V both for giving his support to this work as a whole and for making available to me many unpublished family letters and papers. For the years covered by Volume II much more has survived. After 1930 the bulk is formidable, despite some losses from air-raid damage during the Second World War. Before 1930 the pattern of survival is rather uneven though far more has remained from before 1914 than might have been thought from the terms of the 1921 Board minute. The papers of individual directors have proved especially useful as a means of interpreting the formal proceedings recorded in Board or committee minutes. By no means all of such papers have survived; for the years after 1920, however, the retention of virtually the complete business correspondence of Samuel Courtauld IV and Sir John Hanbury-Williams has provided an indispensable source. In this context of directors' papers I would like to record my thanks to Mr. H. L. Johnson. Not only did he give me much valuable help on technical matters but he also made available to me many letters and papers, business and private, both of his own and of his father.

Complete and unrestricted access to all records relevant to the period covered is a vital prerequisite to a history of this kind. This I have had. Businessmen, like statesmen, both blunder and triumph. If business history is to lay claim to serious regard it must include analysis of loss as well as gain, of mistakes along with victories. The author of such a work must be free to express responsible judgement upon the firm's achievement. Because it was agreed, during the preliminary discussions, that this was to be an objective history, 'warts and all', I have enjoyed this freedom and exercised it. In reaching agreement to permit of such an approach the problem of the terminal date of the history has obviously to be solved. Too often in the past it has been solved, in this country at least, by ending the effective history at the First World War; or by ensuring that any chapters which covered subsequent years were little more than bland narratives of events. A terminal date too close to the present can be patently undesirable. Historical judgement on very recent developments may be extremely difficult; and if adverse may be inimical to the current functioning of the business. The date at which this study is brought to an end seems to meet both these dangers. The onset of the Second World War created a sufficiently new situation to mark a turning-point in the company's history. I have not indeed examined any of the immediate effects of the war on production, sales, or general policy. Their history properly belongs to a third volume. One war-time event only has been treated in detail: the enforced sale of Courtaulds' subsidiary in the U.S.A., the American Viscose Corporation. The loss of this in 1941, perhaps even more effectively than the outbreak of the war itself, marked the end of an era in the company's history. The era which followed was initially part of the longer war-time and post-war phase. The sale itself, though not its aftermath, properly belongs to these volumes, and thus it ends them.

As every economic historian knows, his craft is always liable to attack on two flanks. If he takes heed of the economist, then the orthodox historian will complain of him that his work is too theoretical or prone to unsupported generalizations; is weighed down by statistics and made incomprehensible with jargon; and, because of its obsession with trends and patterns of development, that it ignores the individual and reduces the force of the human spirit to a point on a graph. Conversely, if he is more disposed to the ways of thought of the historian, then the economist will complain that the resulting economic history is inadequately based upon economic theory; that it lacks the precision which can be given by the use of sound statistics and properly constructed economic models; and that, because of its excessive concern with the individual, it fails to reveal the true economic function of the phenomena under examination. If the economic historian tackles the task of writing a commissioned business history, he adds to these hazards of his craft a further peril. His work is then open to the suspicion that it is conditioned by the simple maxim: he who pays the piper calls the tune.

The precautions taken against this last hazard have already been indicated. Those to whom such a work as this is simply a piece of capitalist apologetics will doubtless remain unconvinced, and little that I can say is likely to convince them of its objectivity. Of others I would ask simply that they judge by what they read. To the more general problem my approach has been eclectic. I have not set out to reconcile the sometimes conflicting approaches of the economist and the historian—if only because I am not sure that they are ultimately reconcilable. The quantifiable aspects of this history have, however, been presented in statistical form, thus to give them some precision; and the simpler tools of economic analysis have been used as a method of dealing with certain problems. In contrast, a good deal of attention has been paid to the character and performance of leading figures of the firm, to the influence exercised by their attitudes of mind upon the company's reaction to external stimuli; and to the social context of their activities. The particular mixture will not please everybody. All I would claim of it is that it attempts to present, in the context of wider economic relationships, the development of a big firm as an example of human endeavour, with some small part at least of the infinite complexity which such endeavour implies.

These two volumes have been prepared and written during the course of my normal work as a university teacher. The text of the first volume was completed in 1965; that of the second at the end of 1967. They are the product neither of a team of assistants nor of a computer. Nevertheless, in the course of six years I have had the incidental help of a great many people. Were I to thank them all by name the roll call would cover a couple of pages or more and still I would not be certain that there had been no omissions. However churlish it may seem, I have decided to eschew the pleasure of thus extinguishing my debts of gratitude. Those who helped me were various indeed: colleagues at the London School of Economics and elsewhere in the university world; archivists and librarians; past and present employees of Courtaulds Ltd. or subsidiary companies; members of families in some way or at some time connected with the firm; businessmen and trade unionists; directors and accountants, managers and chemists. They have included the humble as well as the eminent, the outspoken along with the cautious. I thank them all. I would like also to thank those who, at the Clarendon Press, Oxford, did so much to ease the process of publication. Some help has been of a highly specific kind. Without technical advice I would not have been able to understand the significance of various processes; without the assistance of certain persons or firms I would not have been able to consult records in their possession; without some research assistance on specific problems my task would have taken much longer. My thanks to those who have helped in these ways has normally been recorded at appropriate places in the footnotes to the text.

A history of a functioning business necessarily requires the permission and co-operation of the company's directors. I am grateful to Sir Frank Kearton, Chairman of Courtaulds Ltd., and his colleagues on the Board not only for their sanction which made this history possible but also for their co-operation in furthering my work.

There remains a particular debt which I owe to four persons who, in very varied ways, have been concerned with this project ever since it started. Had it not been for the kindness of Professor Richard Sayers I would never have written these volumes; Mr. H. R. Mathys, Deputy-Chairman of Courtaulds Ltd., has provided the warm and continuous support without which enterprises of this sort can never succeed; and Mr. Miles Pitts-Tucker, who was Courtaulds' public relations officer during the greater part of the time whilst this history was being prepared, opened doors and removed obstacles with a bonhomie which was as irresistible as it was unflagging. Finally, I wish to record my especial gratitude to Miss Bernardine Gregory, whose devoted help as research assistant and secretary throughout, has been wholly invaluable.

D. C. C.

London and Cavendish
1962–8

CONTENTS

VOLUME I

LIST OF GRAPHS, MAPS, AND DIAGRAMS

LIST OF PLATES

LIST OF TABLES IN THE TEXT

SOURCES

MOST of the sources which have been used in the compilation of this volume are indicated in the footnotes to the text and in the list of abbreviations given below. There are, however, certain exceptions to this.

In 1964 Courtaulds Ltd. agreed to deposit the firm's early records at the Essex County Record Office (E.R.O. Catalogue reference: D/F 3). This collection of deposited records comprises the bulk of what had survived, both in the London office and at the Company's mills in Essex, and which appertained to the period covered by this volume. Excluded from it, however, are two main categories of documents:

(a) All Head Office documents from 1891 onwards, i.e. from the time when the business first became a joint-stock company. These include Board Minutes, Letter Books, salary books, etc.

(b) Documents from the mills which though starting within the period of this volume continue into the present century significantly after 1904. These include certain registers of employees, reports to the main board from the mills, note books and letter books of mill managers, etc.

As records in these two categories are not available for public use there are no footnote references to these sources.

ABBREVIATIONS

B.P. British Patent.

B.P.P. British Parliamentary Papers.

C.F.L. [S. A. Courtauld, ed.], *Courtauld Family Letters, 1782–1900* (7 vols., Cambridge, 1916).

Courtauld MSS. Letters in the possession of members of the Courtauld family. A selection of these letters is due to be published in Vol. II of *The Huguenot Family of Courtauld* (ed. S. L. Courtauld).

D.N.B. *Dictionary of National Biography.*

Econ. Hist. Rev. *Economic History Review.*

E.R.O. Essex County Record Office.

G.C.B. [S. A. Courtauld], *George Courtauld: A Biography* (London, 1922, printed for private circulation).

Hist. Tech. [C. Singer, E. J. Holmyard, A. R. Hall, T. I. Williams, eds.], *A History of Technology* (5 vols., Oxford, 1954–8).

Mitchell & Deane. B. R. Mitchell and P. Deane, *Abstract of British Historical Statistics* (Cambridge, 1962).

P.R.O. Public Record Office.

Report of the Proceedings . . . *Report of the Proceedings of a Public Dinner given to S. Courtauld, Taylors & Courtauld by their Workpeople* (Chelmsford, 1846).

Taylor. P. A. Taylor, *Some Account of the Taylor Family* (London, privately printed, 1875).

Ward-Jackson. C. H. Ward-Jackson, *A History of Courtaulds* (London, 1941).

Warner. Sir Frank Warner, *The Silk Industry of the United Kingdom: its Origin and Development* (London, 1921).

Some first names have been repeated in the Courtauld family for several generations. Whenever any doubt might arise on which Augustin or George or Samuel is in question, I have added numbers, viz. Samuel III, George Courtauld II, etc. The system of numbering is that used by the late Sir Stephen Courtauld in his *The Huguenot Family of Courtauld*, and it can be seen in the family trees, Figs. 1, 4, 17, and 25 in Vol. I, and Fig. 9 in Vol. II. In the footnotes equivalent abbreviations have been used, viz. S.C. III, G.C. II, etc.

PART I

CHAPTER I

Huguenots and Silversmiths

I

A<small>T</small> the end of 1819 young Samuel Courtauld III, at the age of 26, was just managing to keep his small silk business alive, with the aid of capital and credit from friends, relatives, and obliging bankers. Sixty-two years later he died, leaving a fortune of nearly £700,000. For the preceding ten years, simply from his share as senior partner in the business, and wholly apart from his other investments, he had drawn an average income of £46,000 a year, representing an average return on his capital of 35 per cent. per annum.

From these bare testimonies to successful money-making it is not difficult to move on to the customary picture of the determined tycoon, resolute from his youth, bold and far-sighted in his deeds. Such a picture would be, largely though not wholly, wrong. The creation of Samuel Courtauld & Co., out of which ultimately emerged Courtaulds Ltd., was at once more complex and more interesting than any simple-minded Samuel Smiles epic can suggest. Before going on to examine in some detail these textile achievements of the grandson of a London silversmith, it is necessary first to consider two things: the early history of the Courtauld family; and the nature of the English silk industry at the time of the Industrial Revolution.

II

The Courtaulds came from France. In the later sixteenth century, which is as early as diligent family inquiry has traced the family name, they were living on the small island of Oléron, just off the French coast near

La Rochelle.[1] A document of 1584 mentions a Christophe Courtauld, described as *marinier*. Like many of his contemporaries, he was unable to write. But this family of seamen and small traders, linked by marriage ties to others of similar occupations and status, was gradually moving upwards in the social and economic scale. Though Christophe had to make his mark his son Augustin I had learned to write; and the witnesses to the marriage contract of his grandson Augustin II in 1619—a local judge, a lawyer, and four merchants—suggest some further elevation in status. Confirmation of material ascent comes from scraps of evidence about the next generation in the person of Pierre II who, in an inventory of his property made in 1677, was described as 'Sieur Pierre Courtauld, marchand'. His success had brought him into the possession of such local property as a vineyard, land, and houses. Some of this passed, in turn, to his son, Augustin IV, on the occasion of the latter's marriage in 1677 to Julie Giraud, daughter of a local merchant and master tailor.

Augustin IV emigrated to England. He came for the same sad reason that has shifted so many people from country to country: religious intolerance. Precisely when the Courtauld family were converted from the Roman Catholic faith to the Protestant faith is not known, though certainly the marriage contract of Christophe's daughter Anne, dated 1594, shows that she was to be married in the reformed church. The Ile d'Oléron and the neighbouring Ile de Ré had come, in the seventeenth century, to form part of a general stronghold of Huguenots centred on La Rochelle and the surrounding area; about a fifth of the total population was said to be Protestant. Huguenot merchants, amongst whom were probably the Courtaulds, dominated the local wine, salt, and coasting trade.[2] Periods of alternating violence and peace, of limited tolerance and unlimited intolerance, stretched from the bloody and bitter religious wars of the sixteenth century, through the hopeful Edict of Nantes of 1598, the hostility of Richelieu in the 1620's, to the final onslaught of violent persecution of which the central feature was the revocation of the Edict of Nantes in October 1685. In order to be free from further restrictions and harrying the main possibilities now open to Huguenots were abjuration and/or flight. Perhaps two hundred thousand fled,[3] amongst them many pros-

[1] The genealogical information about the Courtauld family used in this chapter is largely derived from S. L. Courtauld, *The Huguenot Family of Courtauld*, vol. i (privately printed, London, 1957), and J. L. Chester, *Some Earlier History of the Family of Courtauld* (printed for private circulation, London, 1911).

[2] W. C. Scoville, *The Persecution of Huguenots and French Economic Development, 1680–1720* (California, 1960), pp. 9–10, 56, 133, 135–6.   [3] Ibid., pp. 119–20.

perous merchants and financiers as well as craftsmen and artisans; their arrival in Holland, England, Brandenburg, Switzerland, and elsewhere enriched the industrial and commercial life of those countries as it impoverished that of France.

Pierre II, at the age of 65, was too old for the perils of illegal flight, so he abjured and stayed. Augustin IV abjured but did not stay. He left for England at some date between 28 September 1685, when both he and his father signed the same abjuration document, and 10 March 1689, when he remarried at the French Church in Glasshouse Street, London. His first wife, who had died some time between November 1685 and January 1687, was succeeded by another Huguenot, Esther Pothier, also a refugee from the La Rochelle area. The only surviving son of the first marriage, Augustin VI, also crossed the Channel, joining his father in London some time between 1687 and 1700. With this move the transference of the main branch of the Courtauld family to English soil was complete.

The immigrant naturally seeks to pursue the calling with which he is familiar. So it is hardly surprising to find Augustin IV, who was naturalized in 1696, described as a merchant in 1690 and, more specifically, as a wine-cooper in 1701 and a vintner in 1705. A merchant who came from so near to Bordeaux can scarcely have failed to detect the likely profitability of selling wine in a country where the substantial thirst of the upper classes for claret was matched only by that for port and madeira. It was perhaps less immediately obvious why both his sons, Augustin VI and Peter, born 10 January 1690, should have been apprenticed to the wholly different trade of goldsmith. The answer probably lies partly in the chance fact of personal acquaintanceship within not only the separated Huguenot colony in London but also that particular stratum of small merchants and skilled craftsmen in which the Courtaulds now moved. For it was to a fellow Huguenot, Simon Pantin, that both Augustin VI and Peter were apprenticed, the former in 1701, the latter in 1705. But it may also have owed something to the discernment by Augustin IV that whilst the French wine trade was being pushed into the dangerous underworld of smuggling, the work of the gold- and silver-smith—well represented amongst the Huguenot immigrants—was equally likely to be in demand by the prosperous English middle and upper classes. For their fashions were already much influenced by things French and their growing wealth was being made manifest in the quickening pace of conspicuous display.

The main achievements of the Courtaulds as gold- and silver-smiths lay in the work of Augustin VI and, to a lesser extent, in that of his son,

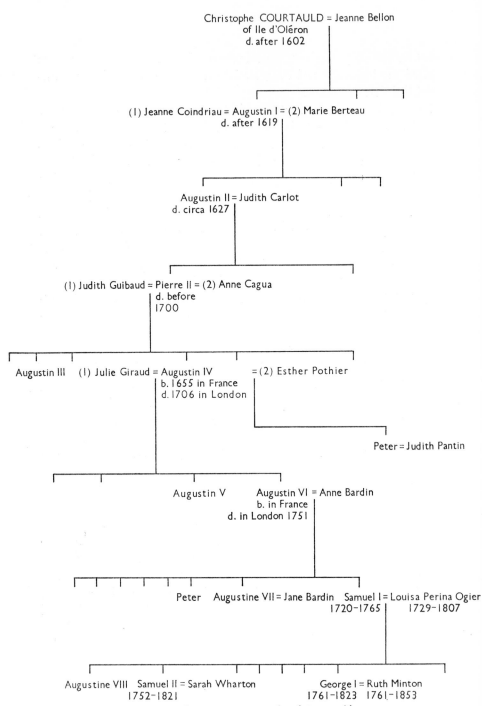

FIG. I. *The Huguenot Family of Courtauld*

PLATE 1

AUGUSTIN COURTAULD VI (*c.* 1686–1751)

Samuel I.[1] Peter's life was short. He completed his apprenticeship, was admitted a freeman of the Goldsmiths Company of London in 1712, registered two marks at Goldsmiths Hall in 1721, when he was established in Litchfield Street, Soho, and died in 1729. No work by him has been identified; nor is anything known of another Peter, possibly his son, who in 1751 was described as a jeweller. Augustin VI, meanwhile, had moved into the upper ranks of his trade. Made a freeman of the Goldsmiths Company after the completion of his apprenticeship in 1708, he went to live and work in Church Street, near St. Martin's Lane, moving later to Chandos Street nearby, where he was in 1729; he died, aged 65, in 1751. One or another of his four marks appear on a fair number of surviving silver pieces, which pay tribute, if not to any great originality, at least to sound and sometimes very fine craftsmanship. His range was wide, including domestic and ecclesiastical plate as well as the State salt of 1730–1 at the Mansion House and a silver tea-table of 1742–3 which was bought by the Empress of Russia. Samuel I, after apprenticeship to his father in 1734–41 and subsequent election to the freedom of the Goldsmiths Company, set up shop as goldsmith and jeweller first at Chandos Street and then later in Cornhill, near the Royal Exchange. His work continued in his father's tradition though branching out also into florid rococo ornamentation. But his years were fewer and his output smaller: he died at the early age of 45 in 1765, two years after having been made a liveryman of the Goldsmiths Company. The business passed into the hands of his widow, Louisa Perina Courtauld, who carried it on first under her own name, until 1768, then in partnership with George Cowles until 1777, and finally with her son Samuel II until 1780, when it was sold. Silver work, competent but undistinguished, from each of these periods has been identified. It was the last phase of the Courtaulds in this trade: Samuel II migrated to America, where he pursued, without any very striking success, a career as a merchant, dying there in 1821;[2] Louisa Perina lived on to die in London in 1807; and her other children moved into a world different in economic interest and no longer dominated by Huguenot connexions.

For most of the eighteenth century, the Courtauld family established in this country had remained, at least in its main line, at the centre of two interlocking economic and social circles: it had remained in the middle

[1] See E. Alfred Jones, *Some Silver Wrought by the Courtauld Family* (privately printed, Oxford, 1940), and Joan Evans, 'Huguenot Goldsmiths in England and Ireland', *Proceedings of the Huguenot Society of London*, vol. xiv, pp. 496–554.

[2] He was described by his brother George I in 1815 as being 'low in pocket', and as having been 'a kind of itinerant merchant'—Courtauld MSS.: G.C. I to S.C. III, 11 July 1815.

ranks of the London *bourgeoisie* and it had remained firmly embedded in the nexus of Huguenot families of similar status. Throughout the period, the Courtaulds were working goldsmiths, employing journeymen and apprentices. There is no support for the too-easily made assumption that because they were goldsmiths they were likely to be bankers. The successful goldsmith banks, such as Hoare's or Child's, Gosling's or Martin's, had shed their goldsmithery by the second or third decades of the century.[1] As small goldsmith bankers were notoriously unstable at that time and as the Courtaulds survived as working goldsmiths for three generations it seems unlikely that they did more than add, as was commonly done, a certain amount of pawnbroking and diamond dealing to their gold and silver work. The solid but moderate prosperity which they attained never took them into the ranks of the landowning gentry, with its habits of primogeniture and strict settlement. So by following the practice, common to the French and the English urban middle class, of equal division amongst heirs, their gains were evenly spread; no large capitals were accumulated, no richly endowed daughters dangled before the socially elevated. Most of Augustin VI's wealth was probably in his house and his stock in trade; he may have had some investments in Government securities, 'The Funds', as they were then known, he had none in Bank of England stock, though he did hold £500 of East India stock from 1732 to 1739 and £1,000 thereafter until his death.[2] The portion which he gave to two of his daughters—£400—was typically the sort of sum given by substantial yeomen; and the gifts or bequests of identical sums to his other three children, each also left one-fifth part of his estate at death, was a procedure commonly followed in other generations and in similar and related families.[3]

For the three generations of Augustin IV, Augustin VI, and Samuel I, those related families were entirely Huguenot. Peter was apprenticed to

---

[1] D. M. Joslin, 'London Private Bankers, 1720–85', *Econ. Hist. Rev.*, 2nd series, vol. vii, No. 2, 1954.   [2] Bank of England Record Office: East India Company stock ledgers.

[3] The book by J. L. Chester has a number of misleading historical comparisons which combine to give an inaccurate impression of the social and economic status of the family in the eighteenth century. In this context a word should perhaps be said about certain of the early family portraits. That of Augustin VI reproduced in the books by Chester, S. L. Courtauld, and Jones certainly looks a likely portrait of a successful early eighteenth-century goldsmith; but the additional and very fancy portrait, bought by a member of the family in 1913, also alleged to be of Augustin VI, and reproduced only in Jones, seems thoroughly unlikely. Then there is the portrait of Louisa Perina attributed to Zoffany. The story related in S. L. Courtauld, op. cit., pp. 82–84, of another portrait by Zoffany painted in lieu of rent owed, not only lends support to the attribution but also suggests that not too much in the way of social significance should be read into the possession of a portrait by so distinguished and fashionable a painter.

one goldsmith Pantin and married the daughter of another goldsmith Pantin; the families of Bardin, Goujon, Jacob, and Ogier provided more brides or bridegrooms for the Courtaulds; and the Huguenot settlements and their churches in Soho, Westminster, and Chelsea were the scenes alike of baptisms, marriages, and burials. John Jacob, who married Anne Courtauld in 1738, was yet another Huguenot goldsmith; and even George Cowles, the working goldsmith whom Louisa Perina took in as a partner after her husband's death and who hardly sounds a Huguenot, was in fact a nephew by marriage. Samuel I's marriage to Louisa Perina Ogier fell within the general pattern, but it did provide one significant variation: it linked a representative of the Huguenot settlement in the western end of London to its counterpart in the eastern end—Spitalfields. For Louisa Perina was the daughter of a silk weaver.

The manufacture of paper and textiles, of hats and glass, the trades of goldsmith and jeweller, and the sundry doings comprehensively labelled commerce and finance: these and like activities absorbed most of the 40,000 or so Huguenots who came to England. They went to Norwich and Canterbury, Southampton, London, and elsewhere, but probably the best known of all their settlements was that in Spitalfields. England had its silk industry and Spitalfields its textile workers before the Huguenots came; but among the results of their arrival was the stimulation of English silk manufacture and the filling up of this area of eastern London with a substantial colony of interrelated Huguenot families. Their wealth and status varied from master weavers or throwsters employing large numbers of journeymen to humbler men working at their own looms. The Ogier family, who came from Poitou at the beginning of the eighteenth century, apparently belonged to the former group, at least by the 1720s, when Peter Abraham Ogier was living in the 'rich' weavers' area of Corbet Court, Spitalfields. Other members of the family also settled in the district and by the 1740s there were several Ogiers living and working in Spital Square and Princes Street. The family expanded and ramified as the silk industry grew: by business partnerships or family relationships it was soon linked with a score of other Huguenot families, with Bigot, Byas, and Courtauld, with Godin and Grellier, Mazé and Merzeau, and more besides.[1]

---

[1] N. K. A. Rothstein, 'The Silk Industry in London, 1702–66' (unpublished London University M.A. thesis, 1961).

Giles Godin and Françoise Catherine Merzeau were godparents to Louisa Perina Courtauld's daughter Catherine, born April 1760; and Louisa Perina in turn stood as one of the sponsors to Louise, daughter of Pierre Merzeau and M. C. Mazé, in April 1777. Chester, op. cit., p. 58.

In 1777 when Louisa Perina took her eldest son Samuel II into partner-ship in the Courtauld family business, he was 25. The three brief years of the partnership, the subsequent sale of the business, and the migration of Samuel II across the Atlantic, all combine to suggest some disenchant-ment with the silversmith's trade. It is not perhaps surprising that when Louisa Perina came to the task of deciding upon a vocation for her other surviving son, George I, the seventh of her eight children, she should have turned to her own family trade and its connexions. In the 1770s the silk business was booming. So in 1775, at the age of 14, young George was apprenticed to Peter Merzeau, silk throwster of Spitalfields. With this move, and with the subsequent and diverse activities of that most im-probable of businessmen, George Courtauld I, the family were on their way to making their début in the silk industry.

CHAPTER II

The English Silk Industry

I

SILK was for long an exotic luxury to the English. Lustrous to the eye, soft to the touch, and high in price, silk fabrics, here as elsewhere, symbolized wealth and power. They were often the subject of medieval sumptuary laws; and disapproving commentators could always be found to sniff at 'silks and wines with all such like kinds of wares which be here only things of superfluity for the richer sort of men to bestow their money upon'.[1] Such sentiments, of which this expression belongs to 1549, were given plenty of economic stiffening by the fact that these silks were not in any significant quantity the product of native skill and capital, but had instead to be imported. And in practice, whatever the views of moralists, English Governments made many, though rather haphazard, efforts to encourage the growth of silk manufacture in this country. For the establishment of the industry here was seen as potentially productive of a trio of useful things: lessening our bill for imports; striking a blow at France, from whom at that time we bought most of our silks and whose power, so Burghley observed in 1581, 'England ought not to increase';[2] and creating employment for the poor. These efforts achieved little until Protestant refugee artisans from the continent of Europe—who came in two main waves, in the late sixteenth and in the later seventeenth centuries—brought technical know-how to a struggling English silk industry. Silk weaving of some sort had been going on in London from the fourteenth century, but little in the way of an organized silk industry appeared until three hundred years later. A company of silk throwsters was incorporated in London in 1629; and amongst James I's efforts to promote the industry was an instruction to the Lords-Lieutenant of counties to encourage the planting of mulberry trees.[3]

[1] Quoted in R. H. Tawney and E. Power, *Tudor Economic Documents* (London, 1951), vol. iii, p. 343.

[2] Ibid., vol. ii, p. 124.

[3] E. Lipson, *Economic History of England* (4th ed., London, 1947), vol. ii, p. 100.

This rare, and fruitless, exhortation serves to focus attention upon a long continuing problem of the English silk industry—the nature and origins of its raw material and its consequent difficulties in competing with foreign producers who had more immediate access to that material. For even after it had vastly improved its techniques and was in its greatest period of expansion, in the eighteenth and nineteenth centuries, the English industry, despite pockets of remarkable prosperity and success of which Samuel Courtauld & Co. was one, never became one of the major industries of this country. It will perhaps be helpful, in order to understand both its early economic problems and the course of its growth, to examine briefly the techniques of silk manufacture.

II

The making of silk involved (and still does involve) a series of processes which can be considered under six main headings: the production of silk by the silkworms; reeling; winding, drawing, and throwing; warping, spooling, and weaving; dyeing; and finishing. This sequence was not immutable, and variations for particular purposes will normally be explained as they are encountered.[1]

Silk has the oddest origin of all natural fibres, starting as a filament extruded from the head of the silkworm which is in fact a caterpillar called *bombyx mori*. For thirty-five days after it has hatched from the eggs laid by its parent moth, the silkworm spends the bulk of its time eating. It consumes large amounts of the leaves of the mulberry tree. It then, in the course of two or three days' spinning, surrounds itself in a cocoon which consists of a continuous and very fine filament of silk. This filament is in fact a double thread held together by a sticky gum, sericin, extruded together with the filament from the spinneret in the creature's head. Once enclosed inside the cocoon the silkworm turns into a chrysalis and then, in the natural course of events, into a moth which escapes by making a hole through the cocoon; it then mates, lays its eggs, dies, the eggs hatch, and

---

[1] This description of silk manufacturing processes is mainly based upon early nineteenth-century accounts, notably D. Lardner (ed.), *A Treatise on Silk Manufacture* (London, 1831), A. Rees (ed.), *Cyclopaedia of Arts, Sciences and Literature* (London, 1819), C. Tomlinson (ed.), *Cyclopaedia of Useful Arts* (London, 1844), G. Dodd, *The Textile Manufactures of Great Britain* (London, 1844), and A. Ure, *Dictionary of Arts, Manufactures and Mines* (ed. R. Hunt, London, 1878). I have also been much helped by Mr. W. H. Nankivell, who has put me right when I have gone astray on various technical matters, and by Mr. S. J. Bloomfield who, in the course of introducing me to old records in his care at Bocking Mill, told me much about silk and its manufacture.

the sequence starts all over again. For the purpose of silk cultivation, however, nature is frustrated by heating the completed cocoon, thus killing the chrysalis. The undamaged cocoon can then be reeled.

The process of unwinding the silk filament, which could be as much as a mile long, was called reeling, and the establishment in which this was carried out was known as a filature. Cocoons were steeped in very hot water to soften the gum, and the ends of the double filaments in each of six or more cocoons were found. The filaments were then laid together and, whilst the cocoons remained floating in hot water, they were reeled off together to form one single, strong thread, the individual filaments of which cohered by reason of the gum. The product of this process was raw silk, reeled in skeins and packed into 'books' and bales.

In this form the raw silk was received by throwsters or manufacturers. The first process to which they then subjected it was known as winding. For this purpose the skeins were put on to large reels, known as 'swifts', and wound off on to bobbins, broken threads being joined together by attendant labour. The silk was then cleaned by being drawn through cleaning devices on a drawing engine where it was wound on to a further set of bobbins ready for throwing.

The next process, that of throwing, consisted, or might consist, of more than one procedure, according to the type of silk yarn required. The yarns had various special names, but before considering these, it is important to stress one point: silk, as a continuous filament and not, like other natural fibres, a series of short lengths, was not spun but twisted. Hence the term 'throwing', rather than 'spinning', although the latter was sometimes, and very confusingly, used to describe all or part of the processes involved in throwing. The effective action of the twisting or throwing mill, whatever its motive power, depended on the revolving of two sets of bobbins at different, carefully adjusted, speeds. The bobbin containing the silk to be thrown was attached to a spindle to the top of which was fastened a flyer. The silk was drawn off the bobbin through the eye of the flyer and the rotating action of the latter inserted twist into the yarn. The amount of twist was determined by the relative speeds of the two bobbins, the first feeding the silk to be thrown, the second taking it up after the flyer had twisted it. Thrown silk yarn which consisted simply of a single thread, taken from the winding and cleaning process, and then twisted on the throwing mill, was known as 'singles'. Unthrown silk was called 'dumb', and yarn in the form of a single thread taken directly from winding and cleaning and without any throwing was known as 'dumb singles'.

A yarn consisting of two or three 'dumb singles' wound together on to a single bobbin on a doubling mill was known as 'tram'. And finally, the strongest of all the types of yarn which need concern us here, and which was commonly used for warps, was known as 'organzine'. In this two or three 'dumb singles' were twisted in one direction, doubled, and then the resulting compound thread twisted in the opposite direction, in the manner of a rope. In all thrown silks the amount of twist was measured in terms of twists per inch. A yarn with a low throw would have from 10 to 30 twists per inch; a high throw, 30 to 70 or more. Highly twisted yarns were known as crapes or crape yarns because they were used in the making of crape fabrics—a confusing double usage which we shall meet again. The fineness of a silk yarn was denoted by its 'denier', which was the weight in grams of 9,000 metres of yarn. The lower the denier, the finer the silk.

Once the yarn had emerged from the hands of the throwster, the remaining processes were not greatly different from those accorded to other natural fibres. Warping, i.e. the setting up of the warp for the loom, weaving, spooling, dyeing, and finishing differed only in details, for example the use of particular types of looms for particular silk fabrics, or of special finishes. For many purposes dyeing was done not at this later stage, 'in the piece', but earlier, in the yarn. One procedure was peculiar to silk, viz. boiling off or degumming. This was not always done and when it was did not always occur in the same place in the cycle. The remarkable lustre and texture of silk only came with degumming. This was normally carried out before weaving, the degummed yarn being known as 'soft silk'. Conversely, silk with the gum still in it was known as 'hard silk', and certain fabrics, including crape, were woven from hard silk and then variously finished.

Much of this broad outline of the techniques of silk manufacture and many of the technical terms still apply today.[1] Methods remained similar for hundreds, perhaps thousands, of years, though of course with vast improvements in productivity and speed after the advent of power-driven machinery. At what state had the English industry arrived by the time that George Courtauld I made his first formal acquaintance with it in 1775?

III

Silk, like paper, came to Europe from China via the Middle East, and then to England via the European countries bordering the Mediterranean, notably Italy, Spain, and France. In the course of this long-drawn-out

---

[1] Cf., for example, J. G. Cook, *Handbook of Textile Fibres* (Watford, 1964).

diffusion of a skill the first two processes of manufacture, silkworm cultivation and reeling, failed, to all practical purposes, to cross the English
Channel. The English silk industry had to draw its supplies of raw material
from a wide range of countries: Italy, France, Spain, Syria, Turkey, and,
later, Bengal and China. Some of it came in as raw silk to be thrown in
England; some of it as thrown silk, usually organzine and mainly from
Italy, to supply English weavers.

During this early period most of the winding and throwing as well as

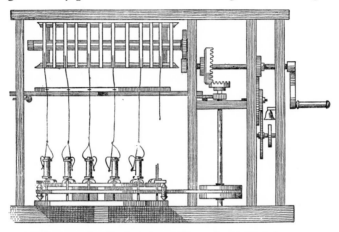

Hand-operated silk throwing mill—early nineteenth century

all the weaving was done by hand. The equipment was simple and could
readily be accommodated in the workers' dwellings; so much of the
industry was organized on the 'putting-out' or 'domestic' system, though
master throwsters and weavers also employed people on their own
premises. Silk-winding was one of the simplest and worst-paid of all
industrial jobs. In Spitalfields, by the mid eighteenth century, much of it
was casual labour performed by women, children, and the poorest of the
poor. It had become a common occupation for the inmates of London
workhouses.[1] Throwing was done on a crude wooden-framed mill turned
by hand. There were various patterns of these mills, some of them continuing in use into the early nineteenth century. The machine illustrated
above belongs to that period. These, too, demanded large amounts of
unskilled labour plus some appropriately experienced supervision. The
bigger throwsters employed large numbers of women and children in

[1] M. Dorothy George, *London Life in the Eighteenth Century* (3rd ed., London, 1951),
p. 184.

tending such machines, putting on new bobbins and tying broken threads. One London throwster, for example, stated in 1755 that he employed about 800 persons, some of whom worked on his premises, others in their homes, winding and doubling.[1] In weaving the work varied from simple weaving done by women, who quickly learnt this semi-skilled task, to the skilled work of those weaving figured fabrics on a draw-loom. The use of the hand-loom again permitted much of this work to be organized by master manufacturers and put out to workers in their own dwellings. The use of the so-called 'Dutch engine loom' in weaving ribbons was no exception to this, for it was not a power-driven loom but merely an ingenious device enabling several plain narrow ribbons to be hand-woven at once.[2]

The main centres of the industry in the early eighteenth century were London (notably Spitalfields), Coventry, and Norwich. Most of the fancy trade was concentrated in London; Coventry had a growing manufacture of ribbons; in Norwich, an important centre of immigrant textile workers, much of the silk went into the weaving of mixed fabrics of silk and worsted.[3] Although the English silk industry had made substantial strides in the later seventeenth century, it did not continue to advance rapidly during the first half of the eighteenth century. The accompanying graph, Fig. 2, showing English consumption of silk, raw and thrown, does not suggest more than a very slow rate of growth during that period. The early steep rise in imports of thrown silk while the trend of imports of raw remained virtually stationary, suggests some increase in English weaving capacity. Thereafter, from approximately 1720 to 1750, the industry seems to have gone through a period of stagnation, even depression.

Recovery during the 1750s, however, was sustained and brought the industry into a period of appreciable expansion. The changing circumstances which induced this expansion were of four main sorts: the gradual adoption of power-driven machinery; the increasing supply of silk from the Far East; the consequences of State action, notably war and protection; and the general rise both in population and in national income.

The introduction to this country of the power-driven silk-throwing

[1] George, op. cit.

[2] Ibid., p. 187, and J. Prest, *The Industrial Revolution in Coventry* (Oxford. 1960), p. 47.

[3] In general on the early silk industry, see F. Warner, *The Silk Industry of the United Kingdom, its Origin and Development* (London, 1921), which is comprehensive but rather out of date and sometimes inaccurate. Two unpublished London University M.A. theses contain valuable detailed inquiries into various aspects of the industry's history: N. K. A. Rothstein, 'The Silk Industry in London, 1702–66' (1961), and W. M. Jordan, 'The Silk Industry in London, 1760–1830' (1931).

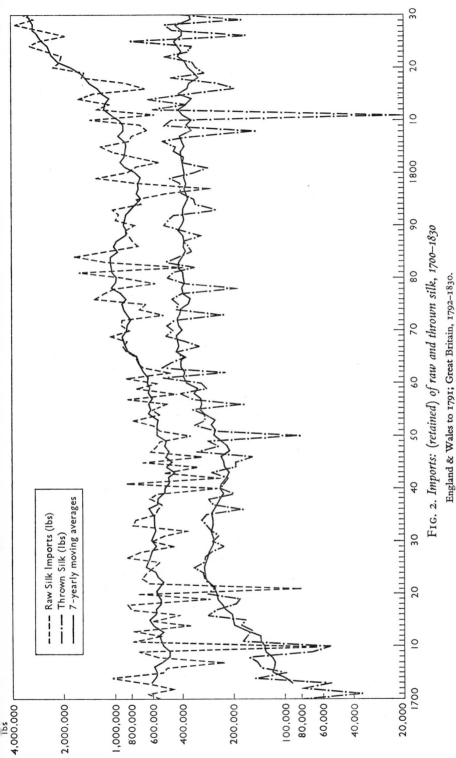

lbs

4,000,000

2,000,000

1,000,000
800,000
600,000

400,000

200,000

100,000
80,000
60,000

40,000

20,000

1700   10   20   30   40   50   60   70   80   90   1800   10   20   30

- - - - Raw Silk Imports (lbs)
— · — Thrown Silk (lbs)
———— 7-yearly moving averages

FIG. 2. *Imports: (retained) of raw and thrown silk, 1700–1830*

England & Wales to 1791; Great Britain, 1792–1830.

Sources: Mitchell & Deane; E. B. Schumpeter, *English Overseas Trade Statistics, 1697–1808* (Oxford, 1960); P.R.O.: Customs
3 and 5; *B.P.P.* 1821, vol. VII

mill, its patenting by Sir Thomas Lombe in 1719, and his erection of what can claim to be the first power-operated textile factory of the Industrial Revolution: all this, decorated by sundry romantic trimmings, is one of the best-known episodes of English industrial history.[1] Accounts of it tend to be garbled and its significance invariably exaggerated. Sir Thomas Lombe, son of a Norwich weaver, was a prosperous London mercer who imported Italian silk. With the assistance of his half-brother John, he discovered how the Italian throwing mills worked, patented the idea in this country, and set up what was for the time a large water-powered mill, completed in 1721, on an island in the Derwent near Derby. On the expiry of the patent in 1732 it was not renewed, but Lombe, after Parliamentary discussion, was given a reward of £14,000 on the condition that a model of the machinery was displayed at the Tower of London. Neither the romantic garnish about industrial espionage and sinister Italians nor the goggling wonderment and inflated claims of interested contemporaries need detain us. Suffice to note that water-powered silk throwing had been known in Italy since the fourteenth century.[2] Lombe's mill was preceded by another on the same island, erected in 1702 by Thomas Cotchett and containing water-powered Dutch silk-throwing engines.[3] It failed; Lombe's own mill was far from an unqualified success; and even a century later power-throwing had still not wholly ousted ancient hand-operated mills.

Nevertheless, Lombe's venture stimulated interest in the possibilities of reducing costs in silk throwing, and after his patent expired, water-powered throwing mills began slowly to appear. They appeared first not near the old weaving centres of London and Norwich, but in the new and developing areas of the Industrial Revolution: in the Midlands and north-west, at Stockport, Macclesfield, Congleton, and Derby; by the 1770s isolated examples were to be found as well in such diverse counties as Hampshire, Somerset, Gloucestershire, and Dorset. But before any substantial growth could occur the economic environment of the industry in this country had to be changed. Some part of these conditions was satisfied by an improvement in the quality and reliability of the raw material supply. Italian raw silk was the best in quality and Italian rulers were correspondingly anxious to retain it for their own industry. Just as the English Government had long forbidden the export of raw wool, so did

[1] A useful, brief, and recent account of Lombe's enterprise will be found in W. H. Chaloner, *People and Industries* (London, 1963), pp. 8–20.

[2] M. Postan and E. Rich (eds.), *The Cambridge Economic History of Europe*, vol. ii (Cambridge, 1952), p. 329.

[3] Chaloner, op. cit., pp. 10–11.

the King of Sardinia prohibit the export of raw silk in 1724. The poor quality of the silk from such alternative sources as Turkey, India, and China remained for long an obstacle to their effective use, despite their lower price. So English weavers had for the most part to use foreign-thrown silk, much of it Italian, at least for their warps: in 1765 it was estimated that only about one-ninth of the organzine used in England was thrown in English mills.[1] And so, in turn, competition with the imported fabrics of Continental producers continued to be difficult. But from the 1770's the English East India Company, which controlled the import of Asiatic silk, began to take steps which resulted in some improvement in the quality of these silks; and some English silk throwsters also began to think it worth their while to invest money in filatures in Bengal and in other efforts to ensure better raw material supplies.[2] They had probably been helped to think in this way by the change in duties on imported silk. Table 1 below indicates the general trend towards favouring raw silk as against thrown silk imports and towards the equalizing of duties on Italian and Asiatic raw silks.[3]

TABLE I

Silk import duties, 1704–84

(per lb. of 16 oz.)[4]

	Raw			Thrown	
	China	Bengal	Italy		
	s. d.	s. d.	s. d.		s. d.
1704–47. .	2 6	1 3	11	1704–47	3 2
1747–50. .	3 2	1 7	1 3 ⎫	1747–65	4 0
1750–65. .	3 2	1 3	1 7 ⎭		
1765–79. .	10	10	10	1765–79	4 6
				⎧ 1779–81	4 9
1779–84. .	11	11	11	⎨ 1781	4 11
				⎩ 1782–4	5 2

In consequence of these shifts, however precisely motivated, 84 per cent. of an average annual import of raw silk totalling 746,000 lb. in 1780–4

[1] *Journals of the House of Commons*, vol. xxx, 1765, p. 213. This report of the proceedings of a Select Committee on the silk trade provides much of the evidence for the state of the industry in this period.

[2] *Hist. Tech.*, vol. iv, p. 309; B.P.P. 1831–2, vol. xix, pp. 695 ff.

[3] B.P.P. 1831–2, vol. xix, p. 265.

[4] For much of the eighteenth century a lb. of 24 oz. was used for raw silk: the figures have been converted to facilitate comparison with later data (see below, p. 20).

came from Bengal and China, as compared with only 35 per cent. out of the much smaller annual average of 400,000 lb. in 1730–4.

These trends in tariffs were, however, only one part of a policy towards silk which took its major protective step in 1766. French silk goods—in common with virtually all French commodities in the eighteenth century—had to pay very high import duties; the imports of ribbons had long been forbidden; and there was plenty of recurrent agitation for a general prohibition on all foreign silks. The pressure mounted in the 1760s after the end of the Seven Years War (1756–63), during which this country had captured much of the French trade in silk manufactures. As Fig. 3 shows, this period witnessed a quite exceptional rise in English exports of silk goods which in normal times were fairly sluggish. But peace brought a slump. As it was put in the House of Commons in 1766: 'during the late war the silk trade was very brisk, and since the peace it has declined very much'.[1] After much discussion the appeals for protection were answered. In 1766 a prohibition on all imports of foreign silks and velvets was granted for five years;[2] it stayed in fact for sixty years. Under this protective umbrella the industry sheltered and grew. But it proved, for some years at least, a capricious and unreliable shelter. For tariffs are fiscal as well as commercial devices, and the urgent demands of war brought stiffer duties on raw silk as well as variously, sometimes helpfully, sometimes unhelpfully, distorting the channels of trade. As the following figures show, the import duties on raw silk moved up sharply, even more than those on thrown:[3]

TABLE 2

Silk import duties, 1779–1823

(*per lb. of 16 oz.*)[4]

		Raw			Thrown	
		China	Bengal	Italy		
		s. d.	s. d.	s. d.		s. d.
1779–84 . .		11	11	11	1782–4	5 2
1784 . .		3 0	3 0	3 0	1784	7 4
1797 . .		3 3	3 3	3 3	1797	8 0
1801 . . .		5 1	3 9	5 1	1805	11 5
1807 . . .		5 5	4 9	5 5	1807	12 2
1817–23 . .		5 6	3 6	5 6	1814–23	14 7

[1] Quoted George, op. cit., p. 373.   [2] 6 Geo. III, c. 28.
[3] B.P.P. 1831–2, vol. xix, p. 265.
[4] Converted as for Table 1: see also note below, p. 20, n. 1.

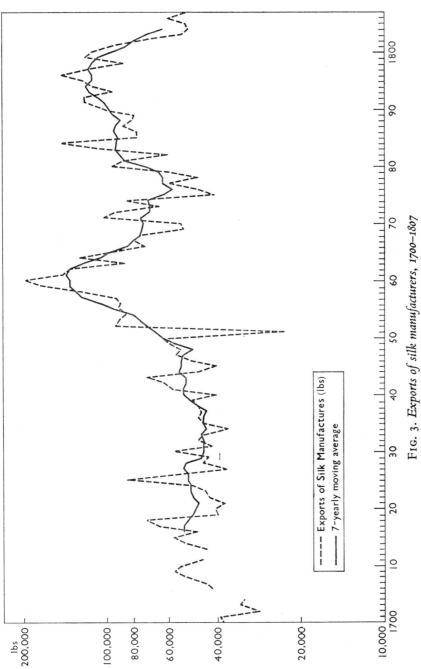

FIG. 3. *Exports of silk manufacturers, 1700–1807*

England & Wales to 1791; Great Britain, 1792–1807. The series ends in 1807 because of a change in definition thereafter.

Source: Mitchell & Deane

The result of these complex circumstances was a marked expansion of the industry, starting in the 1750s, i.e. before the import prohibition of 1766, and continuing until the 1780s, followed by a period during which that expansion was curtailed. For almost three decades, as is evident from Fig. 2, the industry, at last as measured by the quantity of its inputs, was in effect again stagnating; real growth was not resumed until after 1810.[1] Meanwhile, however, concealed by these aggregate figures, the structure, location, equipment, and products of the industry were changing. Comparison of the curves of thrown and raw imports in Fig. 2 suggests a significant growth in throwing capacity during the period 1760–80. This is indeed confirmed by evidence of the continued establishment of water-powered mills and of the decline of the Spitalfields hand-throwsters. It was not only in throwing, moreover, that Spitalfields was beginning to feel the wind of competition from outside. For along with the new throwing mills in Cheshire, Lancashire, and elsewhere came the development of silk weaving—still on hand-looms—in these same areas.

A further complication in the economic position of the London manufacturers arose from the passage in 1773 of the well-known Spitalfields Act. The ready but poorly paid employment which many persons found in Spitalfields, in silk winding and throwing or as journeymen and apprentices to weavers, meant that in times of trading depression thousands were thrown out of work, that destitution, misery, and violence spread in an area where poverty was endemic and the gulf between rich masters and poor labourers was wide. The depressed years following the end of the Seven Years War were just such times. The flooding of work-houses by destitute silk workers, rioting, and various forms of industrial violence by combinations of journeymen against wage-cutting masters: these made up the background to the protective measure of 1766 and to

---

[1] For some general statistical estimates of the industry's growth, see P. Deane and W. A. Cole, *British Economic Growth, 1688–1959* (Cambridge, 1962), pp. 207–11.

It is important to note, however, that in so far as these estimates are concerned with the eighteenth century they seem to be built upon erroneous statistical data for the imports of raw silk before 1787. The change, at that date, from the lb. of 24 to the lb. of 16 oz. for raw silk (thrown and certain other types were consistently weighed in the 16 oz. lb.) has apparently eluded both Deane and Cole as well as E. B. Schumpeter, *English Overseas Trade Statistics, 1697–1808* (Oxford, 1960), and Mitchell & Deane. Hence all the published figures of eighteenth-century raw silk imports before 1787 have to be multiplied by 24/16 in order to get a homogeneous series for the century. With the corrected figures (as used in Fig. 2) the stagnation of the industry from about 1784 to about 1812 is seen to be appreciably more marked. Similarly, the widening gap between imports of thrown and of raw silk after the protective change in the duties in 1765 also becomes more evident.

the Spitalfields Act of 1773. This Act, at a time when the practice of wage regulation had been virtually abandoned, empowered the local Justices of the Peace and the Lord Mayor of London to regulate the wages of Spitalfields silk weavers by fixing weaving prices, limited the number of apprentices that could be taken at any one time, and forbade combinations. In the short run the Act seems to have helped to improve and stabilize conditions in Spitalfields—though it prevented neither combinations on both sides of the industry nor acute distress in times of depression, as for example in 1796–7 and 1810–12—but in the longer run it also furthered the work of those other economic forces which were already, before its passage, gradually driving the silk industry away from Spitalfields.[1] For available labour at lower, and uncontrolled, wages was increasingly to be found outside London, as the massive rise in population got under way, especially in the newly expanding industrial areas of the Midlands and north-west. So the big London silk manufacturers, trying to reduce costs and improve their competitive position, began both to invest in water-powered throwing mills in rural areas and country towns and to put out work to weavers in these same districts. They looked particularly towards East Anglia, and it was precisely in this sequence of economic striving that the first George Courtauld was to be involved and his family established in north Essex.

IV

So far this chapter has been chiefly exercised with the circumstances of production, with raw materials, techniques, organization. The industry's markets, the nature of its products and the demand for them must now be examined.

The notion of prestigious luxury attaching to silk ensured for a long time that the manufacture of such fabrics as damasks and brocades represented the acme of attainment in the industry. Since the baroque splendours of the age of Louis XIV, European fashion had come to mean French fashion. So it was against French standards that the English industry was measured. On this score the same plaint can be heard in the eighteenth and nineteenth centuries alike:

The plain silk weaver requires but little ingenuity but the weavers of flowered silks, damasks, brocades and velvets are very ingenious tradesmen: these ought

[1] On conditions in Spitalfields in the second half of the eighteenth century and on the Spitalfields Act, see particularly Jordan, op. cit., *passim*, George, op. cit., pp. 176–95, and, for further details of riots and violence by silk workers, G. Rudé, *Wilkes and Liberty: a Social study of 1763–1774* (Oxford, 1962), pp. 98–103.

to learn drawing to design their own patterns, the want of which gives the French workmen the greatest advantage over us. Were our weavers as expert at designing as their rivals, the weavers in Spitalfields need not be obliged to send to Paris for new patterns....[1]

This comment of 1747 could be matched by others of the same period. Here is the same problem as it appeared to a Royal Commission and to one of its witnesses almost a century later, in 1840:

... a great abundance of figured silks is sold in London, and those silks are the produce of foreign looms. The natural inquiry is, What can be the cause? ... The sole cause is that figured goods are not made in this country in such taste as to secure a preference.
... The French people are accustomed daily to have before their eyes the finest works of art, and naturally and imperceptibly acquire a good taste from that cause ... I think it would be beneficial if children from an early age were accustomed to view beautiful figures, as of flowers, statues, animals and elegant designs ... if only a few should thereby be excited to a love of the fine arts, the expense would be abundantly recompensed: by such means we should become able to rival, or even excel, the pattern drawers of France.[2]

However ludicrous in its flattering vision of 'the French people' or naïve in its picture of English children absorbing 'taste' by gazing at flowers, statues, and animals, this was nevertheless a typical expression of what was seen as the aims and the failings of the English silk industry. That Spitalfields should have been easily the most important centre for the production of these fashionable fabrics was natural enough. Yet there is reason to think that the Huguenot inspiration which earlier had shaped this industrial area towards the satisfaction of the London market later failed to maintain its vigour. Members of the close-knit, interbred Huguenot community tended to grow conservative.[3] Hand-throwing lingered late; and the Jacquard loom, invented in 1801 and characteristically a French invention, came but slowly to Spitalfields. Though French silks were smuggled into the country in substantial amounts, the protective wall after 1766 could hardly have acted as a stimulus to imagination. But with its proximity to the 'West End trade', dependent on the current of fashion which travelled across the Channel from Paris and reached London before anywhere else, Spitalfields clung to the weaving of the elegant fabrics.

[1] R. Campbell, *The London Tradesman* (London, 1747), pp. 259–60.
[2] *B.P.P.*, 1840, vol. xxiii, p. 227.
[3] On the Huguenot community see especially Rothstein, op. cit.

The simpler fabrics were the first to move out. The straightforward weaving of silk for handkerchiefs, scarves, shawls, and the like was soon established in Lancashire and Cheshire. In Norwich, the eighteenth century saw the gradual decay of its worsted industry, and to counterbalance this, in part, a growing manufacture of silk and worsted mixtures, of camlets, crapes, and bombazines. Some of them, notably crapes, later became wholly silk fabrics, and their manufacture, once also pursued in Spitalfields, became part of the East Anglian silk output.

Expansion into plainer fabrics with simple weaves intended for a wider and less exclusively rich and fashionable market was indeed the essence of this whole phase of growth in the English silk industry. It was in part a logical economic reaction to the failures, frustrations, and vicissitudes attendant upon efforts to match continental styles. It owed much to the growth in both population and national wealth and especially to middle-class demand. But it was also a consequence of the economic logic of the problem posed by raw material supply. Most of the high-quality Italian-thrown organzine went to Spitalfields, for there it was needed for the warps of expensive flowered silks. Many of the simpler fabrics made in the provinces, however, could use English-thrown silk, the cheaper sorts Bengal silk; and, moreover, some of them could be woven with tram instead of organzine in the warp. In brief, this meant lower labour costs and cheaper silk for the water-powered throwster, lower raw material costs and cheaper labour for the provincial manufacturer. This in turn implied not only that different markets were being tapped but that, to some extent —and this must not be exaggerated, for silk still remained the dearest of fibres—there was a limited move away from the luxurious exclusiveness of silk.[1]

The particular fabric with which this volume is primarily concerned demands the attention of a separate chapter.

[1] See in general *Journals of the House of Commons*, vol. xxx, 1765, pp. 208–19, and the minutes of evidence in B.P.P. 1831–2, vol. xix, and 1840, vol. xxiii.

CHAPTER III

The Early History of Crape

I

LIKE many English names for fabrics made of fibres other than wool, crape is a term of foreign origin: *crêpe* (Fr.), *crespo* (It.), both from the Latin *crispare*, to curl. At some stage of history, certainly in the Middle Ages, the word came to mean a gauze-like fabric woven wholly of silk, with a craped, crimped, or curled effect in its texture which was basically dependent on the use of a highly thrown yarn made, in one way or another, to untwist itself after weaving. In the course of time two main sorts of crape were developed: soft and hard. In eighteenth and early nineteenth-century England the former category included fabrics which were called Canton or China crape, French crape, and Norwich crape; in the hard category was Italian or Bologna crape. Both sorts were woven of hard silk, but whereas the former ended up as a soft and usually coloured fabric, the latter was subjected to various dressing and finishing processes and ended up as a stiff and usually black fabric. The manufacture of the soft type later developed on the continent of Europe, particularly in France; the manufacture of the hard type slowly moved away from Italy and became a peculiar speciality of England. Both sorts of crape, when dyed black, were at one time or another associated with mourning, but especially the Italian and, later, English sort. Consequently the word crape alone came eventually to mean mourning crape, and when in the later nineteenth century the other variety became fashionable in England it was distinguished from its mourning relative by being called *crêpe de Chine*, whilst English mourning crape was known across the Channel as *crêpe anglaise*.

It was not, however, until about the middle of the nineteenth century that the word crape alone came to have this immediate identification with this particular type of mourning fabric. So before that time we cannot always be certain from contemporary documents what type of fabric was meant. Sometimes clear distinctions were made. For example, a silk manufacturer, Joseph Grout, giving evidence before a Parliamentary Committee in 1831, when asked what articles he made, answered unequivocally: 'Every type of crape, namely China, Italian and French.'[1]

Crape, like other silk fabrics, had come to Europe from the Orient by way of the eastern Mediterranean. Bologna had become an important centre of its manufacture in medieval times, and in the sixteenth century, if not earlier, Bologna crapes found their way northwards to the great European market of Antwerp. Their association with mourning can similarly be traced back to this period.[2] As the English silk industry grew, from the late seventeenth century onwards, attempts were naturally made to copy the imported fabrics. Early records of these efforts testify both to the origin and to the uses of these Bologna crapes. In 1698 Francis Pousset was given a patent to make black and white silk crape, having, he claimed, 'after many years of trouble and great expence found out the true art of making black silk crape and white silk crape, such as formerly were and now are used for veils, hoods, scarves and hatbands for mourning'. He also claimed to have brought it to such perfection that those he could make were indistinguishable from those imported from Italy. Despite his claims and his fourteen-year patent, similar claims and another fourteen-year patent, went to John Gastineau and William Mons, two Spitalfields weavers, in 1730. Their patent spoke of 'mourning crapes made of silk and commonly known as . . . vallee cypress or Bologna crapes'.[3] The wish to dispense with Italian imports led to the encouragement of other sorts of English silks as a substitute for Bologna crapes:

For the encouragement of our English silks called a la modes, His Royal Highness the Prince of Denmark, the Nobility, and other persons of quality, appear in Mourning Hatbands made of that silk, to bring the same in fashion in the place of Crapes, which are made in the Pope's country where we send our money for them.[4]

That these early patents had little or no success is suggested by the fact that in 1765 the Society for the Encouragement of Arts, Manufactures and Commerce was offering a prize for Italian crimped crape. 'The Italian method of crimping Crapes has been attempted by many of our ingenious silk manufacturers', but nothing much had been achieved; so the Society offered its premiums for 'the greatest quantity of English crimped crape

---

[1] B.P.P. 1831–2, vol. xix, p. 691.

[2] R. H. Tawney and E. Power, *Tudor Economic Documents*, vol. iii, p. 163; *Enciclopaedia Italiana, sub* 'crespo'.

[3] B.P. 357 (1598) and 520 (1730).

[4] Quoted R. Davey, *A History of Mourning* (London, 1889), p. 110.

for mourning, not less than an hundred yards, and nearest in quality to the Italian Crape'. Though three candidates appeared, no one produced the requisite amount of crape, so no prizes were awarded. One candidate said he had been to Naples on purpose to 'make himself master of the art of crimping crapes'; another spoke of it as 'Mourning Crape or Cyprus gauze'.[1] It seems clear, however, that other manufacturers were experimenting with this type of crape, for in 1772 members of the Society were shown 'a large specimen of crape, crimped and manufactured so exactly like the Italian, as not to be distinguished therefrom'.[2]

Unfortunately it is not possible to tell to whom should be given the credit for developing the manufacture of this Italian crimped crape. More than one patent for it was taken out at about this time. Some were obviously useless, such as that in 1768 of James Crookshank and William Norton, who merely recommended that boiling water should be poured on the woven gauze; this, they said, would produce 'the shrivel or curdle in the crape'.[3] Much more interesting, however, was that taken out in 1772 by a man with the appropriate name of John Crumpler. His method of imitating Italian crape involved a machine for dressing the crape in which one can recognize a crude anticipation of the crimping or embossing machine such as came into use at a later date.

My engine [he said] . . . is two large upright pieces of wood, fastened to the place top and bottom where erected, between which posts I have two large rounds, discretionally hot, which open and close, with a figure between, which engine it being properly prepared, the silk has been thrown and operated on and wove, is put in such a manner as to make it pass as even as possible through the operation which must be done with all possible care. Then there are two handles to work the machine . . . which is done by hand labour or by springs or water. . . .[4]

Crumpler does not appear to have had any success with his invention, so presumably, like many an inventor, he had difficulty in its practical application. These various eighteenth-century essays do, however, tend to make nonsense of the claim, which appears in Warner's book and elsewhere, that Joseph Grout was responsible, early in the nineteenth century,

---

[1] An eighteenth-century undertaker's card referred to 'all sorts of Black Cyprus for scarfs and hatbands', Davey, op. cit., p. 109.

[2] W. Bailey, *The Advancement of Arts, Manufactures and Commerce or Descriptions of the Useful Machines and Models contained in the Repository of the Society for the Encouragement of Arts, Manufacture and Commerce* (London, 1772); Royal Society of Arts Library: Guard Book, vol. ii; Minutes of Committees, 1765–6.

[3] B.P. 912 (1768).

[4] B.P. 1013 (1772).

for the invention of crimped crape.[1] Another earlier and perhaps more likely candidate is Peter Nouaille, 1723–1809, a member of a prosperous and important Huguenot family of Spitalfields silk manufacturers. It has been said, without supporting evidence, that he was 'the first to introduce the manufacture of crepe into England, it having previously been brought from Bologna'.[2] Certainly he was a crape maker, of London and Seven-oaks, Kent, in the later eighteenth and early nineteenth centuries, and certainly he patented, in 1770, an improvement in silk-throwing machinery, but we do not know precisely what sort of crape he was making.[3]

A further source of confusion is the existence at this period of a fabric called 'Norwich crape'. This almost certainly owed its existence to the im-migrant weavers who had settled in that city. It was a silk and worsted mixture, a soft, dull fabric which, in the earlier part of the eighteenth century, was also used for mourning attire. So, too, was another silk and worsted fabric much associated with Norwich, bombazine. These two were united in some of the published orders for Court mourning which were issued by the Lord Chamberlain. On the deaths, for example, of the Princess Caroline in 1759 and of George II in 1760 there were to be found amongst the prescribed materials for ladies' mourning '. . . black bomba-zines . . . crape hoods . . . crape fans . . . and dark Norwich crapes'.[4] Norwich crape, however, was deteriorating into bombazine, which itself was degenerating into a cotton and worsted mixture, and both were losing their connexion with mourning. Crape meanwhile was coming to mean, though not exclusively, the all-silk, Italian-style crimped crape. To make confusion worse confounded, however, a new sort of Norwich crape was developed around 1820. This was a coloured, striped, silk and worsted mixture which had nothing whatever to do with mourning.[5] At the same time, moreover, the all-silk crimped mourning crape was

---

[1] Warner, p. 286. According to Warner, 'the first patent for embossed crape was taken out by the firm in 1822'. I have not been able to trace this patent. A patent, No. 4614, taken out by Joseph Grout in 1821 relates to weaving coloured crape and has nothing to do with embossed or crimped crape.

[2] *Victoria County History: Kent*, vol. iii, p. 415.

[3] See further on Nouaille, Rothstein, op. cit., pp. 21 and 133; and below, p. 36.

[4] *London Gazette*, 8 September 1759, 26 October 1760.

[5] Much of this extra confusion arose from the patenting—B.P. 4776 (1823)—by J. Francis of a new fabric of silk and worsted which he called Norwich crape, but which was obviously quite different from what had earlier been called by that name. The misleading account which appears in *B.P.P.* 1840, vol. xxii, p. 145 seems a likely source of the confusion. Warner's version, op. cit., pp. 278 ff., however, makes it clear that more than one type of fabric was involved.

being made in and around Norwich and other parts of East Anglia. And it was this type of crape, no longer imported, which was meant in the Lord Chamberlain's orders for Court mourning at royal funerals in the nineteenth century, with their prescriptions for crape fans, crape hatbands, and similar solemn trimmings.[1]

Meanwhile, until English all-silk mourning crape established itself, Italian crape was specified in the purchases of the Lord Chamberlain's department for royal or Court funerals. Although it was said that during Walpole's administration, and so long as Norwich had friends at Court, 'public mournings were always ordered to be in Norwich crapes', nevertheless hundreds of yards of 'broad black Italian crape' were ordered on such occasions as the funerals of the Duke of Cumberland in 1765 and the Duke of York in 1767. Then, as later, the stiff, crimped crape was used for decorative or trimming purposes, the softer material for clothing. Thus, for example, at the funeral of the Duke of Cumberland, in order to cover the sashes of twenty-nine officers and a quartermaster, 105 yards of this Italian crape were bought at a cost of £34. 2s. 6d.[2]

The protocol of the Court went far to determine the national demand for mourning materials. The display of grief at death, the association of black with that grief, the conspicuous wearing of black: these are merely constituent elements within the piece of very ancient ritual which is called mourning. They do not in themselves depend upon the presence of a Court. But when Crown and Church, the two greatest founts of magic and ritual, are so interconnected that the former is the legal head of the latter, as in England; and when they both exerted great social power as they did in eighteenth- and nineteenth-century England: then a doubled force is given to ritual enactments of the Court, their consequences rippling through social and economic life. So the ostentatious display of black at the funerals of members of the royal circle and the attendant orders demanding Court mourning for lengthy periods combined to form an expression of power sanctified by ritual. Those who hurried to don the appropriate clothes included not only the Court but all those of the upper classes who liked to be regarded as part of the Court; and so in lessening degrees the relevant attire spread out through the faithful. What Crown and Church prescribed for royal occasions was surely right, with suitable modifications, for private occasions. Conspicuous grief for deaths in

---

[1] See, e.g., *London Gazette*, 21 June 1837 (death of William IV) and 15 December 1861 (death of the Prince Consort); also Davey, op. cit., pp. 99–103.

[2] Warner, p. 282; P.R.O., L.C. 2/33.

private families thus became at once a symbol of social status and an act of loyal piety. Naturally this procedure started high in the social scale. Slowly it worked its way to the middle classes, though it probably did not penetrate very far down the social scale—except, of course, for household servants—even in the nineteenth century, by which time an elaborate code of private mourning, thought fit and proper for ladies and gentlemen, had been developed.[1] This will be considered later (see below, Chapter VII), but meanwhile it is perhaps worth emphasizing the extent to which deep and elaborate mourning had become an accepted part of English social ritual—and thus a fount of economic demands—long before Queen Victoria came to the throne of England. Private and public grief had become of sufficient business consequence for 'family mourning and funeral furnishing' to appear on eighteenth-century trade cards; and in the later years of that century at least one London shop or warehouse seems to have been specializing in the sale of mourning materials.[2]

Because public display of mourning was royally determined, silk, the most expensive and exclusive of fabrics, long the mark of high rank, was the fabric for the occasion. And the technical equivalent of the transference from lustrous, gleaming display to funereal darkness was retention of the gum, high throw, black dye, and certain methods of manufacture and finish which crape makers surrounded in industrial mystery, and which will be examined in detail in later chapters.[3]

This substantial English demand for mourning silks was an economic tool with a double edge. On one side it hit the makers of bright colours and flowered fashions. The elaborate public mournings ordered to mark the death of a royal notable could last for several months. Those most affected by such orders were also consumers of the fashionable colours. The small manufacturer concentrating on figured fabrics and already at the mercy of a capricious, fashion-ridden market did not find adaptation easy. More than once in the eighteenth century London silk weavers petitioned for a shortening of the length of these public mournings, and some shortening was in fact conceded in 1786.[4] 'The grievances of those concerned in the silk trade . . . occasion'd by frequent and long public

---

[1] C. W. Cunnington, *English Women's Clothing in the Nineteenth Century* (London, 1937).

[2] Alison Aldburgham, *Shops and Shopping, 1800–1914* (London, 1964), p. 58.

[3] On the mysteries of crape finishing, see below, pp. 88–89.

[4] Aldburgham, op. cit., pp. 58–61; Rothstein, op. cit., p. 475. Miss Rothstein's thesis contains a most interesting account of the effects of public mournings, especially on the fancy silk trade; see esp. pp. 328 ff. and 474–6. For mournings and the ribbon trade, see Prest, op. cit., p. 44.

mournings' were aired in tracts and pamphlets.[1] In 1731 one literate weaver was vainly hoping to limit the social range of mourning: 'if the mourning went no further than the Court and drawing room, and if women of inferior rank should make no alteration in their dress, it would be full as well'.[2] The larger employer, on the other hand, with many hand-loom weavers on his books and with stocks, or ready command, of various types of yarn could switch to the production of black fabrics. This, at least, is how it seemed to one of the bigger Spitalfields manufacturers, William Hale. In the course of evidence which he gave to a Parliamentary Committee in 1821 he made a most interesting statement on the subject of English mourning customs and their effect on the silk industry which deserves to be quoted at length. Admitting that the French industry had the advantage of being closely linked to French fashions, he contended, however, that:

. . . we have one advantage, I conceive, in Britain, in employing our poor in the silk manufacture, which is unknown in any part of the world. It is no uncommon thing for the poor on the continent to be employed for three or four months, and then to be out of work two or three months; but not so with our best hands, either in the silk trade or the broad cloth. The general mournings and mournings for private families, being at least three months, while on the continent they are only for a few days, there is always a great quantity of goods manufactured for the black trade, for the purposes of mourning; and this being so sure an article, it serves for the principal manufacturers to repose upon to employ their hands at the time when, but for that circumstance they could not know what to do with them.

He went on to draw a striking picture of the dependence of this section of the silk-working population upon the whims of fashion and how this could be tempered in its impact by the steady demand for black.

Sometimes, in the months of June and July, it cannot be ascertained what colours will be wanted for the winter or what colours will be most fashionable. The lower classes of society would be destitute of work for two or three months, till some Duchess might make her appearance in Brighton with a new colour just from Paris, and they might be then set to work upon it; but during those seasons the manufacturer will not turn off his best hands, but will employ them on black, as being sure to go at one time of the year or another; for black being so much worn on general and private mournings, it is sure to go within

---

[1] Some examples are given in L. W. Hanson (ed.), *Contemporary Printed Sources for British and Irish Economic History, 1701–1750* (Cambridge, 1963),

[2] *Gentleman's Magazine*, vol. i, 1731, p. 161.

six or twelve months; and I conceive this to be a very great blessing to our poor.[1]

Fascinating as is this picture of the poor being maintained by the economic consequences of ritual gloom, it overlooks a number of important points. Hale did not mention that the wages obtained by weavers working on mourning fabrics were likely to be much less than they would have gained on the figured silks. From Hale's viewpoint the other alternative to this latter work was no wages at all: mourning work was better than unemployment. This was no doubt true, but it implies that there did not exist an already adequate manufacturing capacity engaged on making mourning fabrics. This was ceasing to be true. For the other economic edge of this curious English enthusiasm for conspicuous grief was of course that it gave positive encouragement to the growth of that specialized branch of the silk industry which was crape making.

The encouragement which thus sprang from unusual demand also gained strength from the fact that technical and economic circumstances such as were mentioned in the preceding chapter favoured the making of this particular fabric in England. So far from needing expensive, highly taxed, high-quality Italian organzine, crape was usually woven with singles, thrown from less-taxed, lower-priced, poorer-quality silks in both warp and weft, though sometimes tram was used in the weft. So far from needing draw-looms or Jacquards, and the labour of the better-paid and more skilled weavers who used them, it could be woven on simple looms by lower-paid, semi-skilled men or women; indeed it was peculiarly conducive, as will be shown later, to the early application of power-loom weaving.[2] And once successful embossing or crimping machines were developed they could be driven by water- or steam-power, the use of which was spreading so strikingly in the England of the Industrial Revolution. Crape was un-affected by the urge either to seek original designs or to imitate the latest French fashions. And though its costs could be kept low its price could be kept high. Its consumers were ultimately the richer classes; and its usage, springing as it did from the command of the Court, was heavily charged with the powerful electricity of social esteem. For this the buyers paid, and from it the makers profited.

Not surprisingly then we hear in the early nineteenth century of the establishment of a number of crape manufacturers and/or throwsters of

[1] *B.P.P.* 1821, vol. vii, p. 439.
[2] Lardner (ed.), *Treatise on Silk Manufacture*, p. 297; *B.P.P.* 1840, vol. xxiii, pp. 218–19 and *passim*.

crape yarn. How much earlier specialization of this sort had developed it is difficult to say. Though to judge from the fact that most of the crape makers or throwsters seem to have operated in southern or eastern England—appropriately near to London and the Court—their coming into existence was probably part of the same economic process by which some of the Spitalfields makers invested in the country (see above, p. 21). Virtually all of this initial development of crape making was contained within the period 1790–1830. And it was in this context that the firm of Courtauld came into being.

PART II

CHAPTER IV

The Courtaulds Enter the Silk Industry

I

O F the first George Courtauld's education and upbringing we know little; of his political and religious views we know much. These will be considered in a later chapter. For the moment it will suffice to note that he did not follow the Calvinistic Nonconformity which was the normal religious position of Huguenots in England, but instead became a Unitarian; that he was influenced in this direction by one of the most famous Unitarian thinkers of the time, Dr. Richard Price; and that he also adopted Price's radical and republican opinions with their vigorous sympathy for the American Revolutionaries in the fight against George III's Government. These political and religious sentiments informed his whole attitude to life; exhortations to pursue 'rational Christianity' jostle in his letters with details of throwing machinery and business transactions; and his enthusiasm for America took him to and fro across the Atlantic, four times out, three times back. But for George Courtauld I the process of going to and fro was not confined to movement across the Atlantic. A kindly, spirited man of high principles and virtuous intentions, he changed his mind with notable frequency and was remarkably deficient in business acumen.

In about 1782, after he had served his full seven years of apprenticeship to Merzeau, he set up in Spitalfields, as a throwster, with the help of £500 left to him by his father. His master's throwing mills were hand-operated, his own are said to have been turned by a horse.[1] These already out-of-date techniques could hardly flourish in the difficult days of the 1780s. Although

---

[1] *C.F.L.*, vol. i, pp. xxix, xxxvii, xxxviii.

in 1785 he was performing official duties at the French chapel in Spitalfields,[1] in the same year he sold his mills and made his first visit to America, where Independence had not long since been formally won. There is nothing to suggest that this move was much influenced by the presence in America of his elder surviving brother, Samuel II. Certainly it did not make George I a merchant, for he bought land in New York State and started to farm. As the years passed he could not have been much attracted to return by such news as that which he received from a friend and former fellow apprentice: in December 1787 'the throwing business in general is most wretched bad indeed, particularly in London',[2] in April 1788 'trade is most dismally bad indeed . . . all Mr. M[erzeau]'s engines are still'.[3] (Fig. 2 certainly confirms these reports.) But return he did, for whatever reason, and found a bride, in the person of Ruth, daughter of Stephen Minton of Cork. The visit was brief. He was soon back in America, and married Ruth Minton in New York State on 10 July 1789. Starting in 1790, as a glance at Fig. 4 will show, she bore him, over the next seventeen years, eight children, of whom seven survived.

Fig. 4 also reveals that in two generations there were three marriages between the families of Courtauld and Taylor. The latter soon became closely involved in the business activities of the former and demands a brief introductory digression.[4] The first connexion between the families seems to have arisen from the fact that, like George Courtauld I, William Taylor also served his apprenticeship, from 1771 to 1778, with Peter Merzeau. In 1783 he married his fellow apprentice's sister, Catherine Courtauld I. She bore him fourteen children. From amongst the twenty-one children, and their descendants, of the two marriages, George Courtauld to Ruth Minton and William Taylor to Catherine Courtauld, were to come most of the partners or directors of the Courtauld business for nearly a century. Behind the common Spitalfields apprenticeship of George Courtauld and William Taylor as an ostensible cause of the union of two families, both, as a descendant put it many years later, 'in the middle ranks of life',[5] lay also a common interest in 'rational Christianity' and Radical Dissent. William Taylor was the youngest child of Rev. Henry Taylor

[1] Chester, op. cit., p. 38.

[2] C.F.L., vol. i, p. 33, Kilner to G.C. I., 17 December 1787. Kilner had apparently also been one of Merzeau's apprentices.

[3] Courtauld MSS.: Kilner to G.C. I, 26 April 1788.

[4] Information on the Taylor family largely derived from P. A. Taylor, Some Account of the Taylor Family (London, privately printed, 1875).

[5] Taylor, p. 587.

PLATE 2

GEORGE COURTAULD I (1761–1823)

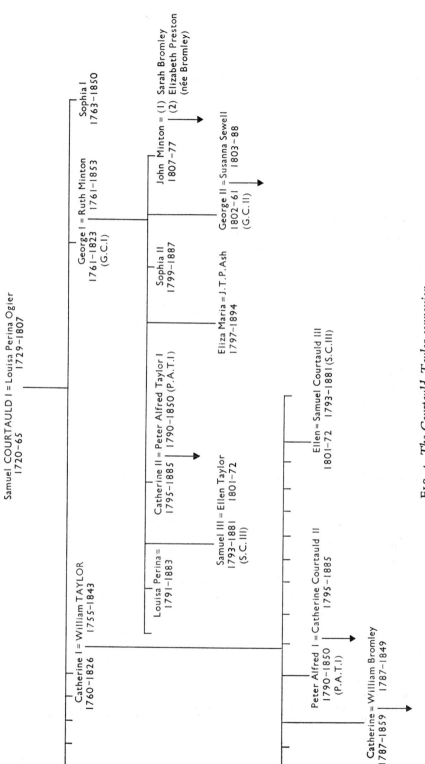

FIG. 4. *The Courtauld–Taylor connexion*

(1711–85). The latter, an unorthodox churchman, was a close friend, again, of the celebrated Dr. Price, and the author, under the pseudonym of 'Ben Mordecai', of theological writings of a markedly rationalistic flavour. And when his son William, aged 27, was courting Catherine Courtauld in 1782 it was at 'Dr. Price's Meeting', which Price was then regularly conducting in Hackney, that they met.[1] At this time Taylor had already been set up as a Spitalfields throwster for some four years. He, too, felt the economic trend of the times for the London throwsters. His annual income of £300 in 1782 hardly suggests massive profits; in April 1788 'almost all his mills [were] standing',[2] But unlike the visionary George the matter-of-fact William did not heed the call of 'the most desirable country in the world'.[3] He went not to America but to Tottenham Court Road. Here, in partnership with a Mr. Jones, he ran a tin and hardware business, Jones, Taylor & Co., in which his old master Merzeau was also a sleeping partner.

Meanwhile, in the land over which George Washington now presided, George Courtauld I had recommenced a life of farming. He took up also the manufacture of pearl-ash. He had by now a farm of 300 acres and another 300 acres in Kentucky. But in 1793 or 1794, leaving his farm leased and with 'a few hundred pounds clear of all incumbrances',[4] he and his family returned to England. The reason for this move may well have owed something to his wife. She did not like the wilds; she wanted comfort and a minimum of service. Nor, indeed, did she and George much like each other. And this fact undoubtedly influenced both his business career and, indirectly, that of his son. George contended, in 1814, that they had 'lived miserably together for 25 years during which time I have been reproached as the worst of men'. Conversely, she, a kind but prosaic person, resented his energetic and continuous attempts to treat the children as his own especial responsibility, to 'companionize' them, as he called it; she also mistrusted, not without some reason, his capricious ways with money.[5]

His return was not only to England but to silk. August 1794 found him working in a capacity which he described as that of a 'superior assistant' at the silk mills of Peter Nouaille at Great Ness, near Sevenoaks, Kent.[6] Nouaille, as already mentioned, was a Huguenot silk manufacturer of

---

[1] Taylor, pp. 249, 602. See also *D.N.B. sub* Richard Price.

[2] Taylor, p. 602; Courtauld MSS.: Kilner to G.C. I., 26 April 1788.

[3] Taylor, p. 649, also *C.F.L.*, vol. i, p. 47.   [4] *C.F.L.*, vol. i, p. xxxii.

[5] Ibid., vol. iii, pp. 1000, 1010–13; Courtauld MSS.: G.C. I to S.C. III, 20 January 1814; Ruth C. to S.C. III, 17 January 1814, to G.C. I, 22 May 1822; G.C. I to his children, 21 July 1821, etc.   [6] *C.F.L.*, vol. i, p. xxxii.

some consequence to whom has been ascribed the introduction into England of Italian-type crape.[1] He was certainly using these mills in Kent to throw crape yarn and he was certainly also a crape manufacturer.[2] What type of crape he made is unknown; nor, if he did make crimped crapes, is it known where the finishing process was being carried on, at Great Ness or in London. However, to George crape seemed apparently to hold out splendid prospects. He exulted, William Taylor pondered. 'If only half of G.C's expectations are realised . . . I cannot do better than withdraw from tin to crape. However, the pudding is only proved by the eating.'[3] In fact George's job lasted for only three years. His employer is said to have disapproved of his political sentiments and activities. As these now included not only his existing enthusiasm for America and republicanism but also a new enthusiasm for the French revolutionaries, this disapproval was not perhaps wholly surprising in the war-scared years of the 1790s. Nouaille is alleged to have declared of his 'superior assistant' that he would not 'continue such a man in business for 500 a year'.[4]

Having made what was presumably the first Courtauld contact with the crape business, George followed this up with a brief and undocumented foray into the paper industry in London in about 1797–8[5] before his next recorded enterprise in silk. This took him, for the first time, into East Anglia. For the London silk firm of Witts & Co. he established and managed a water-powered throwing mill in the tiny north Essex village of Pebmarsh.[6] He converted an existing flour mill and built dwelling-houses. The work started in about 1799; for a while he lived in Sudbury, and then early in 1801 he and his family set up house in Pebmarsh. He received a salary of £350 per annum, together with a house and some five to six acres of land rent free. But his engagement did not stipulate any term of years, and he encountered some difficulty with his employers in trying to secure a more definite agreement. He was therefore attracted, according to his own account,[7] by an unsolicited invitation 'from a gentleman largely engaged in mercantile and manufacturing pursuits (but not in the silk trade) respecting the establishment of silk mills and the manufacture of crapes'.[8] So once again crape reappears in the story. Witts & Co. were known to

---

[1] Above, p. 27.

[2] *Victoria County History: Kent*, vol. iii, p. 415; see also E.R.O., D/F 3/2/94.

[3] Taylor, p. 589.   [4] *C.F.L.*, vol. i, p. xxxiii; Taylor, p. 649.

[5] *C.F.L.*, vol. i, p. xxxiii.

[6] Witts & Co. were Witts & Rowley, later Witts & Roddick. See *B.P.P.*, 1834, vol. xx, p. 377, and *House of Lords Papers*, 1823, vol. clvi.

[7] This is mainly to be found in E.R.O., D/F 3/2/94.   [8] E.R.O., D/F 3/2/94.

have been making crape at this time,[1] but there is nothing to show that George Courtauld was in any way concerned with this side of their business. Through this unnamed entrepreneur, seemingly impressed by the profitability of the crape business, he met in April 1806 Joseph Wilson of Milk Street, Cheapside. Wilson carried on business as a silk manufacturer under the name of Remington, Wilson & Co., and it was thought that he 'might be induced to add the establishment of throwing mills and the crape manufacture to his other extensive concerns'.[2] The unnamed businessman then withdrew, and for the next three years Wilson and George Courtauld I maintained a sporadic correspondence about the proposed mills, Wilson being evidently reluctant to commit himself. After considering the merits of various possible sites, including a water mill at Hertford, once used for cotton-spinning, a decision was finally reached in March 1809 to acquire a former flour mill at Braintree, a mere twelve miles from Pebmarsh (see Fig. 5 below, p. 61). Wilson bought the land and property, George Courtauld carried out the conversion, undertook the management, and received an initial salary of £400 per annum, plus house and land rent free. The agreement was signed on 2 May 1809.

Eight years later, it took a Chancery action to disentangle the affairs of Messrs. Wilson and Courtauld, to put an end to years of strife, to write an epitaph on the business career of the first George Courtauld, and, as an unintended by-product, to start the next generation of Courtaulds independently in the silk business. What happened, what went wrong, and why?

II

The bare, factual outline can be sketched easily enough.[3] The conversion was a fairly substantial operation: the old premises were demolished, a new and larger building erected, together with a mill house, the water deepened, and a larger wheel put in. Throwing started some time in 1810 and weaving soon after. The silk, Italian, Bengal, or Chinese, came by carrier from Wilson in London to Braintree; there, under George Courtauld's supervision, it was wound and thrown, as directed, into singles, tram, or organzine; the thrown yarn was then either returned to London or woven into crapes. The crape gauzes were also returned to Wilson, who had them

---

[1] *House of Lords Papers*, 1823, vol. clvi.   [2] E.R.O., D/F 3/2/94.
[3] The account that follows is derived from E.R.O., D/F 3/2/94; Courtauld MSS.; *C.F.L.*; and the Chancery pleadings and answers in P.R.O., C. 13/2134/38.

dyed and finished. Again, it is not clear what sort of crapes were being made. George was not concerned in the finishing processes.

Despite a number of complaints by Wilson about both the throwing and the weaving, the business evidently made some headway. For Courtauld invested £1,000 in it, and, after much pressure, Wilson agreed in 1813 to raise his salary to £500 per annum. At about this time George Courtauld, whose interest in technical inventions was matched by some real capacity for making them, completed work on a new device for throwing organzine. This was a double spindle designed to carry out in one operation the three operations necessary for throwing organzine, i.e. twisting the separate threads in one direction, doubling, and then twisting together in the opposite direction. In the course of 1814 the possibility of a partnership between Courtauld and Wilson was discussed at length, with the new spindle as a central feature of the discussions. After the rejection of a scheme to take out a patent in their joint names, George Courtauld patented it in his own name in August 1814.[1] In the following month the two men entered into partnership for a fourteen-year term which was to come into force as from 25 March 1815.

By the article of partnership the business was to be known as Wilson & Courtauld. The premises remained the former's property, but the latter, as manager, was given a share of the profits. Further expansion was planned: Courtauld's £1,000 advance was returned to him, but he was directed to instal machinery at Wilson's expense up to a maximum of £1,000. Any capital expenditure over this limit was to be repaid, with interest, to Wilson whenever the total profits of the business exceeded £1,320 per annum and George Courtauld's share exceeded £600 per annum. These profits were to be computed and divided in the following manner. An agreed scale of charges for throwing was set out, based upon the computed cost of the joint operation of winding and drawing, thus:

	s. d.	s. d.	s. d.	s. d.	s. d.	s. d.
If the weekly cost of winding and drawing per lb. was:	6	7	8	9	10	above 10
Then, add for Organzine	7 6	7 10	8 4	8 8	9 0	9 4
Total charge for throwing Organzine	8 0	8 5	9 0	9 5	9 10	10 2
Add for Trams	4 6	4 8	4 10	5 0	5 2	5 4
Total charge for throwing Trams	5 0	5 3	5 6	5 9	6 0	6 2

[1] B.P. 3834 (1814).

From the aggregate of these charges, the whole current expenses of the mill were to be deducted. The remainder was then the computed profit of the business, and was divided as to 6/11ths to Joseph Wilson and 5/11ths to George Courtauld.

For several months the partnership seemed to work satisfactorily. But the mutual antagonism of the partners soon became apparent: by November 1815 they were 'almost at open war'.[1] This time the main object of their dispute was the scale of charges. Wilson contended that general changes in trade had lowered throwing prices, but that the new scale, so far from producing a similar reduction, had in fact led to charges higher than those prevailing before the partnership. 'There is no modification of the scale of prices that will satisfy me', he wrote in October 1815. 'The whole must be done away with and the prices compare with the Trade generally.'[2] Early in the new year he began to withhold supplies of silk. In February 1816 George Courtauld proposed a scale based not on winding costs but on deniers and types of silk. It was not accepted, and in March Wilson refused to supply any more silk. The mills came to a stop, and so too did George Courtauld's income. There was no compensating stoppage, however, in the cost of maintaining thirty apprentices, in taxes and incidental expenses, all of which Courtauld had to bear. Lawyers were consulted and a great many acrimonious letters written. In December 1816 George Courtauld began to use his partner's mills to throw silk procured from elsewhere. Accordingly in January 1817 Wilson published a notice saying the partnership was dissolved and commenced an action in King's Bench for possession of the mills and the ejectment of his partner. Courtauld countered this by securing an injunction and starting an action in Chancery. The case was heard in July 1817 and Courtauld won. By a deed of dissolution, the partnership came to an end on 28 January 1818; Wilson paid Courtauld £3,500, retained the premises, and took over the apprentices; and Courtauld for his part agreed not to engage in silk throwing or any branch of silk manufacture within ten miles of Braintree (excepting the parish of Pebmarsh) before 5 April 1829.

III

The reasons for this last of George Courtauld's industrial misadventures are complex. Their elucidation may help to illustrate some of the

---

[1] Courtauld MSS.: G.C. I to S.C. III, 15 November 1815.
[2] P.R.O., C. 13/2134/38.

problems of early business management; and, at a different level, to point
to the hazards of operating in business whilst equipped with an over-
developed sense of unrewarded virtue.

First we must note that the affairs of Wilson and Courtauld came to
grief, as so often happens, at a time of general economic depression. The
banishment of Napoleon to Elba in April 1814 had been followed by
a rising wave of business optimism; production and trade boomed,
interest rates fell, investment rose. But before 1815 was over, the boom had
collapsed; industrial prices fell, bad harvests in 1816 and 1817 brought
high grain prices and a drop in real earnings; business confidence slumped.[1]
In the silk industry, the manufacturers and throwsters who had been
expanding their operation behind the protective tariff wall found that this
gave no protection against falling demand and prices at home. Boom and
slump alike can be seen reflected in Fig. 2 over the years 1814–17. The
lure of crape making had brought too many producers to so seemingly
promising a field.

'I must concede that the silk business in general is very dull and the
crape trade particularly bad', George Courtauld wrote to Wilson in
September 1815, and continued in his long-winded way:

I understand that you mean to lessen that latter manufacture as soon as possible
yet not so violently as to render it difficult to resume or increase it in future
should that demand require it. I induce it cannot be supposed (unless by some
national arrangement the whole silk business should be materially injured) that
the article of crapes should permanently cease or become suddenly and irretriev-
ably worthless. I have taken measures immediately to lessen our quantity, and
of course also to improve our quality. Some hands I have dismissed, others
alarmed by the fear of losing their work, have taken an opportunity of getting
different employment, and I have reduced the quantity allowed to be made by
one hand to 1½ pieces per week. Our night work at the crape mill will cease this
week. . . .[2]

It was one thing to dismiss hands, but quite another to persuade a partner
to forgo rewards to which he was legally entitled. But economic circumstances forced Wilson to try somehow to alter the scale of charges,
the very nature of which made for rigidity. On Courtauld's own calcula-
tions, the average charges for throwing at Braintree in the year ending
March 1814 had been 9s. 11¼d. per lb. for organzine, 5s. 11d. for trams;

[1] T. S. Ashton, *The Industrial Revolution* (Oxford, 1948), p. 152.
[2] E.R.O., D/F 3/2/94, G.C. I to Jos. Wilson, 25 September 1815.

for the corresponding year 1815–16 they rose to 10s. 3½d. and 6s. 3¼d. respectively. His claim that the increase was due to poorer quality silk and the taking on of untrained apprentice children may or may not have been true, but it availed little in the face of a market so falling that by the end of 1816 prices had dropped by 20 per cent.

This economic context of the dispute does not, however, explain either its course or its nature. Amongst the specific problems which faced the enterprise, that of finding and supervising the labour force proved particularly intractable.

The tasks demanded of those attending the machinery of throwing mills were neither difficult nor arduous. To contemporaries they seemed peculiarly well suited to the children of the poor, from whom indeed industrial labour had long been demanded without thought of disapproval. For the manufacturers who had invested in water-powered mills in rural areas there seemed a promise of adequate supplies of cheap labour in the facts of growing population and the existence of lower wages outside London. To some extent this was true, and not least along the Essex–Suffolk border with its decaying woollen industry. But as throwing mills multiplied— and several were established in this area at this time—they began to find themselves in competition for a particular sort of labour, i.e. young women and children. Moreover, as labour costs could account for up to 50 per cent. of the cost of throwing, there existed a powerful incentive to keep down these costs and to maintain productivity by training and supervision.

During the earlier phase of their association, i.e. before the partnership, the girls and young women in the throwing mill were locally recruited. By 1812, however, George Courtauld was writing of the need for 'more exertions . . . to obtain sufficient work-people',[1] and in 1813 he was busy doing what some cotton mill owners or managers were doing in the industrial north—recruiting parish children from workhouses to be bound apprentices. Sometimes he went to local parishes, such as Glemsford, but increasingly these young workers were garnered from the pauper children of parishes nearer to London. Characteristically, he saw in this process a vision of social advance:

I have 8 children coming from Islington on Tuesday next and 8 or 10 more on Thursday . . . I had my choice from upwards of 50 girls of different ages and accepted all but 1 that were within the age of 10 and 13. They are from a very

[1] Courtauld MSS.: G.C. I to S.C. III, October (?) 1812.

PLATE 3

BRAINTREE OLD MILL

well-conducted workhouse and I really expect and earnestly hope that by continued care and attention my establishment of apprentices will prove a nursery of respectable young women fitted for any of the humble walks of life.[1]

In fact, between 1813 and 1816, the business took children, girls only, from St. Pancras and St. Sepulchre, in London, as well as from Islington, the highest number at any one time being fifty-five. They were sent 'with a complete change of strong common clothing, or an allowance made for it, and £5, half paid upon their being bound and half after the expiration of the first year'. Bound apprentices until the age of 21, 'by the wish of the several parishes', they were then taken on at wages ranging from 6s. to 8s. per week. However, the firm, as George Courtauld explained, accustomed them, from 17 onwards, 'to attend to their own expenses and in a great measure support themselves by suitable agreements with them respecting the product of their employments'.[2] The costs to the business of maintaining and training the apprentices was expected to lead to increased costs in the first year and then to fall as the children learnt their simple tasks—which they could certainly do in less than seven or eight years' apprenticeship—thus, it was hoped, providing adequate, very cheap, and legally bound labour. An establishment of up to 100 such apprentices was the ultimate aim.

But always there were problems of supervision. At various times one or another of George Courtauld's four daughters, Louisa Perina, Catherine, Eliza, and Sophia, whose ages in 1814 ranged respectively from 23 to 15, worked in the mill and supervised the children at the winding engines. Weaving was also done on the premises, and in November 1812 George was seeking a new overseer at the mill who would know 'how to maintain order and attention to business . . . in the weaving room'.[3] There was trouble in 1814 over a woman supervisor who was alleged to have beaten the apprentices. Girls ran away; an angry father and uncle of one of them came to Braintree; there were threats and scenes between them and George, who denied all knowledge of the 'petty tyranny' of the supervisor. He complained to Wilson that it was impossible to get proper supervision for the wages which Wilson was willing to pay. He proposed instead the attendance of his four daughters, and in particular that

. . . the winding, drawing and doubling floor, where the scale is fixed, should at every instance of time during working hours have one of them

---

[1] E.R.O., D/F 3/3/94, G.C. I to Mr. Mann, 11 December 1813.
[2] Courtauld MSS.: G.C. I to R. W. Oldham, 8 February 1816.
[3] Ibid., G.C. I to S.C. III, 24 November 1812.

present that their constant eye and whole attention be given to the people of that floor in maintaining perfect silence except the singing of hymns which we find a useful relaxation and a help to industry, attention and orderly conduct.[1]

This musically alleviated toil was to be accompanied by a system of marks for blame or praise, exhibited on slates.

Overseers, supervisors, daughters—they came and went in the mill. And this failure to maintain constancy in supervision was surely a potent cause of the stream of complaints about poor throwing, bad weaving, and excessive waste which flowed from London to Braintree. 'I receive continual and great complaints of the badness of my crapes', wrote George in July 1811; and, admitting that they were generally still far from good, he put it down to 'so many new hands compared with those who are experienced'.[2] A year or so later: 'I have carefully looked over all the crapes and am sorry to say that they do *not* please me', grumbled Wilson in June 1812; in August, 'the uneven and foul silk cannot be endured'; in November, 'I must beg your particular care with the Organzine'; in February 1814, 'I have very carefully examined our goods . . . and also compared them particularly with many pieces of other houses. Our's are evidently irregularly thrown . . .'; in January 1816, 'the truth is that you have an unworthy reluctance to engage suitable help and you allow ignorant and idle children to do as they please'.[3] These are but a few variations on a theme which seems to have been heard throughout this inharmonious association.

One alone of George's assistants and supervisors might have improved matters, but, alas, he too came and went: his eldest son, Samuel Courtauld III. For behind this failure of labour relations lay a failure of personal relations. George Courtauld I managed to fall out with his business partners, his wife, some of his daughters, and certainly his eldest son, the son who was by far the ablest member of his family. By the spring of 1813 his relations with his wife had grown so bad that a scheme for formal separation was being discussed, and he wrote a pathetic *cri de cœur* to his son: '. . . I am not in spirits. You have left me, the two girls talk of leaving me, I shall seem to be without help and without friends.'[4]

[1] E.R.O., D/F 3/2/94, G.C. I. to Jos. Wilson, 24 September 1814.
[2] Courtauld MSS.: G.C. I to S.C. III, 1 July 1811.
[3] E.R.O. 3/3/94, Jos. Wilson to G.C. I, 16 June 1812, 10 August 1812, 9 November 1812, 26 February 1814; G.C. I. to Jos. Wilson, 16 January 1816.
[4] Courtauld MSS.: G.C. I to S.C. III, 6 March (?) 1813.

IV

Born in Albany, New York, on 1 June 1793, Samuel Courtauld III first began work at Pebmarsh mill in 1807 at the age of 14. He helped his father in setting up the Braintree mill and in the early years of running it, thus acquiring a fair knowledge of the machinery of silk mills, of the water works for mills, of throwing and weaving, as well as some idea of the problems of management.[1] But hard work and filial affection were hardly proof against four years of George Courtauld I. At the end of 1811 or beginning of 1812, Samuel left home, having, as George I characteristically put it, 'left your father's house very properly, and with his entire approbation because from various causes your temper and manners were so far unsuitable to his, as to render it highly improbable you could at that time continue living there, connected as you were in every way, with comfort and advantage to either.'[2] Through the agency of his uncle, William Taylor, he got a job in Jones, Taylor & Co. in Tottenham Court Road. The post had been occupied by his slightly older cousin, Peter Alfred Taylor I, eldest son of William Taylor. He stayed there for some two and a half years. Whilst Samuel had been at Braintree, his father had paid him a salary; when his son left George continued to debit the business with this amount. Not surprisingly, when Wilson discovered this early in 1812 he was 'rather crusty' about it.[3] But he seemed unwilling to pay for, and George unwilling or unable to hire, adequate assistance; and so the complaints multiplied.

Meanwhile, a clerk in London, Samuel was the target for a steady barrage of very frequent and very long letters fired by his ever-zealous father. That he should have been warned against 'the allurements of vice' and the dangers of 'wandering about the streets of an evening'; or that he should have been recommended to a detailed, not to say exhaustive, programme of self-improvement by reading good books:[4] such counsels were likely enough. But he got more than that. George provided accounts not only of the quarrels with his partner but also of conflicts with his wife, who wanted to go back to Ireland, and with his eldest daughter, Louisa, who wanted to start a school. In letter after letter came reproaches, moralizing, and all manner of exhortations. Dotted here and there with bits of

[1] Ibid., G.C. I to S.C. III, 14 March 1813.
[2] Ibid., G.C. I to S.C. III, 17 August 1812.
[3] Ibid., G.C. I to S.C. III, 1 April 1812.
[4] Ibid., G.C. I to S.C. III, 1 July 1812, 23 March 1813.

technical information about spindles, these exhausting and orotund homilies, sometimes running to two, three, or four thousand words, went weekly or bi-weekly from Braintree to London. Exhorted to piety, meekness, humility, love, truth, forbearance, and charity, Samuel, not surprisingly, remained turbulent, ambitious, sensitive, critical, opinionated, and able. Nor did he allow himself to be ruled by the most significant of his father's adjurations. He became dissatisfied with Jones, Taylor & Co, so his father, suggesting that if he stayed on there long enough something might turn up for him, offered him these precepts:[1] 'Remember . . . that the greatest and wisest men must be governed by circumstances—we cannot command events—our wisdom lies in seizing the favourable opportunities which Providence often supplies most bountifully', and again: '. . . Circumstances over which we have often no control throw opportunities of getting forward in our way. It appears to me our wisdom and our duty, thankfully to a kind Providence, to seize the opportunities.' Fortunately for himself and the Courtauld family, Samuel III did not content himself with waiting for Heaven-sent opportunities.

In the summer of 1814 Samuel returned to the Braintree mill. A number of reasons combined to influence this decision. First, George had for some time been trying, in connexion with the negotiations for the partnership, to get his son back with the offer of a salary of £150 as an assistant. Evidently terms were agreed with Wilson on this, though at precisely what salary remains unknown. Second, Samuel was now 21 and so might have considered that, though with his father, he would perhaps have more chance than formerly of independent behaviour. Third, aware of the responsibilities which attached to him as eldest son, he saw, in the boom year of 1814, promising prospects in the silk business. And finally and most pressing of all, he was in love with a girl, Christina Anderson, who lived not far from Braintree. The comments of a friend on the proposed return underline both the nature of the position and the distance between Samuel's attitude to circumstances and what his father thought it should be:

. . . I am pleased to find that the desire of obtaining the object of your wishes has made you resolve to give the thing a fair trial and sincerely hope ere this that you have had such an answer from Miss A as will confirm you in the resolution to relax a little in what seems to be a fault in your disposition, too uncomplying in a submission to circumstances.[2]

[1] Courtauld MSS.: G.C. I to S.C. III, 20 April 1812, September 1812.
[2] Ibid., John Newberry to S.C. III, 15 October 1814.

He had not, however, long been back before his relations with his father were again in disorder. His cousin, Peter Taylor, who also observed that 'your attachment to Miss A . . . seemed to have no other chance of a happy termination but by continuing with your father', warned him against further injury to his temper, and embittering his father's happiness.[1]

These distressing relationships were brought to an end in about May 1815 when Samuel fell seriously ill, so seriously that it was at one time thought that he would not survive.[2] However, recover he did and in the autumn went, presumably to convalesce, to stay with his maternal uncle, John Minton, in Ireland. His pending departure gave his father the opportunity of sending him some fulsome advice on social conduct in general and Samuel's manners in particular. This letter deserves quotation not simply because it presents a picture of young Samuel, as he appeared to his father, but also because it exactly captures the flavour of the father, the well-meaning but stupefying literal-mindedness, the belief in simple rational expositions both of principles and of actions as the path to human perfection. He exhorted Samuel to:

> . . . endeavour to profit by the opportunity this excursion is so well calculated to give you, of throwing off a certain stiffness and distance of manner, which is so apt to repress cordiality, and to chill the first impressions of the benign affections. We should aim not only to be loved where we are *known*, but by a cordial friendly manner *invite* those benevolent feelings which should induce a *wish* to know *more* of us. . . .

> . . . Upon the subject of appearance and manner, allow me, and with the hope of being useful, to add another remark. When we go into a new place—among new people—the circumstance offers a very fine opportunity for adopting *any* alteration we deem expedient in our conduct or manners; *because* the alteration cannot seem 'odd'—cannot appear remarkable as contrasted with our yesterday's self. Now I would recommend your particular attention to your manner of first addressing upon any occasion, or receiving the first address of others. Our manner may be *respectful* and kindly; or *familiar* and kindly, as circumstances may appear to warrant; for the first we should with a pleasant smile proceeding from kindly feelings *bend* gently forward—head, shoulders and back together— (I do not mean anything resembling a dancing master's bow)—with a How d'ye do or anything that may appear most suitable; for a person we would wish to treat rather with good natured *familiarity* than polite and kindly *respect*, we should still *bend* in much the same manner, but more *quickly*; the slower bend

[1] Ibid., P.A.T. I to S.C. III, 15 November 1814.

[2] The nature of the illness is not clear, though references in letters suggest a pulmonary disease of some sort—see Courtauld MSS.: G.C. I to S.C. III, November 1815.

THE ANGUS L. MacDONALD LIBRARY

ST. FRANCIS XAVIER UNIVERSITY.

ANTIGONISH, N. S.

would seem to say—'My dear and respected Sir, I hope you are well'—the quicker motion would say—'My dear Sir, I am happy to see you and hope I shall soon have the pleasure of being better acquainted with you'. In both cases you see I think a polite *bend* (respectful or more familiar according to circumstances) essential in accosting those to whom we are strangers or with whom we have but slight acquaintance; and this, my dear Sam, you are aware I recommend in opposition to your adopted mode of standing *bolt upright* as if you said— 'Here I am—ready' (for I give you credit for frequently expressing this) 'ready to receive any attentions you may think proper to show, but—I make no first advances.' The mode I recommend—the kindly benignant *Bend*—says most plainly 'You see—I wish to treat you with kindly and polite attention—and if *you* are willing to return it you may be *assured* it will give me pleasure.'

Now, my dear Samuel, you must not reply that everyone has a manner of his own, and that to assume what is not natural to him will never do; I should reply to this, were it urged, that we should always aim to adopt what is *proper* in manner as well as in conduct; and *USE* will soon render it natural . . .[1]

The 'kindly benignant Bend' had not, alas, done much for George's own relationships.

Some months after he had dispatched this to his 22-year-old son, George was imploring him to return. Early in 1816 he was still holding out hopes of re-establishing Samuel in the business with Wilson. But as the dispute became warfare, so by March he began to beg his son's return to help him in the fight. Typically, George managed on 10 March to write two long letters in one day, asking in the first for Samuel's immediate return, in the second deciding that this was not necessary. However, later in the month he changed his mind again, and sought his urgent return: 'our affairs greatly need every attention we can procure; your assistance, long wished for, may soon, very soon, be essentially requisite'.[2]

Samuel III returned to Braintree and, in about July or August 1816, took the crucial step of setting up as a silk throwster on his own account. His 'silk manufactory on a very small scale in this vicinity', as he described it in a letter to John Minton on 31 August 1816,[3] was on a site in Panfield Lane in the contiguous parish of Bocking, only a very short distance from the Courtauld and Wilson mill. Its finance, development and future were all bound up with the history of Samuel III's enterprises and will be examined in the next chapter. Meanwhile, it must be em-

[1] Courtauld MSS.: G.C. I to S.C. III, October 1815. More of the same sort about Samuel's 'bolt upright figure' arrived in the following month (13 November 1815).

[2] Ibid., G.C. I to S.C. III, 4 March 1816, 10 March 1816.

[3] *C.F.L.*, vol. i, p. 202.

phasized firstly that Samuel's small enterprise enjoyed an immediate success, and secondly and more important, that its establishment arose directly out of his father's dispute with Joseph Wilson.

By cutting off silk supplies, and with them George Courtauld's means of supporting his wife and younger children, Wilson chanced to bring about concerted action in the Courtauld family, with some far-reaching results. Until this time, Samuel, evidently weary of both his father and the silk business, remained in Ireland, undecided about his future. He contemplated agriculture, trade in America, business in London, the study of medicine. But faced with news of pending legal actions, of dismissals both of hands in the mill and of the two servants at home, of business and domestic outgoings totalling over £1,000 a year and of no income, Samuel returned.[1] Wilson's tactics engendered a degree of family harmony hitherto absent. Under the threat of being starved out George I stopped vacillating and added consistency of actions to his existing energy and spirit. Samuel's newly found purposefulness obviously helped to stiffen his father's resolve, and father and son acquired a new regard for each other in joint action against the common enemy. Samuel's own enterprise formed a part of their concerted plans. In August 1816 he wrote that 'our hopes of affecting Wilson's proceedings depend on my getting forward before he has starved us out'.[2] Though still wary of his father's schemes ('I dare hardly trust my father's plans on paper') he lavished praise on his father's conduct: 'heroic constancy of purpose . . . intrepidity of soul . . . tenderness of heart, cheerfulness of spirit, and pious resignation . . . We are all too near to appreciate the grandeur of the rock to which we cling'.[3] The other side of the medal to all this was that by December 1816, Samuel was not only hard at work throwing silk on his own machinery but was also supplying silk to his father, getting it thrown in the Braintree mill of Messrs. Wilson and Courtauld, and then selling it in the market at prices below those of that notorious scale agreed to some two years earlier by his father and Joseph Wilson.[4]

These developments wrought a change in Samuel's situation. He was gradually moving towards the position not simply of responsibility but of ascendancy which he was later to occupy in the Courtauld family circle.

---

[1] Courtauld MSS.: G.C. I to S.C. III, 13 November 1815, 19 January 1816, 29 January 1816, 6 February 1816, 21 March 1816; J. N. to S.C. III, 5 February 1816.
[2] *C.F.L.*, vol. i, p. 203. [3] Ibid., vol. i, p. 204–5.
[4] P.R.O., C. 13/2134/38. S.C. III's reference (*C.F.L.*, vol. i, p. 203) to obtaining the 'assistance of mere workhouse children' suggests that he was probably also using the Courtauld–Wilson apprentices.

The legal processes ground forward in the course of 1817, and meanwhile 'the mills above and below [i.e. both in Braintree and in Bocking] go merrily round. Sam has silk pouring in from every quarter.'[1] George wrote to his favourite daughter Sophia II, then a governess in Bristol, told her of the current state of the battle, and observed:

> ... But the best of all is that Samuel succeeds so well, has in the short space of 6 months so well established his reputation as a Gentleman, an upright man of business, and a superior manufacturer, that he has more silk than either he or I together know how to proceed with ...[2]

Their relations continued on these harmonious terms through the Chancery hearings of July 1817 to the final formal dissolution in 1818, a dissolution which left George Courtauld I out of the silk industry and his son Samuel Courtauld III in it. He was in it on his own account, but yet as a by-product of his father's dispute with Joseph Wilson. And in that dispute, though general economic circumstances, the problems of labour and supervision, and the personal relationships between George Courtauld and his family had all played their part, what perhaps ultimately brought the partners to legal battle was their irreconcilably opposed personalities. Indeed, in retrospect the wonder is not that they quarrelled, but how they ever came to sign the partnership deed of 1814. Joseph Wilson wrote sharp, curt, and often tactless letters, bristling with complaints. George Courtauld answered with interminable expositions of moral principle, long quotations from past letters, and a vast array of detailed information: the net result was usually to blot out the point at issue. Wilson took the illegal step of breaking the agreement and paid for it. The dispute ended George I's business career, but it started the much more important one of his son.

V

The remaining years of the first George Courtauld's life formed an interesting but sad epilogue to his career.

Once the threat to the family represented by Wilson had been vanquished, internal strife reappeared. 'I feel, more I dare say than you can suppose, the widening breach in our sympathies', wrote Samuel to his father in December 1817. His father's ideas, he observed to his sister Sophia, 'are very inconstant and much governed by feelings, violently

---

[1] C.F.L., vol. i, p. 239.   [2] Ibid., p. 236.

excited it may be by circumstances perfectly unconnected with the subject on which they are exhibited'.[1] George, for his own part, after settling the details of the dissolution remained undecided about his future. Then he took a characteristic decision. Having in February 1818 gone to Berkshire with the idea of looking at a silk mill there, he heard by chance of an English settlement in Illinois. So he decided to take another trip to the U.S.A., with, as he said, the intention of acquiring 'an American estate for myself and those of my family who may desire to accompany me in my second trip next spring'. Samuel looked at the venture without enthusiasm: '. . . this American undertaking! Well, well, without philosophy we can do nothing, and with it we can endure all things.'[2]

The family departed to Edinburgh, where not all was harmony between mother and daughters, Samuel stayed at Braintree, and George departed, in time, to Ohio. Here he bought land. He tried his hand, without luck, at speculation. He hoped to sell some of the land 'for immediate payment at a very handsome advance. I certainly had very fair ground for this conclusion, but it has proved fallacious'.[3] However, he persevered with his land, and in the spring of 1819 returned to England. Here, living in London for some of the time, he wrote and published a tract advocating migration to America and tried to establish a joint-stock association for that purpose. Meanwhile he was making preparations for returning to Ohio with such of his family as would accompany him.

So in August 1820 he sailed for America again, and for the last time. With him went his daughters Sophia II and Eliza, his sons George II and John Minton. On this side of the Atlantic there remained behind Louisa, a governess in Edinburgh, Catherine, who in 1818 had married her cousin Peter Alfred Taylor I, Samuel III, hard at work at his Essex mills, and George's wife, who stayed behind with her eldest son. In the autumn of 1821 he tried to set up a community of migrants in Ohio, and a further group, including Peter and Catherine Taylor, left to join them. But the 'association' quickly failed, and George I and Peter Taylor soon fell out with each other. Letters passed to and fro across the Atlantic containing proposals for Samuel and his mother to join the American party or for George I to return to silk in England. But nothing came of them. There were too many reproaches by Ruth Courtauld to her husband, and too many doubts about renewed contacts between Samuel and his father. In June 1822 Samuel, in his most assured, not to say haughty, manner, was

---

[1] C.F.L., vol. i, pp. 323–4, 331–2.   [2] Ibid., pp. 352, 359.
[3] Ibid., vol. ii, p. 465.

telling his father that he was 'quite satisfied . . . that your particular view of business in this country is impracticable';[1] in September Ruth Courtauld was telling her daughter Sophia that she could not go to America 'under the dread of being sent adrift when your father spends all his money, which experience teaches us would be soon'.[2] By April 1823 all notions of Samuel going to America—and the previous year he had been near to going—had been abandoned.

And then news came that George Courtauld I had caught a fever and, on 13 August 1823, died. With his death, Samuel moved into that position of responsibility and ascendancy both in the family and in its business affairs which he had been moving towards since 1816 and which he was now to occupy and to consolidate for the next fifty-eight years.

[1] Courtauld MSS.: S.C. III to G.C. I, 12 June 1822.
[2] C.F.L., vol. ii, p. 929.

PLATE 4

PANFIELD LANE MILL

All that survived of Samuel Courtauld's original venture of 1816, just before demolition in 1926

CHAPTER V

The Origins of Samuel Courtauld & Company

I

T HE twelve years from 1816 to 1828 which separate the setting up by Samuel Courtauld III of his own business in Panfield Lane and the signing of the deed of partnership which brought into being the firm known as Courtauld, Taylor & Courtauld were in many ways the most crucial in the origins of this family concern. It was a period of trial and error, of near-failure and final success. This success would not, however, have been readily predicted in the difficult days of 1819–21 when the business was near to being sold. Nor would it have seemed reasonable at that time to guess that this small venture, then wholly concerned with throwing, would have grown by 1850 into perhaps the biggest crape manufacturing firm in the country.

In historical retrospect the period clearly falls into two parts, the dividing event being the death of George Courtauld I in 1823. Samuel III dominated the enterprise throughout. In the first phase he was struggling with hesitations, doubts, fits of depression, and acute financial difficulties; in the second, he was grappling with the quite different problem of organizing a larger concern which had to function in economic circumstances substantially changed by the Government's lowering, in 1824–6, of the protective wall around the silk industry.

II

The fluctuating course of Samuel III's enterprise in its early years did not immediately make itself evident. At first all went well. 'Sam is going on better and better', as Ruth Courtauld told her younger son George II in January 1817.[1] After the action against Wilson had been won, Samuel, so far from seeing any reason to withdraw, sought expansion. In the

---

[1] *C.F.L.*, vol. i, p. 233.

summer of 1817 he persuaded his cousin Peter Alfred Taylor I to join him in the silk business. Between November 1817 and January 1818 the partners of this first firm of Courtauld & Taylor spent some time looking for a suitable water mill to replace the hand- or horse-powered Panfield Lane factory.[1] Negotiations for mills at Canterbury, Newbury, and at Coggeshall, nearby in Essex, proved unfruitful, so in January 1818 they bought a piece of land in Braintree on which to build 'a factory for horse power large enough to about treble our present business'. In November 1817 the Panfield Lane establishment had been yielding a profit of nearly £1,000 a year; from the new premises Samuel was hoping in February 1818 for '£1,200 or £1,500 per annum by May'. Whether these expectations were fulfilled remains unknown, but at least the 'New Mills' at Braintree were finished on time, and the business continued in a thriving state until around the end of the year.[2] As can be seen by reference to Fig. 2, this phase of prosperity in 1817–18 seems to have coincided with an up-turn in the industry as a whole.

But the following year brought a down-turn alike in the industry's production and in the affairs of Courtauld & Taylor. Increasing financial difficulties were now combined with family opposition to his schemes. In July 1819, Samuel admitted that although in general the business was good, the Braintree mill had not fulfilled expectations. 'But truly', he complained to his sister Sophia, 'I am weary of the one unalleviated course of up-hill drudgery that is my lot. To oppose at every step the desires of the friends and family is as a mountain on the brain.'[3] Business fell off, relations with Peter Taylor grew strained. But Samuel, despite recurrent moods of fierce depression, kept his faith in the business and renewed his search for a water-powered mill. In this he succeeded, finally securing a lease, with option to purchase, of a former cloth-fulling mill, in the possession of the local family of Savill, at Bocking. Meanwhile the financial circumstances of business worsened. So in November 1819, as part of a rearrangement which will be examined shortly, the New Mills at Braintree were sold; the Panfield Lane establishment was given up; Peter Taylor was dropped from active partnership and dispatched with his recently acquired wife, Samuel's sister Catherine, to live on very little at Ostend;

---

[1] In the later 1820s it was certainly manually operated (see below, p. 64); in 1817 S.C. III referred to it as 'this donkey place', though whether literally or figuratively is not clear (C.F.L., vol. i, p. 295).

[2] C.F.L., vol. i, pp. 293–5, 297–9, 305, 313–14, 332, 337, 358–9, 370–1; vol. ii, p. 471.

[3] C.F.L., vol. ii, p. 551.

and the business was concentrated at Bocking mill.[1] For a while Samuel's younger brother George II, now 17 years old, was working with him, but his departure for America with his father, in April 1820, left Samuel alone with his water-powered mill, his mother, and a pile of debts.

The next three years were the true testing-time of Samuel III's career. Improvement was at first very slow; the burden of debt remained heavy; and Samuel moped about his thwarted passion for Christina Anderson.[2] Advertising, in October 1820, for an apprentice throwster—and thereby a premium—brought no responses.[3] By the autumn of 1820 he had decided, he told his father, 'to get the concern into as good a state as possible, and to use the summer and autumn of 1821 in endeavours to dispose of it decently . . . and to . . . join you in the spring of 1822 . . .'.[4] He felt the separation from his brothers and sisters. Yet, though he lamented to George II that he often wished he were with him, he also told the latter of improvements in the business, recalled the value of his past services, and dangled some bait obviously designed to induce him to return.[5] Samuel's 'unsettled state of purpose', as his friend John Newberry aptly put it in January 1821, continued. At the same time as he was telling his sister Sophia that business was better and that despite disadvantages his 'habits [were] identified with it' and that he would 'hardly again find [himself] so well-off for a living', he was trying to sell it for £3,000 to a prospective buyer, Andrew Taylor—of whom more will be said later. The deal fell through. So Samuel tried to get a partner: he failed. In July 1821 he advertised the business for sale: he got no worth-while replies. But by this time, it was 'doing more comfortably than I have ever known it for a long season and I doubt not that it will still improve'. Although his throwing was still done on a commission basis, he now no longer had to solicit for silk to throw, but was himself solicited to take it; and his efforts to sell, though they continued, seem to have become rather half-hearted.[6]

Substantial progress in business now coincided with one of the changes

[1] Ibid., vol. ii, pp. 578, 602–3, 620–1; Courtauld MSS.: J.N. to S.C. III (? June) 1819; Ruth C. to S.C. III, 13 July 1809; Sophia C. III to S.C. III, 13 July 1819; G.C. I to Ruth C., 20 December 1819.

[2] Courtauld MSS.: J.N. to S.C. III, 2 March 1820.

[3] Ibid., J.N. to S.C. III, 6 October 1820.

[4] Ibid., S.C. III to G.C. I, 18 September 1820.

[5] Ibid., S.C. III to G.C. II, 20 September 1820, 19 November 1820; S.C. III to G.C. I, 19 November 1820.

[6] C.F.L., vol. ii, pp. 758, 777, 807; Courtauld MSS.: J.N. to S.C. III, 12 January 1821, 23 March, 1821; S.C. III to G.C. I, 23 June 1821, 24 July 1821; J.N. to G.C. I, 3 August 1821; S.C. III to G.C. I, 14 March 1823 and 23 April 1823.

of personal life which, like the length of Cleopatra's nose, seem random occurrences in the context of a narrowly economic calculus but which in historical fact often tilt the scales of decision. Samuel fell in love with Ellen Taylor, younger sister of his cousin, brother-in-law, and absent partner, Peter Alfred Taylor. In December 1821 Ruth Courtauld wrote to report to her husband in Ohio that Ellen's father, i.e. George I's former fellow apprentice, William Taylor, 'came down . . . to inspect Sam's situation, and seems much pleased'.[1] In July 1822 they were married. Though George I continued to hope for family reunification in America, it would clearly now have needed serious economic depression in the silk industry to have pushed Samuel out and to have induced him and his new wife and his mother to cross the Atlantic. Instead, the country as a whole was enjoying an economic boom, and its force was felt in Bocking as elsewhere. In November 1822 Samuel's profits were again running at around £1,000 per annum. He started looking for land for the erection of another factory; the little Panfield Lane establishment was brought back into use in March 1823 as an auxiliary winding and doubling plant. An important stage in his career as a throwster was reached, for he tried hard to induce his brother George II to return to the business.[2] In this endeavour he did not immediately succeed, but it mattered little. For when George I died in August 1823, though the general economic boom was past its peak, Samuel's business and confidence alike were in good shape. Now there was no turning back.

III

How had these early years of difficult endeavour been financed? Just as Samuel's move into the silk-throwing business on his own account arose from his father's involvement with Wilson, so were his early years in business still dependent, in more ways than one, upon his father, despite the latter's departure to America. The most important of these ways was the provision by George I of long-term capital. When Samuel first started up in Panfield Lane in 1816 his financial support was, as he put it, 'the romantic liberality of a friend'.[3] This friend was John Newberry, who, during the crucial years that followed, provided Samuel with the short-

---

[1] C.F.L., vol. ii, p. 859.
[2] Courtauld MSS.: S.C. III to G.C. I, 30 November 1822, 14 March 1823, 23 April 1823; C.F.L., vol. iii, pp. 991–5, 1001; E.R.O., D/F 3/2/95 (i), Durant & Co., to Courtauld & Taylor, 25 February 1823; E.R.O., D/DQC. 1, S.C. III to Wm. Bromley, 12 February 1823.
[3] C.F.L., vol. i, p. 203.

term credit which complemented the long-term loans made by George I. It was on these two bases, together with some overdrafts from his bankers, that the business struggled along.

George's first main contribution of long-term capital was the loan to the firm of Courtauld & Taylor of £1,000; this was used to finance the construction of the New Mill premises at Braintree (the land cost £120), upon which it was secured by a mortgage. A further £800 was later loaned personally to Samuel as part of a scheme by which George was to become a sleeping partner in a separate and new concern. The scheme was abortive, but the money became lodged in Courtauld & Taylor, and in January 1819 George, not unreasonably, was asking to know: 'the exact state of your pecuniary concerns and whether I may speedily expect the return of this £800 in the family funds'.[1] Some part of this total of £1,800 now loaned to Samuel was itself a loan to George I from his unmarried sister Sophia I, who in March 1817 had helped him with 'several hundreds' during the battle against Wilson.[2] Once again the influence of the Courtauld–Wilson conflict on Samuel III's business is underlined. But George's chances of early regaining his £800 grew less as, in the course of 1819, Samuel's business position worsened and his indebtedness to John Newberry increased.

John Newberry was a personal friend of Samuel III, some nine years older than the latter, and their friendship may have dated from Samuel's years in London in 1812–14. He lived at 54 Upper Marylebone Street. Although the exact nature of his trade is not clear, it is evident from the surviving correspondence that he had no direct concern with the silk business.[3] It is also equally clear that from 1819, perhaps earlier, he was providing short-term finance for Samuel Courtauld by means of the well-worn contemporary device of accommodation bills. These were bills of exchange drawn simply to provide accommodation; they were not drawn to secure payment for goods or services, as none had in fact been provided. They were consequently sometimes called 'fictitious bills'. In the ordinary way A lent his name, and creditworthiness, by accepting such a bill drawn on him by B who was to be accommodated. It could then be used as an instrument on which cash could be raised. Thus did Newberry write to Samuel Courtauld in February 1819, evidently confirming arrangements made:

[1] Ibid., vol. i, p. 339; vol. ii, p. 478.   [2] Ibid., vol. i, p. 249.

[3] Courtauld MSS.: Letters S.C. III and J.N., 1819–23. According to contemporary London directories John Newberry, father or son, carried on business as a leather gilder, a maker of leather covers, and was connected with the Manchester velvet and upholstery warehouse.

'You will therefore please to draw as you proposed and it shall be regularly accepted.[1] The personal nature, and also the dangers, of the procedure are, in part at least, testified to by Newberry's comments in April 1819:

> ... You ask me if you may draw again on me for to make good this deficiency with your banker. I can only say certainly if you need it. I have been puzzling my brains to find out why you have put the question so seriously as involving our friendship, but in vain. I have sufficient confidence in you to know you draw for no more than you can in prudence, and that is the only limit I would set to your demands. By prudence of course, I mean that you can comfortably provide payment for. 'Tis true I did say I was sorry to see you were obliged to make this fictitious capital larger than at first proposed, but my sorrow was on your account, not on my own, as I should like to see the bales destroy the bills.[2]

Before 1819 was out the total amount due to Newberry on such bills was nearly £800.

The rearrangement which then ensued was largely dictated by the need to dispose of this burden of short-term debt. The sale of the unsuccessful New Mills brought £900 and so cleared Newberry's claims; George I, having relinquished his mortgage upon these mills, then left his £1,800 in the business; Samuel was to pay 5 per cent. thereon, to repay the capital by specified annual instalments, and to be limited to £150 per annum until these annual charges were met. As sleeping partner Peter Taylor was to receive £100 a year from the profits. Then any profits that remained were to be divided so as to give Samuel as managing partner £200 more per annum than Peter Taylor.[3]

In the months of slow recovery that followed, the accommodation bill account at first mounted again: over £400 in March, reduced to £250, around £380 at the end of the year. Newberry's friendship and help were real. Samuel's bankers were kept happy: 'I suppose you will be drawing on me again soon for the purpose proposed of leaving a more respectable balance in [the] bank.' In November, when cash was short, Newberry managed to discount bills in London and send the proceeds to Bocking to enable Samuel to meet bills due. In March 1821 Newberry reported on: 'the bills now out between us ... £440 in bills afloat wholly yours and of this sum £252 are discounted by your banker.' Only with the turning of the tide in 1822 did this dependence end. Unfortunately, the evidence in the shape of Newberry's letters also comes to an end. All that can be said

[1] Courtauld MSS.: J.N. to S.C. III, 8 February 1819.
[2] Ibid., J.N. to S.C. III, 29 April 1819.
[3] Ibid., G.C. I to Ruth C., 20 December 1819.

is that in February 1823 the amount outstanding to Newberry was only
£96.[1]

If this precarious short-term financing somehow worked, continuing
shortage of long-term capital made itself felt in the hampering of Samuel's
efforts to expand. Leasing and borrowing were inevitable. Peter Taylor's
initial capital contribution remains unknown, but it was probably only
very small. The loans of George I and Aunt Sophia were invaluable, but
apart from interest, George's capital had to be repaid and Sophia's contribution discharged in the form of payments to a life annuity. The Panfield Lane premises were obtained on a lease at £30 per annum both in
1816 and again in 1823; the New Mills were built with the loan from
George I; the mill at Bocking was also finally leased, at £100 per annum,
although the original negotiations for this entailed purchase at £2,500, the
money to be raised by a mortgage at 5 per cent. to Savill.[2] Samuel's vain
efforts in 1821 to find a partner were part of the search for capital. So, too,
was an unsuccessful attempt in 1822 to sell a share in the business, which,
he claimed, would have yielded the buyer 20 per cent. on his capital. He
added: 'I have now no expectation of getting capital unless I bid higher for
it, as I have been in treaty with a vast number of persons to no purpose.'[3]
By this time the business horizon was clearing, and he could tell his
father: 'I am now making £1,000 a year by my business and have already
saved £902 by living so very much within my income.' The instalments of
repayment were still due and the need for capital no less. So he went on to
say: 'Should you be better pleased by my parting with it or retaining it?
I believe £150 is now due to you on the instalments—for this sum you
may draw, on receipt of this if you please—*but if you let it remain in my
hands, I will pay you 12 per cent interest thereon, and likewise on any further
instalments which you may please to let remain after they fall due*'[4] (my italics).

Although it is not clear precisely what was done, this willingness to pay
12 per cent. highlights Samuel's need for more capital. It emphasizes,
moreover, both the high rates which that capital could be made to earn in
the silk business and the advantageous position in which Samuel was to
find himself on his father's death a few months later. His own achievements in saving can be seen by the comparison of two fragments of early
accounts which have survived. In August 1820 out of a total of £2,324,

[1] Ibid., J.N. to S.C. III, 28 March 1820, 16 November 1820, 2 March 1821, S.C. III to
G.C. I, 14 March 1823; *C.F.L.*, vol. ii, p. 709.
[2] *C.F.L.*, vol. ii, pp. 637–8, 709; E.R.O., Savill MSS., F. 30.
[3] Courtauld MSS.: S.C. III to G.C. I, 30 November 1822.
[4] Ibid.

the main creditors were George Courtauld for £1,725 and John Newberry for £383; in February 1823 out of £2,801, they were George with £1,436 and Samuel himself with £1,005; similarly the main debit item, machinery, advanced from £1,712 to £2,604.[1] But the claim of frugal living as the source of the saving must not be taken too literally. Certainly he was limited in his income by the terms of the 1819 agreement, and certainly in past years sheer survival depended on cautious spending. But if in good years profits of £1,000 per annum could be made on a capital of £2,800, or even on probably less in the first fine flush of the Panfield Lane business in 1817, then the willingness to pay 12 per cent. for more capital becomes as understandable as the idea of frugality becomes inappropriate.

IV

Further inquiry into the economic and technical circumstances of these early endeavours is necessary in order to reveal the nature of the capital employed and why more was needed.

Perhaps the most striking fact about the Panfield Lane and New Mills enterprises was that they were horse- or man-powered. Although the search for a water-powered mill was ultimately successful at Bocking it was still worth while having the Panfield Lane plant as a man-powered auxiliary. How could it even seem possible to enter the industry with such apparently out-of-date equipment when water-powered throwing mills had been increasingly used in the industry for many decades? Courtauld & Taylor were not alone in using ancient methods, nor were old methods confined to sources of power. In 1828 a writer on the silk industry made the following observation:

At the commencement of the year 1824, I can safely assert that no machinery throughout Great Britain, upon which so great a result depended, was of so barbarous a nature or so wanting in improvement as that employed in the throwing trade; and it unfortunately happens that nine out of ten mills at the present moment, are of a similar nature.[2]

There were two main reasons for the existence and survival of what in economic terms would seem to have been marginal or sub-marginal producers: the high degree of protection which the industry enjoyed, and the low labour costs in many of the mills which had sprung up in low-

[1] Courtauld MSS.: S.C. III to G.C. I, 18 September 1820, 14 March 1823.
[2] Richard Badnall, *A View of the Silk Trade* (London, 1828), p. 78.

wage areas. The protective tariffs around the industry and the economic situation which led to London producers investing in rural throwing and weaving were considered in Chapter II. The particular circumstances of the East Anglian branch of the silk industry now demand a closer look.

FIG. 5. *East Anglia: places named in text*

The three counties of Norfolk, Suffolk, and Essex (see Fig. 5, above) already formed an area of declining industrial and commercial life when the Industrial Revolution first began to make its mark in the Midlands and northern England. The old and famous worsted industry of Norwich; the woollen and worsted trades of north Essex and south Suffolk, once occupying scores of small towns and villages around such places as Colchester, Bocking, Sudbury, and Hadleigh; the shipbuilding yards of Ipswich and Woodbridge; the commerce of King's Lynn, Yarmouth, and Colchester: all were in varying degrees of decay. Agriculture and its concomitant processing industries—milling, malting, and brewing—did not share in this decline; but of those new spurs to human advance in the age of steam—coal and iron—the area was wholly devoid. Though the Industrial Revolution passed it by, population growth did not—at least in the early stages of the great upsurge which formed so obvious a landmark in this period of English history. After a time, of course, the rate of growth fell off as people migrated from the area to other parts of the kingdom which offered more and better jobs. These painful adjustments took time, and during the early decades of the nineteenth century East Anglia, as the following figures suggest, was an area of more than average poverty and less than average population growth.[1]

TABLE 3

Population growth and poor relief: England and East Anglia,
1801–41

	Expenditure on poor relief per head of the population			Percentage increase in population	
	Average for England and Wales	*Average for Norfolk, Suffolk, and Essex*		*Average for England and Wales*	*Average for Norfolk, Suffolk, and Essex*
	s. d.	s. d.		%	%
1801 .	9 1	11 11			
1811 .	13 1	21 3	1801–11	14·5	9·7
1821 .	10 7	16 9	1811–21	17·5	16·0
1831 .	9 9	16 11	1821–31	16·0	10·7
1841 .	6 2	9 2	1831–41	14·5	6·9

Thus to the endemic underemployment of the time was added the structural unemployment of an area of decaying industry; and to both were added the problems arising from an increase in population which, though less than the average for the country, was still far more than could be absorbed at current wages in local jobs. It is not surprising to find that during the first half of the nineteenth century in East Anglia agricultural wages—a good indicator of the general level of wages in such an area—fell below the national average and were well below those in such

[1] *B.P.P.* 1843, vol. xxii, p. 12; G. R. Porter, *The Progress of the Nation* (London, 1847), pp. 94–95.

ding industrial areas as Lancashire and the West Riding of Yorkshire.[1]
strial wages were correspondingly lower than elsewhere; and those
k weaving some two-thirds of what was paid in Spitalfields.[2]
nese were the general economic circumstances in which silk mills were
ing into operation in East Anglia, especially around the Essex–Suffolk
er and in and around Norwich. Apart from the mills at Pebmarsh and
atree with which George Courtauld I was concerned, others were
ed at Colchester, Hadleigh, Coggeshall, and Bocking. The London
ence, evident in the Pebmarsh and Braintree mills, was widespread:
at Coggeshall, for example, John Hall, who set up a mill in 1818, was
concerned with his partner Thomas Sawyer (or Sawer) in a firm of ribbon
manufacturers of London and Coventry.[3] If the supply of young women
and children promised well for the labour requisites of the throwing mills,
unemployed hand-loom weavers and a long tradition of textile manufacture were an invitation to silk weaving. In and around several towns
of the area—Braintree, Bocking, Coggeshall, Colchester, Hadleigh, Halstead, Haverhill, and Sudbury—the hand-loom weaving of silks developed,
much of it put out by the manufacturers to be done in the weavers' own
homes. Many Spitalfields manufacturers were putting out work to this
region in the 1820s; by 1840 almost all such employers were London firms,
so much so that it was said that 'these towns are . . . so far as their silk
manufactures are concerned, merely outposts or dependencies of London'.[4]
In the early decades of the century the biggest of the East Anglian silk
manufacturers was Joseph Grout. In 1826 the firm of Grout, Bayliss & Co.,
with offices in Foster Lane, London, employed over 3,500 persons in Norfolk and Suffolk: their throwing mills were to be found at Norwich,
Yarmouth, Bungay, and Mildenhall; they employed hand-loom weavers
not only in Norfolk but in Essex as far afield as Sible Hedingham, Saffron
Walden, Bocking, and Braintree; and, according to Grout, had a capital in
1834 of £150,000–£160,000.[5]

Grouts, Courtauld & Taylor, and other firms had both water-powered
twisting mills and hand-operated winding and doubling engines.[6] Of the

[1] See M. Blaug, 'The Myth of the Old Poor Law', *Journal of Economic History*, vol. xxiii,
No. 2, pp. 182–3.

[2] B.P.P. 1840, vol. xxii, p. 125; *House of Lords Papers*, 1823, vol. clvi.

[3] B.P.P. 1831–2, vol. xix, pp. 124–6, 372–84; 1834, vol. xx, pp. 369, 373, 375, 377; 1839,
vol. xlii, *passim*.

[4] B.P.P. 1840, vol. xxiii, pp. 125–38; 1821, vol. vii, pp. 436, 441

[5] B.P.P. 1831–2, vol. xix, pp. 691–4; 1834, vol. xx, p. 1109.

[6] B.P.P. 1834, vol. xx, *passim*; 1840, vol. x, pp. 217–18.

technical equipment of these early East Anglian mills in general we know little, but it can hardly be doubted that so long as protection lasted, low wages and an adequate supply of young women and children helped to slow down the adoption of improved techniques and make it worth while to keep slow, manually operated plants in existence. For driving the twisting mills, however, water-power was rapidly becoming necessary for economic working. Hence the search by Samuel Courtauld and Peter Taylor in 1817–18 and, probably, the failure of their horse-powered New Mills. The conversion of a flour mill, the improving of water-courses, the installation of machinery: these absorbed the long-term capital. But as a form of capital-saving rather than labour-saving, winding and doubling could be done, as it was at Panfield Lane, on machinery turned by old men and tended by young children.[1] Entry into the silk industry was relatively easy; but for growth, effective competition, and ultimately for survival, access to capital was vital.

There is some evidence to suggest that Samuel Courtauld III was soon alive to the need for technical improvements. Newberry told him that the machinery in some silk mills he had seen in Surrey was 'exceedingly clumsy and heavy in comparison to yours'; Samuel wrote to his brother George II in July 1821 telling him of a new, better method of cleaning and winding he had introduced; and it seems likely that he was well aware of the value of using metal rather than wood in the construction of machinery. Certainly it is clear that George II, both when he worked with Samuel in 1819 and later, had a real mechanical aptitude.[2] And their father's patent spindle proved, temporarily at least, to be an invention of some value. Although fuller evidence on this relates only to the years after George I's death, Samuel was evidently exploiting his father's patent earlier, for in April 1820 he wrote: 'I obtained a handsome sum from Sawyer & Hall [i.e. at Coggeshall] for my aid in the construction of their works, for patterns of some parts of my machinery, permission to their people to take measures of the whole, and privilege to use the patent for a certain number of spindles.' Two years later, having experienced some difficulty in the sale of patent rights, he asked his father for a general power of attorney to

---

[1] [John Williams], *The Story of My Life by an Octogenarian* (Braintree, undated, but *circa* 1895) gives a description of the Panfield Lane works in the writer's boyhood. It is substantially confirmed by the surviving Panfield Lane Pay Book (E.R.O., D/F 3/2/18), even to the names and wages (5s.–8s. per week) of the men who turned the winding and doubling engines.

[2] Courtauld MSS.: J.N. to S.C. III, 6 April 1819; Ruth C. to G.C. I, 22 May 1822; G.C. I to S.C. III, 12 June 1823; C.F.L., vol. ii, pp. 836–40, vol. iii, p. 956. See also below, pp. 116–17.

: future transactions of this sort.[1] Once again the link between
I's enterprise and that of his son is apparent.

did Courtauld & Taylor get through these early years: short of
dependent on George I's loans and Newberry's accommodation
id, like all other producers of the area, using lowly paid East
abour in a protected national market. The firm derived something
orge I's patent, something from the mechanical initiative of the
Samuel III and George II, and a great deal from the drive, pur-
energy of Samuel III. It was basically this combination which
y to face and to triumph in the changed economic circumstances
e 1820s.

V

Free Trade and economic liberalism in Britain took a major step forward in the 1820s. Under the aegis of Frederick Robinson, later Viscount
Goderich, as Chancellor of the Exchequer, and especially of William
Huskisson as President of the Board of Trade, a series of acts cut down
protective tariffs and sundry commercial and economic restrictions. The
economic teachings of Adam Smith and David Ricardo and the political
philosophy of the Utilitarians, Samuel Bentham and James Mill, seemed
strongly and increasingly to be reinforced by the facts of current economic
expansion. Cotton-spinners, ironmasters, and other representatives of the
growing, mechanized industries of the Midlands and north sought cheaper
raw materials and wider markets.

The silk manufacturers were divided in their attitude: all favoured the
removal of import duties on raw silk; some throwsters hoped for continued protection against imported thrown silk; many manufacturers
trembled at the thought of removing the protection against imported silk
fabrics; a few members of the industry were thoroughgoing Free Traders.
In the event, the industry got modified Free Trade. Table 4 (p. 66) shows
what happened to the import duties on raw and thrown silk (cf. Table 2
above, p. 18).

These rates stayed in force until 1845, when, during Sir Robert Peel's
further instalment of Free Trade, what remained of protection for the
throwster was swept away. Meanwhile, by an Act of 1824 coming into
force in July 1826, the prohibition on imported silk manufactures was replaced by a scale of specific duties intended to average about 30 per cent.
ad valorem, thus to give some measure of protection and to discourage

---

[1] *C.F.L.*, vol. ii, p. 709; Courtauld MSS.: S.C. III to G.C. I, 30 November 1822.

smuggling. Falling prices increased the effective protection, and the rates were recast in 1829; the aim was to achieve the desired 30 per cent., but in practice by 1832 the average rate was around 35 per cent. Peel's anti-protective dose of 1845 reduced the rates again to an average, *ad valorem*, of about 15 per cent. In 1860, when Gladstone administered the final dose of Free Trade medicine, even this protection was finally removed from the industry, with consequences to be considered later. The reduction of the silk duties in 1829 was accompanied by the introduction of a system of

TABLE 4

Silk import duties, 1817–29

(per lb. of 16 oz.)[1]

	Raw			Thrown (undyed)		
	China	Bengal (British India)	Italy		s	d.
1817–23	5s. 6d.	3s. 6d.	5s. 6d.	1814–23	14	8
March 1824		3d.		March 1824	7	6
				November 1825	5	0
July 1826		1d.		July 1826 { organzine and crape	5	0
				tram and singles	3	0
July 1829		1s. per cwt.		July 1829 { organzine and crape	3	6
				tram	2	0
				singles	1	6

drawbacks designed to replace the former bounties on exports of silk manufactures. And finally in this chronicle of the advent of economic liberalism, the determination of weavers' wages in Spitalfields was thrown on the market by the repeal in 1825 of the Spitalfields Act.

Not all of what followed these enactments was caused by them, though contemporaries obviously thought so. Many of the writings and speeches about the silk industry at this time were in reality attacks upon or defences of the idea of Free Trade. The argument achieved its most voluminous expression in the minutes of evidence—running to nearly 1,000 pages—given in 1832 before the House of Commons Select Committee on the Silk Trade, set up as a result of protests by the protectionists, to inquire into the effect of the legislative changes since 1824.[2] The Committee,

[1] See above, p. 17, n.4.   [2] B.P.P. 1831–2, vol. xix.

battered and bewildered, found themselves unable to come to any conclusions, a result neither surprising to the unprejudiced nor unacceptable
to the Free Trader.

This is what seems to have happened. There was an increase in the number of water- and steam-operated throwing mills, especially in the north,
as firms prepared to take advantage of possibilities opened up by the
removal of the duties on raw silk. In the Manchester area, for example,
the number of silk mills rose as follows:[1]

1820	1822	1824	1826	1828	1830	1832
3	5	6	10	12	14	16

Imports of thrown silk declined, those of raw and waste[2] silk increased (see
Fig. 6). Prices of raw silk fell sharply (see Fig. 11). So did those of thrown:
Italian organzine, of 24 to 28 denier, for example, selling at about 42s. per
lb. in 1823, had fallen to 21s. 9d. in 1831. Both imports and exports of silk
manufactures increased (see Fig. 7), and again there was an appreciable fall
in prices: certain sorts of ribbons, for instance, fetched 30 to 60 per cent.
less in 1832 than in 1824.[3] Falling prices and sharpened competition put a
premium upon resourceful throwsters with large units, up-to-date throwing machinery, and efficient sources of power; it put at a disadvantage
small, remote, old-fashioned mills. In manufacture, it encouraged enterprising men to look to the power-loom, which had already made a spectacular mark in the cotton industry, but in the early 1820s had hardly
appeared in silk. Everywhere the need to cut costs became urgent as the
boom of 1824-5 passed, as competition intensified, and as the trade cycle
moved into a downward phase from 1828 to 1832. Wages were pushed
down, hours lengthened, machinery driven faster; cheaper silks and cheaper
power were sought. Specialization on simpler fabrics went a step further;
makers of figured fabrics and users of conservative designs, as in Spitalfields, found themselves hard hit. Marginal producers were gradually
driven out of business.

In brief, some of the reactions to the changed circumstances added up to
a continuation of trends long apparent in the industry. The use of cheaper
silks and the making of simpler fabrics, the decline of Spitalfields and the

---

[1] A. Redford, *Manchester Merchants and Foreign Trade, 1794-1858* (Manchester, 1934),
p. 238.

[2] Waste silk was the raw material of a small but growing spun silk industry. It became much
more important later in the century, see below, pp. 160, 164.

[3] B.P.P. 1831-2, vol. xix, pp. 109, 315, and *passim*.

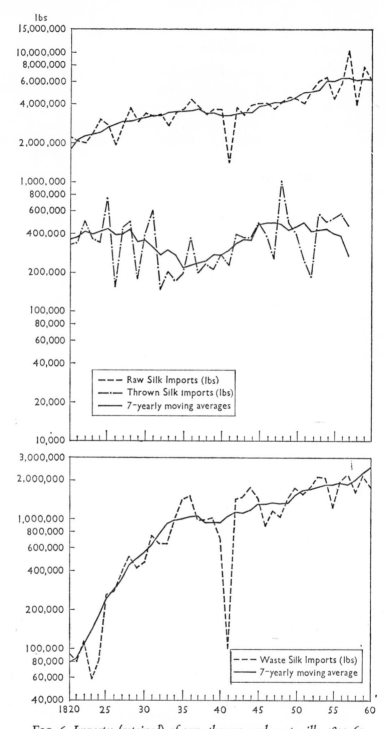

FIG. 6. *Imports: (retained) of raw, thrown, and waste silk, 1820–60*

Note: Thrown silk imports are not shown after 1857 because of some negative figures
for retained imports which cannot be plotted on the logarithmic scale. (See also Fig. 22)
U.K. *Sources*: Mitchell & Deane; P.R.O.: Customs 5

rise of Lancashire and Cheshire: these we have seen before. They were now given an impetus by the removal of the circumstances which had allowed the retention of antique methods and high-cost producers. For forty years

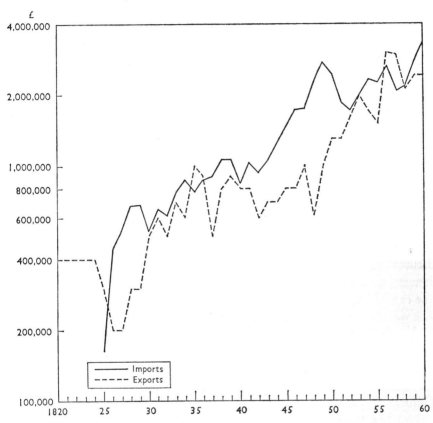

FIG. 7. *Imports and exports of silk manufactures, 1820–60*
U.K. *Sources*: Mitchell & Deane; P.R.O.: Customs 5

or so after the first draught of Free Trade the British silk industry grew; but in the process many firms and more employees were hard hit.

VI

The successful Courtauld responses to these challenges, which led to the firm's most rapid period of expansion in the nineteenth century, will be examined in the next chapter. Meanwhile, the steps by which Samuel enlarged the business and created a family firm demand attention.

For about a year after George I died those who had accompanied him to the U.S.A. stayed there. Samuel redoubled his efforts to persuade George II to return; in June 1824 he told him: 'your determination to remain in America is a great disappointment to me'. But reports of booming business in England, not least in silk, and his brother's latest moves and offers finally turned the scale. 'The silk business was never so flourishing as at present ... Sam is very high in the trade ... everybody that can is getting into the silk business': to these happy tales were added specific offers of a job in connexion with Samuel's latest venture.[1] By September, George II, Sophia II, Peter and Catherine Taylor, John Minton Courtauld, Eliza and her husband Joseph Ash, an Englishman whom she had married in Ohio in 1821, were all back in England. Samuel's new venture bore a striking similarity to that upon which his father had ventured fifteen years earlier. He entered into an agreement with another firm to erect a mill to throw crape yarn. The lure of the crape business was still strong; George I's high hopes with Nouaille in the 1790s and Wilson in the 1810s were echoed again in these boom days of the 1820s. This time both the other party and the result were different. The agreement was made with Stephen Beuzeville, another Spitalfields silk manufacturer of Huguenot origin; it was embodied in a deed of 19 January 1825. Beuzeville was to provide the capital and supply the silk; Samuel Courtauld was to convert the mill —a water corn-mill called Town Mill in the neighbouring Essex town of Halstead—erect machinery, run the works, and take a share of the profits. The terms of the agreement—which not surprisingly included provisions obviously aimed at preventing the situation which had arisen between George I and Wilson—suggest that it was Beuzeville who was to manufacture the crape from the yarn.[2]

Not everything went smoothly for the family on returning from the U.S.A. The work on the conversion at Halstead proceeded in 1824–5, and George II worked at Bocking in helping to prepare the machinery. To judge from his letter to his sister Sophia he embarked on this without enthusiasm and with a good deal of nostalgia for life in the Ohio countryside, where, as he wrote in December 1824, 'this time three years', I was a blacksmith's man'. Joseph and Eliza Ash were set up in Coggeshall with some winding machinery, but after initial successes had to close up at the

---

[1] C.F.L., vol. iii, pp. 1179–81, 1182–3, 1187–8, 1188–9.

[2] E.R.O., D/F 3/2/97; C.F.L., vol. iii, p. 1179. On Beuzeville, see W. A. Beuzeville, 'Notes on the Family of Beuzeville', Proceedings of the Huguenot Society of London, vol. xii, pp. 417–18.

PLATE 5

HALSTEAD OLD MILL

The original 'Town Mill' converted by Samuel Courtauld in 1825

end of January 1825, all their hands having left them. John Minton, now 18 years old, worked for Samuel. Peter Taylor, equipped with a loan from another brother-in-law, William Bromley, sought, unsuccessfully, for a water mill, to set up on his own in the silk business; and his wife complained of poverty and disappointment.[1] But by the summer of 1825 all had been ordered under the general dispensation of the dominant Sam —also assisted by loans from William Bromley.[2] Halstead mill was working and Joseph Ash installed as resident manager; Peter Taylor had rejoined his former partner—the business entity, Courtauld & Taylor, still existed at Bocking; more buildings were put up at Panfield Lane; George II had also joined up with Samuel at Bocking in another business entity, Courtauld Brothers, to make silk-throwing machinery and in particular the patent organzine spindles; and young John Minton, settled with his eldest brother and earning 16s. a week, noting how his world had changed, added a final Panglossian touch which perhaps he had got from his father: 'I suppose all things will go the way that is best on the whole.'[3]

The particular pattern of organization did not last long. Sam was set upon expansion, and despite the marked turn for the worse in the general economic climate which appeared in 1826, he continued to prosper. A small steam engine was installed at Bocking. This had been presaged earlier, in the hard winter of 1822–3 when ice and frost were followed by floods: 'the summer after next, I look to need a 4-horse engine as a short-water aid', he had written in February 1823. Towards the end of 1825 or early in 1826 there was built the machine shop which was to be the special preserve of George II; it adjoined Savill's old mill at Bocking and came to be known, within the business, by the evocative name of 'Steam Factory'.[4] Despite distress in Spitalfields and unemployment in Halstead, the Courtauld business continued to increase: in the throwing of crape and other yarns, especially of a type of highly thrown yarn called 'marabout', in which they were now starting to specialize, as well as in the manufacture and sale of spindles. In June 1826 Sam was asking anxiously of William Bromley: 'Have you any good news to tell me about money matters—

[1] C.F.L., vol. iii, pp. 1215–16, 1233, 1235, 1249, 1250, 1253, 1255, 1256–7.
[2] E.R.O., D/DQC. I. William Bromley (1787–1849), the husband of Peter Taylor I's elder sister, Catherine, was a member of Gray's Inn and had been George Courtauld I's lawyer at the time of the Courtauld v. Wilson case. Loans to Samuel of £500 and of £200 are mentioned in a letter of 26 December 1824.
[3] C.F.L., vol. iii, pp. 1267–8, 1287–8, 1291–2, 1293; E.R.O., D/F 3/1/1; B.P.P. 1834, vol. xx, p. 369.
[4] C.F.L., vol. iii, p. 993, 1432–3; B.P.P. 1834, vol. xx, p. 369.

such would be most welcome';[1] in July 1826 a legal action about water rights at Halstead went against him. Nevertheless he continued to plan for further expansion, and in 1828 a 6 h.p. engine was installed at Halstead.[2] Though in August he confided to his sister Sophia that 'we have lost a little fortune by bad debts and our future trade is to a certain degree *in nubibus*', he impressed upon her that this was to be forgotten as soon as read. 'You must not know that we have lost a farthing or that our successes have received any check. We have', he added, 'many things on the *tapis*, and some of them I hope will succeed to the filling up of the place of those which pass away.'[3] By October 1826, soft-silk winding machinery was being set up at Halstead; and George II was observing that the business was being weekly enlarged. Of his own branch he remarked that 'we seem to be able to get into a more general trade than that of manufacturers merely of organzine spindles or even of silk machinery in general'.[4] But of the various 'things on the *tapis*', that which soon engaged their attention was the weaving and finishing of crape. This was the logical development of the crape-throwing at Halstead; it followed, moreover, from the knowledge which Sam had gained whilst working with his father, not only of throwing but of crape gauze weaving.

There is no evidence that before 1827 Samuel's business—to be more exact, the firm of Courtauld & Taylor—had done any weaving whatever. Not only does no mention of it appear in all the correspondence between Sam and his father or Newberry in 1817–23, but the contents of some of the letters make it reasonably certain that he was only a throwster; and indeed he was described in various legal documents of 1825–6, not as 'silk manufacturer', but as 'silk throwster'.[5] In September 1827, however, in the recently enlarged Panfield Lane factory, in addition to the winding and doubling, some twenty or thirty girls were at work making gauze;[6] and in 1827–8 a finishing factory was in course of building at Bocking, alongside the existing Steam Factory and Bocking Mills.[7]

---

[1] E.R.O., D/DQC. 1, S.C. III to William Bromley, 2 June 1826.

[2] *C.F.L.*, vol. iii, pp. 1413–14, 1420, 1422, 1431, 1432–3; vol. iv, p. 1467; E.R.O., D/F 3/2/97, *Ruffle* v. *Ash* deeds; B.P.P. 1834, vol. xx, p. 369; 1831–2, vol. xix, p. 199.

[3] *C.F.L.*, vol. iv, p. 1473.   [4] Ibid., pp. 1508, 1517.

[5] E.R.O., D/F 3/2/96 and 97. The large folio account book (E.R.O., D/F 3/4/2) containing accounts of silk put out to, and received from, domestic hand-loom weavers over the years 1819–25 probably came from another firm. There is nothing to identify it as relative to the Courtauld enterprise at that time. It is not in the handwriting of Samuel Courtauld or Peter Taylor. It may perhaps have come from the former Wilson–Courtauld mill at Braintree which S. Courtauld & Co. took over in 1842.

[6] [J. Williams], *Story of My Life*; E.R.O., D/F 3/2/18.   [7] E.R.O., D/F 3/2/17.

At about this time a new opening for expansion appeared, Beuzeville went bankrupt. He already owed Samuel £2,000; so by an agreement of 16 October 1827 with Beuzeville's Commissioners in bankruptcy and by a formal deed of sale of 11 April 1828 the mill (subject to charges of £3,000) was sold to Samuel for a cash payment of £1,500. This transaction, coming on top of the expansion already under way, put a strain on the financial resources of the business. So once again Sam tried to bring in a partner with money. And this time he was successful with the man who might have bought the business in 1821—Andrew Taylor. Unrelated apparently to the other Taylors, Andrew Taylor was connected with the silk trade, probably as a 'silkman' or silk broker.[1] He evidently had sufficient confidence in Samuel Courtauld to be willing to put money into the business. Negotiations proceeded in December 1827, and on 18 February 1828 a deed of partnership was signed by Samuel Courtauld III, George Courtauld II, Peter Alfred Taylor I, and Andrew Taylor. The total initial capital is not known, though it was probably £15,000. On 3 January 1829 the partners were attributed with a total of £15,418, or £15,858 after profits had been credited. This £15,858 was divided: Samuel £4,718, George and Peter Taylor each £1,888, and Andrew Taylor £7,364. After Andrew Taylor had been paid a prior claim, the division of profits was: Samuel Courtauld 5/12ths, George Courtauld and Peter Taylor each 2/12ths, and Andrew Taylor 3/12ths. A revision and renewal, for seven years, of the articles of partnership in 1837 made these proportions: Samuel Courtauld 5/9ths, George Courtauld and Peter Taylor each 2/9ths, and Andrew Taylor 10 per cent. on his capital. Although Andrew Taylor worked in the early years at the London office, 42–43 Gutter Lane, which was opened towards the end of 1828, failing health led to a less and less active share in the management of the business, and he became a sleeping partner after 1837. In 1844 the partnership was renewed for a further seven years and Andrew Taylor's return reduced to 8 per cent. Before this final seven years was up the partners decided to bring the partnership to an end in February 1849, after it had run a successful term of twenty-one years.[2] The firm was formally called Courtauld, Taylors and Courtauld, but it soon became known to the public as it was known in practice to the partners: Samuel Courtauld & Co.

[1] E.R.O., D/F 3/1/1. This shows that S.C. & Co. bought silk from him in 1828. He is described in later deeds as of Bromley, Kent.

[2] E.R.O., D/F 3/1/8, D/F 3/1/18. The original deed of 1828 has not survived. See also C.F.L., vol. vii, pp. 3290, 3378.

CHAPTER VI

Expansion

I

Q. The Committee understand that you are a very considerable manufacturer, perhaps the most considerable in England, of Crape.

A. (Samuel Courtauld) Yes.

THIS terse affirmative to a Parliamentary Committee[1] in May 1851 must have given some subdued satisfaction to its author if, at least, he recollected that about thirty years earlier he had been trying vainly to sell his business so as to migrate to America. Once the enterprise had been provided with a reasonably firm financial base, in the partnership of February 1828, and once it had solved certain technical problems, then, as is usual in modern industrial development, there followed an initial phase of rapid growth, both in output and in profits. The productivity of greatly improved machinery and the economies of larger-scale production were being realized. The £15,418 of partners' invested capital in January 1829 had become £173,253 twenty years later.[2] This high rate of growth could only have been sustained by high profitability. For the years from 1830 to 1848 inclusive, the annual rate of return to the partners in the shape of profits plus interest on capital averaged 26·5 per cent.[3] Fig. 8 illustrates the course of growth in profits and in capital.

The outward sign of this growth to the people of northern Essex was the building, and extension, of power-driven factories at Bocking, Braintree, and Halstead; and the gratifying fact of the growing employment which they offered, so that by the end of the 1840s some 2,000[4] local inhabitants were, directly or indirectly, dependent upon this new manufacturing complex.

Of the component parts of the firm's productive plant, the Bocking nucleus was, for more reasons than one, the most important. Around and

---

[1] *B.P.P.* 1851, vol. ix, p. 59. [2] E.R.O., D/F 3/1/1, D/F 3/1/8.

[3] After charging depreciation on capital. See below, Appendix to vol. I.

[4] *Report of the Proceedings . . .*

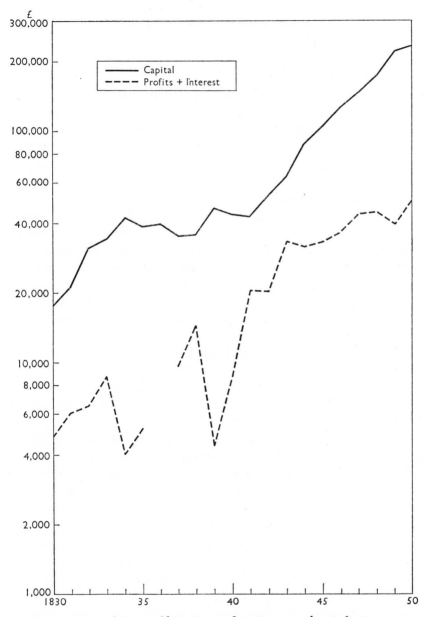

FIG. 8. *Samuel Courtauld & Co.: profits+interest and capital, 1830–50*

Note: The capital figure used is the partners' capital less profits at the balancing date, normally 31 December each year, i.e. the opening capital for the following year. 1836 is missing in the profits curve because there was a loss that year (see p. 106)

Source: E.R.O.: D/F 3/1

adjoining Savill's old mill on the Blackwater, three interlocking entities grew and ramified: they were known in the firm's books as Steam Factory, Finishing Factory, and Bocking Mills. The first became the machine shop. It sprang from George II's early work with his father's patent spindle, was nourished by his own mechanical abilities, and burgeoned into a substantial piece of engineering plant. In this vital part of the firm's structure much of its throwing, weaving, and finishing machinery was not only maintained and repaired but, as will be shown later, devised and built. The Finishing Factory started in a small way as a dye-house and a shed where girls carried out simple finishing tasks. Once the making of mourning crape had become the firm's main activity, it grew into a central and, so far as the outer world was concerned, most mysterious pillar of the enterprise, where biasing, crimping, dyeing, and dressing gave to Courtauld's crape its selling appeal. On the expiry in 1833 of the fourteen-year lease of Bocking mill itself, Sam exercised his option to purchase. Its expansion in the course of years made it not only the main centre for winding, drawing, and throwing but also the administrative headquarters of the enterprise. The partners concerned with production, Sam and George, lived not far from it. Sam and his wife had settled in 1825 at High Garrett between Bocking and Halstead. (Their residence, much less grand than that which Sam was later to occupy, was called Folly House, 'an appropriate name', it seemed to Ellen Courtauld at the time, 'for its inhabitants'.)[1]

The crape mill at Halstead had initially the highest book value of any single part of the business, as Table 5 indicates. This reflected its greater size (it included a mill house where the current mill manager lived) and more convenient site; and it testified to its equipment of machinery, installed originally for Beuzeville, which in 1828 included 9,300 throwing spindles and 1,430 winding, drawing, and doubling spindles. But the site had useful possibilities for expansion, and advantage was taken of these when the firm's experiments with power-loom weaving had proved successful and the time had come for full production. Land adjoining the mill was acquired and the first building of what came to be called the Power Loom Factory was opened in 1832, the second in 1836, the third in 1842. In this way weaving capacity was expanded and concentrated at Halstead, coming in time to overshadow the throwing mills there. Meanwhile, of course, much weaving continued to be done on hand-looms, perhaps some still at Panfield Lane, but far more put out to domestic weavers, mainly in Braintree and Halstead. The little Panfield Lane factory was still in

[1] *C.F.L.*, vol. iii, p. 1318.

operation in 1833,[1] though some time shortly after this it was given up. Finally, the Braintree nucleus developed during these years in a different way. For some unknown period, probably beginning in the 1830s the

TABLE 5[2]

Fixed assets 1828–48

	Halstead Mill	Power Loom Factory	Bocking Mills	Steam Factory	Finishing Factory	Braintree Mills
	£	£	£	£	£	£
As taken in stock 18 Feb. 1828	6,000	..	..	1,700	545	..
Balance sheet values as at						
Jan. 1829	7,194	183*	..	3,180	1,214	..
Dec. 1831	9,320	618*	..	3,077	2,368	..
Dec. 1838	7,875	7,891	7,862	3,045	4,141	..
Dec. 1848	6,984	15,864	13,470	7,655	7,511	5,868

* 'Power Weaving Machinery'; the Power Loom Factory had not yet been built.

firm leased a building there which was described in 1842 as the Broad Silk Warehouse, Braintree. It was certainly used as a storehouse for hand-looms and silk and as a depot for putting out materials to domestic hand-loom weavers. In 1843, however, Samuel Courtauld & Co. bought the Braintree mill which George I had originally converted, with such remarkable consequences, for Remington, Wilson & Co. Though not much expanded in this period, it was used for winding and throwing.

Outside north Essex, the firm's London office and warehouse at 42–45 Gutter Lane was held on a lease, as was its successor in Carey Lane after fire had seriously damaged the Gutter Lane premises in 1845.[3] Not until 1859 was a freehold site acquired in London for office and warehouse development.

II

During these early years mourning crape was far from the only commodity made by Samuel Courtauld & Co. in their new mills and factories. The company's activities can be divided into four main categories: machine

---

[1] *B.P.P.* 1834, vol. xx, p. 369.   [2] E.R.O., D/F 3/1/8.
[3] *C.F.L.*, vol. vii, pp. 3112, 3113–14.

making; silk throwing; the manufacture of soft-silk fabrics; and the manufacture of hard-silk fabrics, notably crapes of various sorts.

The intention of developing the machine-making side of the business
was revealed as early as April 1825. George II wrote: '. . . I am still engaged in constructing this machinery for Halstead; as soon as may be, i.e.
as soon as Sam has his time a little disengaged, we shall commence as
machinists. . . . Sam is quite undecided at present as to where to place this
same machinists' establishment. . . .'[1] A year later Steam Factory had been
built. George was telling of having to spend from 5.30 in the morning
until 9 at night in the factory, 'taking for meals only just enough time to
dispatch my chop'. He added: '. . . tomorrow we finish 400 organzine
spindles and next week 500 more, and when these are gone and the money
received I shall have time to look about me'.[2]

Courtauld's patent spindle evidently achieved a certain fame, albeit
limited and temporary, for some other manufacturers spoke favourably
of it in the 1830s. In 1838-9 both John Hall at Coggeshall and Brown &
May at Colchester used 'Mr. Courtauld's patent spindle', though it was
noted that the patent had expired.[3] Such terms as 'patent spindle' or
'patents' continued to be used, as often happens, after the legal monopoly
had ended. As well as supplying the spindle, by licence or sale, to other
throwsters, the firm itself used it in throwing silk for the market. So the
spindle was obviously closely linked with the second of the categories of
activity mentioned above: throwing silk, not only for their own use as
weavers, but also for sale or on commission.

Samuel Courtauld & Co. had two specialities in their early years as
throwsters: marabout and the patent organzine. It is clear that the firm
early acquired a reputation as throwsters of marabout, a special sort of
highly thrown tram which was then used particularly in the manufacture
of gauze ribbons.[4] A west-country throwster, named Lamech Swift, who
had been throwing marabout on commission since 1826, was asked by the
1832 Select Committee on the Silk Trade if he knew who else threw marabout in England. He replied: 'Messrs Courtauld & Taylor in Gutter Lane;

[1] C.F.L., vol. iii, p. 1287.
[2] Ibid., vol. iii, p. 1432-3. George II's speciality is made quite clear from a number of
apprenticeship indentures of this period (E.R.O., D/F 3/2/96), in which he is described as
'machinist' whilst Sam is called 'silk throwster'.
[3] B.P.P. 1840, vol. xxiii, p. 129.
[4] In the making of marabout yarn three threads were first slightly twisted, then dyed, and
then twisted again to give a very hard yarn. It was dyed in the gum. See B.P.P. 1831-2,
vol. xix, p. 197; and for evidence of its use for gauzes, pp. 96, 134, 197-9.

they were I believe the first marabout throwsters, they were throwing it twelve months before I was.'[1] Much of this marabout found its way to the ribbon-weaving centre of Coventry. Here the firm apparently had some sort of temporary warehousing facilities, for in the 1830s and 1840s the stock books periodically record stocks of marabout, or silk for marabout, at Bocking and at Coventry. The purchase of Braintree mill in 1843 was made with a view to increasing the firm's capacity for throwing trams for marabout; and the tram mills at Bocking were removed to Braintree.[2] But the trends of business justified those witnesses in 1832 who, testifying to the better quality and lower price of French gauze ribbons made from French marabout, bewailed the decline of Coventry ribbons in general and gauzes in particular. In March 1848 Sam spoke of the marabout trade as 'worn out'; although the firm was still throwing marabout in 1849, in 1850 its marabout stock was nil.[3]

The precise nature and merits of the organzine thrown on the patent spindle is not unfortunately made evident by the flattering mention which it received during the 1832 hearings. Cleophas Ratliff, a Coventry ribbon manufacturer, said:

. . . there is a description of silk thrown in this country, superior to any I have been able to obtain from Italy.

Q. In what does that superiority consist?

Ratliff. In the throw; there is a patent taken out by Courtauld & Taylor, which throw is superior to any foreign silk we procure.

He added that he used it in the manufacture of satin ribbons. Another witness, when asked if any decided improvements had taken place in throwing since 1824, praised a mill which he described as being 'on the principle of Mr. Courtauld'.[4] In 1838–9, the silk thrown on the patent spindle was said to be 'well-known to manufacturers'.[5] The contexts of these remarks make it clear that the thrown silk was organzine; and, as I have not been able to trace any other relevant Courtauld patent, the assumption that it was George I's patent of 1814 seems reasonable. But these swallows hardly made a summer for Sam. The patent spindle and the organzine which it produced made no great or lasting impression, presumably because there

[1] *B.P.P.* 1831–2, vol. xix, p. 199.

[2] Ibid., p. 200; *C.F.L.*, vol. vii, p. 3356; E.R.O., D/F 3/1/8.

[3] *B.P.P.* 1831–2, vol. xix, pp. 94 ff., 109 ff., 134, etc.; *C.F.L.*, vol. vii, pp. 3290, 3356; E.R.O., D/F 3/1/9.

[4] *B.P.P.* 1831–2, vol. xix, pp. 99, 277.   [5] *B.P.P.* 1840, vol. xxiii, p. 129.

was neither reduction in costs nor improvement in quality adequate to justify its continued use. In 1841 the old organzine mills at Bocking were dismantled and it was 'uncertain whether they will ever be put in their present state'; after 1842 organzine disappears from the stock book category of 'silk as thrown for sale'.[1] The firm continued to throw organzine for its own use in making fabrics other than crape, but there is no evidence to show that the patent spindle was used; and probably it was not.

Although these two branches of the firm's activities fell away during this period, the manufacture of fabrics other than crape certainly did not. Indeed it formed a significant and, for a while, perhaps even a growing part of the firm's business. Despite their obvious limitations, in merely

TABLE 6

Stock values in main productive activities, 1829–65

Year or period	(1) Crape gauzes and finished crapes	(2) Broad and fancy goods	(3) Soft silk and broad and fancy machinery (hand-looms, etc.)	(4) Silk thrown for sale (organzine and marabout)
	£	£	£	£
1829 (Jan.)	6,100	..	463*	[140]†
1830 (May)	2,642	498	834*	[370]†
1831 (Dec.)	8,732	698	990*	[630]†
1838–40	22,600	1,500	200	2,700
1841–3	23,300	7,500	400	2,500
1844–6	36,800	16,200	900	600
1847–9	55,200	22,600	1,000	100
1850–2	50,700	18,900	900	..
1853–5	57,700	25,900	700	..
1856–8	60,700	29,700	600	..
1859–61	68,300	15,300	400	..
1862–4	77,400	2,200	100	..
1865 (Dec.)	90,000	..	50	..

* In these early years the description sometimes used in the stock books, 'hand weaving machinery', certainly included hand-looms used for crape as well as for soft-silk weaving.

† These are only rough estimates. The early stock entries do not distinguish clearly between silk in the course of being thrown for internal use or for sale.

[1] E.R.O., D/F 3/1/8. In 1848 Peter Taylor reported that 'we have been nearly stationary for several years in our sale of patents', but it is not clear from the context whether this means spindles, yarn thrown on them, or fabrics made of yarn thrown on them—C.F.L., vol. vii, p. 3287.

representing stocks, the figures in Table 6 may give some idea of the changing relative importance of these various activities, for some forty years from the beginning of the 1828 partnership.[1]

Columns 1 and 4 of this table probably give a reasonably accurate impression, at least after 1838, of the rise and the decline of the two different branches of the firm's business. But column 2 demands one immediate qualification. The high value of the stock of non-crape silks in the mid 1850s certainly reflects sales difficulties. In 1856, 'this stock being very large and not rapidly selling', its book value was depreciated more than usual; two years later, though some £10,000 worth had been made in the current year, the remaining old stock, to about the same value, was said to be in excess of needs.[2] Soon, stocks were sold off at reduced prices and this line of business was stopped. Before this final phase, the manufacture of sundry soft-silk goods had obviously enjoyed a decade of boom. Nevertheless, this branch often seemed to be in an equivocal position in the firm's structure, which was so closely geared to hard-silk operations, i.e. to throwing crape yarn and weaving and finishing crape fabrics.

In February 1826 Courtauld & Taylor's fancy silks were said to be doing well, and in October of the same year Sam was installing soft-silk winding machinery 'on a new principle' at Halstead.[3] But soft-silk weaving, all done on hand-looms, was always a marginal activity to the firm. It was pursued or dropped according to the state of the market. Various economic factors, including sharp fluctuations in silk prices, prejudiced its position in 1836–8 (see below, pp. 96 et seq.), and so soft-silk work was stopped. Stocks of broad and fancy goods in 1838 were nil; and the value of soft-silk machinery only £39. Dr. John Mitchell, investigating for the Royal Commission inquiring into the condition of hand-loom weavers, reported of Braintree that here 'Messrs. Courtauld had formerly men employed at soft-silk goods, now they confine themselves to crapes'.[4] Then there was renewed enthusiasm, even a boom, starting particularly in about 1842; this was presumably a part of the general revival of trade which can be seen reflected in Figs. 6 and 7. It seems reasonably certain that when Samuel Courtauld & Co. took over Remington's mill at Braintree in 1843 they also took over, and subsequently expanded, the hand-loom weaving business which that firm was carrying on. Hence the sharp rise in columns 2 and 3 of Table 6 in the years after 1843. In 1845–6 soft silk was being put

[1] E.R.O., D/F 3/1/7–11. [2] E.R.O., D/F 3/1/10, 11.

[3] C.F.L., vol. iii, p. 1420; vol. iv, p. 1508.

[4] E.R.O., D/F 3/1/8; B.P.P. 1840, vol. xxiii, p. 127.

out to weavers in both Braintree and Halstead; and the stocks of satins and velvets damaged in the fire at Gutter Lane in 1845 were surely the products of their labours.[1] Yet by 1847–8, with falling prices for such goods and the firm's ever-increasing concentration on crapes, 'it is determined to reduce the Braintree looms'. The complete abandonment of this line of business was discussed but rejected; instead, the looms at Braintree were called in and lay idle in the mill there, and weaving was concentrated at Halstead.[2] So soft-silk work continued for another decade; but as its significance declined and sales became harder, its further stoppage could not be long delayed.

The firm's concentration upon mourning crape was neither complete nor immediate. At the very beginning they were certainly turning part of their output into crape handkerchiefs and scarves; and the manufacture of 'aerophanes', a flimsy, coloured fabric of crimped crape gauze, was soon started. The hemming and fringing of the handkerchiefs was proceeding in the Finishing Factory, certainly from 1830; and aerophanes were being made from December 1831 onwards.[3] The powerful market magic of mourning crape soon, however, made its mark. Handkerchiefs seem to have been given up after about 1832, and, as the following figures show, aerophanes did not form a large proportion of the total amount, nor did they advance commensurately with crapes.[4]

TABLE 7

Crapes and Aerophanes: average annual finish (packets), 1832–54

Period	Crapes	Aerophanes
1832–4	3,542	952
1842–4	15,316	774
1852–4	24,504	1,360

Once certain technical problems were solved the pattern was set. And the extremely rapid rate of growth in total output (see Fig. 9) was overwhelmingly due to mourning crape. In 1834 the Finishing Factory had in

[1] E.R.O., D/F 3/1/8; *Report of the Proceedings . . .*; C.F.L., vol. vii, p. 3113.

[2] E.R.O., D/F 3/1/8; C.F.L., vol. vii, pp. 3287–8.

[3] E.R.O., D/F 3/2/1–7, D/F 3/2/8–12, D/F 3/2/19. The statement in Ward-Jackson, p. 26, that hemming and fringing were carried on from 1821 to 1830 must originally have been based on a misreading of the date (1821 for 1831) in a loose sheet (which is in fact watermarked 1829) in D/F 3/2/19.

[4] Figures for 1832–4 based on E.R.O., D/F 3/2/17, D/F 3/2/1–12.

operation two crimping machines for aerophanes and two for mourning
crape; ten years later there were still two aerophane machines at work, but
now nine were crimping crape.[1] When in 1848 Sam Courtauld observed that 'our crape trade has progressively advanced even up to the

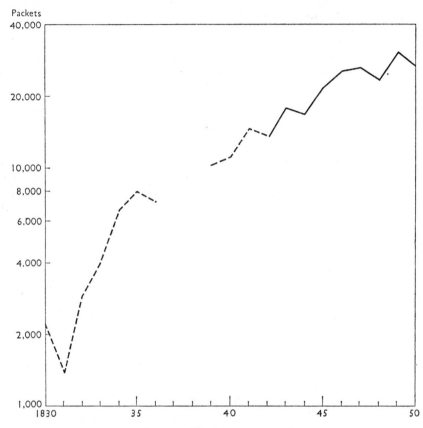

FIG. 9. *Samuel Courtauld & Co.: output of crape, 1830–50*

Based on annual numbers of packets finished; 1830–6 and 1839–41 are reasonably reliable estimates
from surviving records

Source: E.R.O.: D/F 3/2

present time',[2] he was in effect speaking of the firm's growing share of
the market in ritual mourning attire.

In trying to discover how this expansion had been achieved it is useful to
consider the reasons under three heads: technical, economic, and financial.

[1] E.R.O., D/F 3/2/17.   [2] *C.F.L.*, vol. vii, p. 3290.

III

The techniques of making crimped crape were for long surrounded by a deal of mumbo-jumbo. 'Different manufacturers [of crape]', wrote the author of a treatise on the silk industry in 1831, 'affect a degree of mystery with regard to their peculiar methods of dressing crape, possessing or imagining thence some superiority over their rivals in the manufacture.'[1] Eighty years later the *Encyclopaedia Britannica* in its edition of 1910 told its readers that the details of crape-making processes are 'known to only a few manufacturers, who so jealously guard their secret that, in some cases, the different stages in the manufacture are conducted in towns far removed from each other'. We have already seen[2] the sundry efforts, from the 1690s onwards, to master the exotic art of crimping crapes in the Italian manner. The absence of effective patents covering the processes made the practical possession of the relevant knowledge all the more precious and consequently liable to be shrouded in mystery. And so it was. Secret rooms, specially locked doors, industrial espionage, the painstaking interrogation of employees newly secured from competitors, secrecy clauses in contracts: all these and more were practised in the course of the nineteenth century by Samuel Courtauld & Co., and some, probably all, by the small number of their competitors in the mourning crape trade. At the heart of the mystery was the crimping room. Here the efforts to preserve the mystery achieved their highest expression. Up to the First World War Samuel Courtauld & Co.'s crimpers were still being sworn to secrecy before a Justice of the Peace.[3]

The seductive haze of the unknown should not, however, blind one to reality. It is possible that this secrecy may have helped to discourage entry of other firms into this prosperous branch of the silk industry. But the Justice of the Peace was not the real guardian of Courtauld's nineteenth-century success. It was rather the effective development of a series of technical devices precisely suited to the various processes of one job—making

---

[1] D. Lardner (ed.), *Treatise*, p. 297.   [2] Above, Chap. III.

[3] It is not clear precisely when this procedure started. Testimonies to the secrecy surrounding the crimping processes abound in several of the firm's nineteenth-century records. In 1857 George II's son George III, then aged 27, was allowed into the crimping room for the first time, though he had been working in the family firm for ten years. It was the occasion for a piece of mock ceremonial, described in *G.C.B.*, pp. 67–68. It is a tribute to the extraordinary continuity of the solemn secrecy which lay behind such apparently harmless foolery that the compiler of this piece of family piety should, in 1922, have provided to the account an equally solemn footnote saying: 'this is, of course, all fun; but the crimping-room was always kept strictly private'.

crape; and crimping, with all its aura of mystery, was only one of these processes.

The first of these devices was the crape mill. This was simply a throwing mill, wooden-framed, with iron or steel working parts and tin bobbins. There was probably nothing very original in its design, but it was simple and specific to its task of twisting the highly thrown crape yarn. How far George Courtauld II was responsible for the design of these mills it seems impossible to discover. Nor do we know how they compared with, for example, 'the most modern and improved silk throwing machinery such as is made by Messrs. Fairbairn of Manchester . . . in which the old-fashioned leather bands and straps are done away with' that Samuel was extolling in 1845.[1] Suffice to say that they were built at Steam Factory under the direction of George II, that in the early years they bore 1,500 and later 2,170 spindles each, that they were valued in this period at about £600 each, and that they were turned out one after the other during this period of rapid expansion. By the end of the 1828–49 partnership, the tenth crape mill had been installed at Bocking and the sixth at Halstead.[2] Including tram and organzine spindles at Bocking and Braintree, this gave the firm a throwing capacity of roughly 25,000 spindles there and 12,000 at Halstead.[3]

More noteworthy than the crape mills were the power-looms. The striking fact here is that in the silk industry in general the use of power-looms before about the mid 1830s was virtually confined to narrow goods and hard-silk weaving. In the textile industry as a whole at this time the power-loom, as Table 8 shows, had made its mark chiefly in

TABLE 8

Power-looms: England and Wales, 1835 and 1850

		Cotton	Wool and worsted	Silk	Flax and other fibres
1835	.	90,678	5,105	1,714	66
1850	.	223,626	41,787	6,092	1,083

the weaving of cotton fabrics.[4] Technical problems were largely, though not wholly, responsible for these variations. The delicate and readily broken fibres of degummed silk created particularly difficult obstacles

[1] E.R.O., D/F 3/2/98. S.C. III to M. Jeanneau, 10 February 1845.
[2] E.R.O., D/F 3/1/8; E.R.O., D/F 3/2/75.   [3] B.P.P. 1850, vol. xlii.
[4] B.P.P. 1836, vol. xlv; 1850, vol. xlii.

to the use of power-looms in weaving broad goods of soft silk. Conversely, the tougher fibres of hard silk and especially of highly thrown hard silk, could be woven into narrow fabrics or ribbons and also tolerate the stresses and strains of the early models of power-loom. In 1832 John Brocklehurst of the important Macclesfield silk firm of J. & T. Brocklehurst & Co. was questioned about the use of the power-loom in the silk industry. It had been successfully applied, he agreed, to the weaving of 'common narrow ribbons'; and it had been valuable for the weaving of crape gauze, 'the crape thread being hard twisted and capable of bearing the friction of this mode of weaving'. But he despaired of ever using power-looms in the making of broad goods, fancy ribbons, figured fabrics, and similar soft-silk wares.[1] Brocklehurst was an extreme protectionist, so his evidence is likely to have been prejudiced against the supposed merits of power-looms as a method of competing with foreign imported goods. Nevertheless, the gist of his contention was borne out not only by Free Trade opinion of the time but also by the factory returns.[2] The 1,714 silk power-looms were distributed as follows:

TABLE 9

Distribution of silk power-looms: England and Wales, 1835

Cheshire	414	Staffordshire	119
Lancashire	366	Essex	106
Norfolk	300	Devonshire	80
Derbyshire	166	Worcestershire	7
Somerset	156		

Of these, 132 in Somerset were certainly used 'solely for the manufacture of crape', the 300 in Norfolk were all in the Norwich works of Grout, Bayliss & Co., then probably the largest crape makers in the country; it was generally known that many of the power-looms in Cheshire, Lancashire, and Derbyshire were engaged on simple, coarse goods such as handkerchiefs and scarves, on plain ribbons, or, again, on crape; and the 106 in Essex were all in Samuel Courtauld's Halstead mill.[3]

After Edmund Cartwright's original invention of the power-loom and his own improvements thereto (1786–92), a number of engineers, notably

---

[1] B.P.P. 1831–2, vol. xix, pp. 796–7.

[2] See, e.g., Lardner, *Treatise*, p. 275; factory returns in B.P.P. 1836, vol. xlv, p. 152.

[3] B.P.P. 1836, vol. xlv, p. 152, 1831–2, vol. viv, p. 693 and *passim*; B.P.P. 1834, vol. xliii, p. 479.

PLATE 6

a. CRAPE THROWING MILLS AT HALSTEAD. This photograph, taken towards the end of the nine-teenth century, shows some of the wooden-framed crape mills, of Courtauld's own design and manufacture, still then in use

b. A COURTAULD CRAPE LOOM. The name on it—Courtauld, Taylors and Courtauld—means that it must have been made before 1849

William Horrocks and Richard Roberts, improved it still further. By the later 1820s, when Sam Courtauld came to consider the installation of power-looms, various models would have been available.[1] What looms he first used and precisely when we do not know. But the type which soon came into use was the simple loom illustrated opposite, which, as can be seen from the name 'Courtauld, Taylors & Courtauld' on it, belongs to the period of this first partnership. From whatever origins these looms sprang they were, like the crape mills, made by the firm at Steam Factory and turned out in large and growing numbers from the 1830s onwards. Valued at about £15 each in the 1840s, they were small, light in weight, and, like the crape mills, specifically and successfully designed for their task. In June 1838 Sam claimed that these looms were 'a discovery that gave considerable pecuniary advantage' though he 'had no patent to protect his discovery'.[2] The 'discovery' may or may not have been Sam's, but the mechanical skills which went into the design and construction were, once again, almost certainly those of his younger brother, George, whose role in the company's development must not be underestimated.

The £182. 18s. 1d. of 'Power Weaving Machinery' in the balance sheet of January 1829 may have represented about eight to ten looms, thus suggesting that the initial installation was in 1828. The corresponding balance sheet values rose to £618 in December 1831.[3] The first major investments in power-looms came with the first and second buildings of the Power Loom Factory of 1832 and 1836, bringing the total to 106 in 1836. The ensuing fourteen years of this period of expansion then saw a tremendous bustle of building these little looms and cramming them into the Halstead factory.[4]

TABLE 10

Number of power-looms at Halstead, 1829–50

1829	(?8–10)
1836	106
1838	178
1840	243
1845	477
1850	570

[1] *Hist. Tech.*, vol. iv, pp. 299–302.   [2] *B.P.P.* 1840, vol. xxiii, p. 224.
[3] E.R.O., D/F 3/1/7. The Stock Book (E.R.O., D/F 3/1/8) valuations give about £15 per loom as prime cost in the 1840s. Grout, however, gave a figure of £34. 10s. for his power-looms (but including reeds, harness, driving gear, and space) to the 1832 Committee— *B.P.P.* 1831–2, vol. xix, p. 694.
[4] E.R.O., D/F 3/1/8 and 9; *B.P.P.* 1836, vol. xlv; 1850, vol. xlii.

Leaving for later consideration[1] the economics of this notable investment in power-looms and its relation to the hand-weavers whom the firm still employed, we must now consider the third technical basis of the firm's achievement in crape: the crimping and finishing processes.

The path by which the eighteenth-century efforts to imitate the 'Italian method of crimping crapes' were finally transformed into the techniques of nineteenth-century English crape makers is hard to trace. No account survives of the processes followed at Bocking during the first half of the nineteenth century; and I know of no such account from any other firm or source. From the second half of the century, however, a fair amount of evidence on this subject survives in the Courtauld archives.[2] By using these in conjunction with certain records of machinery and output for 1830–50, it is possible to obtain a rough idea of the methods used.

The lengths of undyed crape gauze went from the looms first to be 'biased' or 'angled'. This was done on a device normally and not surprisingly known as a biasing or angling machine. In almost all of Samuel Courtauld & Co.'s early records, however, the process was called 'turning on' and the true nature of the machines concealed under the unrevealing name of 'turning-on machines'. On these machines the gauze was first passed over a steam box, which softened and slightly untwisted the highly thrown yarn, thus allowing it to be drawn tight and free from wrinkles, and then, under tension, was pulled sideways so as to lay the weft thread askew to the warp. The distorted gauze was then passed through the rollers of a crimping machine. This, like the biasing machine, was power driven. It consisted essentially of two rolls which could be run together under controlled pressure: the upper of brass, capable of being heated internally, and on the surface of which was engraved a 'figure' such as that which can be seen on the piece of crape illustrated in Plate 14; and the lower of compressed paper. The latter was 'worked in' so that the figure was transferred in reverse on to its surface. When the crape was between the two rolls, under heavy pressure and with the brass roll heated to 275°–300° F., the figure was embossed upon it. At this stage the purpose of the biasing becomes apparent. Silk does not possess as much elasticity or stretch as wool; consequently, any attempt to emboss silk by this method without biasing would result in the cutting or weakening of the fibres. By artificially lengthening the weft relative to the warp, through biasing, and by using figures which ran with the weft across the roll, the figure could be received upon the fabric without damage to its threads. After crimping,

[1] Below, pp. 102–4.   [2] E.R.O., D/F 3/2/28, 33–38, 40–90, 110–15.

the bias was then pulled out, probably by hand in this period, though later by machine.

Having thus impressed a figure upon the gauze whilst under tension, the next major procedure was to allow the gauze to assume the curl or crimp which would follow from its being made of highly thrown yarn. This was done by steeping the gauze in a liquid at temperatures sufficiently high to cause the twist to unwreathe and thus the entire fabric substantially to contract. In this way the figure was set and the crape made to assume the peculiar craped and crimped quality which apparently made it desirable. What was used in the early days for this 'wetting' process is unknown, but after 1848 the gauzes were steeped in a strong extract of valonia.[2] The temperature to which the steeping liquor was raised varied according to the quality of the gauze and was carefully controlled to ensure the right amount of contraction. The average temperature was about 100° F. and the total contraction about 25 per cent. in area. Biasing, crimping, de-biasing, and wetting added up to produce various changes in the size of the fabric between weaving and finishing: for example, a certain type of gauze woven 38 in. wide would be reduced to 22½ in. by biasing, emerge from crimping at 18½ in., and then be de-biased and end up at 28½ in. Similarly a woven length of 30½ yards would contract to 24 yards.

Aerophanes were crimped with a lighter figure, then had the gum boiled off, and were dyed in various colours. But mourning crapes had not only to be dyed black but also to receive the final process: dressing. For black dyeing in the early years sundry vegetable dyes were used in varying proportions and combinations at different times. Copperas, log-wood, and valonia were amongst the usual ingredients. By the time the silk had emerged from the dye-house it had lost much of the hardness given to it by its natural gum. It might even begin to look bright and soft, which would never do for the authentic mourning crape: the dull stiffness appropriate to this funereal trimming had to be put into it. This was done by passing the crape through a dress into which had been boiled up a variety of glutinous ingredients. Like the black dye, the dress was the subject of change and experiment. Amongst the ingredients used at this time in diverse combinations were gums of various sorts, starch, glue, and even treacle.

About this complex of processes which made up the mystery of crape

[1] Valonia: the name given to the acorns or acorn cups of *Quercus aegilops* and the related *quercus vallonea*, types of oak growing especially in the Mediterranean area. It contains much tannin.

finishing three things can be said. First, there is the noteworthy empirical content, the element of trial and error, so typical of this phase of the Industrial Revolution. This revealed itself not only in the composition of the dye and the dress but also in the angle of the figure on the roll, the temperatures for crimping and wetting, the pressure on the crimping rolls, and much else. There were frequent variations in quality and nobody really understood why. Second, because there were no patents and because of the value of some tested combination of ingredients, pressures, or temperatures, the urge to secrecy becomes intelligible. This urge was reinforced by the possession of the two constituents of the total process which alone may have possessed real elements of originality: the biasing machine and the design of the figure on the brass roll. Third, the importance in the whole procedure of the power and heat available from that characteristically Victorian industrial combination: water, steam, and later, gas.

How, then, did Samuel Courtauld & Co. acquire the knowledge of these processes and how far were they developed in this first phase of expansion?

The use of power-driven rolls in printing or embossing was much in the air at this time. The resemblance between the crimping machine and Crumpler's patent dressing machine of 1772 (above, p. 26) is obvious. The search for methods of making Italian crape as sketched in Chapter III, the successful experiments with calico printing by rollers, the taking out of various patents for embossing, printing, or figuring textiles: all these point to the conclusion that there was nothing especially original in the crimping machines at Bocking, though obviously there may have been particular parts or items which were original. We may not know precisely whence came the idea of these machines, but we do know that, like other machinery used by the firm, they were made at Steam Factory under George II's supervision. Vitally important to the crimping machine was the engraving on the brass rolls, and here Courtauld & Co. seem to have made a major advance when they secured the services of one of the best-known engravers of the time, Henry Le Keux.[1] This arose from the personal friendship of Sam and Le Keux. Various letters between the two survive from the years 1812–15; during one of his periods of depression in 1812 when he found life 'absolutely intolerable', Sam had contemplated,

---

[1] On Le Keux (1787–1868) see *D.N.B.* His elder brother, John (1783–1846), was the more famous of these two well-known engravers. The *D.N.B.*'s garbled version of Henry's connexion with Courtaulds is that about 1838 he 'abandoned engraving and joined in starting a crape manufactory at Bocking, Essex'.

inter alia, becoming an engraver. His father had warned him, however, that 'mere manual labour—though of the higher class—is very rarely indeed so valuable as a business, as those modes of trade or manufacture which allow us a profit from the labour of many other persons'.[1] Some twenty-five years later, when Sam was certainly sampling the profits of the labour of others (and of himself), he added Le Keux to those working for him. Joining the firm in 1837 Le Keux continued to work for Courtauld & Co. until his death in 1868.[2] Like other engravers who later joined him and followed him, he was given favourable terms of work and pay in reward for the lengthy and exacting work of engraving. Some idea of the cost, both in money to the firm and in time and eyesight to the 'gentlemen of the engraving room', may be gained from the fact that it took anything from six months to one-and-a-half years to engrave a roll and that in the 1840s the approximate valuation of a new crimping machine was:[3]

	£
Frame	50
Brass roll . . .	45
Engraving on Brass Roll .	100
Paper Roll . . .	90
Other parts . . .	15
	£300

There is no doubt whatever that the market success of a particular pattern or 'figure' was vital to crape sales; competition between crape firms was as much in design of figure as in price and quality. So Le Keux's work probably made an important contribution to the firm's early success.

If the significance of the crimping lay less in its originality than in the quality of the engraving and the skill of its operation, there seems to have been something original in the biasing machine. I know of no patents covering this nor of any discussion of it. Other crape makers must have known of the need to bias the gauze—Nouaille or Grout or half a dozen other crape makers may have found this out. But did they discover how to mechanize this process? Although by the 1880s other types of angling or biasing machines certainly existed, and were used by some manufacturers, Courtauld & Co. regarded them as inferior to their own, and it was known that most other crape manufacturers, including Grout & Co., still

[1] Courtauld MSS.: G.C. I to S.C. III, 17 August 1812; John Newberry to S.C. III, July 1814; Le Keux to S.C. III, 30 August 1815; J.N. to S.C. III, 2 March 1820; *C.F.L.*, vol. I, pp. 132–3.

[2] E.R.O., D/F 3/2/52, p. 21.   [3] E.R.O., D/F 3/2/17 and 32.

biased by hand.[1] Was the machine invented at Bocking, perhaps by George II? The very absence of any claims that it was might seem to testify against this supposition, though it might just as well testify to the power of the whole crimping mumbo-jumbo. At least there was such a machine at Bocking in the very early years, for the first surviving account of the Finishing Factory, March 1833, records, along with three 'craping' machines ('crimping' machines as from 1839), one 'Turning-on machine, with brass band, complete—£24'.[2]

Just as no claims seem to have been made to suggest that the biasing machine was a Courtauld invention, so have the legends which have grown up about the firm's early possession of the crimping techniques as a whole tended similarly to suggest that the knowledge was surreptitiously bought from outside. Two legends are available. One is that Sam paid Grout & Co. a sum of money to go into their crimping room and learn all he could of their machinery.[3] This story is linked with the claim that Joseph Grout invented crimped, figured, silk crape, and patented it in 1822. This, as already shown in Chapter III, is untrue. On the other hand, in the 1820s Grout certainly had a large and flourishing crape-making concern. The centre of the business was Norwich, with other establishments in various towns of East Anglia, including Braintree; and until 1828–9 their London office was at 42 Gutter Lane, which Courtauld & Co. then took over.[4] So Sam may or may not have bought information from him: it seems unlikely but is unprovable. The second story, current amongst old people in Bocking at the end of the nineteenth century, is that Sam got the requisite technical information from a crape maker called Leny Smith, by paying him a lump sum and promising employment both for him and his son at the factory.[5] There certainly was a firm of this name, listed as Leny Smith & Son, silk and crape manufacturers, 6 Paternoster Row, from 1817 to 1824; and the story seems to get some credence from the fact that a Leny Smith, presumably the son, appears in the firm's records as employed

[1] E.R.O., D/F 3/2/34, June 1886; D/F 3/2/37, August 1890; D/F 3/2/69, 26 March 1886, D/F 3/2/40, 41; 17 January 1888.

[2] E.R.O., D/F 3/2/17.

[3] The *locus classicus* of this story is Warner, pp. 289–90; it is also mentioned in Ward-Jackson, p. 28.

[4] B.P.P. 1831–2, vol. xix, pp. 691–700; *Johnstone's London & Commercial Directory* (1817); *Robson's Classification of Trades & Street Guide* (1829); *Pigot's London & Provincial New Commercial Directory* (1822–4). Grout & Co. moved to Foster Lane.

[5] This story is hinted at in Ward-Jackson, p. 28, though the garnering of the full story from local verbal sources is the result of the inquiries of Mr. Thomas Rayner, who kindly passed the information on to me.

in some capacity, at various dates from 1852 until his death, aged 65, in 1885.[1] There is, furthermore, a faint hint of an enterprising Smith in the silk business in a letter from George I to Sam in 1812. In this, George, referring to his son's 'idea of applying to Mr. Smith or other manufacturers of silk', presents Smith's story as a long tale of speculative inventiveness and failure, evidently designed to frighten Sam away from his notions, and finishes with ironic references to making 'a craping machine that shall far exceed all others'.[2] Smith, alas, is a depressingly common name.

The unspoken implication common to both these stories is that there was a secret technique which Sam Courtauld did not possess and which he had somehow to acquire from someone else. This ignores too much. It ignores the complexity and empirical nature of the crape-finishing processes, and the efforts which had been made by various people to master these processes for the previous fifty years or more; it ignores the experience which Sam Courtauld had had of the silk industry since he was 14 years old, and the fact that he and his father had been concerned with throwing crape yarn and weaving crape gauzes; and, finally, it ignores the fact that he had taken over Halstead mill from a crape manufacturer, Stephen Beuzeville. Both Stephen Beuzeville and his son James then worked for Courtauld & Co. What may they have contributed?[3] Sam's experience, vigour, and abilities, allied to George II's mechanical aptitudes, would together have gone a long way in the task of breaking into the crape business. What mattered far more in the long run was the skill, drive, and good fortune which kept the firm going and built it up.

During the early years, however, Samuel Courtauld & Co. did have to get some crimping, and perhaps dressing and dyeing, done outside. As Fig. 10 shows, during the years 1833–6 most crapes were crimped in London, while Bocking concentrated more on aerophanes.[4] But who did

---

[1] *Johnstone's London Commercial Directory* (1817), *Pigot's London & Provincial New Commercial Directory* (1822–4); E.R.O. D/F 3/1/9; D/F 3/240, 41, p. 53; D/F 3/2/56, p. 222 (27 February 1872).

[2] Courtauld MSS.: G.C. I to S.C. III, 14 April 1812.

[3] Stephen Beuzeville died at Bocking in 1862—W. A. Beuzeville, op. cit. It is not difficult to think up sundry wholly hypothetical influences. A man called Vavasseur was on the pay roll of the Finishing Factory in 1831: what relation, if any, did he have to Carter & Vavasseur, a firm of London silk manufacturers who were employing hand-loom weavers at Braintree in the late 1830s? Or again, a certain Beckwith apparently had something to do with the crimping rolls in the early 1830s: what relation, if any, did he have to William Beckwith, of Wood St., London, who was putting out weaving work in the Coggeshall area in 1838?—E.R.O., D/F 3/2/17; *B.P.P.* 1840, vol. xxiii, pp. 125–8.

[4] E.R.O., D/F 3/2/1–12.

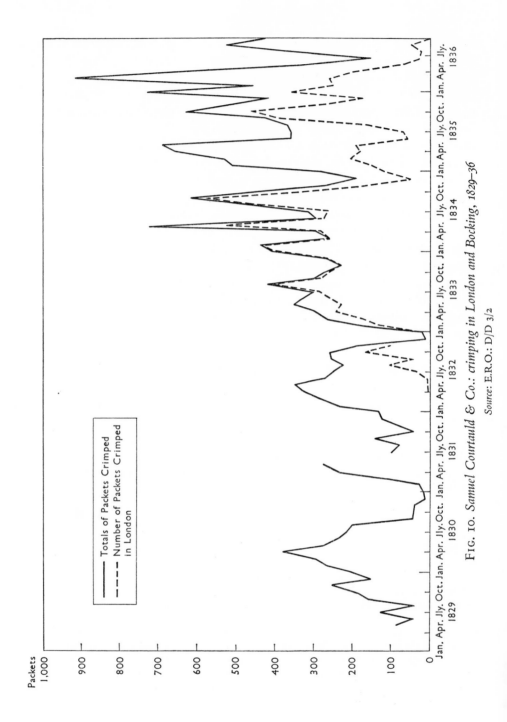

Packets

1,000

900

800

700

600

500

400

300

200

100

0

Jan. Apr. Jly. Oct. Jan. Apr. Jly.Oct. Jan. Apr. Jly. Oct. Jan. Apr. Jly. Oct. Jan. Apr. Jly. Oct. Jan. Apr. Jly. Oct. Jan. Apr. Jly. Oct. Jan. Apr. Jly.
     1829   1830   1831   1832   1833   1834   1835   1836

Totals of Packets Crimped

Number of Packets Crimped
in London

FIG. 10. *Samuel Courtauld & Co.: crimping in London and Bocking, 1829–36*

Source: E.R.O.: D/D 3/2

the work in London, and by what methods, it is hard to tell. These questions are intractable. Such words as 'crimped in town' or 'crimped in London' in surviving records reveal little. There were certainly specialist firms in London listed in the commercial directories of the day as 'Crape dressers'. Probably the packets marked in July 1833 as 'crimped in town by Lowe' went to Daniel Lowe of Goswell St., crape dresser; and that of May 1834 labelled 'to be dyed and sent to Godefroy to be dressed' presumably went to Peter Augustine Godefroy, crape and bombazine dresser and dyer, of Sydney Place, Cambridge Road. All that can be said with certainty is that by the summer of 1836 London crimping was coming to an end and that, scribbling in the margin of a crape book, Sam was demanding to know of certain unsatisfactory pieces: 'Why are these crimped in Town?'[1] Soon no more were. More machines had been installed, more rolls engraved and Le Keux's services secured, more experience gained with the practical problems of the whole group of finishing processes. The technical corner had been turned.

Water-power, steam-power, gaslight: this Industrial Revolution trio was the final technical basis of the firm's early achievement. Crape mills and light crape-looms did not require as much horse-power to drive them as heavier types of industrial equipment. According to Sam Courtauld in 1838, whereas 1 h.p. could drive 14 or 15 cotton power-looms, it could drive 40 of his crape power-looms. This was probably more hopeful than accurate, though the general principle remained true.[2] So light steam-engines were installed to match the investment in throwing, weaving, and finishing machinery. At Bocking, the 8 h.p. of water and 4 h.p. of steam of 1826 had become approximately 40 h.p. of steam by 1850. The engines installed were such as the two beam, condensing engines supplied by James Horn of Whitechapel in 1845 and 1847 at £330 apiece. These and other engines there drove throwing mills, as well as the crimping and biasing machines. At Halstead the 8 h.p. of water and 6 h.p. of steam of 1828 had grown to some 45 h.p. of steam in the power-loom factory, whilst in the old crape mill the steam engine still functioned only when there was not enough water to drive the mills. Braintree remained

[1] E.R.O., D/F 3/2/1–7, *passim* and especially 17 July 1833, 13 May 1834, 11 August 1836; *Johnstone's London Commercial Directory* (1817); *Pigot's London & Provincial New Commercial Directory* (1823–4).

[2] For Sam's statement see *B.P.P.* 1840, vol. xxiii, p. 225. His calculation would obviously have been based on the earliest, lightest, and smallest of the Courtault crape-looms; in 1870, the company's engineer James Finney calculated that 12 looms needed 1 h.p. and a crape mill of 2,170 spindles required 2 h.p.—E.R.O., D/F 3/2/54, 30 June 1870.

wholly a water mill of 10 h.p. in this period.[1] Gas lighting, installed at Halstead in 1838, illuminated the power-looms there; and in 1846 a complete gas storage plant was put up at Bocking to provide gas not only for lighting the factory but soon also to be used for heating the crimping rollers.[2] By the mid century this mechanized early Victorian crape works was firmly planted astride these three towns of north Essex.

IV

Without the economic circumstances, external and internal, these technical problems and achievements tell us little.

The economic attractions of East Anglia which appealed to silk throwsters and manufacturers have already been considered.[3] But once the long summer of protection which helped to lure them there, and elsewhere, during the first quarter of the century turned into winter after the legislation of 1826–9 and the general economic depression of 1829–32, then the problems of business survival were not everywhere solved. Nor were the difficulties simply those induced by the winds of Free Trade. As Table 3 in Chapter V showed, the rate of population increase in the East Anglian counties fell sharply in the decades 1821–31 and 1831–41; more and more people began to drift away from the area, to London, to the rapidly expanding textile districts of Lancashire and Yorkshire, or to seek better prospects overseas.[4] Difficulties of the sort which George Courtauld I had encountered[5] in recruiting an adequate supply of young girls and women became more acute as silk throwing and weaving expanded in the boom days of the mid 1820s. 'The opportunity of getting Poulter's set of hands', wrote Sam in February 1823 of a throwster who had left Braintree for Halstead, 'determined me instantly to put up some winding and drawing at Panfield Lane'. But two months later, having started up Panfield Lane again, he was 'labouring under difficulties . . . for want of hands', for most of Poulter's hands 'went to weaving, and Grout sending down very recently orders to put up 100 more looms has robbed me of many of my oldest and best hands.'[6] Now wages were rising and employment spreading in an area which had formerly known so much poverty and unem-

[1] On steam-engines see E.R.O., D/F 3/2/30; D/F 3/2/43–90, *passim*; D/F 3/1/88–89; and B.P.P. 1839, vol. xlii, 1850, vol. xlii.

[2] E.R.O., D/F 3/1/8 and 9; 3/2/43–90.   [3] Above, pp. 21, 61–64.

[4] A. Redford, *Labour Migration in England, 1800–50* (Manchester, 1926), pp. 42, 93–94.

[5] Above, pp. 42–43.

[6] *C.F.L.*, vol. iii, pp. 992–3; Courtauld MSS.: S.C. III to G.C. I, 23 April 1823.

PLATE 7

BOCKING MILL

The original part of Bocking Mill, plus extensions, as it was in the later nineteenth century

ployment. Ten years later the economic scene had changed again. Falling prices, sharpened competition, and the inflow of imported silk manufactures hit mainly the soft-silk weavers and the throwsters who worked for the Spitalfields trades. But in the depression years of 1829–32,[1] chilling economic winds were felt everywhere in the industry, and not least in East Anglia. The difficulties of adaptation to the new circumstances, in an area of lower-than-average population growth and lower-than-average wages, now presented themselves.

The dependence of early nineteenth-century silk throwsters upon the labour of young girls was everywhere great, but especially so in East Anglia, as the following figures suggest:[2]

TABLE II

Employment in silk and cotton factories, 1833

	Females as percentage of all employees	Females under 11 as percentage of all female employees	Females under 16 as percentage of all female employees
Silk			
Norfolk, Suffolk, and Essex .	96	14	53
Somerset	80	12	39
Derbyshire	63	8	35
Cotton			
Lancashire	50	4	33

Numbers and proportions do not, however, tell the whole story. Whatever may have been the situation in the boom days of competition for labour a decade earlier, now, despite the migration from the area, East Anglian throwsters, or some of them at least, were able to use double sets of hands for night work. This was in complete contrast to the position in the more industrialized areas of the north-west; the overwhelming majority of silk throwsters and manufacturers in Cheshire, Lancashire, Derbyshire, and Staffordshire found their labour supply inadequate. J. & T. Brocklehurst at Macclesfield, for example, maintained in 1833 that even when work was abundant, no second set of workers could be found for

[1] In general, see A. D. Gayer, A. J. Schwartz, and W. Rostow, *The Growth and Fluctuations of the British Economy, 1790–1850* (2 vols., Oxford, 1953).

[2] B.P.P. 1834, vol. xix, pp. 291–4. The county with the highest silk mill employment in the country, Cheshire (unfortunately excluded from the report from which these figures are derived), probably had a similarly heavy concentration of young female labour.

night work. One Derby throwster said quite bluntly that for night and day working not enough children could be had at sufficiently low wages. But in north Essex, along with some others, Samuel Courtauld & Co. used a double set of hands and worked their mills day and night.[1]

In East Anglia the wages paid, for a twelve-hour day, such as was common everywhere, were notably lower than those in other areas. As the following comparisons demonstrate, this was true within the same age-groups and was not simply a result of employing more young people.[2]

TABLE 12

Average weekly wages of girls and young women
in silk and cotton factories, 1833

Area	Ages						Average poor-rate per head of pop. in 1831
	Below 11	11 to 16	16 to 21	21 to 26	26 to 31	31 to 36	
	s. d.	s. d.	s. d.	s. d.	s. d.	s. d.	s. d.
Norfolk, Suffolk, and Essex (silk) . .	1 5	2 7	4 0¾	5 0	4 11	4 4	16 11
Derbyshire (silk) .	1 11	3 6½	5 11	7 0½	7 7	7 0½	6 7
Lancashire (cotton) .	2 4¾	4 3	7 8½	8 5	8 7¾	8 9½	4 8

These, it must be stressed, are wages, not earnings, and for the most part they apply to those tending machinery—winding, throwing, drawing, doubling, spinning, and so on. The sample from which the figures were drawn included a return made by Samuel Courtauld & Co. The earnings of those on piece work, on the other hand, could obviously be more. The women employed on hemming and fringing in the Finishing Factory made average weekly earnings which varied widely from around 3s. to 7s. per week;[3] and this was still less than the wage rate of their machine-tending counterparts in Lancashire cotton mills. As Table 12 shows, low wages and high poor-rates went together. For various reasons, not too much should be read into this correlation.[4] But at least it helps to em-

---

[1] *B.P.P.* 1834, vol. xx (Answers by factory owners to a questionnaire sent out by the Central Board of Commissioners on Children's Employment in Factories), pp. 305, 314, 369–72 (Samuel Courtauld & Co.'s answers), 374, 493, 495–6, 497, 573, 577–8, 581, 583, 591, 599, 627, 724; *B.P.P.* 1840, vol. x, pp. 781–3.

[2] *B.P.P.* 1834, vol. xix, pp. 291, 298.   [3] E.R.O., D/F 3/2/19.

[4] The sample from which the wages were drawn was small, and various factors helped to determine the level of the poor-rates—see Blaug, op. cit.

phasize both the economic circumstances of the time and the place and the value to the local population of the employment created by industrial growth.[1] The factory owners got cheap labour; for the worker, there would have been less employment and still more poverty had the factories not been there; and when the fluctuations of the market curtailed the factories' operations or shut them down completely, unemployment and poverty came again.

The wages paid to East Anglian hand-loom weavers were consistently lower than in Spitalfields, both before and after the repeal of the Spital-fields Act in 1825. It was generally maintained, moreover, that although rents were lower than in London ordinary living expenses were not greatly different. Braintree, it was said in 1840, 'is sufficiently near London to be within the vortex; cheapness is not felt until farther down in the country: London is a sure market, and all articles of subsistence are drawn to it'.[2] Irregular employment often meant that many hand-loom weavers' earnings were less than those of agricultural labourers. If they were married men with children the household was glad enough of the earnings which mother and daughters could get from such employment as Courtauld's and other mills offered. According to the type of fabric, average hand-loom weavers' earnings around the Essex–Suffolk border area at the end of the 1830s varied from 7s. to 13s. per week; at the same time agricultural labourers in the area earned about 10s. plus some benefits in kind, e.g. beer or malt. By contrast, average weekly wages of men between the ages of 21 and 41 working in Lancashire cotton and Yorkshire woollen mills ranged from about 17s. to 22s. 6d. per week.[3]

Initially, of course, the East Anglian silk throwsters and manufacturers tackled the problem of stiffening competition by the common expedient of reducing costs by employing cheaper labour for longer hours. But how were they to continue to function in the changed circumstances of com-petition in the 1830s, even after the worst phase of the depression was over? As the foregoing account of the labour situation suggests, the opportunities for further action on these lines was virtually nil. According to Joseph Grout in 1831, the average rate of wages paid to all his employees had risen from 7s. 6d. in 1822 to 8s. 8½d. in 1825—a rise which certainly agrees, as we have seen, with Sam Courtauld's experience of the competi-tion for labour in Braintree and Bocking at that period—and then fallen to

---

[1] Sussex, with virtually no industry, consistently had the highest poor-rates in the country in the early nineteenth century—Porter, op. cit.

[2] *B.P.P.* 1840, vol. xxxiii, p. 128.   [3] Ibid., pp. 125–38.

3s. 8½d. in 1831.[1] John Hall, of Coggeshall mill, stated in 1832 that he had reduced the wages of the children he employed by 20 per cent. in the past two years, 'a great and principal reduction in my annual expense'.[2] Although reductions were confined neither to East Anglia nor to the silk industry, wage rates in the area were now running at levels which permitted of no further reduction. By the 1840s, hand-loom weavers' wages had fallen 20 per cent. in the Norwich area since 1829; Grout paid 12s. for weaving a piece of crape in 1822 and 7s. for a slightly larger piece in 1831.[3] In Braintree a pool of underemployed weavers kept wages down. In 1812 George Courtauld I reckoned that a journeyman crape weaver on a hand-loom could earn 12s. to 15s. per week; in 1837–8 Samuel Courtauld & Co. paid an average of 7s. 2d. a week to men and 5s. 1d. to women for the hand-loom weaving of crapes.[4] But at least they still offered some work, and, as already shown, they also put out work to soft-silk weavers in the 1840s. Silk weaving at Coggeshall and Hadleigh, on the other hand, had been given up by this time, and Grout, who employed over 3,900 persons in the boom days of 1825, gave work to only 1,871, less than half this total, in 1831.[5] Despite the employment, albeit at low wages, which C ourtaulds offered, the Braintree–Bocking area was a poor one. In 1833 the Poor Law Commissioners noted the former dependence of the population there on woollen weaving, and observed of the recently introduced silk weaving that it had at first paid high wages and given full employment, but now, since the reduction of the duties on foreign silks, many were unemployed and wages were made up out of the poor-rates. At Braintree the cost of poor relief per head of the population was 18s. 2d., at Bocking and Cogge-shall 18s. 6d. in the £; by contrast at Chelmsford it was 6s. 6d. and at Saffron Walden 4s. 10d.[6]

For the throwing mills, with their demand for juvenile hands, the labour situation in the 1830s looked rather different from what it had in the cosy days of protection. The need to keep down costs was readily translated into a need to keep down wages, but now the falling off in population was beginning to make itself felt as families left the area. John Hall told the Select Committee of 1832 that were he to erect another mill it would not be at Coggeshall but in 'a situation where I should have more hands'; 'at Pebmarsh' George Courtauld I's old employers, Witts & Co.,

---

1 *B.P.P.* 1831–2, vol. xix, p. 692.   2 Ibid., p. 372.
3 *B.P.P.* 1840, vol. xxiii, pp. 149–51; 1831–2, vol. xix, p. 695.
4 Courtauld MSS.: G.C. I to S.C. III, 24 November 1812; *B.P.P.* 1840, vol. xxiii, p. 127.
5 *B.P.P.* 1840, vol. xxiii, pp. 126–38; 1831–2, vol. xix, p. 692.
6 *B.P.P.* 1834, vol. xxviii, p. 229a.

testified in 1833 that 'the population is not superabundant for our employ; to induce fresh hands to settle would not be practicable'. Joseph Grout at the same time bemoaned the shortage of children as having limited the extent of his works: 'after having erected mills at one place . . . we have been obliged to go to another, having found it difficult to obtain a sufficient number of young females for our purpose'. He added significantly: 'the wages we are at present obliged to pay are so very low that no adult labour could be got for the money'.[1] The stick of competition and the carrot of profits bore hard upon the weakest links.

But for those who could survive, there were hands to be got and gains to be made. In the longer run the power-loom weaving of crape was to prove a remarkably sound bet. The market was assured: the English enthusiasm for mourning was unimpaired, and crape, if not quite the rage it was to become in the triumphant days of mid-Victorian mourning,[2] was fashionable enough to sustain a solid middle-class demand. Moreover, the English population was going through the fastest recorded growth in its history: in the fifty years from 1801 to 1851 it doubled, from 9,000,000 to 18,000,000; and grew richer, especially in those reaches of society which could afford the more expensive celebrations of death. So more middle and upper-class bereaved bought more mourning crape. As Catherine Taylor had pointed out to her sister Sophia in 1825 in connexion with the Halstead mill scheme, '. . . crape is far more certain than the throwing' (i.e. organzine and tram throwing).[3] This very belief had, in the shorter run, undoubtedly encouraged an over-investment in crape. But of the many who rushed in during the boom of 1825–6 not all survived. When Joseph Grout lamented the 'ruinous prices' at which, he said, English crapes were selling in 1832, even he, keen protectionist that he was, did not blame this upon massive imports of *black* crape. The English crape industry no longer had much to fear from Italian black crape. It was his white and coloured crapes that had been hard hit by a substantial rise in crape imports.[4] And outside the crape trade it was in the soft silk, figured silk, and fancy ribbon trades that, in particular, the old superiority of France reasserted itself. Yet, for all the outcry of the protectionists, the industry *as a whole* was not instantly ruined. Imports of foreign thrown silk did not rise significantly, and although imports of foreign manufactured silks did, those of raw and waste silk rose still more (see Figs. 6 and 7). These raw materials went to firms who managed to survive the depression years and possessed the

[1] B.P.P. 1831–2, vol. xix, p. 373; 1834, vol. xx, pp. 378, 1110.   [2] Below, pp. 128–33.
[3] C.F.L., vol. iii, p. 1268.   [4] B.P.P. 1831–2, vol. xix, pp. 13, 694.

resources to expand the type of production in which English industry, then had the advantage, i.e. those dependent on power-driven machinery, rather than on artistic excellence of design. It was no longer possible for the English industry to use the capital-saving techniques which, under protection, had allowed manually operated throwing or winding; capital-intensive techniques with higher productivity were now urgent.

Precisely how Samuel Courtauld & Co. survived the depression into which the new firm ran so soon after it was launched is hard to tell in the absence, for these crucial years, of detailed accounts and particularly of data on sales. From what does survive, however, it seems as though their worst time was experienced in 1828–9. A profit of £440 for (probably) the six months ending 3 January 1829 became a mere £82 for the next half-year to June 1829. Then their fortunes changed: the ten months to 1 May 1830 showed a profit of £3,625, and the next twenty months to December 1831 of £8,424.[1] In the short run, revival can hardly have resulted simply from power-weaving, for the firm's investment therein was still less, in value, than that of hand-weaving.[2] The estimates of numbers of packets of gauze crimped, shown in Fig. 10 above, suggest that despite the employment of crimping machines and of crimpers from about 1830 it was not until the general revival in trade in 1833–4 that the firm's output of finished crapes started to increase significantly.[3] Meanwhile, much of the gauze that was produced—mainly by hand—was turned into hand-kerchiefs and the like. Profits, perhaps indeed survival, through these difficult early years may well have depended, to some extent at least, upon throwing the patent organzine and marabout, and the sale of patent spindles. When Grout listed to the 1832 Committee the places in the country where, he said, crape makers other than himself had looms at work he made no mention of Essex.[4] He may have had some reason of his own for wishing to ignore Courtauld & Co., but had they yet been crape

---

[1] E.R.O., D/F 3/1/7.
[2] Ibid.

	Power-weaving machinery	Hand-weaving machinery
	£	£
Jan. 1829 .	182	463
June 1829 .	245	467
May 1830 .	423	834
Dec. 1831 .	618	990

[3] On the general revival, see R. C. Matthews, *A Study in Trade Cycle History: Economic Fluctuations in Great Britain 1833–42* (Cambridge, 1954).
[4] *B.P.P.* 1831–2, vol. xix, p. 694.

makers on a substantial scale he could hardly have done so. Moreover, as
we have seen already, it was entirely as makers of a special spindle, as
throwsters of a special organzine and of marabout, that the firm was
mentioned—and mentioned in flattering terms—during the 1832 hearings.
When the economic tide had turned, when some marginal producers had
been weeded out, and others had contracted their business, then and then
only could Courtauld & Co. really begin to grow. In so doing they no
doubt took over part of the market, and some of the workers, from other
makers who had suffered in the depression. It is tempting to see this as
evidence of Sam's business vision, but for all that we know it was just as
likely to have been good luck. Once the power-looms were at work, the
crape mills and the steam-engines installed, then he had both the economies
of power and the low labour costs of East Anglia, as other throwsters and
manufacturers closed down or contracted. And in weaving, as he himself admitted in 1838, he was now able to use the hand-loom crape weavers
as a buffer against market fluctuations whilst his power-looms did most of
the work. By this time he had supplemented his 178 power-looms with
441 hand-loom weavers. He supplied the looms, the warps, already prepared, and the weft, already wound. It was these weavers who in 1837–8
were making 7s. 2d. or 5s. 1d. a week *when employed*. But as Sam said:[1]

> . . . the crape manufacturer does a great portion of his work in power-loom
> factories; but he also gives out work to hand-loom weavers. Whenever there is a
> slackness of trade he discontinues his hand-loom weavers; a part of them at any
> rate, or perhaps the whole of them. The weavers being dismissed, put him to no
> expense. But he continues on his power looms, because in them he has capital
> embarked, the interest of which he cannot afford to lose. When trade becomes
> brisk, he again employs his hand-loom weavers.

Not only were power-looms cheaper, but they had the great advantage of
regularity and order which was a part of the essence of the new factory
system. For the hand-loom weavers were too liable to the human failing of
irregularity and disorder. They had to be disciplined by the formidable
Sam. Towards the end of 1836 nearly all the looms were called in, but in
the spring of 1837, when trade revived, they were put out again. The work,
however, came in very slowly, and 'Mr. Courtauld . . . was much
annoyed at being unable to supply the goods which he found that he could
sell'. So the weavers were warned that any who took out work must consider themselves obliged to finish at least one piece a week; that those who

---

[1] *B.P.P.* 1840, vol. xxiii, pp. 127, 226–7.

did not were liable to have the looms called back or could expect to be the first to be discharged in the slack season, and in any event would be fined 2*s*. out of the price of weaving a piece. This warning, it was said, 'had a beneficial effect, but not until the penalty in one or two cases was enforced'. These errant weavers had no other employment at the time, and 'their neglect merely arose from the difficulty of throwing off habits of sloth contracted during "play".'[1]

If some parts of the total economic situation could be turned to Sam Courtauld's advantage, others proved less amenable. The supply of raw silk was something which in the main lay quite outside the control of the English throwsters and manufacturers. Some, as mentioned earlier, had invested in filatures in the East with a view to improving the quality of Indian silk.[2] But for the most part raw-silk prices were data to be accepted rather than determined. Apart from the reduction in duties, there was a long downward trend, from 1810 to 1833, in the prices of Indian and Chinese silks (see Fig. 11). This undoubtedly helped to encourage the activities of English throwsters and manufacturers, for, as we have seen, these cheaper silks were much used in the English industry, and especially in crape. Sam Courtauld, not satisfied with this, made efforts to acquire control of some silk supplies. He put money into a filature in Spain, at Vinaleza, near Valencia; and then into one in Syria, at Beirut. Spanish and Syrian silks were coarse but presumably thought to be adequate to make the gauzes of the much-crimped and dressed mourning crape. The Vinaleza undertaking started in 1831. Between April and August of that year Samuel took his wife and his sister Sophia on a trip, via Paris, Lyons, and Milan, to the scene of this Spanish investment. It presumably produced something, for between 1832 and 1838, probably around 1833–4, the firm carried 6,000 lb. of Spanish raw silk in stock. But, for some reason now unknown, it proved an abortive undertaking; after being written down each year, machinery valued there at £257 was written off completely in 1841.[3] In 1845 Samuel Courtauld & Co. set various inquiries in motion about the planting of mulberry trees and the establishment of a filature in France, but abandoned the idea on finding the likely expenditure too great. They then made arrangements for silk reeling at a Beirut filature, but as a result of defalcations by those to whom they had made

[1] *B.P.P.* 1840, vol. xxiii, pp. 126–7.

[2] On Grout's filature in Bengal, see *B.P.P.* 1831–2, pp. 695–8.

[3] On the Vinaleza scheme, see *C.F.L.*, vol. iv, pp. 1829, 1847–8, 1870, 1875; E.R.O., D/F 3/1/8; D/F 3/1/1 and 1A. Stephen Beuzeville's son James became manager of the Vinaleza filature—W. A. Beuzeville, op. cit.

advances of cash, took possession of the filature itself, and in July 1846 bought it and further adjoining land. Repairs were made, buildings put up, and by 1850 the investment was valued at £10,526. But seven years later: 'this property having been offered for sale is put this year at what we may hope to realize, taking it altogether—£1,000'. Next year it was sold.[1]

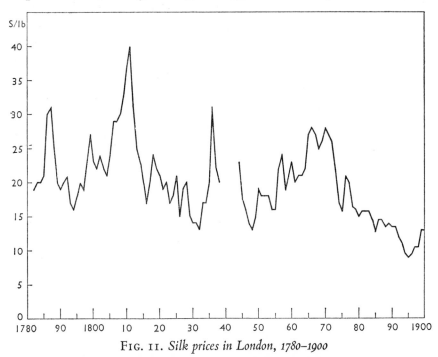

FIG. 11. *Silk prices in London, 1780–1900*

Annual average prices for China or China (Tsatlee) (shillings/lb of 16 ozs)

Sources: 1782–1838, Tooke & Newmarch, op. cit.; 1844–46, 1886–1900, *The Economist*; 1847–85, Sauerbeck index (*Journal of the Royal Statistical Society XLIX*, 1886)

Already in 1848, Samuel had lamented the 'exceptional losses at Beirut and Valencia' which the firm had suffered.[2] The essays into silk reeling were not happy: henceforth silk, mainly from China and Bengal, was bought in London.

These experiments, or at least that in Syria, may have been encouraged by extraordinary fluctuations in silk prices which occurred in 1836–7 and which seem to have put the firm, in common with some others in the industry, in sharp financial difficulties. As Fig. 11 shows, prices, already rising in 1835, rose very steeply in 1836, a rise which turned out to have

[1] E.R.O., D/F 3/2/98; D/F 3/1/8 and 9.   [2] C.F.L., vol. vii, p. 3293.

been largely a product of speculative buying. Very high figures were reached in August 1836, and then the boom burst; prices tumbled, one silk firm holding large stocks failed, another stopped payment in January 1837, and prices fell to levels lower than they had been for two years.[1] In 1836, apparently for the first and only time in the history of Samuel Courtauld & Co. as a partnership, i.e. from 1828 to 1890, a loss (of £2,599) was recorded. Because of the absence of the relevant ledgers for 1836–7, it is impossible to say exactly how it was incurred. It seems unlikely, from the course of output, to have been simply a trading loss; and indeed 1836 was in general a peak year in the trade cycle.[2] It was almost certainly an inventory loss. There had been very heavy capital expenditure in 1835–6, on the second building of the Power Loom Factory at Halstead and on improvements at Bocking; and a crash in silk values towards the end of 1836, plus some deadening of trade, could have put the firm in an awkward position. It was probably this crisis which precipitated the rearrangement of the capital structure which modified the 1828–49 partnership.

v

The finance of the firm during this period of expansion rested on five bases: cash supplied by Andrew Taylor; the maintenance of only small liquid reserves but of large net indebtedness; the ploughing back of profits; mortgages; and the deposit with the firm of savings by friends and relatives who were sometimes also employees.[3]

Andrew Taylor's contributions were of vital importance to the firm during the years up to the change in the partnership at the end of 1837. The capital outstanding to each of the partners in 1829 and 1838 was:[4]

TABLE 13

Division of partners' capital, 1829 and 1838

	S.C. III	G.C. II	P.A.T. I	A.T.	Total
January 1829 . . .	4,718	1,888	1,888	7,364	15,418
December 1838 . . .	13,858	2,283	516	19,126	35,783

[1] T. Tooke and W. Newmarch, *A History of Prices* (1838–57, ed. T. S. Gregory, London 1928), vol. ii, p. 265.

[2] Matthews, op. cit., *passim*.

[3] To this list should perhaps be added the firm's bankers, but unfortunately nothing survives either in letters or in the firm's accounts to suggest how important they were at this time.   [4] E.R.O., D/F 3/1/1 and 8.

Much of the accumulation of Sam's capital resulted from his purchase in 1833 of Savill's mill and his sale of it to the firm, and from the winding up in 1834 of the old firm of Courtauld and Taylor. The former meant that Sam's capital increased by £2,500 for the mill and £1,000 for the machinery; and the latter brought another £2,530 to his account, transferred from that of Peter Taylor's, a measure of his indebtedness to Sam on the termination of their old partnership. The accumulation of Andrew Taylor's capital, however, was largely due to his having paid in large sums of cash during the early years, as well as during the crisis of 1836. This is apparent from the following figures:[1]

TABLE 14

Net drawings by partners, 1833-7

					S.C. III	G.C. II	P.A.T. I	A.T.	Total
1833	.	.	.	.	1,580*	621	493	. .	2,694
1834	.	.	.	.	2,283	787	1,250	1,107	5,427
1835	.	.	.	.	2,684	763	1,037†	3,004	7,488
1836	.	.	.	.	2,373	846	1,066	. .	4,285
1837	.	.	.	.	3,264	1,182	943	1,350	6,739

  * Excludes £2,500 withdrawn to buy Savill's mill, then sold to Samuel Courtauld & Co., plus £1,000 for machinery, and total credited to S.C. III's capital.

  † Excludes £2,530 withdrawn to pay S.C. III and credited to latter's capital, being settlement on the winding up of Courtauld & Taylor.

In 1833 and 1836 Andrew Taylor in fact paid in slightly more than he withdrew. His contribution to the firm's finances was not only very real, but it helped to permit the senior partner to live in an increasingly prosperous fashion and to allow even the junior partners to draw more modest though not skimpy rewards. Until May 1834 George II also drew a salary of £150 per annum; and Peter Taylor had an allowance for residence in London. Andrew Taylor's decision in 1837 to take, as from the following year, a fixed 10 per cent. on his capital rather than a share of the profits, suggests a certain lack of confidence in the business after the early difficulties. It was in fact a bad guess. For ten years later he was still drawing his 10 per cent. on a capital which had grown merely from £19,126 to £24,219; but Samuel and George Courtauld and Peter Taylor were now drawing their 5 per cent. interest plus much higher profits on their combined capital, which had grown from £16,657 to £149,034.

[1] E.R.O., D/F 3/1/8.

Meanwhile, however, much of the working finance had come from the maintenance of a high level of short-term indebtedness. The situation revealed by Fig. 12 was presumably made possible by the combination of trade credit,[1] and the loans from friends, relatives, and employees. Although unfortunately the evidence does not survive for the years between 1831 and 1838, it seems very likely that the position then was much the same. The building up of capital and the withdrawals by the partners were thus being sustained partly by Andrew Taylor and partly by this high indebtedness and low cash reserves. It may well have been this dangerously illiquid position which got the firm into its troubles in 1836–7 and perhaps frightened Andrew Taylor. While the fixed assets were being built up—mainly between 1828 and 1838 and again after 1841—stocks rose substantially, accounting for the largest share of total capital. Raw silk accounted, in general, for about 45 per cent. of the value of stocks during this whole period. After February 1849 the new partnership cut back stocks and maintained a much higher level of reserves of cash and securities: patently a deliberate move (see below, p. 135).

It was the consistently high level of profits in the 1840s which permitted such a move. The ploughing back of profits had obviously been of some importance in helping the early investments to 1832, but in the very difficult five years that followed they helped hardly at all. For 1833–7 average total *net* drawings at £5,327 per annum were virtually identical to average annual gross return (profits plus interest) at £5,389, which represented an average rate of only 14·9 per cent. By contrast the comparable period ten years later, 1843–7, showed total net drawings (including Andrew Taylor's percentage) at an annual average of £13,060 from a gross return averaging £35,636 or 35·4 per cent. on capital per annum. At this rate, particularly with continuingly low liquid reserves, ploughing back could scarcely be avoided. The three active partners drew an average of £4,670 for Samuel, £3,890 for Peter Taylor, and £2,418 for George, per annum.[2]

Finally, there were two other sorts of loans which, whatever their intended use or duration, were in fact allowed to run on for long periods. First, mortgages were obtained to help finance early investment in plant

---

[1] A fair amount of evidence about credit terms in the silk industry is given in *B.P.P.* 1831–2, vol. xix, but arrangements seemed to have varied considerably in different branches of the industry. Moreover, much of the evidence was probably biased towards an overemphasis on the difficult conditions of the time. Unfortunately the particular credit arrangements which prevailed for Samuel Courtauld & Co. at this period remain unknown.

[2] E.R.O., D/F 3/1/1.

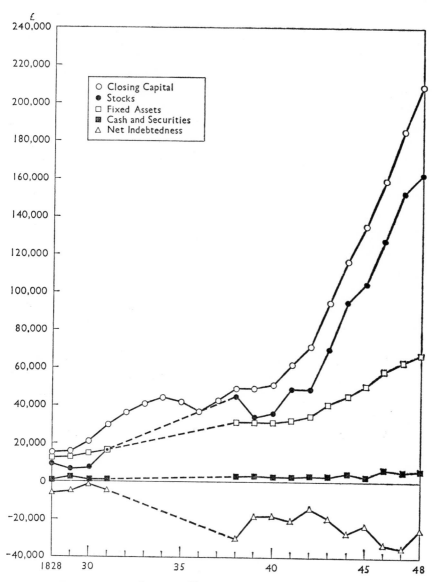

FIG. 12. *Samuel Courtauld & Co.: structure of assets, 1828–48*

Source: E.R.O.: D/F 3/1

and machinery: £2,500 on Halstead in 1829 and £3,000 on Bocking and Steam Factory. They were not paid off until the end of the first partnership. Second, throughout this period, and indeed throughout the succeeding partnerships, money was deposited with the firm by friends and relatives of the partners. Some of these lenders were also employees, but none was, as yet, a partner. Sums of varying size were deposited from time to time and for varying periods by John Minton Courtauld, by the sons of Peter Alfred Taylor I and of George Courtauld II, by William Taylor, Henry Le Keux, and J. T. P. Ash. These loans are reflected in the curve of net indebtedness in Fig. 12. On such deposits the firm paid $7\frac{1}{2}$ per cent. Loans of this sort were the natural successors to the funds which Sam had earlier obtained from George I, Sophia I, John Newberry, and William Bromley. Here, as elsewhere in business the extended family was, in some ways, the essential unit of organization.[1]

VI

The gradual mastery of technical processes, the successful adaptation to economic environment, the solution by various means of the problems of finance: thus can the growth to maturity of the firm of Courtauld, Taylors and Courtauld, alias Samuel Courtauld & Co., be presented. But this ordered analysis of its expansion omits, of course, the vital ingredient of achievement: the men who made it. The chapter which follows will consider them.

[1] E.R.O., D/F 3/1/8 and 9; *C.F.L.*, vol. vi, pp. 2921–2; vol. vii, pp. 3378–9.

CHAPTER VII

Courtaulds, Taylors, and Crape

I

THREE characteristics give to the thirty-five years from 1850 to 1885 a certain unity and coherence as a recognizable phase in the history of Samuel Courtauld & Co. First, it was a period of sustained, though not spectacular, growth in the firm's capital and output accompanied by a generally high, sometimes extremely high, level of profits. In this respect these years stand apart both from the preceding era of rapid expansion which set the business on its feet and from a succeeding phase of declining output and falling profits which, as will be shown in later chapters, brought important changes. Second, this period saw the greatest concentration by the firm upon one fabric. So striking did this specialization become that towards the end of the period Samuel Courtauld & Co. were making virtually nothing but mourning crape in sundry widths and qualities. This concentration in turn reflected the fact that fashionable, crape-using mourning reached its apogee in England during this same period. Finally, the third characteristic of these years in the company's history is that they encompass the passing from the scene, one by one, of all the original partners. By 1885, when the market for mourning crape and the profits of Samuel Courtauld & Co. were alike set for change, the business had neither partners nor managers of the founding generation.

The concern of this chapter will be to look at these three features of the period. It will do so by examining first the achievements and personalities of the men who had built up the firm; second, the nature of the remarkable demand for mourning attire; and third, the performance and organization of the business which, in this period of its high prosperity, was doing so well out of that demand.

II

Of the four partners who had signed the deed of February 1828 the first to go was Andrew Taylor. Apart from his ill health, which was the stated reason for his retirement from active participation in management, the circumstances surrounding the changes in the partnership in 1837 seem to have caused some friction between him and the other partners. The dispute may perhaps have been connected with the loss which the firm recorded in 1836 and Taylor's heavy financial involvement therein.[1] Legal advice was taken. A few years later the size of the lawyers' bills was the subject of complaint amongst the other partners. Peter Taylor grumbled to George Courtauld that it had been Andrew Taylor's objections which had increased the bill, and, moreover, 'most unnecessarily, as he was wrong in all his objections'.[2] Sam's letters suggest disenchantment with Andrew Taylor. In 1821 when Sam was trying to sell him Bocking mill, Andrew Taylor was 'a nice sort of young man'; but in 1832 'A.T. is now in his bed and has been so from a mental exertion, which tho' not great, was *too* great for him'; and by 1850 Sam was urging on his brother George the desirability of completing quickly the process of paying off their former partner so that they could 'have done with him for ever'.[3] This was indeed done. In correspondence[4] between the active partners in 1848 concerning the future partnership arrangements there was never any suggestion that Andrew Taylor would remain. Certain unspecified acts of charity were attributed to him in the course of an employee's speech on the occasion of a dinner given in 1846 for the partners by the firm's workers, but it was also observed that he had 'not been personally so well known to us as our other employers'. He made no answering speech, his state of health allegedly preventing this.[5] His contribution to Courtauld, Taylors & Courtauld had been almost wholly in money, and in the difficult days of 1836 this was of vital importance. His subsequent retreat and the worsening relations with the active partners form a prelude to the final disappearance of Andrew Taylor, a shadowy figure, from this history.

The departure of Andrew Taylor brought no greater problem to the business than that of repaying some £24,000 of capital.[6] The death on 14 March 1850, after a protracted illness,[7] of Peter Alfred Taylor I was a more serious matter, although it remains difficult precisely to define his contribution to the firm and his character as a man. In age he was the senior of the three active partners, three years older than Samuel Courtauld; in his share of capital and profits he stood equal to his cousin George

---

[1] See above, pp. 106–8.   [2] *C.F.L.*, vol. vi, pp. 2922–3 (4 March 1842).
[3] Ibid. vol. ii, p. 758; vol. v, p. 2035; vol. viii, p. 3452.
[4] Ibid., vol. vii, pp. 3277 ff.   [5] *Report on the Proceedings . . .*, p. 10. See below, p. 254.
[6] The repayment was done in instalments paid for a few years after his departure.
[7] See *C.F.L.*, vol. vii, pp. 3360, 3391, etc.

Courtauld, eleven years his junior. The record, such as it is, of his early business career makes a depressing tale and hardly suggests the future founding partner of what was to become a highly successful enterprise.

Until 1812 he was employed as a clerk in the family tin and hardware firm of Jones, Taylor & Co. It will be recalled that it was on Peter Taylor's vacating this post that Samuel Courtauld moved into it.[1] The two young men were evidently on close terms around this time. In 1814 Peter was drawing upon his twenty-four years to enlighten the then lovelorn 21-year-old Sam upon his own experiences of passion. '. . . it is some, if it did not sound very antiquated, I might say many (considering my short life) years since I first felt the inspiration of love, indeed I have never felt it with half the enthusiasm in any attachment I subsequently form'd. . . .'[2] How he earned his livelihood in the years immediately after 1812 is not clear, but just before he joined Sam Courtauld in the latter's new silk business in 1817 he seems to have been a commercial traveller, perhaps for Jones, Taylor & Co. Young George Courtauld II found the new partnership all very surprising, as he wrote to his elder sister Sophia:[3]

. . . So I hear Peter and Sam are partners! ! ! What can it be that has brought them together? I thought Peter had not much knowledge of the silk business and I did not know that either of them were overstocked with money. What can have made Peter leave off his comparatively pleasant business of travelling to come to mope about at a silk mill at Braintree?

Sam reported 'some unreserved conversation' with Peter, which, he said, had 'increased my respect for and attachment to him, and . . . more strongly cemented our connection'.[4] Rather over two years later the cement had been broken up. The disintegration of that partnership certainly owed something to personal friction between the two men. The evidence on Peter comes largely from Sam and his friends, so it is hardly conclusive. Nevertheless, it is worth noting that in 1819 John Newberry was warning Sam against the latter's plan of 'convincing Peter that he is not so attentive to his business as he ought to be'; that George I maintained that were the business to be left under the sole guidance of Peter it would 'surely go to ruin'; and that two years later, when Peter lurked on the other side of the Channel and Sam's business improved, Mrs. George Courtauld, not normally given to agreement with her husband, was asserting her convic-

[1] Courtauld MSS., G.C. I to S.C. III, 17 August 1812; see also above, p. 45.
[2] Ibid., P.A.T. I to S.C. III, 15 November 1814.
[3] C.F.L., vol. i, p. 282.
[4] Ibid., p. 296.

tion that 'as soon as that unlucky partnership was done away, success would again visit Sam, and not till then'.[1]

For six years after the *de facto* disruption of Courtauld & Taylor, Peter Taylor's life seems to have been a miserable and dispiriting sequence of inertia, action, and failure. At Ostend and then Bruges he lived with his wife Catherine on the allowance made to him, under the terms of the 1819 agreement, out of Sam Courtauld's enterprise. He contemplated business, but apparently did nothing.[2] In August 1820 Newberry observed to Sam Courtauld that Peter should have gone with George I to America instead of wasting his life in Europe as 'the drone which consumes the honey instead of the industrious bee adding to the general store'.[3] Sam lamented that 'Peter's hopes still cling so tenaciously to our shattered bark', contended that he should do some work instead of subsisting on the 'liberality of his father and the exertions of myself', and spoke of his situation as 'really very deplorable'.[4] Finally in April 1821, declining an offer from his father of a job as a warehouseman at a salary of £120,[5] and assisted by an extra £100 from Sam,[6] Peter, accompanied by his wife and child, sailed for America. Joining George Courtauld I's community or 'association' in Ohio, he rapidly quarrelled with George I, a familiar conjuncture. George I accused him of being strongly prejudiced against such associations, of possessing 'a too lofty spirit for republican arrangements', and of exhibiting the same selfishness earlier evident at Bocking and now 'rendered more keen and eager by his late necessities'.[7] George was 61, Peter 31 years of age; and George, looking for a scapegoat for the collapse, within four weeks, of his 'association', found one in Peter. Further quarrels followed. In 1822 Peter Taylor's sister Anna wrote to Sam urging the desirability of getting Peter and Catherine back to England. They were said to exist 'in such a state of suffering, poverty and wretchedness as in England would be quite impossible'.[8] The following year Peter tried his hand at a brewing venture, but 'made very poor sales of his porter'.[9] Even

  [1] Courtauld MSS.: J.N. to S.C. III, (?) June 1819; Ruth C. to G.C. I, 12 September 1821; C.F.L., vol. ii, p. 578.

  [2] Courtauld MSS.: S.C. III to G.C. I, 19 November 1820.

  [3] Ibid., J.N. to S.C. III, 9 August 1820.

  [4] Ibid., S.C. III to G.C. I, 18 September 1820.

  [5] Ibid., J.N. to S.C. III, 12 January 1821.

  [6] Ibid., J.N. to S.C. III, 2 March 1821; S.C. III to G.C. I, 24 July 1821.

  [7] Courtauld MSS.: G.C. I. to Ruth C., 24 September 1821; G.C. I to S.C. III, 9 October 1821; G.C. I to P.A.T. I, 22 January 1822.

  [8] Ibid., Anna Taylor (later Mrs. J. P. Malleson) to S.C. III, 4 May 1822.

  [9] Ibid., G.C. I to S.C. III, 12 June 1823.

PLATE 8

PETER ALFRED TAYLOR I (1790–1850)

PLATE 9

GEORGE COURTAULD II (1802–61)

in 1825 when back in England, after the death of George Courtauld I, failure and Peter Taylor seemed inseparable. He borrowed money from his brother-in-law William Bromley and tried to set up on his own account in the silk industry at Chelmsford, Hedingham, and elsewhere, but could not find suitable premises. His wife's lament, written to her sister Sophia in January 1825—'I am so sick of detailing disappointments' —sums up several years of frustration.[1]

Yet a quarter of a century later Peter Taylor left some £35,000 in the very successful firm of which he was a partner, and had acquired some reputation in a wider circle as an important figure in the Anti-Corn Law League.[2] It would be easy to suggest that Samuel Courtauld & Co. did more to make him than he did to make the firm. But in practice there is too little evidence to confirm or refute such a suggestion, to show precisely how the transformation was accomplished. Did Samuel take him back, first in 1825 and then to the main partnership of February 1828, because of a sense of responsibility for his sister Catherine, Peter's wife, or because he thought Peter had something to offer (which was certainly not capital)? In any event he was surely influenced by the very close family ties, for he and Peter were not only cousins but doubly brothers-in-law after Sam's marriage to Ellen Taylor, Peter's sister; and in February 1822 he had sufficiently forgotten the earlier quarrel with Peter (or was sufficiently in love with Ellen) to be writing to Peter to suggest his return to the silk business.[3] What is at least clear is that from the early 1830s onwards Peter lived in London and concerned himself wholly with the commercial side of the business. In the over-charged atmosphere of speech-making which pervaded the 1846 dinner, to him was ascribed 'a great portion of the success which has attended the efforts and enterprize of the firm'; and the 'greatly extended sales effected annually in your department' were 'proofs of an honourable career in commercial dealing'. In his reply—which soon became an anti-Corn Law, pro-Free Trade harangue—he admitted that it was nearly fourteen years since he took any active part in the manufacturing side of the business.[4] Perhaps salesmanship was his real vocation, perhaps separation from continuous contact with Samuel was a safeguard against quarrelling with that fearsome engine of enterprise. In the 1840s, there are signs of the forthright though slightly querulous individualism which had earlier so distressed George I in Ohio and was now fortified by business success. A small number of surviving business letters to George II reveal

[1] C.F.L., vol. iii, pp. 1250, 1255, 1256, etc.   [2] See below, pp. 224–5.
[3] C.F.L., vol. ii, p. 876.   [4] Report of the Proceedings . . ., pp. 9, 15.

vigorous views on the firm's methods of book-keeping, which he held to be antiquated; on the imposition of the income-tax, which he naturally considered monstrous; and on the terms for renewing the partnership after 1849.[1] He seems indeed to have grown into his job.

In 1847, George Courtauld II's eldest son, George III, entering the business at the age of 17, saw Peter Taylor presiding over No. 2 Carey Lane, 'a fine handsome man, always very kind to me and to young people generally'.[2] But not even the fifty miles from Bocking and the confidence of success could prevent a sense of resentment against Sam Courtauld. His had been the hand that fed; it was also the hand to be bitten. An inevitable ambivalence prevailed. The resentment emerged in letters written to George II in 1848 about proposals for the new partnership. Sam's wealth rankled: 'S.C. in addition to the large share he has received of the profits for 21 years . . .'. So did the necessity for the junior partners to plough back and thus accumulate capital proportionate to their shares of the profits: 'you and I had been toiling all our lives (or the best part of them) and had not realised a provision for our families' (Peter and George II each had five children). Drawn along in the wake of Sam's thrusting ambition, Peter saw himself and George as less prone to self-advancement: they had 'never wanted to be put forward in the world'.[3] And yet there was respect, esteem, even affection between the two cousins who had consoled each other in the years of their adolescence. For all the difficulties, 'I am satisfied', wrote Peter to George II, 'with nothing that does not satisfy S.C.'[4] It seems fair to believe that Peter's widow was right in her comment on their relationship: 'there was a peculiar bond between those two spirits . . . tho' the peculiarities of each made some antagonism unavoidable'.[5]

Eleven years after Peter Taylor's death at the age of 59, George Courtauld II died, on 17 April 1861, within a few weeks of his fifty-ninth birthday.

His character and his contribution to the firm are alike easier to discern than those of his cousin. All available evidence testifies to his rule over the mechanical equipment of Samuel Courtauld & Co.'s success. '. . . our machinery being peculiar to ourselves . . . we should feel no doubt willing to give a good deal to keep this machinery from the possession of other parties.'[6] This comment, of March 1848, was not a self-tribute but a state-

---

[1] C.F.L., vol. vi, pp. 2920–3; vol. vii, pp. 2929–31, 2991–2, 3005–6, 3248–51, 3261–4.
[2] G.C.B., pp. 34–35.   [3] C.F.L., vol. vii, pp. 3271–3.
[4] Ibid., vol. vii, p. 3266.   [5] Ibid., vol. vii, p. 3417.   [6] C.F.L., vol. vii, p. 3300.

ment, if not of fact, at least of a belief which seemed, reasonably, to be supported by the firm's success. '. . . it is in my department to make the craping machines . . . if I have a "turn" for Mechanics it is at least possible that I may desire to try this or the other novelty which to the best of my judgment will make such a machine as was never seen before.'[1] Unfortunately, as has been shown in the preceding chapter, it is very difficult to know precisely what novelties in the machinery are attributable to George II's own inventiveness. Just as his father's patent organzine spindle had provided a useful basis for the firm's early successes, so had it provided practical experience for the son's mechanical abilities. Thereafter all evidence is general rather than particular. Crape mills, power-looms, crimping and biasing machines: George II's Steam Factory turned them out and George II himself probably made important improvements in their design. The ' "turn" for Mechanics' had impressed itself on his elders at an early age. His father commented approvingly on the 'correctness and minuteness of his observations of mechanical operations'; and Sam upon his patient and painstaking methods and his 'habit of minute attention to detail'. Combined, as such characteristics were said to be, with a 'quiet domestic taste', it is not surprising to discover that he was at one time attracted to the idea of becoming a schoolmaster.[2] After his first spell with Sam at Braintree in 1819, he left 'the spindle business' without much apparent reluctance; he feared that the silk trade would go the way of the cloth trade, and acceded to his father's request that he should accompany him to America where life seemed more promising.[3] Three years later, in the course of his endeavours to get him back to the business, Sam was trying to warn him off the 'schoolmaster's trade'.[4]

These endeavours by Sam, between 1820 and 1824, to induce young George to return contrast clearly with Sam's attitude towards Peter Taylor. From 1820 to 1822 Sam's letters across the Atlantic kept his brother informed on technical progress at the Bocking mill and also lamented the loss of his services. Once business was better, and Sam had abandoned the idea of himself selling up and going to America, he began to concentrate in his letters upon the idea of ensuring that his brother returned and his father did not. The manner became more cajoling, and if one should not read too much into the change from 'My dear George' to 'My very dear

[1] Ibid., vol. vii, p. 3360.
[2] Courtauld MSS.: S.C. III to G.C. II, 20 September 1820; Ruth C. to G.C. I, 22 May 1822; G.C. I to S.C. III, 12 June 1823; C.F.L., vol. viii, p. 3448; G.C.B., p. 40.
[3] C.F.L., vol. ii, pp. 602–3; vol. iii, p. 1001.   [4] Ibid., vol. iii, p. 955.

brother', at least there is no reason to doubt that Sam meant what he said in June 1824: '*I much want your assistance* in the preparation of this machinery which will be required of *seven* times the extent of my present mills! And neither Peter nor John can give me the assistance I want.'[1] George returned with neither haste nor enthusiasm. When he did finally take ship he came probably as much from the worry of his sister Sophia's poor health as from the high inducements and heavy expressions of disappointment dispatched westwards from Bocking.[2] For several months after his return in August or September 1824 he found his work monotonous and irksome, pined for a return to the Ohio woods, thought of giving up the job, and consoled himself by learning to play the 'cello.[3]

But as crape mills and patent organzine spindles were joined in time by power-looms and the whole crimping complex, George, like Peter, grew into his job and found an outlet for his capacities. He found it mainly in running Steam Factory but also in looking after the accounts at Bocking. For the whole of the first partnership he kept the books there in precise and methodical detail in his own hand, for which he was upbraided in the 1840s by Peter Taylor.[4] The long hours of unremitting attention to detail were followed by the years as a junior partner demanding much ploughing back to accumulate the capital appropriate to his share of the profits. The result was the amassing of something approaching £120,000 by the time of his death, and the drawing of an income from the firm which averaged nearly £9,500 per annum for the years 1851–60.[5] Yet, throughout, George retained an agreeable humour which must have softened those pedantic-seeming and much-praised qualities of painstaking attention to detail, order, method, and the like. His letters remain pleasingly free from the heavy sententiousness which the age knew so well, and of which Sam's sometimes had their ample share. If they never thundered, as did Sam's in another mood, they never piped like Peter's. At their best they have a light irony and a sensitivity to life and its hardships which suggest that George Courtauld II was the most humanly sympathetic of the three active partners of 1828.

. . . Mr. Jefferis six months ago one of the dashing silk people, now an unfortunate, but very pleasing and gentlemanly man, was here the other day. His

[1] *C.F.L.*, vol. iii, p. 1180.
[2] Ibid., vol. iii, pp. 1114, 1158, 1179–81, 1182–3, 1187–8.
[3] Ibid., vol. iii, pp. 1207, 1215–16, 1235, 1287–8.
[4] Ibid., vol. vii, pp. 3248–51, 3271–3.
[5] E.R.O., D/F 3/1/3–5; Somerset House: Will of George Courtauld.

opinion is that the silk trade is under a cloud—that it will again shine and gladden our hearts with the beams of prosperity. Indeed he says that this is a peculiarly auspicious time to set an establishment connected in any way with this trade going, as in consequence of this universal depression, labour and everything is low. If he can persuade others to think so too, and to act upon this opinion, we shall do. Want of persons of this mode of thinking, having the power and will to put their ideas into practice, is the only thing that prevents my becoming rich . . .[1]

Samuel would never have been able to write about such a matter in such a way. But that, perhaps, was part of the price of the fortune he made and the jobs he created. In 1832 George was finding the business of making money agreeable but guilt-laden.

. . . I can't help making haste to be rich—or rather feeling more anxiety to become so than some people might think right. Very likely I *may* have motives for this I do not suspect. One, however, I know is a growing feeling of discomfort at doing nothing for Mother—or anyone else in the world—but alack! . . .[2]

A concern for the welfare of the firm's workers[3] formed an increasing share of his interests. To the inevitable eulogies upon his 'mechanical skill and inventive genius' were joined at the 1846 dinner praise for his consideration of the employees' welfare.[4]

George, like Peter, felt his subordination to his elder brother. There was, however, a difference. After the 1819 disruption of Courtauld & Taylor, Samuel in 1825 and 1828 did something to help a man who was his cousin, doubly his brother-in-law, and formerly his active partner. In practice, this worked out well enough. But George he actively wanted, and this George did not forget. In the course of a furious battle of words about the partnership he was able to write in these terms to Samuel in 1848:

. . . I will take this opportunity to say . . . that I look back upon your conduct towards me since my return from Ohio which resulted in my becoming a partner in this business with unalloyed and grateful pleasure. I shall ever cherish the recollection of the care and solicitude for my welfare (which could not have been exceeded had you stood in the relation of a father instead of a brother) which induced you to make to me, then with small experience and small capital, the generously liberal offer of a sixth share in the business which was then entirely yours, and which, promising *then*, has more than fulfilled its promise now.[5]

---

[1] *C.F.L.*, vol. iv, p. 1471.   [2] Ibid., vol. v, p. 1958.
[3] See below, pp. 248–50.   [4] *Report of the Proceedings* . . ., p. 10.
[5] *C.F.L.*, vol. vii, pp. 3316–17.

A further and verbally more unpleasant conflict ensued over George's purchase of a farm. In the course of this he justifiably complained to Sam of the latter's 'intolerably overbearing style'. But again the matter was finally resolved with mutual expressions of cordiality and to the obvious relief of both sides.[1] A long-enduring quarrel with George II was unthinkable. We will leave him in 1857—a few years before he died of cancer of the stomach[2]—with a letter containing the only traceable light-hearted remark about the awful mysteries of the crimping room. It was addressed to his son George III.

> . . . I am well pleased the crimping room ceremony is over; I believe Mama swallowed it all. Didn't you and William gaze with awe and admiration on the wonders you saw in that long interdicted sanctum? I suppose he and you spend every spare minute now during the day—(regularly devoting the time before breakfast of every day, except Sunday, to the same purpose)—to the study of the intricate and deeply interesting and highly instructive operations there carried on?[3]

In a mere twelve years, 1849–61, three of the partners of 1848 had gone. Another twenty years went by before Samuel Courtauld III died, a few months short of 88 years of age, on 21 March 1881.

To a very substantial extent Sam Courtauld was the firm which bore his name. He made it, shaped it, ran it, dominated it. Even in the later years of his life, when no longer an active partner, he did not hesitate to make his opinions felt on a variety of questions.[4] In the earlier years he did much of the silk buying, took the major decisions of general policy, and exercised himself particularly in matters of manufacturing (i.e. throwing and weaving, as distinct from finishing and selling). Though he consulted his partners and was willing at times to defer to their views, nobody ever had any doubt who was the boss. His personal character and his contribution to the firm were thus in many ways synonymous. He looms large on the horizon of the firm's history in the guise of that classical figure of economic history, the capitalist entrepreneur. Many generalizations have been made about such men. They have been eulogized as virtuous heroes of self-help in the nineteenth-century romantic manner of Samuel Smiles;[5] or perceived as special products of a socio-economic environment in the twentieth-century analytical manner of Joseph Schumpeter.[6] So a close

---

[1] *C.F.L.*, vol. viii, pp. 3444–505, *passim.*   [2] Ibid., vol. viii, p. 3870.

[3] *G.C.B.*, p. 68.   [4] See below, p. 148.

[5] e.g. *Lives of the Engineers* (3 vols., 1861), *Men of Invention and Industry* (1884), etc.

[6] e.g. *The Theory of Economic Development* (Engl. trans. 1934), and *Business Cycles* (2 vols., 1939).

examination of Sam Courtauld's character and personality seems desirable for more reasons than one. In trying to assess him, it is important to remember what he did not contribute. First, he did not contribute capital; but he did contribute the ability to borrow it. In 1816, he started with nothing save the credit supplied by John Newberry and the circumstances supplied by his father's conflict with Joseph Wilson. His contribution then was the successful exploitation of that credit and those circumstances. George II's reference to him in October 1826 as 'the capitalist in our business'[1] testified merely to Sam's accumulations over the previous seven years. Even in 1828, his own capital was inadequate; what mattered was his ability to bring in Andrew Taylor's capital. Second, he did not contribute technical innovation; but he did contribute an awareness of the need for such innovation and the ability to procure it. Aside from minor improvements and ingenuities for which he may have been himself responsible, it seems reasonable to assume that such technical innovation as there was had come from George I and George II. And, third, he contributed nothing that was peculiar to the silk industry or indeed to industry in general. The qualities which he brought were to be found in other regions of life. He might readily have become a lawyer or a merchant; he hankered at one time after medicine and agriculture.[2] Only a succession of chances kept him in the industry to which his father had early trained him; only random circumstances prevented his departure to America and the abandonment of silk. He was, in short, no special breed of entrepreneur produced by an environmental complex, nor did he bring qualities which were unique to industrial life.

His positive contributions were certain qualities of mind and body which together created the psychological entity known as Samuel Courtauld. It is obvious that he was a man of prodigious energy. Apart from the illness of 1815–16, and some occasional minor indispositions, he enjoyed good health, and used it to expend immense physical and mental energy during a long life. He worked very long hours himself, he liked others to know that he worked such hours,[3] and he was contemptuous of those unable or unwilling to work likewise. In his later years, by the customary

---

[1] *C.F.L.*, vol. iv, p. 1517.

[2] See above, p. 49. For some discussion of the possible relationships between his achievement and his Unitarianism, see below, pp. 213–15.

[3] Amongst sundry examples is a letter of 1857 to his brother John Minton Courtauld which begins: '*I wish my partners to know* that altho' I am now hardly ever at Steam Factory, and have not been able these two weeks to get to London, I am nevertheless to the best of my ability and strength—*working* . . .' (*C.F.L.*, vol. viii, p. 3823).

trick of the self-made, he found a peculiar virtue in his own practices and preached a philosophy of work and energy. He told George II in 1857, in connexion with the education of the latter's youngest son, Sydney, that the sound foundation for Sydney's future course in life was 'a practised habit and power of applying himself with energy and perseverance to the accomplishment of a specific purpose by appropriate definite means'.[1] In March 1880, within about a year of his death, he accompanied a twenty-first birthday gift of £1,000 to a great-nephew, George Courtauld IV, with a 2,500-word homily on the power of energy and the merits of work. Convinced that energy had been the most marked characteristic of his own life, he advocated that if his young relative were to pose the question 'What shall I do with my life?', he should answer it with the response '. . . anything that will most and best stimulate and sustain all my powers of work'.[2]

Such elderly expressions of this stunted and unlovely philosophy must not be allowed to obscure the reality of Sam Courtauld's own experience of life. Energy was not enough: it never has been. His was supplemented by an above average intelligence, a practical and shrewd perceptiveness of immediate circumstances, and a flair for organization and careful super-vision. His sisters' consideration of him as 'rather lynx-eyed'[3] was merely a personal mirror of, for example, the fact that he alone was successful, even as a youth, in exercising effective supervision in the mill which his father managed. But neither his energy nor his intelligence operated in a continuous flow, unaffected by upbringing and environment, untouched by the eddies and whirlpools which lie below the surface of what can look in retrospect like a stream of conscious decisions, of deliberate acts of will. In reality his life, and consequently the creation and shaping of the business, was just as likely to have been 'determined' by his psychological characteristics as by the economic and social environment in which they worked.[4] And when we look at those characteristics it is neither difficult to detect nor surprising to discover a mild flavour of the paranoid and faint symptoms of the manic–depressive; nor is it hard to find evidence of reaction to the suffocating emotionalism of his well-meaning father.

Driven on by an ambition whose nature he never understood and whose uncomprehended goals he never reached, Sam Courtauld oscillated

[1] C.F.L., vol. viii, pp. 3834.
[2] Ibid., vol. viii, pp. 3888–95.   [3] Ibid., vol. iii, p. 1397.
[4] In some, though certainly not in all, respects Sam Courtauld's character fits in with the psychological features of the 'innovational personality' outlined in Everett E. Hagen's *On the Theory of Social Change* (Cambridge, Mass., 1962; London, 1964). This fact does not, however, necessarily provide support for Prof. Hagen's theory of economic growth.

throughout his life between deep dejection and intense euphoria. Exhorted from an early age to embrace humility, piety, meekness, and love, he yearned for proud achievement and battled with circumstances to attain it. When in the conflict there were setbacks he drooped into melancholy and self-abnegation, only in turn to swing up again to a fresh drive of energetic action. He told a tale in his eighty-seventh year that as a small boy, when asked what he wanted to be, he answered: 'anything, in a large way'.[1] It may or may not have been true, but his very telling of it seems to testify to a blind ambition, to a high need for achievement. When he was young he was berated by his father for his 'high unyielding conduct' and a taste for 'sharp, pointed censure', yet warned against his excessive sensitivity to 'supposed insult or disrespect'.[2] His father looked askance at the 'very high notions of appearance and respectability'[3] which he claimed his son had adopted; and he was himself hurt and bewildered by the fact that the earnest, emotional 'companionizing' search for filial love which he sought in his son brought little but mounting irritation.

To document all the swings of Sam's emotional surges would be tedious beyond measure. A few examples must suffice. Already in 1814 his cousin Peter Taylor had warned him against 'degrading yourself unnecessarily in your own estimation'.[4] In 1820, in the course of a letter to George II, he praised his brother's patience 'under the direction of so irritable, inconsiderate, and unhappy-minded a tutor as myself', and went on to provide, at the age of 27, this piece of sententious depressive talk:

> May you escape the moral evils that have operated so potently to baffle all the promise of my early youth; or if some experience of the character of similar evils be destined to work out the ultimate advancement of your character, may its elements not require so severe and protracted a state of discipline, as has fallen to my lot.[5]

His sister Sophia, a frequent confidant of his inner feelings, received from him in 1832 a comprehensive damnation of business, politics, friends, hopes, and fears, and a complaint: 'I am not well used.'[6] But by far the bitterest cries came in letters to his wife. His marriage to Ellen Taylor lasted happily for nearly fifty years, until her death in 1872, but their only

[1] C.F.L., vol. viii, p. 3888.
[2] Courtauld MSS.: G.C. I to S.C. III, 14 January 1812, 17 August 1812.
[3] C.F.L., vol. i, p. 368.
[4] Courtauld MSS.: P.A.T. I to S.C. III, 15 November 1814.
[5] Ibid., S.C. III to G.C. II, 20 September 1820.
[6] C.F.L., vol. v, pp. 2034–5.

child, born in 1840, died after barely a year. He had grown older and become richer and yet, hurt perhaps by some of the reactions to his political activities,[1] he remained periodically desolate in his too ill-defined ambitions. Thus he could send such a groan of despair as this, in 1852, when he was almost sixty years of age.

> . . . Tomorrow and Tuesday all the world—save the mere muck worms—will be alive with all the active interests of society, and I shall be at home, with no part nor place, just going through the daily routine of business. . . . A stranded life—I am not good enough for my position in one sense—as you are, being heart-satisfied in doing good and for the good-sake alone, and yearning for nothing in the shape of action or honour on the world's stage. And my position is not good enough for me in one sense, in that it shuts me out and blots me out from all that action, and interest, that is congenial to my race, and at least as much so to me as to men commonly. . . . It does not agree with me at all to be so utterly nothing and nobody, so alien and isolated so outcast and objectless, in the midst of the world's civilization . . . I wish I had nothing of what men call an honourable ambition, or else that I had something to feed it withal. . . .[2]

The converse phases of his inner life exhibited themselves in utterances of striking confidence, in simple boasting, or in a highly autocratic and domineering manner. They could be plain, such as this beginning to a letter of 1820: 'I have been very successful in everything I have done';[3] or they could be coloured, such as this a few years later: 'conscious of the prudence and activity with which my concerns are conducted and of my general success in business, I am satisfied your confidence will not be lessened . . .'.[4] As he moved into a position of ascendancy after his father's final departure to America, he was now able to dismiss a singularly unhappy suggestion by George I—to the effect that he should return to England to serve as some sort of assistant or foreman to his son—in a fashion revealing of his attitude to business subordinates:

> . . . I am quite satisfied, my dear father, that your particular view of business in this country is impossible. However earnestly I should wish to be near you, I should tremble both for your sake and my own, at the idea of our being so connected in business as you suggest. Are we not still flesh and blood? . . . My foreman is my servant; he executes my will without scruple or gain-saying; he is found regularly at his post, however his employer may find occasion to vary

---

[1] See below, pp. 218, 222–3.
[2] Courtauld MSS.: S.C. III to Ellen C., 4 July 1852.
[3] C.F.L., vol. ii, p. 708.
[4] Courtauld MSS.: S.C. III to G.C. I, 14 March 1823.

his own engagements, or whatever personal indulgence he may see fit to take. It is the very object of his office to bear the fag and routine drudgery of application, as the business is rendered to myself an interesting, agreeable and successful pursuit.[1]

The high-handed manner which he adopted in the negotiations about the renewal of the partnership in 1849–50 had the ironic effect of leading his brother George II also to appeal to their kinship. Finally exhausted with Sam's attitude, George protested against his carrying on the discussions 'in the character of a Lord with his vassal, endeavouring to convince—it is true—but if the poor devil will not be convinced then, prepared to ride him down and crush him to the dust'.[2] One of the most striking pieces of condescension was the letter with which Sam accompanied a tip to his brother-in-law Joseph Ash—husband of Sam's sister, Eliza, and never a partner in the business.

Carey Lane
23 June 1849

'Thou shalt not muzzle the Ox that treadeth out the Corn'
'Live and let live'

My dear Ash,
    On the 18th of February last our term of 21 years partnership had run out its prosperous course; and through all that long term you had been a fellow worker with us in it, sharing our labours—and if in respect of affairs of business you have not been much called upon to weep with us when we wept, you have at least rejoiced with us when we have rejoiced. . . . In token of this fellowship, and to the end that you may be laying up something against the days when nature craves 'rest after toil', we the 3 partners of the Old Firm beg your acceptance of £1000. . . .

Yours my dear Ash
most sincerely
Sam Courtauld.[3]

A powerful engine of his arrogance was his dominating position not just in the firm but in the family. In this he exhibited almost a sense of a 'calling'. He knew at an early age that, as the eldest son of an idealistic and forever wandering father, he would probably sooner than later have to support the family. He told his sister Sophia in 1817 that he had no ambition to become rich: 'I have already quite outlived all pleasure in the

---

[1] Ibid., S.C. III to G.C. I, 12 June 1822.   [2] *C.F.L.*, vol. viii, p. 3472.
[3] Ibid., vol. vii, pp. 3378–9.

pursuit of gain.' In the light of his subsequent career this may seem simply a pleasing irony, yet he went on to add: 'that will be my day of triumph when I can feel my duty to others no longer urging me to continue it'.[1] This was not humbug. Money-making, of course, soon acquires a momentum all of its own which, for the successful, is hard to resist. Several years earlier, his mother had made a prophetic remark when he was only about 16: '. . . consider, dear boy, that the comfort of your old Mother and young brothers and sisters may yet depend on your care and industry.'[2] In less than a score years their dependence was complete. Already supporting his mother when his father left for America, he had soon provided, on the family's return after the latter's death, not only an annuity for sister Sophia but jobs for George and John and for the husbands of Catherine and Eliza. In 1850 Catherine summarized the position clearly in a consoling letter to her brother George at the height of the quarrel in which he was then engaged with Sam. The reference to her late husband's feelings is obvious:

. . . I do believe he is unconscious of wrong to you and this belief would make it easy to me to yield. I have often urged the same to one who felt sometimes most keenly the control over him. There's the mischief, the element ever operating unfavourably, the power, the almost uncontrolled power which circumstances have placed in Sam's hand . . .[3]

So, like his father but in a different way and for quite different reasons, Sam fell out with many people in the course of his life. George III recalled that his father, on his death-bed, had said to him: 'George, you must try to get on with your uncle; I know it is not easy.'[4] Quarrels with his partners were scarcely to be avoided, and they were not uncommon. He did not have much regard for his partners' business abilities, and as he grew older and younger generations took over he had still less. So, despite his semi-retirement, in the later sixties and seventies, his manner of making his presence felt was far from agreeable to younger men enjoying the fat profits which the business was then yielding. The respect and awe with which he had once been regarded had been replaced by a resentment which hurt him in turn.[5] A long estrangement starting in the 1860s separated him from Peter Alfred Taylor II, and this did not end until 1880; relations were not always happy with his youngest nephew Sydney Courtauld; but the main object of his scorn was his eldest nephew George III, who became

[1] C.F.L., vol. i, p. 294.
[2] Courtauld MSS.: Ruth C. to S.C. III, 28 July (?) 1809.
[3] C.F.L., vol. viii, p. 3494.   [4] G.C.B., p. 557.   [5] Ibid., p. 34.

PLATE 10

SAMUEL COURTAULD III (1793–1881), in later middle age

PLATE 11

GOSFIELD HALL (West and South fronts)

the senior partner of the business on his uncle's death.[1] The nature of, and justification for, Sam's views will be considered later, but meanwhile it is worth noting that, as a final gesture of disapproval, although he gave legacies of some £30–35,000 apiece to George III and Sydney as well as many smaller bequests to sundry relations he left the bulk of his very substantial estate to two adopted children.[2]

Sam Courtauld's fortune, approaching £700,000, was not enough to put him amongst the handful of millionaire businessmen of his day; certainly his wealth was nowhere near that of the great Victorian landowners. Even so, during the years 1871–80 he drew, simply from the firm, an average annual income of £46,000,[3] and his total income at that time may well have been nearly £70,000 a year. Such incomes, barely touched by direct taxation, should be compared, to gauge their relative size, with the £62. 10s. per annum which he paid his foreman dyer or the £15 or so a year which, in the 1870s, constituted the average annual earnings of power-loom operatives at Halstead.[4] He had bought in 1854 the estate of Gosfield Hall. For this massive mansion, originally Tudor but greatly enlarged in the eighteenth century,[5] he paid £33,400. With it came about 2,000 acres of land, to which he added, by further purchases at about the same time, neighbouring land costing another £29,850.[6] He finally became a local landowner to the extent of some 3,200 acres. He bought Gosfield Hall partly because, in addition to railway shares, Government stock,

---

[1] Courtauld MSS.: S.C. III to Ellen C., 22 March 1864; G.C.B., pp. 286, 299, 303, 304, 308, etc.

[2] Somerset House: Will of Samuel Courtauld.

[3] E.R.O., D/F 3/1/5 and 15.   [4] E.R.O., D/F 3/3/22, pp. 17–18, 28–29, 82–83.

[5] Gosfield Hall, built by Sir John Wentworth in the sixteenth century, passed through various hands, including those of the fashionable late seventeenth-century doctor, Sir Thomas Millington, before being bought by John Knight in the early eighteenth century. He and his successor, Robert, Earl of Nugent, who married John Knight's widow, substantially enlarged and rebuilt the original Tudor house. Between 1788 and 1825 it was owned by the Grevilles, Marquises of Buckingham, the second of whom put it at the disposal of Louis XVIII of France when he came to this country in 1807–9. In 1825 it was bought by a prosperous shipbuilder, Edward Barnard, M.P. for Deptford. On his death in 1851 the Hall and estate were offered for sale, but it was not until 1854, when the property was auctioned in lots, that Courtauld the crape maker followed Barnard the shipbuilder in the ownership of the big house. See Essex Review, vol. xlix, pp. 190–1; Transactions of the Essex Archaeological Society, New Series, vol. xii, pp. 209–11; Country Life, 2 April 1954; and the 'Gosfield Vicars' Book' at the Gosfield Vicarage. This is a collection of all sorts of useful information, including original photographs, surveys, cuttings, and letters about the Hall and the village. It includes a letter, dated 28 November 1887, about the sale of the house in 1854 from Bedel & Co. of London, who handled the business for Sam Courtauld.

[6] Courtauld MSS.: S.C. III to Ellen C., August 1854.

a London house, and the like, he had to invest his accruing wealth somewhere. In 1853 he had contemplated investment in Irish land. He told his wife: '. . . you, I know, hate rents and detest Irish land—but what would you have—I must be investing money . . .'.[1] The legislation of 1856 which granted limited liability to joint-stock companies had yet to be passed; the day of easy industrial investment on the Stock Exchange had yet to arrive. He bought it also partly because he had known Gosfield Park since his youth. 'I was walking last evening in the "Wilderness" at Gosfield Park . . . among decaying oaks and cedars and yews and laurels . . . and . . . the "stillness of repose that's there".'[2] Some forty years after he wrote this to his sister, now, owning it, he was praising its beauty on his return to Gosfield after a time away.[3] And, finally, he bought it because the great house set in its parkland appealed to those same mildly paranoid yearnings which otherwise revealed themselves in his utterances and actions. He lived in it, remote, autocratic, dominant to the last; after his wife's death, his loneliness was relieved by his adopted daughters.[4] He entertained little save within the family circle. Despite his possessions, and despite an enthusiasm for hunting which began around 1830,[5] he never became a truly accepted member of 'county society'. He exhibited, in a land of Tory squires, all the alarming colourings of the self-made magnate and of a rural Radical Dissenter.[6]

III

Before going on to survey the changing composition and the achievements of the firm during this period, it is time to examine the remarkable mid-Victorian demand for mourning crape.

Victorian—and indeed Edwardian—England was an extremely class-conscious place. A lush, pervasive, and variegated growth of snobbery blossomed along with the new growth of wealth. In manners and etiquette, accent and dress, elaborate codes, explicit or implicit, were developed to insist that all were not as equal, even in death, as the uninitiated might suppose. The pattern of private mourning, socially fashioned and

---

[1] Courtauld MSS.: S.C. III to Ellen C., 2 January 1853.

[2] *C.F.L.*, vol. i, p. 384 (May 1818).

[3] Courtauld MSS.: S.C. III to Ellen C., 7 October 1858. Periodically he also cursed the burdens of maintaining the house and estate.

[4] Sarah Ann Cawston and Louisa Ruth Harris. The latter had married Lieut.-Colonel Arthur Lowe.

[5] *G.C.B.*, p. 61.   [6] See below, pp. 217–43.

Court-influenced, which had existed in Hanoverian England,[1] now achieved more precise definition and, through the medium of new journals of fashion, greater publicity. The process of formalization was probably proceeding during the first half of the nineteenth century; certainly in the second half of the century those aspiring to gentility had no excuse for ignorance of the rules, for they were amply set out in such new periodicals as *The Queen* (1861), *The Lady* (1885), or *Gentlewoman* (1890), not to speak of the coyly named *Sylvia's Home Journal*. Publications such as *The Workwoman's Guide* by 'A Lady' (1840) told their intended readers how to look after crape as well as giving hints on buying it. For London residents and visitors wishing to buy crape and similar accoutrements of mourning, there was Jay's Mourning Warehouse. In 1841 W. Checkall Jay had started in Regent Street his draper's shop which soon became The London General Mourning Warehouse. Here they could buy what contemporaries were pleased to call 'atramental and other lugubrious attire consistent with every gradation of mourning'.[2] Jay's caught the eye.

The sober hue of its decorations . . . must at once attract the attention of the most casual observer. . . . Here may be had every variety of mourning attire, from that which heartfelt affection dictates for the loss of a fond parent or dearly beloved relative to the slight token which friendship or fashion demand, in the newest and most approved material and style. . . .[3]

Mourning boomed. A few years later, and also in Regent Street, Pugh's Mourning Warehouse and Peter Robinson's Court and General Mourning Warehouse opened their doors; and in 1854, again in Regent Street, The Argyll General Mourning and Mantle Warehouse was offering ladies 'every requisite for a complete outfit of mourning . . . at a moment's notice'. The West General Mourning Warehouse was in Holborn, Cater's Mourning Warehouse in the City. . . .[4] There was money in mourning.

The full weight of Victorian mourning fell upon women. Men had long since shed their peacock finery of Tudor or early Stuart times; they were already well on the way towards those sombre suits which, with minor variations in shape and colour, did for weddings and funerals, club and office, day and evening, leaving country pastimes alone to be pur-

---

[1] Above, pp. 27–29.

[2] Quoted C. W. Cunnington, *English Women's Clothing in the 19th Century* (London, 1937), p. 149.

[3] Quoted R. S. Lambert, *The Great Provider* (London, 1938), p. 48. See also Davey, op. cit., p. 95.

[4] Alison Aldburgham, *Shops and Shopping, 1800–1911* (London, 1964), pp. 62–68.

sued in colour. So mourning here was a matter largely of gloves, hatbands, and cravats. But for woman, inferior, frail, Victorian womanhood, the burden of conspicuous woe was heavy, almost humiliatingly so. Although there were minor disagreements amongst the authorities, the general rules were as follows.[1] A widow who wished also to be regarded as a lady had, in the 1870s, to wear black for a year and a day in the shape of a dress of paramatta[2] entirely covered with crape to within an inch or two of the waist; wear a mantle also of paramatta and crape, a bonnet entirely of crape with a widow's cap inside, and a crape veil. After a year and a day the widow 'slighted her mourning' and propriety demanded a black silk dress heavily trimmed with crape for six months, followed by another three months in black with less crape and a final three months in black without the crape trimmings. Even after these two years of full mourning it was said to be 'in much better taste to wear half-mourning for at least six months more'. A daughter's mourning for a parent or a parent's for an offspring lasted twelve or fifteen months, for the first six of which crape was to be worn; brothers, sisters, or grandparents rated six months (three with crape), uncles and aunts three months, and first cousins six weeks. A wife was supposed to wear mourning for her husband's relatives as she would for her own. Household servants went into mourning along with their employers.

These rules of etiquette thus not merely emphasized the role of crape as a symbol of heavy mourning but also formalized what had been evident from the much earlier prescriptions for the use of imported Italian crape at Court funerals.[3] It is not perhaps surprising to hear that to keep a piece of crape in the house was thought to be unlucky.[4] So the sort of persistent stimulus to replacement demand which the advertising man today tries hard to achieve was ensured via ritual and superstition. For much of the nineteenth century such a market was a crape makers' paradise, and it might be tempting to imagine that it was they who invented the formalization of the rules for mourning. Tempting but quite inadmissible. For not only is there no evidence to that effect, but the simple fact is that until this atramental boom burst they did not need to invent them. Heavy mourning was curiously in tune with the earnest moralizing of the Victorians, a moralizing which readily turned into an obesssive sentimentality about

[1] This account of the prescribed attire is derived largely from Cunnington, op. cit., esp. pp. 2, 17, 44, 149, 154, 175, 254–5, 270, 406; see also Aldburgham, op. cit., pp. 63, 180.

[2] A type of bombazine, the weft of worsted, the warp originally of silk but later of cotton.

[3] Above, p. 28.

[4] Cunnington, op. cit., p. 17.

PLATE 12

VICTORIAN MOURNING DRESS

Note the plentiful crape consumption represented by the many yards of crape trimming

PLATE 13

GRANDE MAISON DE NOIR, PARIS

From a French mourning brochure, *circa* 1900

Death. Such comforting grief mingled easily with the profuse snobbery of a society growing rich quickly in the shade of Queen Victoria's Court. This was enough. 'With regard to Isabel's mourning', wrote Mrs. Henry Wood in that celebrated tear-jerker, *East Lynne*, 'he [the Earl of Mount Severn] had desired her to have everything suited to her station and degree.' Fiction mirrored life, and from the crape hatband which Charles Dickens put around Jonas Chuzzlewit's hat up to the thousands and thousands of yards of crape bought by the Lord Chamberlain's department for the funerals of King George III in 1820 and George IV in 1830, the Princess Augusta in 1840, the Duke of Sussex in 1843, Queen Adelaide in 1850, and, of course, the Prince Consort in 1861[1]—demand was steady. The years of crape-laden retirement into which Queen Victoria went after 1861 did not create that demand. Indeed, it must be remembered that her protracted retirement into mourning amongst the mists of Balmoral did not add to her popularity. Nevertheless, her remarkable enthusiasm for crape can hardly have failed to affect its sales, and this despite the first murmurings against its use which can be heard in the later 1870s. Victoria's liking for the full trimmings of mourning preceded the death of her husband. 'I think it quite wrong', she wrote in 1859 to her eldest daughter, the Princess Royal, married to Prince Frederick of Prussia whose mother had just died, 'that the nursery are not in mourning'.[2] The Princess's German relations did not share this English enthusiasm. When her uncle, Prince Ernst von Hohenlohe-Langenburg, died in April 1860, she wrote to Queen Victoria:[3]

... I should like to know about your mourning, although I cannot wear the same as you. ... We were only allowed to wear six weeks for our grandmother Weimar, for the King we should only wear two months, for cousins one week. Therefore in this case the utmost I could wear would be four weeks which according to the curious customs here about mourning is considered a very long time.

I should only wear silk—as crêpe is the very deepest one could wear here. It distresses me much not to be able to wear the same as you. ... And the Prince and the whole family hate mourning as you know.

To this Queen Victoria replied firmly: 'that dislike of it I think positively wrong.' She added that 'darling Beatrice looks lovely in her black silk and crêpe dress'.[4] The Princess Beatrice was then three years old.

---

[1] Details of crape, etc., ordered by the Lord Chamberlain's Department in P.R.O., L.C. 2/45, 46, 74, 78.   [2] Roger Fulford, *Dearest Child* (London, 1964), p. 199.
[3] Ibid., p. 248.   [4] Fulford, op. cit., p. 249.

If the death of Albert, Prince Consort, may have given some temporary additional stimulus to the use of crape for heavy mourning, there were other stimuli likely to have been promoting sales at this time. The continuing growth of the English economy not only brought further amassing of wealth but also put this country into a position of the most striking economic supremacy, relative to other countries, that it has ever known. So more people at home, especially those of the middle and upper classes, were able and willing to afford fashionable expenditure, and furthermore, things English tended to become fashionable overseas. Although at home not every lady of the land obeyed the full letter of the law as laid down by *The Queen*, increasing numbers were likely to contribute to the crape-makers' profits.

Outside England, not every country, as the Princess Royal's remarks indicate, was anxious to imitate this particular English habit. But the absence of Prussian enthusiasm for mourning was only one of a number of far more important ways in which Germany showed little tendency to follow English ways. France showed a greater disposition for conspicuous grief; Paris had its *magasin de deuil*. To maintain the fashion of mourning it imported *crêpe anglaise*. And, for a time at least, it also emulated English economic policy. German economists and German Governments remained unimpressed by that especial English export, the idea of Free Trade; but their French counterparts, and especially the Government of Napoleon III, were more interested. One of the main results of this was the signing in January 1860 of the Anglo-French Treaty of Commerce (known also after its architects and signatories as the Cobden–Chevalier Treaty). This, the final peak of achievement in the adoption of Free Trade in England, was designed to bring to an end what had been in effect some two centuries of tariff warfare between the two countries. For the English silk industry it meant the sweeping away of all the remaining import duties on raw and thrown silk as well as the protective duty on imported silk manufactures. It also meant, for those who could take advantage of it, the opening of the French market by reason of the reduction or abolition of French import duties. The makers of mourning crape constituted one of the very few branches of the English silk industry which could thus take advantage of this freer access to French demand. There is one striking testimony both to English superiority in this limited and specialized field and to French demand for mourning crape. For the most part the French silk industry, conscious of its superiority, welcomed Free Trade, but the French crape manufacturers petitioned, vainly, their own Government for the maintenance of the old 30 per cent. protective tariff. Although their own speciality, in which they had little to fear from the English, was the soft, coloured *crêpe de Chine*, they had spent much money in attempting to discover the process by which the English produced their funereal *crêpe anglaise*.[1] They wanted this information partly to be able to compete at home and partly to compete in another country which seems to have been fond of mourning crape: the United States of America. The latter, with its total rejection of Courts and monarchically inspired fashion, seems an improbable purchaser of that commodity; but, as will be shown later,[2] there was some keenness for it, at least in some areas, and that despite stiff American import duties.[3]

So, in one way or another, fashion, wealth, and economic policy generally combined to favour the consumption of mourning crape at home and abroad. How did this make its mark on the experience of Samuel Courtauld & Co.?

IV

Fig. 13 exhibits in graphical form the experience and performance of the firm during this prosperous thirty-five-year period. The level of profits reached in the later 1840s was generally maintained during the fifties. Over the next twenty-five years, however, an upward trend set in, interrupted only by two short, sharp slumps in 1867 and 1877. Until the end of the sixties the return on invested capital averaged rather less than 20 per cent.; but thereafter, as the following figures show, the return (i.e. profits plus interest) for the very profitable 1843–7 period, 35·4 per cent. (see above, p. 108), was exceeded, and for some fifteen years the average was very high.

TABLE 15

Percentage return on partners' capital, 1850–69 (5-yearly averages)

	Per cent.		Per cent.
1850–4	19·7	1870–4	48·6
1855–9	19·8	1875–9	26·6
1860–4	18·2	1880–4	29·9
1865–9	17·1		

Even these figures do not do full justice to the remarkable profitability

[1] A. L. Dunham, *The Anglo-French Treaty of Commerce of 1860* (Michigan, 1930), pp. 264–5.
[2] See below, pp. 193–4.
[3] There was a 50 per cent. *ad valorem* duty on imports of silk manufactures (*B.P.P.* xxi, 1886).

of the firm, especially when comparing the apparently lower yield of the period 1850–65 with the preceding years.[1]

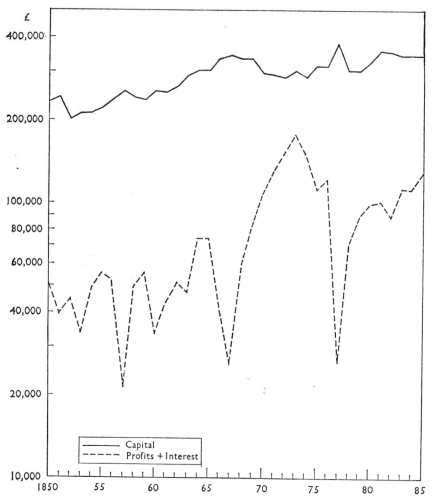

Fig. 13. *Samuel Courtauld & Co.: profits+interest, and capital, 1850–85*
Capital figures used as in Fig. 8
Source: E.R.O.: D/F 3/1

There are various reasons for this. First, the yield as calculated was made lower by two book additions to capital value. At the end of the 1828–49 partnership, £24,000 was added to the book valuations of the firm's fixed

_____
[1] See note on depreciation allowances, below, Appendix to Vol. I.

assests.[1] The decision to do this was carried through by Sam Courtauld in the face of opposition from his junior partners. He saw it as an allowance for goodwill, compensating for the consistent and rigorous depreciation allowances which had been applied since the beginning of the partnership, and justified by the high standing and profitability which the firm had achieved.[2] In exactly the same way, and for similar reasons, a further £25,000 was added at the end of the partnership which terminated on 30 December 1865.[3] Secondly, the financial position of the firm was very much stronger in the 1850s than it was in the 1840s. In the 1870s the cash and security reserves and the often high credit balances on short-term indebtedness provide a still more striking contrast to the position thirty years earlier (cf. Figs. 12 and 14). Simply to compare the situations in the forties, fifties, and seventies, the following averages are eloquent:[4]

	Closing capital (cap. + profits)	Cash and securities	Net indebtedness	Gross return	Percentage return
1843–7	138,169	4,150	−27,878	35,636	35·4
1853–7	260,131	40,839	− 8,794	42,445	18·8
1873–7	422,461	53,672	+10,334	116,907	38·0

Thirdly, the high cash reserves accumulated by the end of the 1865 partnership induced the partners then to agree to a bonus distribution of cash amongst themselves totalling rather over £37,000.[5] And, finally, it is to be noted that this general achievement was not secured by the self-denial of the partners in what they drew from the business. As Fig. 15 shows, the curve of drawings marches along with that of profits and interest with but a small gap. In the longer run this policy, which will be considered later, may well have been unwise; but in the short-run, in the light of the prosperous times, it seemed justified, and so the partners of the day had the enjoyment of substantial incomes.

The causes of this high profitability can, in part at least, be detected by an examination of Fig. 16. The trend in the curve of profits rises at a notably steeper rate than that of output, thus indicating that profit margins were increasing. This might be thought to be a result of further investment in cost-reducing capital equipment. But only to a very limited extent was this so. As can be seen from Fig. 14, it was not until 1869 that the value of fixed assets overhauled that of stocks of silk and other raw materials, of

---

[1] E.R.O., D/F 3/1/8.   [2] C.F.L, vol. vii, pp. 3290 et seq.
[3] E.R.O., D/F 3/1/11.   [4] See Appendix for sources and annual figures.
[5] E.R.O., D/F 3/1/5.

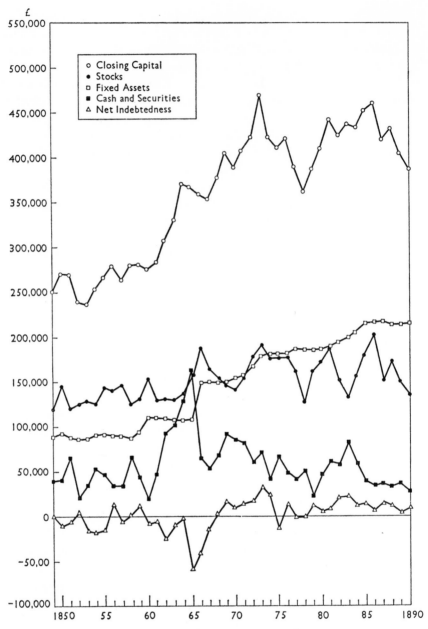

FIG. 14. *Samuel Courtauld & Co.: structure of assets, 1849–90*

Source: E.R.O.: D/F 3/1

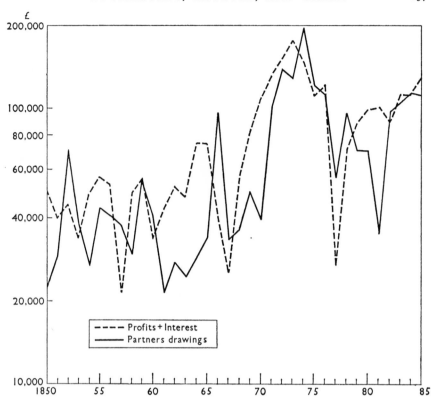

FIG. 15. *Samuel Courtauld & Co.: profits+interest, and partners' drawings, 1850–85*

Source: E.R.O.: D/F 3/1

finished and semi-finished goods. Taking fixed assets only, and including the £25,000 addition for goodwill in 1865, the following ratios suggest that further plant was only a partial answer.

TABLE 16

Profit margins and fixed capital, 1850–82

Period 3-yr. average	Profits (£) per unit of output	Fixed assets (£) per unit of output
1850–2	1·21	3·24
1860–2	1·05	3·61
1870–2	2·95	4·15
1880–2	1·79	4·35

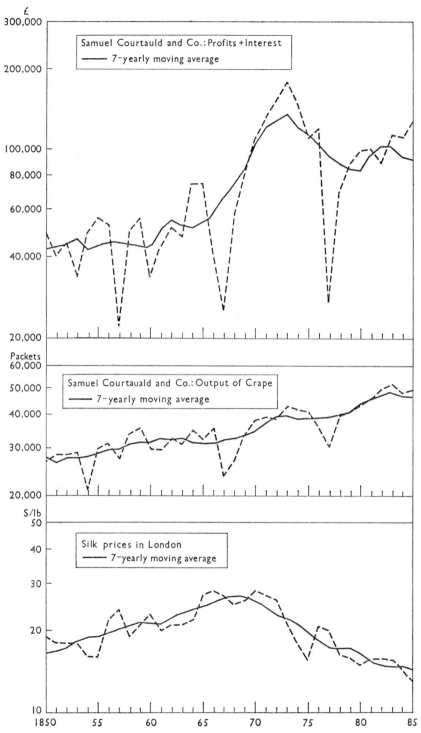

FIG. 16. *London silk prices and Samuel Courtauld & Co.'s profits and output, 1850–85*

Sources: as in Figs. 9, 11, and 13. Output = number of packets of crape finished annually

The profit margins show a 48 per cent. increase from the first period to the last; the ratio of fixed capital to output only a 34 per cent. increase. (For 1860–2 to 1880–2 the contrast is still more striking: 70 per cent. and 20 per cent. respectively.) The nature of the fixed capital investment which was made was not, moreover, such as to lead to markedly increased productivity (see below, pp. 141–2). The answer lay very largely in the course of raw silk prices: as Fig. 16 shows, after the mid-1860s they moved steadily downwards.

Unfortunately no continuous records survive of the prices at which the firm bought silk at this time. It is known that most of the silk which went into the crape was from China; so the prices shown in Fig. 16 may be thought to give an approximately accurate picture of the company's experience in this respect.

Raw silk prices were the main determinant of production costs. A calculation made by one of the firm's managers in 1889[1] showed that at the silk prices then prevailing raw silk accounted for about 63 per cent. of the manufacturing costs of crape or 50 per cent. if to these was added the allowance normally made by the firm for what were called 'common charges'.[2] At the much higher silk prices of 1866–70 the corresponding proportions would have been about 73 per cent. and 58 per cent., assuming that other costs remained constant. Between 1866–70 and 1881–5 the price of raw China silk in London fell by 45 per cent. During the same period Samuel Courtauld & Co.'s profits rose by 100 per cent. The fall in silk prices was due substantially to increasing Asiatic production plus the opening of the Suez Canal in 1869 which together facilitated the movement to Europe of larger quantities of raw silk at lower prices.[3] Moreover, as will be shown in Chapter VIII, aggregate English demand for raw silk declined rapidly after 1872. Circumstances largely outside their control thus put Samuel

[1] E.R.O., D/F 3/2/36, pp. 44–51, etc.

[2] The firm's pricing was based upon the calculation at Bocking of what were called 'White Book Prices' (which white books have not survived). These were compiled first by aggregating the raw material and labour costs entering into all the processes of making a packet of each type of crape. To them was added, for 'common charges', a sum—long fixed, for all types, at 2s. 6d. per packet—to cover 'salaries of officials, depreciation of machinery and stock', etc. The resulting 'white book price' was then used by the London office as a basis for selling prices which varied according to the particular figure and finish of each packet. Very little survives in the records about prices until the late 1880s and 1890s, when long-practised methods began to be questioned (see below, pp. 166–8). E. R. O., D/F 3/2/36, pp. 19, 45–51; D/F 3/2/37, pp. 47, 99, 139–41; D/F 3/2/92, pp. 56–58; D/F 3/2/110, pp. 8, 33, etc.; D/F 3/1/8–12.

[3] R. C. Rawlley, *Economics of the Silk Industry* (London, 1919), pp. 330–1; B.P.P. 1886, vol. xxi, pp. 275 ff.

Courtauld & Co.—and the small number of other English crape makers—in a very favourable market conjuncture.

Information about sales and prices is hard to come by. None of the company's records surviving from this period shows how much of its production it exported or to what countries; crape is not distinguished from other silk goods in national records of the export trade; nor has any continuous series of crape prices been found. We know that the company secured a gold medal at the Paris Exhibition of 1855, and we know from correspondence of the later 1880s and 1890s that the Paris trade was then regarded as very important. In 1893, the earliest date from which figures survive to show the distribution of Samuel Courtauld & Co.'s sales, the value of crape sales to France amounted to over £39,000 out of a total of £163,000. So France was, in that year, by far the largest foreign customer, taking 24 per cent. by value of total sales; of the remainder, 65 per cent. was sold in U.K., the U.S.A. took 5 per cent., and the balance went to sundry countries, mainly in Europe. It seems fair to assume that French sales were already of real consequence to the company in the fat years 1860–85.

Within those social classes which provided the buyers it seems likely that demand for crape was fairly price-inelastic. It was also, as we have seen, capable of extension overseas. If the following figures can be trusted it looks as though crape prices remained remarkably constant over a long period:[1]

TABLE 17

Some crape prices, 1765–1889

	'broad' and 6/4 (i.e. 54 in.)	'narrow' and 4/4 (i.e. 36 in.)
	s. per yd.	s. per yd.
1765 .	6s. 6d.	3s. 3d.
1812 .	..	4s. 6d.
1820 .	6s. 6d.	3s. 0d.
1830 .	..	4s. 0d.
1840 .	6s. 0d.	3s. 6d. (2s.–4s. 6d.)
1843 .	5s. 9d.	3s. 6d.
1850 .	4s. 6d.–5s. 0d.	3s. 6d.
1861 .	5s. 0d.	..
1871 .	5s. 6d.–9s. 0d.	
1889 .	..	1s. 4d.–4s. 0d.

[1] Figures from P.R.O., L.C. 2; Cunnington, op. cit.; *The Workwoman's Guide*; E.R.O. D/F 3/2/35.

These scanty figures must conceal short-run changes as well as variations in quality, but even so they do not suggest any radical fall in selling-prices until the eighties. There can be little doubt that the firm's very high profits during the quarter-century 1860–85 owed much to this particular combination of market circumstances, i.e. the fall in the price of raw silk plus the expansion of crape sales at steady prices. The particular boom in the firm's profits in the early 1870s reflected the general economic circumstances of those years (see below, pp. 157, 163). It may also have been aided by the introduction at that time of a spotted effect in the figure of Courtauld's crape. This turned out to be a very popular sales line;[1] per-haps its success was a tribute to some hidden longing in the crape-buying public for a slight relief from the sombreness of their mourning.

In these conditions it is perhaps not surprising that the firm should have decided to concentrate wholly upon crape. In the early sixties aerophanes still formed a modest share of total output (cf. Table 7 above, p. 82).

TABLE 18

Crapes and Aerophanes: average annual finish (packets), 1852–64

	Crapes	Aerophanes
1852–4. . .	24,504	1,360
1862–4. . .	29,233	3,516

In 1870 aerophanes disappear from the records. The company con-tinued, however, to make small quantities of coloured crapes. At the New York Industrial Exhibition of 1853, for instance, they exhibited both black and coloured crapes; and at the Paris Exhibition of 1878 they were still showing 'silk crape and aerophanes, black and coloured', as well as such insignia of mourning as 'black crape veils'.[2] But the great bulk of their crape was dyed black.

This triumph of crape was similarly reflected in the fact that throughout this period fixed capital investment was largely in more equipment of the same or similar type as existing equipment. The 570 Courtauld looms of

---

[1] E.R.O., D/F 3/2/34, p. 180. The introduction of the 'spot' has been attributed in the firm (see Ward-Jackson, p. 57) to Julien Courtauld, son of John Minton. Julien was indeed in the firm for a few years at this time (see below, p. 148), but I have not been able to find any evidence to support the contention that he was particularly responsible for this innovation, though it may be true.

[2] *B.P.P.* 1854, vol. xxxvi, pp. 231–3; *Report of the Royal Commissioners for the Paris Exhibi-tion of 1878*, vol. i, p. 124.

1850 had grown to 765 in 1870, of which about 80 were at Braintree mill.[1] In 1873 there were 740 at Halstead which were thus distributed in size and type:[2]

TABLE 19

Number and types of power-looms at Halstead, 1873

Width	1-shuttle	2-shuttle	3-shuttle	Total numbers
8/4	..	..	4	4
6/4	..	68	65	133
5/4	..	25	41	66
4/4	156	154	227	537
	156	247	337	740

In brief, much of the firm's weaving was still of the narrower widths of crape and some of it was still being done on simple, even single-shuttle, looms of the original sort. The single-shuttle looms were, however, rapidly being converted, and in 1881 there were only nineteen of them left.[3] Small improvements here and there, but in general more of the same sort: this was the formula. And Steam Factory carried out most of the machine building. In 1872 the engineer in charge there—James Finney, who arrived in 1853 to take over this part of George II's work—estimated that in twenty years the shop had turned out 17 crape mills, 16 winding engines, 4 doubling and 6 drawing engines, 14 creels, and some 300 looms, as well as such other work as installing further shafting and gearing.[4] The component parts of the crimping machinery were presumably now bought in and merely assembled; by 1862 a cumulative total of over seventy crimping machines had been thus made or assembled.[5]

To house these additions to plant, further buildings were erected, especially in the later 1850s, the 1870s, and again in the early 1880s. Apart from extensions to Halstead largely to house new throwing mills, new machinery and steam engines at Steam Factory, and new finishing and dyeing capacity, the largest single increase of fixed plant was the building, and then further extension, of a new mill on the Braintree site. The erection of this new three-story mill was completed in 1859, and in the 1860s Braintree was

[1] *B.P.P.* 1871, vol. lxii, pp. 118–19; E.R.O., D/F 3/3/22; D/F 3/2/54, p. 57.
[2] E.R.O., D/F 3/3/22, p. 40.
[3] E.R.O., D/F 3/3/22, pp. 185–6; also D/F 3/2/60, 61, 62, 63, 65, *passim*.
[4] E.R.O., D/F 3/2/56, pp. 187–9.   [5] E.R.O., D/F 3/2/17.

PLATE 14

COURTAULD'S MOURNING CRAPE

A modern photograph of a piece made in the 1890s, showing the crimped 'figure' and the 'spot' effect

PLATE 15

BRAINTREE NEW MILL
The old Mill can be seen on the left of the picture

being used for power-weaving—as the former hand-weaving of soft silk was abandoned—as well as for winding and throwing. Additional winding capacity was secured by the purchase in 1865 of a small mill at Chelmsford. In 1883–4 another extension to winding and drawing capacity was made by the erection of a small factory at Earls Colne, a village some three miles from Halstead. The land was bought in September 1883, the factory completed early in 1884, and by the end of 1885 over 100 hands were at work there.[1] For the rest, there was some increase in fixed assets through the building of workers' cottages, chiefly at Bocking and Halstead, and finally through the building of new London offices and warehouses on land leased in Aldermanbury in 1860. The main factories were given a very up-to-date air by the installation of electric lighting in the course of the 1880s. Halstead mill saw the first attempts, in December 1880, and the management declared itself satisfied that less silk was wasted under electric than under gas lighting. Dynamos were put in, and by 1886 Halstead, Bocking, and Braintree mills all glowed with the new electric illumination.[2] In the same year George Courtauld III remarked, with satisfaction: 'I believe there are more than 3,000 people that every week take their wages at our pay tables.'[3] Samuel Courtauld & Co. was now one of the largest firms in the silk industry, certainly in terms of numbers employed.[4]

As reflected in the value of fixed assets, all this expansion brought changes from the position indicated earlier in Table 5 (above, p. 77) which are now shown in Table 20 below. The figures include the goodwill additions in 1850 and 1865.[5]

TABLE 20

Fixed assets, 1848–85

	Halstead mill	Power Loom Factory	Bocking mill	Steam Factory	Finishing Factory	Braintree mill	Chelmsford mill	Earls Colne mill	Aldermanbury
	£	£	£	£	£	£	£	£	£
1848	6,984	15,864	13,470	7,655	7,511	5,868	..	..	..
1860	16,076	21,238	15,454	11,580	13,089	14,860	..	..	18,744
1870	17,454	28,510	18,754	16,300	17,308	23,767	3,201	..	28,030
1885	25,039	31,698	19,029	21,538	21,597	33,511	3,302	3,756	26,221

[1] E.R.O., D/F 3/2/67, *passim*; D/F 3/2/7, pp. 71 and 133; D/F 3/2/74, p. 91.

[2] E.R.O., D/F 3/3/22, pp. 177–8; D/F 3/2/64, 65, 66, 67, *passim*; D/F 3/2/72, p. 141; G.C.B., pp. 301, 302.

[3] G.C.B., pp. 389–90.   [4] See below, pp. 230–1.

[5] Both the figures in the table and the account of the extensions are derived from the Stock Books (E.R.O., D/F 3/1/8–12, 14).

Finally, to return to the earlier theme of this chapter: the partners. As the original partners went, their places were taken in the manner shown in Table 21, which also summarizes the entire period of the firm as a partnership, 1828–90. The fractions are the due proportions of the profits.

On the termination of the 1828–49 partnership it was Sam Courtauld's intention to retire from being an active partner.[1] He was fifty-six years old, had worked hard and successfully to build up a profitable business, and perhaps did not urgently covet riches. But just as he feared that his partners were incapable of running the business without him, so were his partners alarmed at the prospect of doing it. Sam wrote to Peter Taylor I in February 1848, confessing to 'discomfort at the idea of leaving my money in the business after myself was out'. Peter Taylor, noting that the amount of capital involved made Sam now less disposed to retire, confessed to George II: 'You and I are already *shaking* at leaving ourselves responsible for the present large plant.'[2] They agreed that John Minton Courtauld and Peter Alfred Taylor II should be brought in as partners. The former, then aged 42, had for some time been in charge of the Finishing Factory, the latter, then 30, had been working at Carey Lane. As Table 21 shows, Sam's retirement from active direction during the brief partnership of February–December 1849 was reflected in the one and only reduction of his share of the profits to an equality with those of the other senior partners. Peter Alfred Taylor I's death undid this arrangement and brought him back to active work in a new partnership in 1850 with, as usual, a larger share of the profits than anyone else. The terms of the deed of partnership permitted him to become a sleeping partner if he so wished. He does not seem ever really to have exercised this right. The problem of paying out Peter Taylor I's capital was solved by leaving it in the business, divided amongst his executors and his widow. His widow was then made a sleeping partner for five years and thus was entitled to both profits and interest. Some of this was allowed to accumulate and build up the capital; thereafter until the end of the partnership in 1865 she ceased to be a partner but left the capital in and was paid interest. Meanwhile, the executors were paid out the remaining amount due for distribution to legatees. Similarly, after the death of George II in 1861 his capital, divided between his executors and his widow, was left in the business, and interest paid upon it until the end of the term of the partnership.[3]

A clean sweep was made at the new partnership of 1866, though in

[1] *C.F.L.*, vol. vii, pp. 3264, 3272–3, 3277–81, etc.
[2] *C.F.L.*, vol. vii, pp. 3279–80, 3287.   [3] E.R.O., D/F 3/1/3–5; 3/1/18.

TABLE 21

The partners and their shares, 1828–90[1]

Period	Sam Courtauld III	George Courtauld II / III	Peter Alfred Taylor I / Mrs. P. A. Taylor I / Harry Taylor	Andrew Taylor / John Minton Courtauld / Julien Courtauld / Sydney Courtauld	Peter Alfred Taylor II	John Warren / Thomas Pickard Warren II
1828–37	(5/12)	George Courtauld II (2/12)	Peter Alfred Taylor I (2/12)	Andrew Taylor (3/12)		
1837–49	(5/9)	,, (2/9)	,, (2/9)	,, (10%) (8% from 1844)		
Feb. 1849–Dec. 1849	(2/8)	,, (2/8)	,, (2/8)	John Minton Courtauld (1/8)	Peter Alfred Taylor II (1/8)	
Dec. 1849–55	(3/8)	,, (2/8)	Mrs. Peter Alfred Taylor I (1/8)	,, (1/8)	,, (1/8)	
1856–60	(3/7)	,, (2/7)	·	,, (1/7)	,, (1/7)	
1861–65	(3/5)	·	·	,, (1/5)	,, (1/5)	
1866–67	(4/13)	George Courtauld III (4/13)	·	,, (3/13)	,, (2/13)	
1867–70	(2/6)	,, (1/6)	·	Julien Courtauld (1/6)	,, (1/6)	John Warren (1/6)
1871–81	(2/5)	,, (1/5)	·	,, (1/5)	,, (1/5)	,, (1/5)
1881–88	·	,, (7/24)	·	Sydney Courtauld (3/24)	,, (7/24)	,, (7/24)
1888–90	·	,, (18/80)	Harry Taylor (18/80)	,, (13/80)	,, (18/80)	Thomas Pickard Warren II (13/80)

[1] E.R.O., D/F 3/1/1–5.

L

practice, because of the family nature of the business, new names often meant old money. Peter Alfred Taylor II retired, not because of his age—he was only 46—nor simply because of the bad relations which persisted between him and Sam Courtauld, but largely so that he could have more time to pursue his political activities.[1] His younger brother, Henry (generally known as Harry, as he always signed himself), took his place in the London office. He was then 35 and much of the money he put in came from his mother. George Courtauld III, George II's eldest son, who had been working at Bocking since 1847 and was now 36, also came in with the assistance of some of his inheritance. Both also now brought in, as partners' capital, money which had been invested at short term in the firm.[2] The other new man, John Warren, as Fig. 17 shows, was the eldest son of the marriage of Peter Alfred Taylor I's sister Wilhelmina to Thomas Pickard Warren I. He was 35. T. P. Warren I, who died in 1867, had been a London merchant and warehouseman of moderate prosperity who had inherited money from two sources: from his father, John, a London merchant and silk mercer, and from his uncle, Edward, the probate of whose will described him revealingly as formerly of Ware, 'malt factor but late of same place, gentleman'. This uncle obligingly died without issue, and worth nearly £80,000.[3] So the John Warren who now came into the business of his cousins the Courtaulds and the Taylors may have been the only one to bring new money into the partnership, but even so he was in part indebted to an existing partner, for Sam Courtauld himself contributed £17,000 to make up the £50,000 which came in in Warren's name.[4]

Under the terms of this partnership Sam managed to retire and yet not to retire. Formally he became a sleeping partner, but the partnership deed[5] recorded that though he was free to absent himself from the business as and when he thought fit, he also had 'full liberty and power . . . from time to time and at any time to take such part in carrying on managing or conducting the said business as he shall think fit and as if he were an active

---

[1] Below, pp. 226–9.

[2] In the closing balance-sheet of the old partnership in December 1865, George III had £21,878 thus invested and Henry Taylor £22,997 (E.R.O., D/F 3/1/11). The new partnership started with both their capitals each consisting of approximately one-half of transfers of these investments and one-half of transfers from their mothers' or executors' accounts (E.R.O., D/F 3/1/5).

[3] Rev. Thomas Warren, *A History and Genealogy of the Warren Family* (privately printed, 1902); and family MSS. in the possession of Mr. Michael Warren, who kindly allowed me to consult them.

[4] E.R.O., D/F 3/1/5.   [5] E.R.O., D/F 3/1/18.

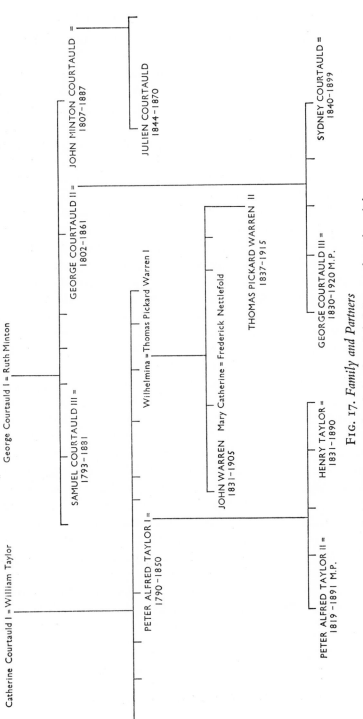

FIG. 17. *Family and Partners*

Note: Active partners at any time during the period 1828–90 are shown in capitals

partner therein'. The deed also gave John Minton Courtauld the right to introduce his son Julien into the business on or after June 1867 and then for himself either to retire completely or to become a sleeping partner on the same terms as Sam. This right he exercised, retiring completely in favour of his son in August 1867 at the age of 60. Although not an original partner, he was of the founding generation. Neither his personality nor his contribution to the firm, in particular to the Finishing Factory, can be indicated with any sort of precision. That he shared some of the interests in machinery and invention possessed both by his father and his brother George is suggested by his having taken out a patent in 1858 for a device to be used in dressing crape or other fabrics.[1] But neither the small number of his letters that survive nor other records suggest that he was a man of any exceptional qualities or that he played an outstanding role in the firm's progress. He died in 1877 leaving nearly £100,000.[2] Meanwhile, however, his son's participation in the family business was brief. Julien Courtauld had worked at Finishing Factory with his father since 1862 and in particular had acquired some ability as a chemist. His period of partnership after 1867, however, ended suddenly, nastily, and rather mysteriously, for on 27 March 1870, on the day before his twenty-sixth birthday, he died from the effects of a dose of potassium cyanide.[3]

The high profits of the 1870s came to an uneasy partnership of three men in their forties and one in his eighties. And when the octogenarian Sam thought fit to busy himself in 'managing or conducting the said business', though conflict with other partners often ensued, lesser men had to scurry to do his bidding. Mill managers were bombarded from Gosfield Hall with lists of questions and ordered to send their replies immediately by special messenger. 'Mr. Courtauld', wrote James Finney, the engineer, in his notebook in 1873, 'gave directions that the alterations in the Engraving Room should be <u>at</u> <u>once</u> proceeded with', and that certain looms should be 'erected <u>immediately</u>'. The underlining of peremptory demands was followed by the seizure of the unfortunate engineer's notebook by Sam Courtauld himself, who then filled several pages of it with a long and furious discourse on looms, boilers, cottage bedsteads, and similar troublesome matters.[4] When death put an end to all this in 1881, George II was now, by a year, the eldest of the three partners. The new man to come in,

---

[1] B.P. 2064 (1858).
[2] Somerset House: Will of John Minton Courtauld.
[3] G.C.B., pp. 152–3; E.R.O., D/F 3/2/54, p. 2.
[4] E.R.O., D/F 3/3/22, p. 39; D/F 3/2/57, pp. 70, 164–96.

complete with a legacy from Sam, was George II's youngest son, Sydney, then aged 41.[1] He had worked at Bocking on the engineering side since 1870, and later took over responsibility for Steam Factory.

These, then, were the four men, George Courtauld III, Henry Taylor, John Warren, and Sydney Courtauld, who now controlled the firm which, after 1885, was to experience great changes of fortune.

---

[1] The intervening sons, Samuel Augustine I and Louis, had died in 1854 and 1878 respectively.

CHAPTER VIII

Depression and Crisis

I

SAMUEL COURTAULD & Co.'s business experience during the twelve years 1886–98 was unlike anything in its previous history. Fig. 18 demonstrates the length and severity of the slump in output and in profits; and it also emphasizes the unique character of those bad years by putting them in the context of the firm's performance during the whole of the second half of the nineteenth century. As the graph shows, all the earlier depressions had been short and sharp, the longest being that of 1866–8. The worst years followed a cyclical pattern of approximately ten-year intervals, 1857, 1867, 1877. All were certainly related to, though not identically synchronized with, the downswings of the business cycle in the economy as a whole; that of 1866–8, for example, coincided closely with the general crisis of credit and confidence sparked off by the notorious failure of the financial house of Overend Gurney & Co. in May 1866. Not even the demand for mourning crape was proof against such pervasive slumps. On such occasions periods of short time were worked; and rumbles of worry were heard, as Sam's in May 1857: 'I have a very uncomfortable sense of unsafety of business.'[1] Yet within a year or two output and profits went up again, confidence returned, and in Samuel Courtauld & Co. as in the wider economic world, the even keel of industrial prosperity—which to some seemed God's special choice for Britain under Queen Victoria—was regained. But the years of real depression brought no such ready comfort; and perhaps nobody in the firm could ever again be quite so contentedly sure, as was George Courtauld III in November 1884, that 'Courtauld's crape' was a synonym for 'everything that is excellent and admirable'.[2]

The conversion of the business into a private joint-stock company in 1891 was surely a move into the haven of limited liability after the tumbling profits of the preceding years had made the unlimited liability of partnership seem too hazardous. Its immediate antecedent, however, was the death of Harry Taylor in April 1890. He left no male heirs; his wife

[1] *C.F.L.*, vol. viii, p. 3824.   [2] *G.C.B.*, p. 360.

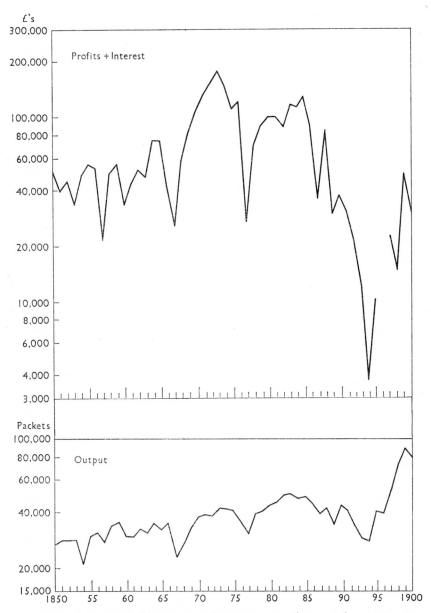

FIG. 18. *Samuel Courtauld & Co.: profits+interest, and output of crape, 1850–1900*

Sources: as in Fig. 13
Output = number of packets finished annually

and family had no such intimate connexions with the business as had earlier generations of Courtaulds and Taylors. So his capital was withdrawn, and the move to limited liability and joint-stock may well have been a necessary condition of the entry of new capital and new men—of whom more will be said later.[1] Samuel Courtauld & Co. thus emulated the actions of many another family partnership at this time.[2]

Although the firm's position in terms of credit and liquidity remained reasonably sound (see Fig. 19), the drastic writing down of the capital assets in 1894, as shown in Table 22, meant substantial losses for those who had entrusted their money to the new company only three years earlier. Nor was this capital reorganization followed by immediate signs of recovery. The dismal record of losses and nil dividends in 1894 and 1896 began falteringly to change in 1897-8, but it was only in 1899 that prosperity seemed to have returned. But even then it was not prosperity of the same order as that of a quarter-century earlier. Although the total quantity of fabric made and sold in 1899 was greater than ever in the company's history, the level of profits only reached that of forty years earlier; and a dividend of 10 per cent. for the ordinary shareholders of 1899 was a return very different from the 29 per cent. which had been the partners' average return on their capital (24 per cent. average profits plus 5 per cent. interest) during that happy quarter-century from 1860 to 1885.

This enduring depression and this limited recovery together formed a part of the business experience of the men who in 1904 were to give Samuel Courtauld & Co. an entirely new slant of interest. So depression and recovery alike demand careful attention, not merely for themselves but also because of what they meant for the future.

How, then, can this depression in the firm's fortunes be explained? There are three angles from which it can be examined, three elements in its causation. It can be seen as simply a fragment of the general circumstances of the British economy at this time; as, more specifically, a part of the experiences of the silk industry; and, still more closely, in terms of the performance of the men who directed the company.

II

In August 1885 there was appointed a Royal Commission to inquire into the 'extent, nature and probable causes of the depression now or

---

[1] Below, pp. 178-82.

[2] See Sir John Clapham, *Economic History of Modern Britain*, vol. ii (Cambridge, 1952), pp. 138-9; vol. iii, pp. 205 ff.

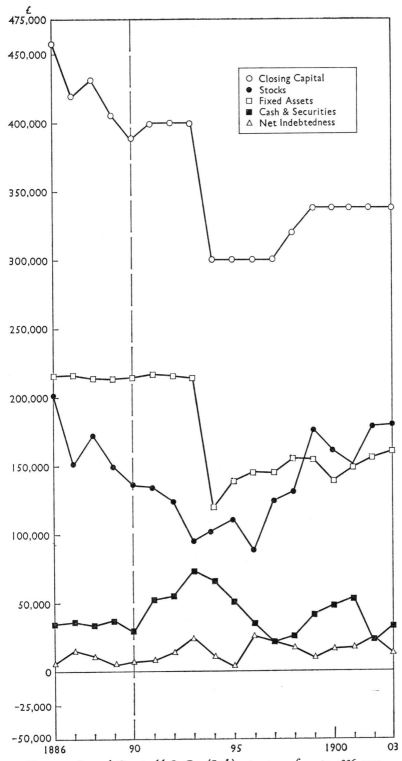

FIG. 19. *Samuel Courtauld & Co. (Ltd.): structure of assets, 1886–1903*

Note: The vertical line at 1890 denotes the change to Samuel Courtauld & Co. Ltd.

TABLE 22

Structure of assets, 1891–9

| Year | Paid-up capital | | | Fixed assets | Stock | Cash and securities | Net indebtedness | Net profit after tax and deb. int. | Total ordinary dividend |
	Ordinary shares	5% Deb. bonds	6% Cum. pref. shares						
	£	£	£	£	£	£	£	£	%
1891	400,000	..	..	217,108	134,390	52,253	+ 7,507	30,758	7½
1892	400,000	..	..	216,129	124,826	54,711	+ 13,977	21,147	5
1893	400,000	..	..	213,659	94,225	73,658	+ 24,073	12,061	3¼
1894	200,000	100,000	..	119,909*	102,768	65,781	+ 10,742	−1,264	Nil
1895	200,000	100,000	..	138,401*	111,888	51,332	+ 2,652	5,173	2
1896	200,000	100,000	..	145,008*	87,651	34,773	+ 25,115	−7,860	Nil
1897	200,000	100,000	..	144,877*	124,083	20,105	+ 20,931	17,450	5
1898	200,000	100,000	20,000	155,037*	131,754	25,739	+ 17,237	9,438	4
1899	200,000	100,000	37,200	154,139*	176,389	41,995	+ 9,174	43,914	10

* Including £13,676 goodwill.

recently prevailing in various branches of trade and industry, and whether it can be alleviated by legislative or other measures'.[1] Its reports and ample minutes of evidence appeared in 1886. Since 1873 there had been a substantial fall both in prices and in profits. This fall affected many branches of industry, commerce, and agriculture; and it was not arrested in 1886 either by the work of the Commission or by the magic of the market. Ten years later, in 1894–6, another Royal Commission sat deliberating on a depression: this time in agriculture; and many businessmen continued to look gloomily at the prospects of industry or apprehensively at stiffening competition in foreign markets. Only in 1896 did the tide of prices and profits seem to turn. Whether there was such an entity as a 'Great Depression' stretching from 1873 to 1896 has been the subject of learned debate amongst economic historians.[2] Various sorts of economic indicators tell various stories. Three different examples are exhibited in Fig. 20. In a comprehensive, weighted index based upon the physical *volume* of industrial production, the so-called great depression is reduced to cyclical fluctuations in a long upward movement: slump years in 1879, 1886, and 1893, boom years in 1883 and 1891. The course of the nation's exports, by *value*, follows a similar, and more striking, pattern of fluctuations, but also shows a long-enduring sluggishness, the high point of 1872–3 only being reached for one year, 1890, and then not again until 1899. The Board of Trade index of wholesale prices exhibits the extreme case, for these cascade downwards almost uninterruptedly from 1873 to 1896. Matching the complexities shown by these—and many more—indicators are the reasons which can be—and have been—advanced to explain these economic movements. Grain prices were sent tumbling by imports from the U.S.A.; prices generally may have been depressed by a shortage of gold relative to the increasing world demand for it; or they may have been brought down by the effects of previous cost-reducing investment; the prices of manufactured goods were falling because of the sharpening competition which Great Britain was now encountering, both at home and abroad, from newly industrializing economies, especially U.S.A., Germany, and France; tariff barriers were rising against British goods; and so

---

[1] B.P.P. 1886, vol. xxi, p. 3.

[2] e.g. H. L. Beales, 'The "Great Depression" in Industry and Trade', *Econ. Hist. Rev.*, vol. v, 1934 (reprinted in E. M. Carus-Wilson (ed.), *Essays in Economic History*, vol. i (London, 1954)); W. W. Rostow, *The British Economy of the Nineteenth Century* (Oxford, 1948); A. E. Musson, 'The Great Depression in Britain, 1873–96: a Re-appraisal', *Journal of Economic History*, vol. xix, 1959; and further contributions in *Econ. Hist. Rev.*, vol. xv, 1963 (Musson), and vol. xvii, 1964 (D. J. Coppock). The debate continues.

on. If business confidence was often depressed and many a firm was liquidated, unemployment, though severe in the slump years, was never

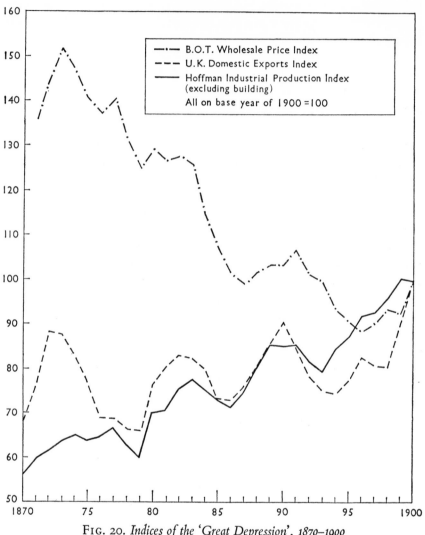

FIG. 20. *Indices of the 'Great Depression', 1870–1900*
Source: Mitchell & Deane

so long and so terrible as it was to be in the 1930's; and falling food prices brought a lower cost of living to many who worked in these years of late Victorian England.

Complex in nature and difficult to explain, the 'Great Depression', if ever such a thing existed or whatever it should be called, was at least something which contemporaries believed to be happening. This is no place to attempt to give precise definition to the phenomenon, least of all to explain it. But it is the occasion to stress how much the business experience of Samuel Courtauld & Co. in these years was a part of a national economic experience. It was not simply the decline of the crape trade, as, naturally enough, members of the firm were at first inclined to think; it was rather, as they came later to understand, that the firm was caught in a phase of general economic experience which demanded skilful and vigorous adaptation to circumstances in order to ensure survival.

The similarities and differences revealed by a comparison of the company's performance with the national trends arise, in part at least, from the fortunate preservation of such evidential rarities as a complete series of profits. And here a clear, albeit limited, confirmation of contemporary laments can be seen. Moreover, if the very high level of Samuel Courtauld & Co.'s profits in the period of prosperity was at all common, then much of the lamenting may well have been tribute to the general maxim: the larger the fall the louder the noise. No significant decline in the firm's profits, however, became apparent until after 1885. After the single bad year of 1877 high levels were soon regained. They were admittedly not quite so high as the boom years of 1872–4 with their average gross return to the partners of 54 per cent.; but a rising trend ever since 1850 and for the period 1878–85 an average return of 30 per cent. hardly called for alarm. It was only after 1885, and until 1896, that, as Fig. 18 shows, every trough and every peak was lower than its predecessors. This maintenance of Samuel Courtauld & Co.'s prosperity in the early years of the so-called Great Depression does tend to confirm a remark made by an otherwise woeful witness giving evidence to the Commission on the depression in March 1886: 'The crape manufacture in England is still as prosperous as ever. I think it is rather more prosperous.'[1] It was the next ten years that brought the damage to that prosperity.

That the collapse in profits, when it did come, was associated primarily with a collapse in selling prices can be seen by comparing the gradients of the curves in Fig. 21. Before the depression the peak year for the company's sales of finished fabrics, both in quantity and in value, was 1883; the trough for both, 1894. The fall in quantity was 45 per cent., in value almost 62 per cent. Expressed in terms of profit margins on sales, the following figures are still more eloquent.

[1] B.P.P. 1886, vol. xxi, 2nd Report, minutes of evidence, p. 284.

TABLE 23

Sales, profits, and margins, 1880–1903

Period	Value of total sales	Quantity of total sales	Sales value per packet	Profits★	Profits per packet sold	Profit margins on sales
	£'000	'000 packets	£	£'000	£	%
1880–2	337	46	7·3	78	1·7	23·3
1883–5	351	49	7·2	100	2·0	27·8
1886–8	266	42	6·4	50	1·2	18·7
1889–91	235	40	5·9	20	0·5	8·4
1892–4	172	30	5·7	11	0·4	7·0
1895–7	194	44	4·4	5	0·1	2·3
1898–1900	344	81	4·3	26	0·3	7·0
1901–3	447	93	4·8	39	0·4	8·3

★ Partners' profits (excluding interest) to 1890; net profits 1891–1903.

Meanwhile the price of the vital component of costs, raw silk, fell by only 41 per cent. during the same years. This squeeze between selling prices and raw silk prices was a crucial element in the firm's plight, the solution to the problems which it posed essential to continued existence. Its causes lay partly in the general price decline which ultimately affected crape as everything else, and partly in circumstances peculiarly relevant to the silk industry as a whole and to the market for crape in particular.

III

The English silk industry of the nineteenth century was structurally diverse and geographically scattered. It had, as shown in earlier chapters, survived the medicinal doses of Free Trade, in the 1820s and in 1845, and continued the expansion which had started so notably under eighteenth-century protection. The industry which was in 1860 to face the final dose of Free Trade—the removal of all protection—comprehended throwsters, manufacturers (who were sometimes also throwsters), and specialized dyers and finishers (though some manufacturers carried out all the processes); it incorporated users of hard silk, of soft silk, and also the most recent and probably the most rapidly growing branch, of spun silk; it still employed large numbers of outworking hand-loom weavers as well as

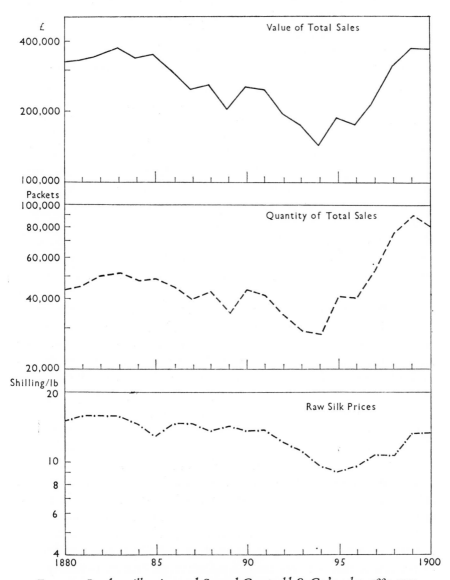

FIG. 21. *London silk prices and Samuel Courtauld & Co.'s sales, 1880–1900*

Prices are for China (Tsatlee)

Sources: as in Fig. 11

using power-looms in large factories; and the constituent firms of the industry were to be found in some twenty-two counties scattered across England and Wales, quite apart from units in Scotland and Ireland.[1]

As Figs. 22 and 23 show clearly, the late 1850s and early 1860s marked a real watershed in the industry's development. The curve of raw silk imports, moving steadily and rapidly upwards since around 1800, turned downwards after 1857 and remained on a steep downward trend for the rest of the century; in 1900 imports of raw silk had fallen to the level of 1820. Exports of silk manufactures and of silk yarn—never very high in value but hitherto moving upwards parallel to raw material imports— remained sluggish in the 1860s, moved up slightly in the 1870s and 1880s and then began their downward trend after 1885. Conversely, imports of silk manufactures moved up sharply after 1860; their trend remained clearly upward for the rest of the century. Thrown and spun silk entered the country in much smaller quantities, indeed hardly at all in the early 1860s though imports increased thereafter. Only one index of the English silk industry's fortunes was promising: imports of waste silk, the raw material of the spun silk industry, grew rapidly, surpassing those of raw in the 1870s and continuing on an upward trend thereafter. By the beginning of the twentieth century the English silk industry was a substantially different entity from what it had been a half-century earlier. It was not simply that after 1860 the home market was entirely open to foreign products, but that it remained open to the products of rapidly growing industries soon to be sheltered by protective tariffs. For by 1880 the Cobdenite mirage of Free Trade had vanished. What was good for Britain in the circumstances of her Industrial Revolution was not necessarily good for other countries trying to emulate her in following the path of industrialization. So in one country after another tariff barriers were erected or existing ones raised. U.S. tariffs moved upwards sharply in the 1860s and still more in 1897; German protection was increased in 1879; in France the policy enshrined in the Cobden–Chevalier Treaty was abandoned in 1881–2 and protection reached a new high level in 1892; Austria, Italy, and Russia increased their tariffs in the early 1880s.[2] In these later decades of the nineteenth century, the silk industries of France, Germany, and Switzerland as well as of Japan and the U.S.A. all grew rapidly. Their products supplied their own home markets, or competed with British

---

[1] B.P.P. 1862, vol. lv, p. 657; 1867–8, vol. lxiv, pp. 823–5.
[2] W. Ashworth, *A Short History of the International Economy* (London, 1954), pp. 132–45.

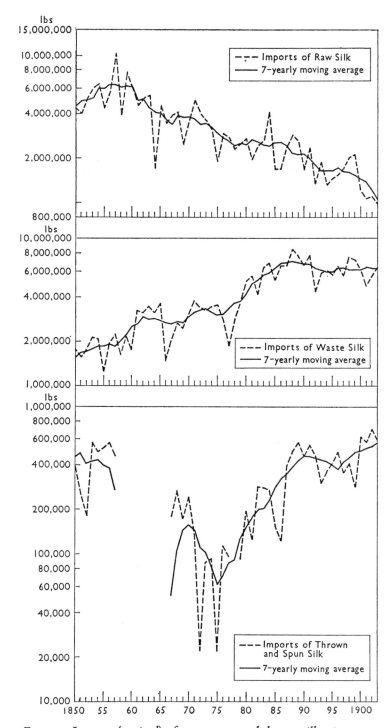

FIG. 22. *Imports: (retained) of raw, waste, and thrown silk, 1850–1903*

Note: Imports of thrown and spun silk are not shown for 1858–1865 because of some negative figures for retained imports which cannot be plotted on the logarithmic scale

U.K. *Source*: Annual Statement of Trade

goods in other markets, or, notably in the case of French and Swiss goods, came across the English Channel in increasing quantities.[1]

The consequence of these developments was that different branches of the English silk industry faced a succession of severe challenges from 1860 onwards. The varying responses to those challenges created the future shape

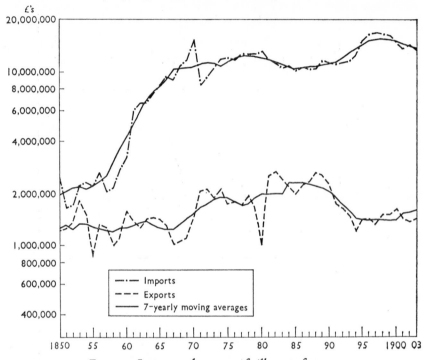

FIG. 23. *Imports and exports of silk manufactures*
U.K. Source: Annual Statement of Trade

of the industry.[2] The soft-silk branches, the users of thrown (as opposed to spun) silk, the makers of fashion fabrics, of dress silks, satins, ribbons, and the like were soon undersold by cheaper and better designed French imports. The Franco-German war helped to stimulate a temporary boom in English exports in 1871–2, but the promise of revival was soon broken by

[1] For a useful, though sometimes rather tendentious, survey of facts, figures, and opinions see the massive Tariff Reform publication, *Report of the Tariff Commission*, vol. ii: *The Textile Trades* (London, 1905).

[2] The section which follows is largely derived from the relevant Minutes of Evidence of the Royal Commission on the Depression of Trade and Industry (*B.P.P.* 1886, vols. xxi and xxiii); the *Report of the Tariff Commission*, vol. ii, part 6: evidence on the silk industry; and Warner, op. cit.

the onset of depression—industrial and agricultural—and the general price collapse. Spun silks and hard silks were little affected by these early challenges. But for the rest, the 'great depression' was the great decline; falling prices, foreign competition, and rising tariff barriers simply piled difficulty upon difficulty. The price squeeze noted in the case of Samuel Courtauld & Co. operated throughout the industry. For it was the world-wide extension of silk manufacture outside the British Isles which prevented the price fall in raw silk being as great as that in silk fabrics in the English markets. Furthermore, the centre of the raw silk market had moved, with the opening of the Suez Canal, from London to Lyons; many foreign producers operated either with lower labour costs, or with newer and better machinery; the inadequacies of English technical education and the unattractiveness of English textile design made themselves felt more formidably than ever. We are back, on some grounds at least, with the debate of the 1760s and the 1820s and 1830s. But this was the last crisis. Before the century was out Coventry and Spitalfields had vanished from the silk industry; so too had most of the scattered throwing mills in such counties as Buckinghamshire and Hertfordshire, Suffolk and Somerset; the silk manufacturers and throwsters of Manchester, Derby, Congleton, Leek, and Nottingham were drastically reduced in number. Though Macclesfield remained as the strongest of the provincial centres, here, as elsewhere, marginal producers were weeded out, and there was a substantial fall in employment. Throughout the silk industry this fall in employment was striking, and much of it was the final contraction of the hand-loom weaving of soft silks.

TABLE 24[1]

Employment in the silk industry: England and Wales, 1851–1901

	1851	1861	1871	1881	1891	1901
Males . .	53,936	43,732	29,225	22,205	19,090	13,859
Females . .	76,787	72,588	53,738	42,630	32,937	25,176
Total . .	130,723	116,320	82,963	64,835	52,027	39,035

In male employment the fall, 1851–1901, was 74 per cent., in female 67 per cent.

Not all, however, was as sombre as these figures suggest. Efficient producers, able to cut costs, to invest in new machinery, to get used to reduced

[1] The figures are those given in the *Report of the Tariff Commission*. They are consistently higher than those given in the Census returns, though this seems to be a matter of occupational definition. The census figures give, however, almost identical percentage falls in employment, 1851–1901, viz. male, 76 per cent; female, 64 per cent.

profit margins: these survived. The spinning of waste silk into yarn had been the subject of various experiments since the eighteenth century, but the major advances in this country resulted from the work of Samuel Cunliffe Lister (later Lord Masham). Inventor and industrialist, wool-comber and silk-spinner, this remarkable man built up, in Manningham Mills, Bradford, one of the biggest textile enterprises of its time.[1] Other large firms, such as J. & T. Brocklehurst of Macclesfield, by using increas-ing quantities of spun silk and concentrating on power-loom production, recovered from the depression; so also did smaller specialized firms such as Warner & Sons, who moved out of London to Braintree in 1878 and concentrated on very high quality products. As a consequence of these developments the statistics of the total number of factories and of power-looms in operation tell a far less catastrophic story than the figures of numbers employed.

TABLE 25[2]

Number of silk factories and silk power-looms:
England and Wales, 1850–90

	1850	1861	1870	1878	1885	1890
Factories (spinning and weaving)	272	761	696	706	691	623
Power-looms . . .	6,092	10,635	12,378	12,546	11,966	11,464

In the hard-silk branch, in effect the crape trade, Samuel Courtauld & Co. were one of a small group of firms. Their main competitors in the 1870s and 1880s were Joseph Grout & Co., the Norwich Crape Co., F. Hinde & Sons, Le Gros, Thompson & Co., Kay & Richardson & Co., and Chorlton & Co. The first three were all East Anglian concerns, Le Gros, Thompson were in Somerset, Kay & Richardson in Cheshire, and Chorlton & Co. in Staffordshire. There is no evidence to show how much of the market Samuel Courtauld & Co. had at this time, but almost cer-tainly they were the largest concern; nor is there any evidence to suggest that the market was other than competitive, in quality and design as much

---

[1] On Lister, apart from the observations of witnesses in *B.P.P.* 1886, vol. xxi, *Report of the Tariff Commissions*, and his own *Lord Masham's Inventions. Written by Himself* (1905), see also *Hist. Tech.*, vol. iv, pp. 296–8, 321–6, and E. M. Sigsworth, *Black Dyke Mills* (Liverpool, 1958), *passim*.

[2] Figures for 1850 and 1861 from *B.P.P.* 1850, vol. xlii, and 1862, vol. lv (both for Eng-land and Wales only); those for 1870, 1878, 1885, 1890 for U.K. from *Report of the Tariff Commission*.

as in price, during the periods of prosperity as well as of depression. If the known prosperity of the trade encouraged entry the difficulties of effecting successful entry must have been considerable. In the 1880s and 1890s competition became more and more rigorous as firms struggled for survival. Not all did survive. Kay & Richardson's mills went under the auctioneer's hammer in January 1888 and Chorlton & Co. had failed by the summer of 1890.[1]

Although the spread to the crape trade in the mid 1880s of the contagious economic ill of falling sales prices was the most immediate challenge to continued prosperity which the constituent firms had to face, there was also the underlying problem of a change in taste and fashion away from the use of their mourning product. Revulsion against the sententious religiosity of high Victorianism brought the beginning of more secular attitudes and in turn a reaction against elaborate ritual mourning; the first cremation in England in 1882 was a symbol of new directions. Women's fashions began to move against the stiffness and rigidity so long prevailing; the flowing lines and Oriental colours pioneered by Liberty's in the 1870s and 1880s were part of the revulsion of fashion—there was no mourning department at Liberty's.[2] It was said in 1889 that:

. . . private mourning in modern times . . . has been greatly altered and modified, to suit an age of rapid transit and travel. Men no longer make a point of wearing full black for a fixed number of months after the decease of a near relative, and even content themselves with a black hat-band and dark-coloured garments. Funeral ceremonies, too, are less elaborate. . . .[3]

The habit of the Court remained an influential determinant. Queen Victoria's sustained retirement and her permanent mourning put her in a position which was contrasted unfavourably with the growing popular enthusiasm for the Prince and Princess of Wales.[4] The use of crape in women's mourning fashion was already waning when in 1892 the Princess of Wales dispensed with it during her mourning for the Duke of Clarence, who died in that year.[5] Too much, however, should not be read into this sign of royal disapproval. The elaborate procedures for feminine mourning

---

[1] E.R.O., D/F 3/2/69, pp. 101–2; D/F 3/2/37, pp. 9–20.

[2] Aldburgham, op. cit., pp. 62, 173–81.

[3] Davey, op. cit., p. 96.

[4] Sir Philip Magnus, *King Edward the Seventh* (London, 1964), esp. pp. 101–2, 121; see also the illustration facing p. 65 for a fascinating visual contrast between the bridal couple and a crape-laden Victoria gazing mournfully at a bust of Albert.

[5] Cunnington, op. cit., p. 381.

were still being set out in the pages of *The Queen, The Lady, Gentlewoman,* and the rest at the turn of the century.[1] The discarded fashions of the *élite* are often adopted by inferior social strata; and falling prices facilitated the spread. So if it was no longer quite so important for a lady to show that she was a lady by smothering her dress with yards of crape, it was at least possible for many lesser creatures to share in the still popular practice of exhibiting grief by crape. By the 1890s the aggregate value of the home market for mourning crape was no longer expanding; only after the death of Queen Victoria in 1901 was it certainly contracting sharply.[2] Meanwhile, however, there was also foreign, and especially French, demand. Despite those tariff walls, despite the existence of continental crape manufacturers, in general *crêpe anglaise* remained an English product and an English export; enterprising firms could hope to capture that export trade.

By 1896 Samuel Courtauld & Co. were already selling more crape overseas than at home; in 1901 they claimed to be the biggest crape makers not only in England but in the world and to have a total production greater than all the other makers combined. They had not only recovered from the depression and avoided the fate of many a firm in the English silk industry, but they had now captured most of the market in this extraordinary product on which they had been built in Queen Victoria's extraordinary century. Before we ask how the recovery was achieved we must examine how they grappled with the depression years.

IV

The years in which sales tumbled and profits became losses acted as a sort of economic purgatory for the easy winnings of decades past. In the course of these dismal times it fairly soon became evident that for Samuel Courtauld & Co., as for many other firms, drastic changes had to come before recovery could be gained.

As the sellers' market ended so were the company faced with a growing inrush of complaints. In May 1886 customers were complaining that their crape wore badly; poor dyeing got the dyers into trouble in 1887–8; Harry Taylor in London was passing on to Bocking between April and June 1888 complaints about irregularities of 'feel' in the crape, softness in patches or on one side.[3] A curious disease known as 'notchiness', a fault in

---

[1] A Courtauld advertising brochure of 1902 contained ample abstracts from such authorities.

[2] See below, p. 196.

[3] E.R.O., D/F 3/2/34, p. 114; D/F 3/2/35, pp. 47, 66, 67, 69, 70–72, 76.

crimping, made recurrent appearances in 1889–90. From Aldermanbury to Bocking went a solemn warning in July 1890: 'this defect is a very serious matter and is becoming even more so. The retail houses are complaining to the wholesale and in some cases absolutely return goods on account of notchiness only.' Then came the significant comparisons, the type of observation which was to recur on several other matters. 'Another point is that notchiness to anything like a serious extent is confined to our goods, the other manufacturers, notably Grouts, are practically free from it.' It was not simply English manufacturers with whom this unfavourable comparison was made: 'foreign crapes never appear to us so notchy as our crapes do'.[1] The most persistent object of complaint, however, was the finish of the goods. Sometimes this was largely a matter of fashion, as in March 1886 when the company's agent reported that customers in Brussels, Lille, Liège, and Cologne wanted a brighter finish; if 'a more brilliant black' could be given then 'a large sale could be made'.[2] Far more serious than this were long-lasting complaints about irregularity and poor quality in finish. From September 1887, when it was said that 'our finish is now anything but good',[3] to 1895, Aldermanbury were sending to Bocking a series of complaints on this score. In May 1894 George Courtauld III read to the Board a paper from Bocking about the 'deplorable state of the finish', and the need for 'a radical change' in the firm's finishing methods. A new method was then in the process of being developed,[4] but this affected only the cheaper grades. In July 1895 the finish of the medium- and high-class goods was still causing trouble: 'our finishing troubles continue very acute'. The blame was put upon the firm's crimping methods, and a most unfavourable comparison was made with the goods of the Norwich Crape Co.:

... again and again we have complaints only too well founded, from Aldermanbury, as to the irregularity of our crapes, and again and again we are told that the Norwich Crape Co. do *not*, as far as we can ascertain, produce bad and good crapes as we do, but that all their crapes (which we see) are alike. Our method of crimping, which has obtained for many years, inevitably produces half our crapes of more or less bad quality. In passing the gauzes through the crimping machine in pairs one above the other, we deliberately sacrifice the quality of one of them by using it as a buffer for the other; and we do this of course because we can find at present no better way. ...

Though improvements were made, perfection remained elusive, and even

[1] E.R.O., D/F 3/2/36, pp. 5, 89.　　[2] E.R.O., D/F 3/2/34, p. 88.
[3] E.R.O., D/F 3/2/35, p. 21 and *passim*.　　[4] Below, pp. 186–7.

in the years of peak recovery, 1898 and 1899, complaints of finish were still being received at Bocking.[1]

These finishing woes were closely linked with a variety of generally unflattering comparisons, in regard both to price and to quality, between the company's crapes and those of sundry competitors. In October 1887 some of F. Hinde & Son's crape was described by Aldermanbury as being 'a better and more saleable article than ours'.[2] Some unpromising attempts were made in the course of 1888 to copy this particular line.[3] In March 1889 London sent to Bocking for their inspection three rolls of Hindes's crapes and observed that the equivalent goods of Samuel Courtauld & Co. were selling at prices which would not compare in value with Hindes's: Courtauld's prices of 1s. 8d., 3s., and 4s. per yard compared with Hindes's, for the comparable fabrics, of 1s. 4d., 1s. 9d., and 2s. 6d. Though Aldermanbury professed no admiration for Hindes's crapes it was admitted that Hindes were the only crape manufacturers then working full time. They were even, it was said, taking on fresh hands.[4] In 1891–2 a series of trials were made to remedy 'the serious way in which our trade is affected by reason of our Doubles being so poor and dull'.[5] The figure and finish of the Norwich Crape Co.'s products were much admired. In November 1892, T. P. Warren from London told the Bocking directorate that 'the question of the competition of *outside* makes' was becoming serious. He added: 'we should like to discuss it with you.' Later the same month the manager of the Finishing Factory sent his assistant on a snooping expedition to Norwich; he produced a report on the location, output, and capacity of the Norwich Crape Co.[6] In a meeting of the Board in December the manufacturing departments were firmly requested to 'produce crapes which can be sold against the cheaper goods produced by our competitors'. One of the lines which Bocking followed in pursuit of this goal during the next few years was a series of determined attempts to analyse and imitate the products of the Norwich Crape Co.[7]

There was, however, another and quite different problem of crape competition which troubled Samuel Courtauld & Co. for a good many years. The weather stops for no man, in life or death; so mourning crape could well be waterproof. But it was not Samuel Courtauld & Co. but Kay & Richardson who at the Paris Exhibition of 1878 exhibited 'Black

[1] E.R.O., D/F 3/2/114, pp. 136–44.   [2] E.R.O., D/F 3/2/35, p. 51.
[3] Ibid., pp. 127, 128, 151.
[4] Ibid., p. 188.   [5] E.R.O., D/F 3/2/37, pp. 65–87, 167–72.
[6] E.R.O., D/F 3/3/92, pp. 49–53.   [7] See below, p. 187.

Crape for mourning attire . . . the newly invented Rainproof Crape, guaranteed not to spot with rain'.[1] Courtaulds had been probing the idea of waterproofing their crape in the 1860s and 1870s. In 1877–8 they commissioned analyses, from Dr. E. Frankland in London and Dr. J. Watts in Oxford, of samples of waterproof crape, presumably the products of various competitors.[2] Trials with waterproofing were under way at the Finishing Factory in 1885 and again in 1888.[3] This time the feared competitor was Le Gros, Thompson, samples of whose weatherproof crape were now analysed. In May 1889 the partners met at Bocking and discussed 'the importance of our being able to make our goods waterproof'; at the Finishing Factory experiments were made with the use of shellac and borax in waterproofing crape.[4] Difficulties were still being encountered in 1889–90.[5] Success was reached soon after this, however, and in 1895 the 'one really satisfactory improvement that has been made is the waterproofing of the ordinary crapes'.

For all these complaints and not always very rapid efforts to improve their products, Samuel Courtauld & Co. nevertheless had an impressive record of awards gained at the exhibitions of the day. And it would certainly be foolish to suppose that their competitors' fabrics were always perfect. At the Great Exhibition of 1851 Sam Courtauld was one of the jurors in the silk section and so the firm was precluded from competing; it had to be content with Prize Medals at the London Exhibition of 1862 and the Chicago Exhibition of 1893, and a mere Honourable Mention at the New York Industrial Exhibition of 1853, where Joseph Grout & Co. gained a Silver Medal; but at the Paris Exhibitions of 1855, 1878, and 1900 Samuel Courtauld & Co. won Gold Medals.[6] How real and rare a tribute to excellence such medals were is not always clear, however, for the official report on the Paris Exhibition of 1855 reveals a somewhat curious story.[7] Apparently in the silk section of the exhibition there were originally awarded four Gold Medals, seven silver, seven bronze, and four Honourable Mentions. This meant that twenty-two of the thirty or so manufacturers who exhibited got some sort of award. Alarmed by so generous a distribution of favours, the Imperial Commission for the Exhibition decided that in aggregate too many Gold Medals had been given and determined that only one should be awarded in this class. It was given to the

---

[1] *Report of the Royal Commission on the Paris Exhibition of 1878*, vol. i, p. 124.

[2] E.R.O., D/F 3/2/105.

[3] E.R.O., D/F 3/2/34, pp. 70, 80–82; D/F 3/2/35, pp. 137–40, 159, 179.

[4] E.R.O., D/F 3/2/35, pp. 23–41.   [5] E.R.O., D/F 3/2/36, pp. 87, 143–5.

[6] B.P.P. 1854, vol. xxxvi, pp. 231, 233.   [7] B.P.P. 1856. vol. xxxvi, part I.

firm which happened to be first on the list, i.e. Samuel Courtauld & Co. This moved the author of the official report to regret the action of the Imperial Commission, for, he said, 'it led to the entire omission of the second and third . . . firms (whose merit the jury, after examination, considered superior) from the lists of medals awarded . . .'.[1] It would be interesting to know how many private axes were being ground here, but at least it looks as though the acknowledgement of Samuel Courtauld & Co.'s excellence at Paris in 1855 may have been helped by a little luck.

Efforts to compete more successfully in quality and in price were not in themselves enough to master the task of survival in the years of depression. It was in the efforts to cut costs and to develop new products that the greatest obstacles were met. These two closely related efforts faced a threefold obstacle. First, there was the very evident fact of the highly specific nature of the firm's entire manufacturing plant, designed to make mourning crape and nothing else. Second was the reluctantly learnt fact that much of that plant was technically obsolescent, not to say obsolete, having been continually expanded on the basic designs of a half-century earlier. And third was the fact which is perhaps more readily apparent in retrospect than it was at the time: the older and senior leaders of the business were out of touch with the latest textile developments and were at their wits' end to know what to do.

It was in the spring of 1887 that the 'falling off in the black crape trade' moved the company to examine the 'desirability of devising a new fabric either in black or colours which might form a subsidiary manufacture'.[2] At first, efforts were made simply to 'look about for fancy fabrics which may be manufactured in our machinery and which might utilize our gauzes'.[3] Such tentative moves turned into experiments with the manufacture of various sorts of *crêpe*: the well-known *crêpe de Chine*, sundry exotically named products such as *crêpe sable*, *crêpe italien*, *crêpe Indien*, as well as crapon and zephyr.[4] The wives of managers or partners bought a few yards of various crapes from West End shops, and Bocking set about analysing and trying to copy them.[5] George Courtauld III suggested in November 1887 that gold or silver thread might be woven into the

---

[1] *B.P.P.* 1856, p. 271. The firms, in order, were: (1) Samuel Courtauld & Co., (2) Winkworth & Procters, (3) Kemp, Stone & Co., (4) Grout & Co.

[2] E.R.O., D/F 3/2/34, p. 180.   [3] Ibid., p. 194.

[4] 'Zephyrs' had been made in very small quantities in 1882–3 but abandoned because of the large amount of finishing involved and the fact that the black crape yielded more profit. E.R.O., D/F 3/2/27, p. 12.

[5] E.R.O., D/F 3/2/35, pp. 7–20; D/F 3/2/15; D/F 3/2/27.

gauzes to produce a fancy *crêpe*; after some gold thread had been bought from Germany and experiments made, Aldermanbury decided in February 1888 that such goods were unsaleable.[1] The possibility of weaving soft-silk goods again soon moved George III's mind towards the revival of hand-loom weaving. In December 1887 he wrote:

> . . . I understand that we still have, here, some soft-silk weavers; and we have also an overseer who used to have a great deal to do with soft-silk, and knows all about the weaving in of it. If desired, I dare say we could, without much difficulty get up a small make of satins and velvets, and increase it if wished. We should have to get some new looms but that would, I fancy, be a very simple matter, for *hand-looms*. If we went into the thing at all largely, we should no doubt desire to buy suitable *power-looms* for *satins* and other similar fabrics: I don't think velvets are capable of being woven in power-houses (?). But for any temporary succedaneum *hand-looms* which could be put up in any chance waste space, and taken down again when not wanted, would be the thing, no doubt. . . .[2]

Although Harry Taylor, after a visit to Paris in May 1888, reported hopefully on the possibilities of a trade in *crêpe sable*, the Finishing Factory manager warned Sydney Courtauld that for the trade in colours the company needed to engage a high-class dyer, adding 'we are not prepared for first-rate trade'.[3]

Trials continued in 1889–90. Patterns of Grout's *crêpe de Chine* and *crêpe sable* were sent to Bocking from London in 1889 with the ominous note that the *crêpe de Chine* was being sold in large quantities at a very low price; samples of *crêpe de Chine* from Lyons were looked at with envy: 'if we could make goods up to this pattern there is no doubt we could sell a considerable quantity'.[4] The brief boom of 1890–1 helped the company's efforts, however, and it managed in those years to start the sale of coloured *crêpes* and push it up to 2,430 packets in 1890 and 5,526 in 1891, before the slump came in 1892–4.[3] The severity of the slump, in black crapes as in coloured *crêpes*, emphasized the need for something much more drastic than had happened hitherto. But the brief and temporary boom of 1890–1 had shown up, not for the first time but now more starkly in the more competitive circumstances of the time, one of the company's greatest technical obstacles: the Courtauld loom.

In 1872 the engineer James Finney had been sent on a tour of loom-

[1] E.R O., D/F 3/2/35, pp. 57, 59, 60.   [2] E,R,O., D/F 3/2/22, p. 387.
[3] E.R.O., D/F 3/2/35, p. 99.   [4] E.R.O., D/F 3/2/36, pp. 17, 18, 55, 91.
[5] For further details of sales of colours, see below, pp. 196–7.

makers in Lancashire and Yorkshire, as the partners were examining the
question of whether to buy in looms or continue to make them at Bocking.[1]
In practice both courses were followed. For the expansion of 1884–5
looms were both bought from outside loom-makers and made at Steam
Factory.[2] But the basic design remained the same, despite the fact that its
limitations had been evident during the boom of the early 1870s. In 1873
the manager of Halstead mill reported to George III on trials made with
looms running faster than the usual speed. 'There is no doubt', he wrote,
'that the looms on fast speed require more attention, cause more breakages,
and do not turn out such good work.'[3] Fifteen years later, in 1888 with the
sellers' market finished, Finney noted that a spare 4/4 loom was being sent
from Halstead 'to have in the shop here for inspection from time to time
while we are considering a design for a loom with a much stronger
framing'.[4] Various imperfections in trial coloured fabrics at this time were
ascribed to the company's looms; 'without some alterations they would
not be got over'.[5] Next year Finney went to the International Exhibition
in Paris principally to look at the 'Palais des Machines'. Here he saw 'a
considerable number of looms . . . the best exhibit perhaps is George
Hodgson's of Bradford, but there are a good many beautiful looms by
foreign makers'. Some of the best silk looms, he thought, were made by
a Lyons firm. He concluded: 'there is one feature in all the looms I saw it
might be well for us to consider, that is the tappet or wiper motion for
throwing the shuttle. In no case did I see shuttles thrown by chuck springs
like ours.'[6] Came the brief prosperity of 1890–1 and again more Courtauld
looms were put in. In February 1891 there were 1,080 looms at Halstead
and Braintree. They were still mainly narrow looms:[7]

8/4	7/4	6/4	5/4	4/4
4	20	181	85	790 = 1,080

And again, this time twenty-two years after his first report, the manager
at Halstead reported on the results of running some looms at 116·5 revolutions per minute, instead of at the ordinary speed of 103·5. The turn out at
the ordinary speed was greater than at the increased speed. 'Our looms', he
said, 'are too slight to stand the increased chuck which faster speed requires,

[1] E.R.O., D/F 3/2/57, pp. 1–7.
[2] Ibid., D/F 3/2/70, pp. 154–5; D/F 3/2/72, pp. 36–37, 45.
[3] E.R.O., D/F 3/3/22, pp. 25a, 26–27.
[4] E.R.O., D/F 3/2/76, p. 53.   [5] E.R.O., D/F 3/2/27, p. 300.
[6] E.R.O., D/F 3/2/76, p. 155.   [7] E.R.O., D/F 3/2/69, p. 164.

the looms therefore stop more frequently, and the silk breaks down much more often.'[1] Not until a few years later were stop mechanisms—such as had long been in use in other branches of textile weaving—fitted on to these looms.

The lightness and simplicity of the Courtauld loom, once merits, were now demerits. But this was not all. Perhaps still more embarrassing was its extreme lack of versatility. The need for diversification inevitably led to attempts to weave soft silk on power-looms. 'We send you', wrote the Halstead manager to Bocking in April 1889, 'our first piece of soft-silk cloth. We are not proud of it, but we have tried several experiments upon it which have been valuable experience for us. . . .'[2] In July Finney went with Sydney Courtauld to Halstead to arrange for the alteration of some of the looms for the purpose of weaving twill.[3]

The first inquiries about buying looms of a quite different sort were made, at last, in 1890 when interest was shown in wide, check looms from George Hodgson of Bradford. One was bought. It did so well that in May 1890 it was decided to have three more; and two wide looms were ordered of Hodgsons in July. In 1891 a very wide (9/4) single-shuttle crape-loom was bought from Rüti in Switzerland. At Sydney Courtauld's instigation and on the strength of the boom of 1891 orders were placed for two more looms from Hodgson and ten of various sorts from Rüti. By April 1892 a total of twenty outside looms of sundry sorts, eleven Swiss and nine English, had been installed,[4] but soon depression came again. The complete re-equipment of the company's weaving sheds had to wait for the stimulus of the really bad years of 1892–4.

What was true of looms was true of other parts of the company's technical equipment. The imperfect crimping techniques and old methods of dyeing and finishing were not rectified until the crisis had made change imperative. Though members of the firm visited various parts of England, usually the great textile districts of the north, to inspect machinery for dressing or finishing, for warping or calendering,[5] little or nothing was done until 1893 and thereafter. The high cost and great slowness of the hand engraving of crimping rolls led to experiments with the electrolytic reproduction of these rolls. After visits to a Birmingham firm in 1884–5, and the expenditure of £357, a trial plant was put up at Bocking; but by

[1] E.R.O., D/F 3/3/22, p. 475.
[2] Ibid., p. 430.
[3] E.R.O., D/F 3/2/76, p. 145.
[4] E.R.O., D/F 3/2/78, pp. 94, 97, 103; D/F 3/2/81, pp. 17, 20, 39, 41–42, 83–115.
[5] E.R.O., D/F 3/2/76, p. 151; D/F 3/2/80, pp. 21 ff., 35; D/F 3/2/35, pp. 137–40; D/F 3/2/37, pp. 9–30, 141.

1888 failure was conceded and Sydney Courtauld decided to dismantle the plant.[1] Success in this, as in other fields, came later.

To assign individual responsibility in economic history is harder than it may seem. How much of business performance is due, over any given short span of time, to the ability or disability of individual partners, directors, or managers and how much to the particular conjuncture of the trade cycle? What might have been George Courtauld I's subsequent career if he and Joseph Wilson had not run into a slump and falling prices in 1816? How much of Sam's success was due to the particular juxtaposition of his father's death and the upswing of the trade cycle in 1823? It is easy enough to talk of foresight or the ability to take advantage of circumstances or the creation of opportunities or flexibility of adaptation, and to say that these are the marks of successful enterprise. It is far less easy for the historian to find conclusive signs of their existence. Such things cannot be quantified and correlated with production curves or profit figures. So too readily he falls back, according to his own prejudices, upon either the blind forces of the market or upon the intelligent enterprise or idiot inaction of individual businessmen. Samuel Courtauld & Co. was not thrown into the crisis of the 1890s merely by the fumbling management of the partners any more than recovery was a simple tribute to their achievements. But if the sheer ubiquity of depression in the English economy is a guarantee against such assumptions, it should not act as a screen for the inertia and complacency of the men of the final partnership. After being sent on a three-day visit to silk factories in Macclesfield and Leek in November 1893, one of Samuel Courtauld & Co.'s assistant managers reported that 'we are far behind other throwsters and manufacturers in various processes at our mills'. The absence of serious dissent from this view, together with all the other evidence of sins of omission, makes it reasonably clear that something had long been wrong with the direction of the company. Who was to blame?

The obvious culprit was George Courtauld III. Though Harry Taylor and John Warren had both become partners at the same time as George III, the latter was not only slightly older but had had the longest experience in the business, having been working at Bocking since he was seventeen years old in 1847. Harry Taylor was entirely concerned with the selling side of the business, like his elder brother and his father before him; and there is no indication that John Warren either had any particular knowledge of the silk industry or was in any way connected with the

---

[1] E.R.O., D/F 3/2/38; D/F 3/3/69, pp. 115–16; and see below, pp. 187–8.

PLATE 16

GEORGE COURTAULD III (1830–1920), as a young man

manufacturing side of the business. John Warren's younger brother Thomas Pickard Warren II came in only in July 1888, and as a junior partner. George III's brother Sydney was some nine years younger than George and was also clearly a junior partner. He had an engineering training and seems to have pursued conscientiously, if unimaginatively, his technical responsibilities. George III, as the heir of a founding partner and eldest nephew of the celebrated Sam, clearly held the position, after Sam's death, of greatest seniority and responsibility. There is, however, a good deal of evidence to show not only that he fell foul of Sam but also that he was a reluctant businessman.

His indeed was the classical case of the second generation in business. Sam had seen the dangers and, in his customary fashion, had lectured his nephew on this subject in the course of a long letter in March 1856. 'It is not', he wrote to George III—whom he accused of degrading business life—'by any means to mere *money* gain so much as *success* in well-contrived and well-conducted action that our interest and satisfaction in our business is found; the money gain is a legitimate result, and no doubt enhances the interest and satisfaction; but it is not the spirit and soul of it, infinitely less is it the *measure* of it.'[1] He was both cogent and fervent on the subject of the fate of businesses through the generations and provided examples from the Peel family:

The parallel between the *inevitable* decline of energy in the life of an Individual Man, and the *ordinary* decline of a family or a business is not correct; the one *must* be, the other probably *may* be, but not of the same necessity; the one implies no neglect of advantages, no defect of will in the exercise of ableness, no moral failure: the other does.

The 'cause' of decline in a business, when it arises from the transference of the energy that had created it to other and higher purposes, may be 'beneficial', e.g. when Sir Robert Peel, the father, had energetically and successfully established a money making business, Sir Robert Peel the son, enabled by inherited wealth to devote his energetic labour to higher action, exemplified the 'beneficial' attributes of the changing phases of business prosperity. On the other hand when the inheritance of easy circumstances simply relaxes strenuous exertion in the affairs of ordinary business without applying the same strenuous exertion to higher purposes, then it is not beneficial; and this is what we see in the 1,000 cases of the history of families and of business enterprises.[2]

Here was Sam's own particular mix of moral ardour and exhortations to energy—similar in kind to that of his father but rather different in purpose and direction.

[1] G.C.B., p. 61.   [2] Ibid., pp. 58–59.

A few years later George got a lengthy homily on the iniquity of wishing to take a holiday of more than three weeks.[1] This was followed in 1864 by a long debate about whether he should remain in the business at all. George had been offered a Captaincy in the local Braintree Volunteers. Sam snarled about: '. . . your incipient disposition to give up business life altogether for the personal ease of what some persons call a gentleman's life upon a moderate competency . . .'.[2] George aired his grievance at not having been taken in as a partner, and promised to carry on in the business. But even after he had been a partner for some nine years and was still only 45 years of age, in 1875, he was hoping that 'matters will so arrange themselves that I shall leave business soon'.[3] In 1879 he wrote to his partners at Aldermanbury that he had decided to remain in the business.[4] By this time he was M.P. as well as J.P. His interests were increasingly in local affairs. He still wondered whether he should not have given up both business and Parliament and instead have settled down 'to work to do some little good (if I could) in the very humble but very real sphere of interests which lies around a man's own house and neighbourhood'.[5] He confessed, to his sister-in-law, Sydney Courtauld's wife, that twenty years earlier he had for a time been bent upon giving up the business and studying for the Unitarian ministry. In practice he lived the life of a prosperous, and increasingly orthodox, country gentleman, surrounded by a large family in a substantial house, Cut Hedge, near Gosfield, and becoming in the course of time the owner of some 3,000 near-by acres. There is plenty of indication that he was conscientious and kindly, that he inherited some of his father's qualities of neatness and order as well as his uncle's autocratic manner, but there is no indication at all that he ever brought to the family business any of those qualities of vigour, perception, intelligence, and enterprise without which it would never have existed.

The period of partnership of these three men, George Courtauld, Harry Taylor, and John Warren, largely coincided with the highest profits of a business which had been put where it was by the efforts of an earlier generation. The very rate of profits enabled them both to draw large incomes and to finance further investments in the same type of physical equipment as that which had served the firm faithfully for so long. There was nothing to tell them to invest in new lines, save the business imagination which they did not possess. So for the twenty years from 1871 to 1890 George III drew out of the

[1] G.C.B., pp. 127–30. [2] Ibid., pp. 134–40.
[3] Ibid., p. 222. [4] Ibid., p. 285. [5] Ibid., p. 288.

business an average income of nearly £23,000 per year, and the other two senior partners drew almost identical amounts. And for most of that time this highly lucrative business, slowly growing in size and slowly increasing its output, was becoming less and less prepared for the future.

CHAPTER IX

Recovery: New Men and New Fabrics

I

'THE Messrs. Courtaulds', wrote a journalist in 1891 in *The Textile Mercury*, 'are fabulously rich, though within recent years their concerns have been converted into a limited liability company—limited in the sense of numbers as well as of responsibility'.[1] The significance of this equivocal remark seems to lie in its hint of tight control and restricted access despite the change in legal form. As in so many of the then frequent conversions of partnerships into private joint-stock companies, this was largely true. Largely, but not wholly, for, as the following figures show, the ownership of the £400,000 ordinary capital of the new private company had been slightly extended outside the dominant men of the old partnership. In August 1891 the shares in Samuel Courtauld & Co. Ltd. were distributed as follows:

	£100 shares
George Courtauld III	959
John Warren	960
Sydney Courtauld	690
Thomas Pickard Warren II	690
Frederick Nettlefold	500
Henry Doughty Browne	200
Samuel Augustine Courtauld II	1
	4,000

The positions of George and Sydney Courtauld, John and Thomas P. Warren were virtually identical to what they had become after the death of Harry Taylor in 1890. They were not materially altered by George's transfer of one share to his eldest son Samuel Augustine, who, now aged 26, had been in the family business since September 1884.[2]

Frederick Nettlefold's entry into Samuel Courtauld & Co. followed a customary path delineated by family connexions. Brother-in-law to John and T. P. Warren II, he was thus also, through his mother-in-law,

---

[1] *The Textile Mercury*, vol. v (1891), p. 269.   [2] *G.C.B.*, p. 358.

tenuously connected to Samuel Courtauld himself[1] (see Figs. 17 and 25). But it also represented something quite different: the entry into this family silk firm, with its roots in London and Essex, of business experience derived from the different world of Birmingham and of hardware.[2] Frederick Nettlefold was the son of John Sutton Nettlefold, who, in the earlier nineteenth century, had an ironmongery business in London and later, with his brother-in-law Joseph Chamberlain, senior, had founded a very successful Birmingham screw-making concern. In 1874, when Joseph Chamberlain, politician and statesman-to-be and son of the founding Joseph, withdrew from the firm of Chamberlain and Nettlefold, Frederick Nettlefold, along with his elder brothers Edward and Joseph, was a partner in this business. In the 1880s, though director and, from 1883 to 1891, chairman of Nettlefolds Ltd., the company which succeeded the partnership, his interests turned more towards London, the locale of his wife's family and its connexions. At the time of his entry into Samuel Courtauld & Co. he was also a director of Nettlefold & Sons, wholesale ironmongers of London, the original Nettlefold family firm; although he remained a director of the Birmingham company until 1901 he had in effect ceased to be a Birmingham businessman and was no longer a director of the firm when it became part of the Guest, Keen & Nettlefold combine in 1904. His connexion with Courtaulds, however, remained both important and close until his death in 1913.

Henry Doughty Browne's links with the Courtauld family business were of a different nature. He was a stockbroker, a partner until 1883 in the City firm of Browne & Griffith. Samuel Courtauld & Co., seeking outlets for their surplus cash, found one such outlet in short-term loans to Browne & Griffith. A loan of £30,000 at 5 per cent., for example, was made in October to November 1881 and repaid in January 1882; £15,000 in January 1882 plus £10,000 in March was repaid in April. Sometimes the loans went on for longer terms: £20,000 was outstanding for most of 1883. During 1883 Browne apparently separated from his partner, but continued in business under his own name. Similar loans continued to be made to him by Samuel Courtauld & Co.[3] He was also a friend of Frederick Nettlefold. When, on the death of Harry Taylor, it was suggested that

[1] His mother-in-law was Sam Courtauld III's sister-in-law and first cousin.

[2] The following account of Frederick Nettlefold's connexions is based on J. L. Garvin, *Life of Joseph Chamberlain* (London, 1932), esp. vol. i, pp. 50–53, 171–4, C. A. Crofton, *The Nettlefolds* (1963), the *Stock Exchange Year Book* and *Directory of Directors*, and information kindly communicated by Mrs. B. M. D. Smith of Birmingham University.

[3] E.R.O., D/F 3/1/14.

Nettlefold should come into the business, he in turn brought in Browne. None of the Courtaulds at this time, George III, Sydney, or Samuel Augustine, held any directorships outside their family firm. But both Nettlefold and John Warren had business interests in companies with which Browne was also concerned. Browne's business interests were in no way connected with textiles. He held directorships in a large number of railway and mining companies, in Britain, the U.S.A., and South America. From 1883 until his death in 1907 he was Chairman of the London, Tilbury and Southend Railway, a company of which John Warren was a director from 1888 to 1893 and deputy chairman from then until 1905. It was presumably Browne's financial and stockbroking activities which had given him directorships in such companies as the Buenos Ayres Northern Railway (of which Frederick Nettlefold was a director from 1886 to 1897), the River Plate and General Investment Trust, and Anglo-Argentine Tramways, not to speak of the chairmanship of the Alabama Great Southern Railway Co. Ltd.

The six main shareholders in Samuel Courtauld & Co. Ltd. were the directors of the company. T. P. Warren took on the job of managing director; George and Sydney Courtauld, as the Bocking directorate, were responsible for the manufacturing end of the business. As the temporary revival of 1890–1 came to an end the Board anxiously addressed itself to the problems which became so menacing in 1892–3. To the attempts to expand the production and sale of colours, or the tentative buying of new types of looms were added such measures as putting the hands on half-time and reducing the numbers employed, cuts in certain managerial salaries, and 'a great reduction in the style of dinners at Aldermanbury'.[1] In February 1893 the new mill at Braintree was shut down. Chelmsford mill, closed in 1889 and reopened in April 1890, was closed again and for the last time in October 1892; in November 1893 it was sold for £1,500. In the summer of 1892 Nettlefold put before the Board a scheme for the financial reorganization of the company by reducing the ordinary share capital from £400,000 to £300,000 and issuing £100,000 debentures at 4 per cent. It is a measure of what was happening that by the time reorganization was accepted in the autumn of the following year, the debentures were at 5 per cent. and the ordinary share capital was reduced not by 25 per cent. but by 50 per cent. (see above, Table 22, p. 154). Nettlefold, T. P. Warren, and Browne were the directors mainly respon-

[1] E.R.O., D/F 3/3/24, pp. 85–90; D/F 3/2/81, pp. 162–3.
[2] E.R.O., D/F 3/2/83; D/F 3/2/39, p. 37.

PLATE 17

b. THOMAS PICKARD WARREN (1837–1915)

a. FREDERICK NETTLEFOLD (1833–1913)

sible for this change. It was Nettlefold and especially T. P. Warren who also seem to have been the prime forces behind a move which, perhaps more than any other single thing done at this time of crisis, indicates how serious and intractable that crisis must have seemed to the Board. For in 1893, in order to secure textile experience of a high quality, the company went outside the family circles, outside the crape trade, outside London and East Anglia, and brought in that experience at top management level and with the promise of a directorship.

On 30 May 1893 a man called Henry Greenwood Tetley called to see T. P. Warren at Aldermanbury. Presumably, though not certainly, he called in response to inquiries made by the company. Tetley, then aged 42, was at that time head of the silk manufacturing department at Manningham Mills, having been working for Lister & Co. for some twenty-two years. He was interviewed by the Board on 22 June and shortly afterwards visited the mills on more than one occasion. In July T. P. Warren and Nettlefold were discussing remuneration with him and Warren was writing to Lord Masham and others for testimonials. But on 20 July, before the latter were received, Warren wrote a revealing letter to Sydney Courtauld:

. . . Tetley has just left us and F. N. [i.e. Frederick Nettlefold] and I have arranged with him so far as to have a preliminary understanding on the points talked over which makes his coming to us practically certain. . . . I believe he is the man for us. . . .

P.S. I may tell you that we mentioned that our finish had been bad as an element in the falling off in trade which we hope to remedy. . . .

In October 1893 Tetley started work at a salary of £2,000 plus a commission on profits above a specified level. In February 1895, 'according to his agreement', he was made a director of the company.

Tetley had obviously been brought in to repair and reorganize the manufacturing end of the business. His appointment apparently owed much to T. P. Warren and to Nettlefold, two men who were little identified with Bocking and the old partnership. Whatever may have been the opinions of George and Sydney Courtauld, they can hardly have looked upon with pleasure, or regarded as a happy necessity, this intrusion into what had always been the family stronghold. George III tried to see to it that a balance between family and outsider should be maintained. Tetley's appointment was formally as *Joint* Head Manager with Samuel Augustine Courtauld; and, in accordance with an agreement between

George III and the company in May 1894, Samuel Augustine, now with two ordinary shares, was made a director in December of that year. Despite the apparent equality of status, their respective salaries reflected the difference in age and experience. After 1893 George III's attendances at Board meetings became less and less frequent. He had virtually retired from the business; which, after all, was what he had been hoping to do for many years.

The modernization of the manufacturing end of the business was not the only necessary change in the new circumstances of crisis. As competition grew fiercer, markets changed, and the company stepped up its output of coloured fabrics, the selling end, the world of Aldermanbury, also needed a new broom. On 9 June 1893 T. P. Warren wrote formally to the Board to resign the salary of £1,000 a year which he received as managing director. He observed that in so doing he also ended 'whatever moral obligation I may now be under to give more time and attention to the business than any of my colleagues can be called upon to bestow'. At its meeting six days later, the Board accepted this resignation, commenting that 'the circumstances of the business now require a manager at Aldermanbury with such a wide knowledge of the silk trade as shall enable him to push the various articles the Company are now in a position to manufacture'. In December of the same year Tetley—not yet a director—reported to the Board that, in accordance with the suggestion of the Board, he had interviewed T. P. Latham with a view to ascertaining whether he would be inclined to accept the position of Sales Manager at Aldermanbury. Thomas Paul Latham, then aged 38, was the company's agent at Manchester. He had formerly represented Lister & Co. both in Manchester and in New York and was therefore almost certainly known to Tetley. Tetley was requested to communicate further with Latham. In January 1894, after an interview with Nettlefold, T. P. Warren, and Sydney Courtauld, Latham was appointed Sales Manager at Aldermanbury at a salary of £1,250 per annum plus an annual commission of ¾ per cent. on all business in excess of that of 1893. Five years later, in April 1898, he became a director.[1] The value of the company's sales in 1898 was 75 per cent. greater than in 1893.

These two men, H. G. Tetley and T. P. Latham, were to dominate the direction of the company for the next twenty-five years. More will be said of them, of their characters and achievements, in Volume II. Meanwhile,

---

[1] Samuel Courtauld & Co. paid Lister & Co. £50 to release Latham from his Manchester agency.

however, let it be emphasized that the reasons which led to this transformation of a family business, a transformation which their ascendancy typified, lay in the depression and crisis of 1886–96. New men with experience outside the world of Bocking and crape, unhampered by close connexions with the founding families and emerging from different social environments: these were vital ingredients of change and recovery. The principle proved itself true of many businesses other than Samuel Courtauld & Co. during this testing period for British industry, as it found that the cushioned comforts of mid-Victorian economic ease had gone. The arrival of Nettlefold, T. P. Warren, and Browne marked the beginning of change. Tetley and Latham were the essential complements, for—and this was particularly true of Tetley—their appointments helped to bring back to the firm the sense of urgency and purpose which Sam Courtauld had himself provided in the earlier years. Of course, the same difficulties arise in trying to assess the responsibility for recovery as for decline. If George Courtauld III and the men of the old partnership were borne down by the weight of general depression, so were their successors helped to float upwards on the bigger wave of returning national prosperity. But not all firms did recover. And there is a good deal of evidence to suggest that the hand of Tetley—a rather choleric and violent man whose vigour was greater than his popularity—was to be seen in many of the changes that took place in north Essex.

II

The process of adjusting the company's weaving capacity was carried another small step further in August 1893 with the ordering of two 4/4 looms for crape weaving, specially designed by Hattersley & Son of Keighley. Built with a stronger framing than the Courtauld loom, they would run appreciably faster.[1] Such measures as these were still somewhat tentative. With the arrival of Tetley changes of a rather different order started to happen. Hattersley & Son were given orders for forty-eight circular box looms, and in February 1894 Finney and Tetley were planning their location at Halstead; by October they had all been installed. These were multi-purpose looms and thus quite different from the old Courtauld looms. In November Tetley suggested to the Board the erection of a new weaving shed at Halstead big enough to hold 200 wide looms, so as to increase the firm's ability to manufacture light silk goods and silk and wool

[1] E.R.O., D/F 3/2/84, pp. 79–81.

mixtures. The Board approved the building, though it decided that only part of it should be fitted up for the present. But in June 1895, Hattersleys were sent an order for 112 looms for the new weaving shed.[1] Already Samuel Augustine Courtauld was reporting that 'the organization at Halstead is slowly becoming smarter, and the turnout from the looms is improving'. In the course of 1894–5 a large number of Courtauld looms were at last fitted with automatic stop mechanisms in the shape of weft forks. Further funds for the new weaving shed were approved in December 1895; and in 1896, as the Hattersley looms were coming in only slowly, eighty-six second-hand Hodgson circular box looms were obtained from a mill in Bradford.[2] By 1898, of the 1,000 or so looms at Halstead, about 740 were Courtauld looms modified in various ways and 260 Hattersley or Hodgson looms, many of which were fitted with Jacquards for pattern weaving.[3] Meanwhile Tetley had been busying himself with such matters as the number of looms actually running at any one moment. In November 1896 he informed the Halstead mill manager that he had calculated that on average 60 per cent. were standing as against 40 per cent. running, and that this order should be the other way round: '60 per cent. of our looms running . . . is the lowest percentage we should admit of', wrote Tetley, '. . . until we begin to see some decided step towards it—I shall not be able to admit that we are making real progress in our weaving'. By 1898 the desired order of percentages had been obtained.[4]

Re-equipment and reorganization in weaving were paralleled by similar moves in other stages of manufacture. In 1894–5 new warping and spool-winding machinery, for example, was ordered, at Tetley's instigation, from firms in Bradford and Macclesfield; and in 1896 five more warping machines were obtained, this time from a firm in Connecticut, U.S.A. Some new winding engines were bought from Macclesfield in November 1893, and directives about changes in winding procedures were soon being sent out from Bocking to the other mills.[5] In 1896 Braintree mill was extended and more winding machinery installed there, including some bought from Lord Rothschild's lately defunct silk mill at Tring, Hertfordshire.[6] Throwing seems to have been one of the few processes for which it was not necessary to order substantially new types of machinery. Indeed

[1] E.R.O., D/F 3/2/84, pp. 149, 167, 171; D/F 3/2/86, pp. 61, 94.
[2] E.R.O., D/F 3/3/24, pp. 53–54; D/F 3/2/83.
[3] E.R.O., D/F 3/3/24, pp. 231–8.
[4] Ibid., p. 236.
[5] E.R.O., D/F 3/2/84, p. 119; D/F 3/2/85, p. 131; D/F 3/3/24, pp. 109–11.
[6] E.R.O., D/F 3/2/87, p. 78.

in 1902, according to Samuel Augustine, 'after investigation in England as well as on the Continent we can find nothing so good as our own crape spinning mills which have been in use for so many years in Essex'. But as recovery got under way and the output of chiffon and *crêpe de Chine* was increased, from about 1897 a shortage of throwing capacity became more and more apparent; by the turn of the century some winding, cleaning, and throwing was having to be done outside on commission. So new mills were put in, old ones repaired and re-erected. In the course of this the decision was made to carry out all the throwing at Braintree. Old crape mills at Bocking, stopped in 1894 and subsequently shifted to the old mill at Halstead, were in 1897 and 1899 moved to Braintree. Water-power at the old, original Halstead mill was now quite insufficient, whilst at Braintree there was ample power from the then newly installed gas engines (see below, pp. 188–90). Accordingly yet another extension was built there, and opened in 1903.[1]

This concentration of throwing at Braintree was part of a general relocation of activities which was gradually carried out during the later 1890s. Warping and weaving were concentrated at Halstead, with a small outpost at Earls Colne where looms were set up in 1897. Weaving at Braintree was discontinued to allow the winding and throwing to be done there, though some drawing and doubling was still done at Halstead. The old winding engines formerly at Chelmsford were brought to Braintree in 1894; and winding was given up at Earls Colne in 1898.[2] Bocking, still the administrative headquarters of all the factories, concentrated entirely upon the complex of finishing processes as well as its engineering activities. Communication between the factories was simplified by the installation of telephones from 1894 onwards, and by the acquisition of motor vans (made by Benz) in 1901. In 1903 Bocking reported that 'the last two horses have now been sold . . .'.

At Bocking re-equipment was pushed along vigorously. At Tetley's instigation new materials, methods, and machines were introduced into the dyeing both of colours and of the traditional black. Stenters and jiggers made their appearance in 1894–5; substantial extensions to the dye-house, with a particular view to colour-dyeing, were made in 1901–2.[3] Not all of Tetley's suggestions were successful. In 1894 he persuaded the Board to authorize the acquisition of a drying machine for drying crape in

[1] E.R.O., D/F 3/2/85, pp. 115, 117; D/F 3/2/87, pp. 146, 152, 161.
[2] E.R.O., D/F 3/3/24, *passim.*
[3] E.R.O., D/F 3/2/85, pp. 43, 178; D/F 3/2/86, p. 87.

continuous lengths; but in 1895 it had proved thoroughly unsatisfactory, the suppliers took it away, and a settlement had to be negotiated. Meanwhile, in the course of this abortive installation, the suppliers' manager fell out with the now rather aged engineer, James Finney, and told him, *inter alia*, that Samuel Courtauld & Co. were 'quite behind other people as was evident by our turn out and the number of people employed'.[1] It was a shrewd blow: productivity certainly had to be improved. But so also had the quality of the finish.

So a major onslaught was directed at the crimping machinery and the techniques of dressing and finishing. Old crimping machines were scrapped, and new machines ordered. An experimental crimping room was approved in July 1894; plans for a new crimping room were put to the Board by Sydney Courtauld in July 1895 and approved. The move from the old into the new room, duly made secret, was completed a year later and work began on the thirty-two crimping machines installed there.[2] For experiments in dressing and finishing, new chemical equipment was needed: so a new laboratory was built in 1896. New machinery for dressing and waterproofing crape was purchased in 1894 from a Manchester firm. Although reasonable success was obtained in this old problem of waterproofing, further trials and improvements continued to be made.[3] Success also blessed the search for a means to a better crape finish. Much of this came as a result of the work of a chemist from Glasgow, named Alexander Guthrie, who was appointed in May 1893. Apparently at the instigation of Sydney Courtauld, he developed, in the course of 1894, a new method of finishing gauzes which permitted a lowering of costs and thus facilitated the sale of cheaper sorts of crape.[4] In what came to be known as 'B make' goods the gauzes were mainly woven of cheap unthrown Bengal silk; the silk was 'put ... to work just as it comes to use',[5] unsorted and uncleaned; the gauzes were dyed before crimping, and were then subjected to a dressing of which the basis was shellac.[6] This advance, however, affected only the 'lower end' of the crape trade, and much work continued to be done to improve the finish of the better quality 'A make'

---

[1] E.R.O., D/F 3/2/85, pp. 31, 127, 147, 157, 181; D/F 3/2/86, pp. 5, 26, 42–43, 46.

[2] E.R.O., D/F 3/2/80, pp. 57, 59, 61, 70, 71, 101; D/F 3/2/86, pp. 87, 101, 135, 168; D/F 3/2/87, p. 52.

[3] E.R.O., D/F 3/2/80, pp. 27, 73.

[4] E.R.O., D/F 3/2/110, pp. 53–55; D/F 3/2/111, pp. 128–9, 141–5, 175.

[5] E.R.O., D/F 3/3/24, p. 66.

[6] E.R.O., D/F 3/2/92, p. 43; and information kindly supplied by Mr. W. H. Nankivell, Mr. Thomas Rayner, and Mr. A. Yeldham.

goods. Various lines of attack were followed. The Norwich Crape Co.'s products continued to fascinate Samuel Courtauld & Co. In 1893 and again in 1899 the idea was entertained of buying shares in that company, but nothing came of it. Instead in 1895-6 Guthrie busied himself with analysing the Norwich Crape Co.'s products; an engraver was set to work on a roll to imitate one of their much-praised figures. This was followed by further imitation of another of their figures, said to sell well in Paris; and in September 1898 by the acquisition of a crimper from the Norwich Crape Co. who revealed his former employers' process of crimping. A finishing machine constructed on the Norwich model was ordered and set up at Bocking, and experiments continued in November and December 1898.[1] Meanwhile Guthrie's new assistant at the Finishing Factory, W. P. Dreaper, who had been taken on from Joseph Grout & Sons in November 1896, made trials with methods of single crimping instead of the double crimping which had been noted earlier as productive of so much waste and bad finishing. He seems to have put his experience at Grouts to good use and in the course of 1897-8 his experiments succeeded. Thereafter, much of the 'A make' was crimped in this way, improved methods of dressing these crapes were developed, and by the turn of the century there seems to have been a general improvement.

At the same time as Dreaper was working on the problem of crimping, he also began to work, under the direction of Sydney Courtauld in 1897, at the old problem, previously abandoned, of the electrolytic reproduction of the crimping rolls. The outcome of this work was both success and trouble. For it resulted in a legal action which illustrates the problem of linking secrecy clauses with possibly patentable work.

In 1899 Sydney died. Guthrie had already taken over the practical management of the whole crape finishing business, and he continued the supervision of Dreaper's work. By 1900 the trials seem to have been successful. Several rolls had been reproduced by an electrotyping process, and Samuel Augustine Courtauld was reporting enthusiastically to the Board: '... the immense advantage of this system of ... reproducing good rolls ... is obvious, and it is both economical and more speedy than the usual method of engraving'. Some difficulties were later encountered, but Dreaper, after being given a special bonus of £50 in 1901, was taken on for a further three years in December 1902 as 'experimental chemist'. In July 1904, just as Samuel Courtauld & Co. Ltd. had announced its intention of going to the public, Dreaper sent the company a letter announcing his

[1] E.R.O., D/F 3/2/114, pp. 16, 20, 27, 66.

application for a provisional patent for the electrotyping process; he offered to sell the invention to the company for £10,000, being two years of what he alleged to be the value of the use of the process to the company, i.e. £5,000. When he had joined the company in 1896, Dreaper had signed a secrecy clause.[1] On the advice of counsel, Samuel Courtauld & Co. dismissed Dreaper in August 1904. Dreaper then sued the company for wrongful dismissal. The case was heard in King's bench, before a judge and special jury in October 1905, and Dreaper won, being awarded £599. 14s. 11d. damages. There seems to be no doubt that Dreaper did bring some knowledge of the process from Grout & Co.; on the other hand, he evidently had assistance at Courtauld & Co.'s expense from an outside expert. The provisional patent remained void, as the specification was never filed. The company admitted that the process had been valuable and had been in use for some years past. Counsel's opinion, given to the company after the judgement, was that it could continue to use the process; that the judge's summing up had been unsatisfactory especially in giving prominence to 'the weakest part of the Defendants case viz the violation of the secrecy clause'; and that they considered 'the successful result of a motion for a new trial a matter of doubt'. Samuel Courtauld & Co. paid up. It was probably a small price to pay.

Throwing and winding, warping and weaving, crimping, engraving, and dressing: all had been reformed in one way or another and to varying degrees. One technical reform of general application remains to be considered: power. In 1892 a total of nineteen steam engines of sundry patterns, sizes, and horse-power were doing their various jobs at Bocking, Braintree, Halstead, Chelmsford, and Earls Colne. They included four beam engines dating from the 1840s and 1850s; one of these, at the old mill at Halstead, was used only when water-power there was inadequate. Braintree had two Corliss steam engines installed in 1876 as well as a water turbine.[2]

Until about 1860 no engines existed, other than the steam engine, capable of working continuously for industrial purposes. In the next two decades, however, pioneer work mainly in France and Germany resulted in the development of the gas engine. Under the patents of the German engineer N. A. Otto (1832–91), Crossley Bros. of Manchester began to

---

[1] It read: 'I promise, whether I remain in the service of Messrs. S. Courtauld & Co. Ltd. or whether I leave it, never to impart to any person or persons information as to such processes or machinery as I may be acquainted with in the factories of Messrs. S. Courtauld & Co. Ltd., or during the time of my being employed by them.' For other aspects of Dreaper's career, see Vol. II, Chapter I.

[2] E.R.O., D/F 3/2/61, p. 65; D/F 3/2/81, p. 87; D/F 3/2/83, 25 August 1892; D/F 3/2/30.

produce large numbers of gas engines in this country.[1] In 1882 Finney made inquiries about Crossley engines,[2] but, as usual, nothing was done until emergencies began to call for economies. Ten years later a tentative start was made with the installation in September 1892 of one gas engine at Halstead.[3] But in 1894, after Finney had been dispatched to some mills in Halifax to see Crossley engines at work and had visited Crossley's works at Manchester, the Board decided to re-equip Halstead with Crossley engines.[4] As was also not uncommon at the time, a gas-making plant was also installed, for it was calculated to be cheaper to run the engines on this home-produced gas rather than off the town main. In the next three years there was a wholesale scrapping of steam engines and a corresponding rush to put in gas engines and gas-making plant. In 1896 and 1897, ten steam engines were sold or broken up; in March 1896 twelve gas engines, of various makes, were at work, six at Halstead, four at Bocking, and two at Braintree.[5] Three steam engines were left at work, and there was an oil engine introduced into the dye-house in 1894, initially to drive the jiggers, but ultimately to drive all the dye-house machinery.[6] Pleasure at the cost reduction secured by gas instead of steam was soon being expressed. 'Large economies are being made by the gas engines', reported Samuel Augustine in February 1896. At Braintree the expected saving was calculated at 16s. 4d. per ten-hour day or £229. 1s. 6d. for fifty-one weeks.[7] The scrapping of the existing steam engines not merely cost money but also demanded the mental adjustment of learning to abandon long-tried and once successful machinery. Too many British businessmen failed to make such an adjustment at this period of our industrial history. What disposing of some of the old steam engines meant in money to Samuel Courtauld & Co. may be illustrated by the chance survival of the following figures:[8]

Engine	Mill	Date bought	Cost price	Valuation at 1 Jan. 1894	Selling price in 1896
1 pair beam engines	Bocking	1845 and 1847	£660	£165	£15
1 pair beam engines	Halstead	1850 and pre-1850	£990	£100	£32. 10s.
1 pair horizontal engines	Steam Factory	1871	£300	£75	£50

[1] *Hist. Tech.*, vol. v, pp. 155–60.　　　　[2] E.R.O., D/F 3/2/67, p. 11.
[3] E.R.O., D/F 3/2/83, 22 September 1892.　　[4] E.R.O., D/F 3/2/84, pp. 175–82.
[5] E.R.O., D/F 3/2/30; D/F 3/2/83 and 85, *passim*; D/F 3/3/24. Of the twelve gas engines, five were Tangye engines, four Stockport, and three Crossley.
[6] E.R.O., D/F 3/2/85, p. 12.　　　　[7] E.R.O., D/F 3/2/87, pp. 43, 45.
[8] E.R.O., D/F 3/2/30; D/F 3/2/85, p. 55.

The massive, not to say precipitate, investment in gas engines was not, however, wholly sensible and satisfactory. For they proved inappropriate prime movers for power-looms. When another and major extension to weaving capacity was made at Halstead in 1903, the gas engines were replaced by a new and better steam engine, and soon the 1895 extension was also operated by this engine. In November 1904 Bocking reported to London on the improved weaving 'consequent upon the steadier drive of the steam engine compared with the gas engines'. A nice irony, but the moral is not obvious. Suffice to say that the rush to buy gas engines seems to have been one of Tetley's less perceptive moves.

The carrying out of all these measures of technical reform was obviously spurred along by Tetley more than by anyone else. One should not, however, overlook the contributions of Sydney Courtauld and the engineer James Finney. There are signs that they had some awareness of the firm's technical problems and shortcomings and were informed on what was going on in the outside world of textile engineering. So it seems reasonable to suppose that earlier re-equipment, before crisis made it imperative, was probably frustrated by the inertia of senior partners and directors rather than hindered by any ignorance or incompetence on the part of Sydney Courtauld and the faithful Finney. But if ultimately it needed the new men at the top to ensure recovery, so also were replacements found at lower levels of management and supervision. In the course of the 1890s most of the older managers, and many of those in similar positions, went. Some died, some retired or resigned with varying degrees of freewill. After the death of one Halstead manager in 1892 his successor was pensioned off (with a gratuity of £500) in 1899. The Finishing Factory manager left in 1893; his former assistant resigned in 1896; death or resignation took away two chief engravers and one other between 1891 and 1897. James Finney, a member of the Bocking staff since 1853, finally retired at the age of 72 in 1898 (with a pension of £300 a year and an understanding that the company would call on him from time to time for advice). The chief salesman at Aldermanbury (a nephew of Harry Taylor), left in 1894 on being told of Latham's appointment; the Chelmsford manager was given notice when that factory closed; the Braintree manager was sacked in 1895. The list could be continued. More important to note, however, is that many replacements came, not from inside, but, echoing the changes at the top, from outside. Assistant managers came to Halstead from Lister & Co., Bradford, and from Macclesfield. On the Braintree manager losing his job in September 1895 his place was taken by a new man, Henry Johnson from Macclesfield, who had been appointed assistant manager only in June of that year. This appointment arose directly from an inquiry made by Samuel Courtauld & Co. of William Johnson, a small Macclesfield silk throwster with whom the firm had dealings. His own trade being poor, William Johnson recommended his son who worked for him. In January 1896, 'Mr. Johnson the new manager there gives us great satisfaction'; in 1914 he was to become a director of Courtaulds Ltd. Engravers were recruited from the Birmingham and Coventry areas;[1] in 1897 foremen and overseers of weaving were engaged from the north of England deliberately to 'strengthen the Halstead staff'; clerks and dyers alike were obtained from Bradford and Manchester.

So in the course of about a decade or so, the existing plant, the staff, the management, and the directorate of Samuel Courtauld & Co. changed. So, too, did its output and the direction of its sales.

III

In July 1893 T. P. Warren told Tetley, in the course of negotiations about the latter's appointment, 'We think you under-estimate the probability of an increase in the profits of our crape trade in 1894'. Fig. 24 indicates the course of recovery, in crapes and in colours, for the final decade of the private company 1893–1903. It illustrates, implicitly, how wrong Warren was; and it reveals explicitly the striking contribution to recovery made by the sale of coloured fabrics.

In 1894, the company's crape sales, in Europe and at home, collapsed; a loss was made. Home crape sales tumbled still further in the other loss year, 1896, though European sales were now reviving. Thereafter the noteworthy fact about the company's crape sales is the falling share of home demand. Even in the great revival year, 1899, when Samuel Courtauld & Co. Ltd. made and sold more packets of crape than ever before, not only was the total value 22 per cent. less than in the last five years of previous prosperity 1881–5, but 65 per cent., by value, of those 1899 crape sales were overseas. In 1893 the proportion had been completely reversed: 65 per cent. of crape sales, by value, had been in the U.K. Much of the recovery was obviously in the expansion of sales of the cheaper 'B make' tapping lower social reaches of the mourning market, and at the same time regaining ground lost to competitors. In March 1896 Latham told the Board about the 'great competition in the crape trade', and it authorized

---

[1] E.R.O., D/F 3/2/80, pp. 90–93, 97, 98, 148, etc.

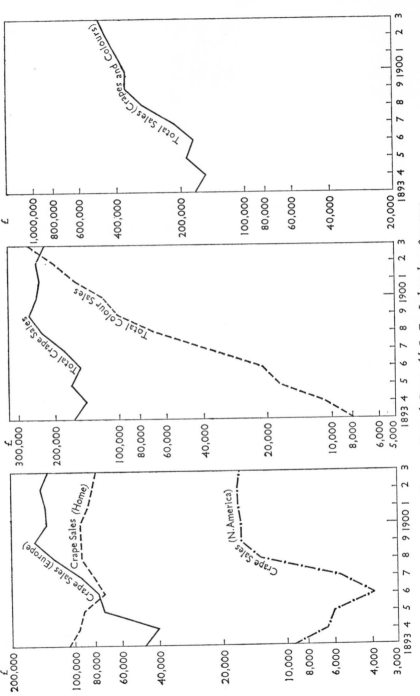

FIG. 24. *Samuel Courtauld & Co. Ltd.: sales, 1893–1903*

him to reduce prices at his own discretion 'in order to maintain the business and increase sales'. Success enabled him to raise crape selling prices by 5 per cent. in October 1899. The increase in overseas crape sales was all the more remarkable in view of the stiffening of tariff barriers. The increase in the company's European crape sales, despite tariffs of 6 to 10 per cent. in France and 25 to 30 per cent. in Germany, contrasts with the woes expressed to the Tariff Commission in 1905 by both the Norwich Crape Co. and by Francis Hinde & Son.[1]

Success was again, in part, a tribute to the new and cheaper make of crape; but it also owed something to the new administration tackling the selling side of the firm and in particular to its vigorous efforts to revive the company's export business. Marketing was done partly through direct sales to London wholesale and shipping firms, partly through agents working on commission. The Manchester and Glasgow agents normally received in the 1890s a commission of $2\frac{1}{2}$ per cent. on crapes, $1\frac{1}{2}$ on colours. Exclusive agencies and guaranteed minima were also sometimes negotiated: the Manchester agent was to undertake no other crape agency and had a guaranteed minimum raised to £300 per annum in 1894. Overseas terms varied, but the usual commission, paid in Paris, Berlin, and Belgium, was 3 per cent. The importance of the Paris trade is reflected in a guaranteed minimum of £1,000, raised to £1,500 per annum in 1899. The Paris trade was indeed the subject of particular efforts, for France was by far the largest of the foreign markets, taking in general around 60 per cent. of all the company's European crape sales. From 1891 onwards Nettlefold and T. P. Warren, Tetley, and Latham, exercised themselves in preparing and revising arrangements with the company's new French agent. Tetley, visiting Paris in February 1894, wrote to the Board, which declared itself as 'much impressed with the contents of the letter and fully recognised the serious position in our Paris trade'. In April he departed to the continent of Europe with a catalogue of selling matters to investigate for the Board. He reported on visits to Frankfurt, Cologne, Vienna, Warsaw, and Berlin. In the course of the next few years agencies were started, continued, or revised for Austria, Germany, Switzerland, Italy, Belgium, Russia, Denmark, Sweden, Norway, Holland, Spain, and Portugal. In all these countries, as well as France, increases in crape exports were registered during the period under review.

So they were, too, across the Atlantic, though the South American agency proved of very minor value, and Canada showed no marked

---

[1] *Report of the Tariff Commission*, vol. ii, part 6, paras. 3500, 3501.

enthusiasm for crape. The U.S. market was the subject of special inquiry. W. G. Hitchcock, of New York, had been selling Samuel Courtauld & Co.'s crape since 1854. Tetley visited him in America in October 1895 and reported that Hitchcock 'has been considered the highest authority on crape in the American market, and it has evidently become a fixed principle with him that it is his duty to devote the remainder of his active business life, which he reckons on as lasting till January 1900, to doing everything that can be done towards bringing the sales of crape up to a high figure'. The company's sale to the U.S. had dropped sharply in 1894 (see Fig. 24). Hitchcock put up a scheme whereby Samuel Courtauld & Co. would contribute towards the capital cost of a retail establishment in New York entirely devoted to mourning, 'just as Jay's does, or at any rate used to do in London'. Tetley reported on this plan and gave it a cautious blessing, observing rather desperately: 'if we take this step, and it does not bring back our crape trade, then nothing can bring it back'. Though some details were secured of a possible store in Fifth Avenue it was decided in April 1896 not to take part in the scheme. The enthusiastic Hitchcock, however, had gone ahead, and in February 1897, Latham, acknowledging photographs of his 'Retail Mourning Establishment' in New York, congratulated him on his 'heroic and supreme efforts to revive the fashion for crape in the United States'. But though after 1896 the tide temporarily turned, the depression had been too much for Hitchcock and his firm failed in October 1897. Latham promptly sailed for New York and negotiated an agreement with the prosperous firm of Briggs, Priestley & Sons for the distribution of the company's goods in the U.S.A. But the ever-increasing tariff barriers, reaching a new high level with the Dingley tariff of 1897, made sales in the U.S.A. very difficult; in 1901 the company was complaining of the 'almost insuperable difficulties in the way of trade with the States'. Even in recovery, crape sales in the U.S.A. were never more than about 6 per cent. of the company's total crape sales.

The flattening in the curve of crape sales in the U.S. market after 1899 is also visible in European sales. But at least there was no really marked fall in total overseas crape sales. In the home market, on the other hand, recovery had been slower and slighter; and after 1899, as Fig. 24 shows, the curve of the company's U.K. crape sales began clearly to turn downwards. In 1903 the home market share of the total value of crape sales was only 31 per cent. The change in mourning fashions during the last decade or so was now making itself felt. Samuel Courtauld & Co. now dominated the crape market, but all its efforts could do little to reverse the trend in fashion. The efforts were real.

In November 1893 the Board resolved to spend £1,000 per annum on advertising. Henry Muller was appointed advertising agent. Soon he was busy with such public relations matters as keeping in with *The Queen*; ensuring that a paragraph about the visit to the company's factories of the Countess of Warwick appeared in *The Queen*; arranging for a reporter from *The Queen* (rather than from *Our Work*, 'a respectable paper but circulating in a lower class of society than *The Queen*') to go down to the factories and write a special article about them. John Warren was assured by that keen crape devotee, W. G. Hitchcock, that *The Queen* was 'the most influential paper in New York'. Year after year the £1,000 annual expenditure on advertising, as well as Muller's appointment, was renewed; agent and appropriation were both still the same in 1903. Additional sums were voted in October 1894 to send 'mourning books' to Hitchcock in New York and to Marshall & Snelgrove in London; and an extra £250 was spent on advertising the merits of crape in conjunction with Jay's. No longer was it possible to rely on traditional ritual, on the magic of Court fashion. Now demand had to be worked for. Softer finishes were given to the crape to conform with the changing trend in women's fashions prevalent at the end of the century.[1] With the aid of that indefatigable spokesman for the English silk interest, Thomas (later Sir Thomas) Wardle (of Wardle & Sons, Leek), the Funeral Reform Association was persuaded to omit from one of its publications certain passages recommending the disuse of crape. The advertising appropriation was increased again in March 1897, by £250, so that 250 sets, consisting of framed photographs of the Queen and of the Princess Beatrice, together with a card showing the etiquette of mourning, could be ordered for distribution to wholesale customers and to the larger retailers. Presumably the Princess's early subjection to crape (above, p. 131) had ranged her alongside her mother as, so to speak, a pro-crape royal party, as against the anti-crape views of the Prince and Princess of Wales. At the end of 1898 Latham arranged for the insertion in trade journals of a statement that in that year Samuel Courtauld & Co. had made and sold more crape than in any other year of the firm's history. Muller got a bonus of fifty guineas for his 'special services' to the company on the death of Queen Victoria in

---

[1] See below; one of the company's brochures *circa* 1902 spoke of its crape being 'of a soft draping character. Such crape', it continued, 'is being used in conjunction with the soft clinging fabrics now so largely worn.'

January 1901. Finally, the last effort by the greatest crape firm of a great crape-using reign: Samuel Courtauld & Co. in May 1901 applied for a Royal Warrant. The company claimed to be the largest makers of crape, not only in England but in the world, and to have the bulk of the highest class of trade in crape throughout Europe and America; Exhibition awards were listed; it was stated that Queen Victoria was 'in the habit of wearing our crapes'. The Lord Chamberlain rejected the application on the ground that the company was not now 'supplying goods habitually to her Majesty'. A letter was produced from the royal dressmaker to support the company's claim. But it was all too late. The reign of Queen Crape was over.

The major contribution of coloured fabrics to the company's renewed prosperity was finally sealed in 1903 when, as Fig. 24 shows, the value of coloured sales exceeded that of crape sales. In 1896 crape had accounted for 88 per cent. and colours 12 per cent. of the value of total sales; the equivalent proportions for 1903 were crape 45 per cent. and colours 55 per cent. By 1905 colours had also surpassed crape in the number of packets produced. In this success the home market was all-important. The company's overseas sales of colours showed some increases in the course of the 1890s, but by the turn of the century remained generally sluggish. In contrast, home sales of colours, growing rapidly in absolute terms, accounted in 1903 for 83 per cent. by value of all colour sales.

If fashion was unkind to Samuel Courtauld & Co. in the slow death of crape, it was kind in another way. For the re-equipment of the company with a view, in part at least, to making fabrics other than mourning crape got under way just at the time that fashion moved in an advantageous direction. Of 1897 it has been said by a great authority on English women's fashions of the Victorian age:

This year introduced a change of style so complete as almost to amount to a new conception. The notion which had prevailed for some years, seemed to have been that the dress should have a clean cut motive, a hard surface, and a distracting colour scheme, conveying a sense of harsh resistance and solidity. The new conception was that the dress should be fluffy and frilly, undulating in movement with ripples of soft foam appearing at the feet; colours harmonising with each other, surfaces broken with flimsy trimmings and revealing submerged depths of tone. The softened outlines, willowy and slender, created the illusion that these very habitations must be occupied by beings composed of stuff less solid than flesh and blood. It was the old 'feminine mystery' but in a new setting.[1]

----

[1] Cunnington, op. cit., p. 402.

Clouds of chiffon, yards and yards of soft China *crêpe* of one sort or another: these were now in demand. Already in 1894 'chiffon [was] much used, and Courtauld's new silk crêpe'.[1] Samuel Augustine reported from Bocking in June 1896 that 'we are constantly being asked to make chiffon'; in July of that year about 30 per cent. of the looms at work were employed on colours, 'that is to say on chiffon'. The Board considered the desirability of increasing the make of colours, of chiffons, and light *crêpe de Chine*. It is from this time onward that sales of colours started to move at a significantly faster rate than those of crape. By December 1900 there were, all told, 576 looms on crapes and 807 on colours. In 1901 Tetley claimed that Samuel Courtauld & Co. were 'now doing a fancy silk business second in volume to only Lister & Co.'; he added, 'appearances point to our speedily being the largest'.[2]

This great increase in the production and sale of colours, taken in conjunction with the recovery of crapes, posed a variety of problems. It affected the raw material intake. Different sorts of silk were necessary—a problem aggravated by rising silk prices towards the end of the century. In the 1880s most of the raw silk used by the company was Canton and China (Tsatlee), together with a small proportion of Messina.[3] But from 1895 Tsatlee began to rise in price (see Fig. 21), and later so too did Bengal; although in 1895 the company's total silk stocks were very large —nearly 103,000 lb. in December 1895—they fell to only 55,000 in August 1896. A year later they were over 91,000 again, but now two-thirds of the stock was Bengal, needed in the B-make crape. In September 1897 Samuel Augustine was writing a warning against being caught by a rising market with only small stocks of China, Messina, or Bengal. Substantial quantities of Italian and Brutia as well as China were being bought for chiffon and other colours; and in 1898 increasing quantities of Canton filature, a silk still cheaper than Bengal, were bought instead of or in addition to Bengal, to make the poorer sorts of B-make crape. In 1897 the weekly requirement of the company for crapes and colours was put at about 3,500 lb. (or 178,500 lb. per annum, assuming fifty-one weeks). In 1899 Canton filature and China (Tsatlee), at prices which averaged around 12s. to 13s. per lb., accounted for about 62 per cent. of the firm's total purchases of raw silk, which were approximately 200,000 lb.; Italian

[1] Ibid., p. 392.
[2] According to Lister himself, Lister & Co.'s profits in 1903 were £83,000, i.e. approximately double those of Samuel Courtauld & Co. (see Lord Masham, op. cit.).
[3] E.R.O., D/F 3/3/22, pp. 404–5, 407.

and Brutia, at about 17s. to 18s. per lb., accounted for a further 24 per cent.; and Bengal and Messina made up most of the remaining 14 per cent.

TABLE 26

Value of raw silk and other fibres bought, 1894–1904

Year	Raw silk	Sundry materials: spun silk, cotton, etc.	Profits (+) or loss (−) on raw silk resale
	£	£	£
1894	72,703	75	−614
1895	77,757	2,673	− 62
1896	57,023	2,438	−239
1897	108,492	5,566	+7,534
1898	124,669	16,523	+1,473
1899	154,060	29,440	+1,811
1900	164,691	24,860	+8,863
1901	136,749	34,466	+ 521
1902	191,115	41,244	+ 22
1903	196,336	48,188	..
1904	151,477	59,673	..

During the years 1896–1900 Samuel Courtauld & Co.'s purchases of raw silk accounted for 10 per cent. of the value of total U.K. imports of raw silk, though the heavy buying of 1902–3, together with a fall in national imports, brought the proportion up to 21 per cent. for the years 1901–4.[1] In addition to this varied list of raw silk purchases, far more varied than in the days of crape's dominance, the company was now also buying

[1] These figures may serve to correct the rather misleading claim in Ward-Jackson, p. 71, that Samuel Courtauld & Co.'s position in the silk trade at this time can be gauged from the fact that the firm was consuming 25 per cent. of all British imports of raw silk. This is based on a statement that in 1899 the company used 252,000 lb. of silk for crape and 125,000 lb. for colours; this total of 377,000 lb. is then compared with average imports for 1896–1900. I have not been able to find supporting evidence for the total of 377,000 for 1899, but even assuming it to be correct, to compare the consumption in the exceptional boom year of 1899 with an average for five years is hardly likely to lead to an accurate picture. If the alleged consumption in 1899 of 377,000 lb. is compared with total British imports of raw silk for 1899, the proportion is in fact 18 per cent.; but if the value of raw silk purchases in 1899 is compared with U.K. imports in 1899, the proportion is 10 per cent.; and the stated requirement for 1897 is again 10 per cent. of total British imports for 1897. This omits to note, however, that the nation's imports of waste silk (the raw material of the spun silk industry) were three and a half times as great in bulk as those of raw silk. Samuel Courtauld & Co., though they were now using spun silk, were not significantly large consumers of it. Even if it is assumed that in 1899 all the 'sundry materials' in Table 26 were spun silk, then the company's total fibre purchases were about 9 per cent. of the value of total U.K. imports of raw and waste silk; on the same assumptions the proportion would be 16 per cent. in 1901–4.

increasing amounts of spun silk for use in the ever-growing colour output, as well as cotton and other yarns for use in mixtures. The figures in Table 26 illustrate the trend.

Apart from the obvious stimulus towards the installation of new and better dyeing equipment, perhaps the most striking impact of this joint boom in colours and crapes in the late nineties was upon the problem of securing adequate modernized weaving capacity and suitable labour. The weaving of coloured fabrics needed more skill than was necessary for the simple crape gauze weaving. The re-equipment and the weaving shed extension of 1895 took time. Meanwhile, as demand revived, looms, adequate in number and suitable in type, had to be found. The first attempt to meet this challenge came in 1895 when it was arranged for a Glasgow weaving firm to make some 1,500 packets of B-make crape gauzes. This arrangement was continued; in 1897 and 1898 this company turned out a regular weekly quantity of these gauzes, at the rate, in October 1898, of 400 packets a week. This left the Halstead looms free for other crape weaving and for colours, though in May 1897 Samuel Augustine reported from Bocking that they were trying to arrange with Glasgow for the production of chiffon—including the throwing of the silk—because the chiffon trade was currently so large. This type of arrangement was not entirely satisfactory, for fairly obvious reasons. But in north Essex labour was no longer as abundant as once it had been. So in 1898 Tetley pushed through a move which, though not momentous in itself, was another symbol of present change—and also a portent for the future. In July 1898 Samuel Courtauld & Co. bought, for £6,000, Brook Mill, Leigh, in Lancashire.

This was not strictly the firm's first move outside the confines of Essex and London—the filatures at Vinaleza and Beirut had been still more distant investments. But Brook Mill was intended for a part of the central manufacturing processes of the company's business; and this shift to one of the great textile areas of the north of England was certainly an important step away from the firm's odd industrial isolation in Essex. The mill was already equipped with a steam engine, looms, winding and doubling machinery, and the like, deemed by Tetley and Harry Johnson to be satisfactory; labour supplies were ample; a small outlay on improvements was needed. By 1900 a tender of £8,000 for an extension was being accepted. Production of 450–500 packets per week in 1900 had become 700 by 1902, with 220 weavers at work there.

Even this, however, was not enough. In January 1902, before newly installed looms at Leigh had had time to make their mark on output, it was necessary again to put out weaving to be done on commission: crapes at Glasgow, and some other goods, including satins with a spun silk warp, at Keighley and Bradford. Reluctantly, commission weaving of crapes had again to be arranged a year later. In May 1903 Samuel Augustine sent a long report to the Board on the weaving problem at Halstead, and recommended that a major extension be built there. Not only was the capacity at Halstead inadequate but the layout of the looms was too cramped, the lighting, shafting, and flooring in parts of the old building were all poor, and the gas engines ran unevenly. The proposal was accepted, and in 1904 work was put in hand on a large new extension which was opened in the following year.

IV

Recovery, reform, and expansion: how were these financed? After the drastic writing down of the capital in 1894, followed by the meagre profits of 1895 and the loss in 1896, the immediate programme of repair was financed by drawing on reserves. As Table 27 shows, there was a change for the worse in net indebtedness, though this never reached the negative figures common earlier in the century; the cash and securities reserves fell sharply. In February 1896 the directors at Aldermanbury were empowered to sell or deal with the company's investments in English railway stocks in case funds had to be raised. After cash and securities had gone down by over one-third between 1894 and 1897, a temporary loan of £10,000 at 5 per cent. was obtained, *pro rata*, from the shareholders in January 1898 until the 1897 balance sheet was completed. The loan was obtained 'in consequence of the great increase in the trade of the company'; and George Courtauld III, who had not attended the relevant Board meeting (he attended only four meetings in the whole of 1897 and 1898), was assured by the company secretary that 'there was no intention of repaying the loan, and indeed it is pretty clear that still more money will be required'. It was in fact dealt with by the issue of preference shares. In May H. D. Browne proposed the immediate issue of £20,000 6 per cent. cumulative preference shares to be offered *pro rata* on the holdings of the shareholders. Liquid funds were still inadequate. In September 1897, £9,760 of the company's holdings of railway stocks had been transferred to nominees of the Bank of England with a view to obtaining temporary advances when necessary. In the course of 1898 the Bank provided a series of such advances or loans; from 31 March, for instance, a temporary loan of £10,000 for fourteen days was repeatedly renewed until finally paid off with interest on 9 June. A committee consisting of T. P. Warren, Nettlefold, and Browne was appointed in February 1899 further to consider the problems of finance. Ultimately, £37,200 was raised against preference shares before the much higher profits which began to be earned from 1899 onwards made further calls unnecessary.[1] The cash and securities position improved; a new reserve fund was created with £10,000 in 1902; it had reached £20,000 in 1903. And in the summer of that year the first intimations were heard that Samuel Courtauld & Co. were contemplating the move of becoming a public company.

There were good reasons for such a move. Modernization, reorganization, and expansion had brought renewed prosperity on a sound financial basis. But the momentum of rapid recovery had slowed down. For the five years 1899–1903, as Table 27 shows, profits had remained good but at much the same level; and margins on sales (see Table 23) remained obstinately sluggish. Further success, in prosperity or in a struggle for power in the silk industry, meant further expansion. For this the resources of the private company were no longer adequate. It was now a concern, if not yet wholly dominated, at least substantially guided in its manufacturing and trading strategy by Tetley and to a lesser extent by Latham. But in 1903 these two men, salaried and with substantial commissions dependent on profits and sales, between them owned a mere £4,000 of ordinary shares. The ownership of the company—ordinary and preference shares and debentures—was still solidly in the hands of the Courtauld-Warren-Nettlefold group, and, to a much lesser degree, of H. D. Browne. Samuel Augustine was the only Courtauld now active in the direction of the business—and there was little love between him and the rampageous Tetley. George III had long effectively retired; Sydney was dead, though his second son, Samuel Courtauld IV, who had joined the company to learn the business in 1898 at the age of 22, was made mill manager at Halstead three years later. In 1903 John Warren was 72, Nettlefold 70 years of age. From a family group so placed it was no longer likely that sufficient funds, in the changed circumstances of the twentieth century, could or would be forthcoming.

Just as in 1893 the family had gone outside to find Tetley, so now, some ten years later, the company had to go further outside for more capital. It was a result of this move, essentially an outcome of the firm's position as a silk business, that Tetley was in turn able to persuade the Board in July 1904 to buy the English rights to the patents for making artificial silk by the viscose process. But that is another matter, and belongs to Volume II.

[1] The issued preference shares totalled £47,200; the called, £37,200.

TABLE 27

Structure of assets, 1894–1903

Year	Capital paid up			Fixed assets	Stock	Cash and securities	Net indebtedness	Net profit after tax and deb. int.	Total ordinary dividend
	Ordinary shares	5% deb. bonds	6% cum. pref. shares						
	£	£	£	£	£	£	£	£	%
1894	200,000	100,000	..	119,909*	102,768	65,781	+10,742	−1,264	Nil
1895	200,000	100,000	..	138,401*	111,888	51,332	+2,652	5,173	2
1896	200,000	100,000	..	145,008*	87,651	34,773	+24,115	−7,860	Nil
1897	200,000	100,000	..	144,877*	124,083	20,105	+20,931	17,450	5
1898	200,000	100,000	20,000	155,037*	131,754	25,739	+17,237	9,438	4
1899	200,000	100,000	37,200	154,139*	176,389	41,995	+9,174	43,914	10
1900	200,000	100,000	37,200	138,337	166,574	47,994	+16,659	24,086	10
1901	200,000	100,000	37,200	148,753	151,670	56,843	+19,934	35,917	12½ tax free
1902	200,000	100,000	37,200	156,141	178,887	21,288	+24,113	40,324	12½ tax free
1903	200,000	100,000	37,200	160,343	179,212	33,035	+12,582	41,863	12½ tax free

* Includes £13,676 goodwill.

PART III

CHAPTER X

Dissenters and Radicals

I

SAMUEL COURTAULD & CO. was supremely the family business in a century of family businesses. The bonds which united the sons and brothers, nephews and brothers-in-law, and the cousins of varying degrees who controlled its fate were not simply those of blood or marriage but also of religion. The Unitarianism that formed the common faith of the extended family unit which was Samuel Courtauld & Co. was one of the most remarkable phenomena of Victorian social history. Its influence upon the course of change, particularly in fields which may be called socio-political, was quite incommensurate with its numerical significance. Along with the Quakers—another body of Dissenters whose influence was out of proportion to their numbers—the Unitarians were one of the smallest of the main Nonconformist sects in Britain.[1] The strength of this tiny group lay in the appeal which Unitarianism had for educated and active members of the urban middle class. The congregations of Unitarian meetings or chapels included many able and influential men and women, a large number of whom were also inter-related. Unitarians married other Unitarians. So of course did Anglicans

---

[1] At the religious census of 1851 the figures, for England and Wales, for those attending the most popular service of the day when the census was taken were:

Church of England	.	.	. 3,773,474
Protestant Nonconformist	.		. 3,153,490
Roman Catholic	.	.	. 305,393
Other groups	.	.	. 28,685

Of the Nonconformists, the largest group, Wesleyan Original Connexion, accounted for 907,313; the Unitarians numbered 37,156 and the Society of Friends (Quakers) 18,172. Figures quoted in H. J. Hanham, *Elections and Party Management* (London, 1953), p. 117 n.

marry other Anglicans, or Catholics or Jews or Baptists do likewise. But none of these bigger creeds possessed that combination of limited class appeal, rationalistic ethic, reforming urge, and humanitarian instincts which were the peculiar and self-conscious qualities of nineteenth-century English Unitarianism.

Before considering the consequences of these qualities as they were demonstrated in the leading members of Samuel Courtauld & Co., it is time first to exhibit simply in broad outline the activities and ramifications of this particular Unitarian family group.

It all started, as already shown in Chapter IV, with the generation of George Courtauld I and William Taylor, and the influence upon them, directly and indirectly, of Dr. Richard Price. It was consolidated by the marriage between William Taylor and George's sister Catherine I; and then spread through the families by a series of further marriages in the next generation. William Taylor was the first avowed Dissenter of his family,[1] a serious thinking, religiously minded, middle-class family. His political views were those of moderate Liberalism. Whatever the political opinions of George Courtauld's forebears, their religious worship and his upbringing were pursued within the confines of the French Protestant community in London, an inbred community group, again essentially of the urban middle class. It was a silk-throwing Huguenot Beuzeville with whom Samuel III entered into business at Halstead in 1824, and it was a Samuel Beuzeville who had been George I's 'worthy schoolmaster' before he came under the influence of 'my worthy pastor, Dr. Price'.[2] The next generation took over not only the Unitarianism and the political radicalism but also the sense of belonging to a small, separate, consciously serious-minded group. The correspondence between its members, at least in the earlier decades of the nineteenth century, was full of religious discussion. Louisa Perina II, Samuel III, Catherine II, Sophia II all displayed in varying ways and degrees much concern with that haunting evil of Unitarian thinking, the menace of Calvinism and Trinitarianism. It was after all Calvin who in 1553 had had one of the earliest of the Unitarians, Michael Servetus, burnt at the stake. 'The whole family of us', observed George II in 1838, 'and I believe every individual of the Taylors and the Courtaulds, were religiously (as people call it) educated.'[3] The Bocking–Braintree–Halstead area was full of Dissenters, mainly Independents, Baptists, and Quakers; the Courtauld–Taylor family was almost alone in being Unitarian.[4] George II,

[1] Taylor, p. 592.   [2] *C.F.L.*, vol. i, p. 242–3.   [3] *G.C.B.*, p. 8.
[4] According to Sam Courtauld III, see *B.P.P.* 1851, vol. ix, p. 72.

who had married into an established local Liberal Nonconformist family, the Sewells, spoke of the Courtault–Taylor family as being 'cut off... from much of our country society'.[1] It was this generation which first displayed some of the constituent elements of Unitarian radicalism on the public stage.

Peter Alfred Taylor I's reforming energies found vent in working for the Anti-Corn Law agitation.[2] Becoming, as he did, a prominent and active member of the League, he formed political and social connexions in London which, along with Unitarianism, influenced his son's outlook and activities. In the doings of Peter Alfred Taylor II, and his wife, the Unitarian radicalism of the family made its most sustained and public impact. Before he entered the House of Commons as M.P. for Leicester in 1862, in which he then sat for twenty-two years, Peter Alfred Taylor II had already become well known in the busy world of Utilitarian-Unitarian activity, a world of intellectuals, politicians, agitators, journalists, Nonconformist parsons, and professional reformers. He became one of the leading representatives in the Commons of advanced middle-class radicalism, his wife an active worker in the cause of women's suffrage.

As the name of Taylor was thus becoming known in Radical reforming circles, that of Courtauld was acquiring related fame. Whilst his partner and brother-in-law campaigned against the Corn Laws, Samuel Courtauld III waged a fight against the levying of church rates on Dissenters. Starting as a local issue in Bocking in 1834, it broadened into a national issue via what became known as the Braintree Church Rates Case; and ended with a substantial measure of success for Sam in a decision of the House of Lords in 1853. Locally Samuel Courtauld & Co., largely through the efforts of George II and of Sam and his wife Ellen, built up a growing reputation as enlightened employers and providers of various schemes of welfare for the local population. Their Unitarianism was transmitted to the next generation through the children of George II. George III successfully contested the Essex borough of Maldon in 1878, and represented that constituency until 1885.

The main lines of the Courtauld–Taylor family group, however, by no means delimited the extent of the Unitarian family connexions. (For aid in following the next two paragraphs the reader is referred to the genealogical tree of the extended family, Fig. 25.) Peter Alfred Taylor I's sisters also married into active Unitarian families. In 1823 Anna Sophia married the

---

[1] *C.F.L.*, vol. vii, p. 3219.
[2] For details of this, and of the other political activities sketched in these two paragraphs, see below, pp. 223–9.

Reverend J. P. Malleson, who was headmaster of a Nonconformist school at Brighton. Their children maintained both the Unitarian and reforming traditions. The eldest son, William Taylor Malleson, who married his first cousin, Catherine Ellen Taylor, worked with his brother-in-law Peter Alfred Taylor II in support of radical causes, and was secretary of the organizing committee supporting John Stuart Mill's successful Parliamentary candidature at the Westminster election in 1865.[1] His sister-in-law, Mrs. Frank Malleson, was active in promoting girls' secondary education; at one time she helped to run a non-sectarian, co-educational school of a very un-Victorian nature which counted Garibaldi's sons amongst its pupils; and occupied such posts as Honorary Secretary of the Working Women's College.[2] Another of Peter Alfred Taylor I's sisters, Louisa Caroline, married a Unitarian minister, the Reverend John Jeffrey. Their only child, Louisa Caroline Jeffrey II, was for a time the 'suitable, discreet and retiring . . . pleasant and intelligent' companion to that quite extraordinary example of Victorian womanhood and product of Unitarianism —Harriet Martineau (1802–76).[3] Popularizer of classical economics, prolific writer of moral tales, journalist, champion of all manner of reforms, she ultimately deserted Unitarianism, first for Mesmerism and then for Positivism, became a celebrated Victorian invalid, and turned down the offer of a Civil List pension. Louisa Caroline Jeffrey II married in 1844 the Reverend J. R. McKee. He was one of Samuel Courtauld III's executors. In 1832 Sam was telling his sister Sophia: 'Wish you knew the Miss Flowers and Miss Martineau (They are quite convenient to the Bromleys). Saw them last Sunday and liked them prodigiously.'[4] The Miss Flowers were Sarah and Eliza Flower; the Bromleys, William Bromley of Gray's Inn and Catherine Taylor, his wife, yet another sister of Peter Alfred Taylor I. Sarah and Eliza Flower (Sarah's main claim to fame lies in having written the hymn 'Nearer, My God, to Thee') were part of a Unitarian group centring around William Johnson Fox. Preacher, orator, vigorous Anti-Corn Law speaker, founder of the South Place Unitarian Chapel in Finsbury and of the British and Foreign Unitarian Association, journalist, and later Radical M.P. for Oldham, Fox was, not surprisingly, a close political associate of the P. A. Taylors, father and son.[5] And Sophia did

[1] M. St. John Packe, *Life of John Stuart Mill* (London, 1954), p. 449.
[2] R. Strachey, *The Cause* (London, 1928), pp. 129–30; H. S. Solly, *These Eighty Years* (London, 1893), vol. ii, p. 428.
[3] R. K. Webb, *Harriet Martineau* (London, 1960), pp. 139–40.
[4] *C.F.L.*, vol. v, p. 2035; and Solly, op. cit., vol. i, p. 403.
[5] F. E. Mineka, *The Dissidence of Dissent* (University of North Carolina Press, Chapel

meet Harriet. For they shared not only spinsterhood, and a Unitarian up-bringing, but also the common bond of deafness; in the later 1840s, during the high tide of Harriet's Mesmeric enthusiasm, correspondence between her, Louisa Jeffrey, and Sophia Courtauld reveals attempts by Harriet to mesmerize Sophia's deafness out of existence.[1] They failed.

To Hove House School, Brighton, kept by J. P. Malleson—and where George Courtauld III was sent in 1838—had earlier gone Henry Solly.[2] After leaving school Solly became one of the earliest students of the new London University in Gower Street, University College, London, as it was later to become. He was accompanied and followed there by many Non-conformists' sons to whom the older universities remained closed until well into the second half of the nineteenth century. They included George II's sons, George III, Samuel Augustine I (1833–54), Louis and Sydney, as well as Warrens and Mallesons.[3] In time Henry Solly became a Unitarian minister, and in 1851 accepted the ministry at Carter Lane Chapel, London. Here the congregation included Martineaus, Warrens, Prestons, Nettlefolds, and Chamberlains: more connexions with the Courtauld–Taylor family group.[4] The Warrens, already Unitarians, were linked, as we have already seen, by the marriage between Thomas Pickard Warren I (whose grandmother had been the sister of a Presbyterian minister in Carter Lane)[5] to Wilhelmina Taylor, yet another of Peter Alfred I's sisters. The Nettlefolds and Chamberlains, already Unitarians, already linked together in religion, marriage, and business (see above, p. 179), were joined to the Courtaulds and Taylors in the next generation by the marriage of Frederick Nettlefold to Wilhelmina's daughter, Mary Catherine Warren. The Prestons were Henry John Preston, a London solicitor, and his wife, who was Elizabeth Bromley, daughter of William Bromley and Catherine Taylor. Elizabeth Bromley's sister Sarah was John Minton Courtauld's first wife; after her death in 1855 and after the death of Henry Preston, John Minton in 1877 went through a cere-mony of marriage in Switzerland with Elizabeth Preston, his deceased wife's sister.[6] The youngest of the Bromley sisters, Mina, became George

Hill, 1944), pp. 169–203; J. Ewing Ritchie, *British Senators* (London, 1869), pp. 134–40; R. J. Hinton, *English Radical Leaders* (New York, 1875), pp. 55–70.

[1] *C.F.L.*, vol. vii, *passim*. [2] Solly, op. cit., vol. i, p. 91; *G.C.B.*, p. 4.

[3] Ibid., pp. 22, 96, 98, 101; *C.F.L.*, vol. vii, p. 3424; vol. viii, pp. 3443, 3784–7.

[4] Solly, op. cit., vol. ii, pp. 83, 87.

[5] Reverend Thomas Warren, *A History and Genealogy of the Warren Family* (1902).

[6] Somerset House: Will of John Minton Courtauld. Marriage to a deceased wife's sister was outside the permitted degree.

Courtauld III's first wife in 1855. Finally, to complete this particular round of connexions, Henry Solly's uncle was Samuel Solly, F.R.S., and the latter's second son, Lewis Barrett Solly, married in 1844 George Courtauld II's only daughter, Susannah Ruth; and, ultimately, a branch of the Martineau family was joined up, with the marriage of Frederick Nettlefold's daughter, Mary Edith, to Sydney Martineau.

A few outlying connexions could be added, but enough has been sketched to indicate the pattern both of activity and of inter-marriage in this extended Unitarian family. Two points remain to be emphasized: location and duration.

Many of the chapels or residences of the members of this group were originally in what is now north London. In the earlier nineteenth century such areas as Highbury, Islington, Newington, Hackney, and Walthamstow were plentifully populated with the prosperous Nonconformist middle class. Dr. Price had been preaching at Hackney and Newington from the 1770s onwards; and it was at the Old Gravel Pit Chapel at Hackney that Catherine Courtauld I and William Taylor met and married in 1783 and that John Minton Courtauld and Sarah Bromley married in 1837. George Courtauld I's mother, Louisa Perina I, after the death of her husband, retired to live at Hackney. The Taylors lived in the Hampstead Road; Peter Alfred I, Anna and Ellen Taylor were all married at St. Pancras; Peter Alfred II later became closely associated with the South Place Chapel at Finsbury. The Sollys were successful City merchants who lived at Walthamstow; the Chamberlains were shoemakers off Cheapside (in the same Milk Street where George Courtauld I's former partner and enemy Joseph Wilson carried on business), and in the 1840s they were living in Highbury. Coming back into the Courtauld business again, the Nettlefolds were ironmongers in Holborn; Thomas Pickard Warren I was a warehouseman of Cheapside and lived in Highbury; Sydney Courtauld married at the Unitarian chapel in Islington and Harry Taylor at the Unitarian chapel in Portland Street. In brief, the originating social and cultural environment of the men who carried on this textile business in three country towns in Essex in the nineteenth century was that of the *bourgeoisie* from these parts of London. In the circumstances of the time when George I had gone from Spitalfields to Pebmarsh perhaps this did not matter. But in the changing circumstances of the textile industries as the nineteenth century wore on, it seems likely that this milieu, quite remote from the textile world of the north, may have been an additional obstacle to successful adaptation in the crisis years of the 1890s.

Just as the family character of Samuel Courtauld & Co. was weakened in the crucial transition between 1890 and 1904, between the end of the partnership and the beginning of the public company, so was the strength of Unitarian and Radical tradition. In 1900, shortly after Sydney Courtauld's death, his widow, commenting on the forthcoming marriage of her son, Samuel IV, noted of her future daughter-in-law: 'Of course, she is not Unitarian, but happily they are not shocked at us, and in these days we are more and more aware how little it matters'.[1] This comment was a measure at once of the former isolation and of the changing circumstances of Unitarian families such as the Courtaulds. Though the wills of Frederick Nettlefold in 1913 and of T. P. Warren II in 1915, like that of Sam Courtauld III in 1881, provided for substantial legacies to Nonconformist charities, the decline of Dissenting Radicalism had set in before the nineteenth century was out. Its death is perhaps seen most strikingly in George III. Brought up as a Unitarian, soon after his marriage he began to attend the Anglican church; elected to Parliament as a Liberal, he soon became a Unionist, and after he had left the Commons became wholly a Conservative; himself attending a Unitarian school and non-sectarian London University, his sons went to public schools, and, some of them, to Cambridge; his father held no office in local government, his grandfather had once been Overseer of the Poor; he became a Justice of the Peace, Chairman of the Bench, and Sheriff of Essex.[2]

Such changes were common form. Nor had they gone unnoticed much earlier in the century. 'A wealthy dissenting family', it was said in 1823, 'is but rarely known to continue steadfast in the principles of Nonconformity for more than two generations.'[3] The religion of dissent and the politics of protest had long been frequent bedfellows in a society in which the Established Church was a department of State. There was nothing unprecedented about the transformation of Nonconformist Victorian industrialists into Anglican Edwardian landowners (with a useful slice of equities). It was no different in principle from the transformation, 200 years earlier, of Puritan Cromwellian merchants into Tory Stuart financiers and Anglican Hanoverian squires. But there was a difference in the practice and achievements of those who, like the nineteenth-century Unitarians, were active in the politics of reform. For by the time the century was over Unitarianism had lost its original character, and most, though certainly not all, of what its more active adherents had worked for in the field of

[1] G.C.B., p. 486.   [2] Ibid., passim.
[3] Quoted Mineka, op. cit., p. 25.

828235.1   P

socio-political reform had either been achieved or looked like being achieved only through quite different means. Whatever may have been the legacy of the nineteenth-century Unitarians their sort of political Radicalism was finished.

II

'Unitarianism', observed Coleridge in 1817, had 'a particular charm for what are called shrewd, knowing men'. It flourished 'in our cities and great manufacturing and commercial towns, among lawyers and such of the tradesfolk as are the ruling members in book clubs'.[1] In 1814 the earnest young Sam Courtauld, who was certainly in his life both shrewd and knowing, was writing to his London friend and future financial supporter, John Newberry, about becoming a member of a 'Philomathic Institute', regaling him with the details of an alarmingly rigorous scheme of work and learning, which involved turning his bedroom into a study, and ordering a list of books which varied from Newton's *Principia* to Brugh's *Art of Speaking*, taking in Mason on *Self Knowledge* and the *Bride of Abydos* on the way.[2] Sixty-seven years later he left, out of the industrial fortune he had accumulated, £4,000 to the British and Foreign Unitarian Society and £2,500 to the Society for the Liberation of Religion from State Patronage.[3]

Is this the perfect example of the Unitarian businessman, and, if so, what did his business success owe to his Unitarianism or Unitarianism to his business success?

This is no place to examine either the origins of the Unitarian sect in sixteenth-century Hungary and Poland or the doctrinal controversies which rumbled around the world of Christian theology. Eschewing, then, the details of Arianism, Socinianism, and more besides, suffice to say that the essential elements in English Unitarianism which separated it from Anglicanism were: firstly, a denial of the doctrine of the Trinity and of the divinity of Jesus Christ; secondly, a denial of the doctrine of atonement; thirdly, an emphasis upon the Bible as the source of religious truth; and fourthly, an insistence upon reasoning, upon rational thought and questioning, in the interpretation of Christianity. Joseph Priestley (1733–1804), scientist and theologian, gave English Unitarianism its markedly rationalistic stamp. He thus provided some of the intellectual

---

[1] Mineka, op, cit., p. 25.
[2] Courtauld MSS.: J.N. to S.C. III, July 1814 and 15 October 1814.
[3] Somerset House: Will of Samuel Courtauld.

content which was later to afford a ready bridge to Jeremy Bentham's Utilitarianism.[1] The appeal of such a creed was obviously limited. Shorn of mystery, deprived of dogma, and deficient in emotion, it had no mass appeal. It was quite unlike the Evangelical revival which, at the time of the Industrial Revolution, swept across the British working classes. Priestley and Richard Price together gave to Unitarianism its particular association with political radicalism, through their public support of the American, and more limitedly, of the French, Revolutions. Unitarians, with their active aid to all sorts of movements towards greater political and religious freedom, were particularly good examples of those who came to be known as 'Political Dissenters'.[2] It is hardly surprising that until the time when the tides of reform began to run strongly, as they did in the 1830s and 1840s, Unitarians were attacked alike by the orthodox in religion and the conservative in politics.

In the second half of the nineteenth century, Unitarianism changed. It was largely under the dominance of James Martineau, Harriet's brother, that 'new' Unitarianism moved away from the reliance upon scriptural authority which had been so important a characteristic of 'Old Unitarianism'. The source of authority was now to be 'in human experience of the divine, in the conscience, soul, and mind of man'.[3] The old fires of theological controversy gradually died away; and if now it was still less clear whether Unitarianism was really part of Christian doctrine, now it mattered less. Unitarianism was a compromise religion for radicals, suiting those who felt the need for a haven of reconciliation between eighteenth-century rationalism and traditional Protestantism. The fervour of its many notable adherents was given to causes not specifically religious, to freedom of thought, of political expression, of economic action, for social improvement, for greater tolerance, for less bigotry. In the half-century between the first and the third Reform Bills, many of these ends were achieved; and their achievement owed much to Unitarians—to such men as Southwood Smith in public health, to Joseph Chamberlain in local administration, or to those with such varied influences on political, economic, and social reform as Bentham, Bagehot, or Sir John Bowring. But for the future, agitation for reform belonged to new secular entities, to the trade unions, to the emergent Labour Party, to organized political

[1] Mineka, op. cit., pp. 145 et seq.
[2] E. Halevy, *History of the English People in the Nineteenth Century* (English paper back edition, London, 1961), vol. iii, p. 156.
[3] R. V. Holt, *The Unitarian Contribution to Social Progress* (London, 1938), p. 342.

machines competing for votes in a mass electorate. The old compromise between rationalism and traditional religion was no longer relevant. Though Unitarianism survived, it had lost its former significance. Already in 1851, Richard Martineau, Harriet's cousin, and one of the Carter Lane congregation which in the same year appointed Henry Solly, observed that the sect could attract no promising young men.[1] Some members were beginning to drift away, like W. J. Fox, to a purely secular ethicalism; others, like Harriet Martineau, to the positivism of Auguste Comte; others, again, were attracted to the Christian Socialism of the former Unitarian F. D. Maurice, a movement which had the advantage of commending itself to High and Low Church alike, in contrast to the doubts felt about the very Christianity of Unitarianism.[2]

In the probably varying ways which Unitarianism allowed, the Courtauld–Taylor family subscribed to these general Unitarian beliefs and, in differing measure, took part in this pattern of achievement. How much, and in what way, was the piece of social and economic history which they represent affected by those beliefs? Could it be said *mutatis mutandis* of Unitarianism in particular what had been said in the eighteenth century of Protestantism in general, 'that the Protestant religion is better calculated for trade than the Catholic', or that Methodism was 'not a religion for a trading people'?[3] Was Unitarianism a religion for 'trading people' like Courtaulds the crape makers as it was for a Unitarian potter like Josiah Wedgwood, Unitarian cotton spinners and manufacturers like the Strutts in Derbyshire, the Gregs in Cheshire, Samuel Oldknow in Stockport, or the Ashtons of Hyde, or Unitarian shippers such as the Holts of Liverpool, Unitarian engineers like Sir William Fairbairn, or Unitarian chemists ranging from Joseph Priestley himself to the John Brunner of what became Brunner, Mond and was in time to grow into Imperial Chemical Industries Ltd.?[4]

It can be argued that the removal of much of the mystery from religion and its replacement by the exercise of reason acted as a stimulus to the mind; and that the critical thought thus provoked was an influence upon upbringing more conducive to the practice of intelligence than the passive learning of dogma. To these possible stimuli to the use of the mind were added the excellent educational facilities of the Dissenting academies, many

[1] Webb, op. cit., p. 283.   [2] Ibid., pp. 283–4; Halévy, op. cit., vol. iv, p. 261.
[3] Dean Tucker, quoted T. S. Ashton, *An Economic History of England: The Eighteenth Century* (London, 1955), p. 19.
[4] Holt, op. cit., pp. 36–68.

of which were generally admitted to be superior to institutions attended
by the religiously orthodox. It is certainly reasonable to suppose that the
education which the first George Courtauld received from his Dissenting
teachers, and which he lovingly passed on to his family, mingled with that
which George II received at the 'Protestant Dissenters Grammar School'
at Mill Hill to produce some of the qualities apparent in the 'machinist'
of Courtauld, Taylors & Courtauld. George I's patent spindle and his
general interest in mechanical matters; George II's engineering work, his
'minute attention to detail', his painstaking book-keeping, his earlier
predilection for being a schoolmaster; the habits of neatness, tidiness, order,
and systematic application commented upon by George III, after he had
attended Malleson's school at Hove: all these may well be tributes to a
certain type of education and upbringing. But, of course, these qualities
were no more necessarily productive of business success than is a degree
in economics or a prize scholarship in mathematics. George I's earnest
desire to bring up his children to 'rational, virtuous and religious views',
his regard for 'that Reason which is the highest privilege of our Natures,
and by which alone we can derive any advantage from Revelation', and
his advice to Sam that their minds should be kept 'above all inordinate
desire for ease, affluence or worldly pleasure':[1] none of these prevented
him from making a complete hash of most of his personal and all of his
business relationships. Left to himself, George II might well have in fact
become a schoolmaster or achieved distinction in a field of intellectual
endeavour. And the £2,000,000 of George III's estate when he finally died
in 1920[2] was the product of having contributed virtually nothing but
inertia to the family business.

Sam Courtauld III, alone of the extended family in the nineteenth-
century firm, possessed real entrepreneurial flair. What formal education
he had is unknown. For six or seven years after he was born his father was
on the move, from New York to London, to Kent, to Pebmarsh; by 1807
at fourteen years of age he was helping his father in the mill. Whatever
school he may have attended, we may be sure that his father's influence
was substantial. Sam took over the Unitarianism which he was given,
retained the humanitarian concern and the political radicalism in which
he was nurtured, but it was not the Unitarian inheritance which made him
a successful businessman. Probably the education which he received helped.

[1] *C.F.L.*, vol. i, pp. 221–2; Courtauld MSS.: G.C. I to S.C. III, 18 June 1812 and 23 June
1813.
[2] Somerset House: Will of George Courtauld.

So perhaps did his curious parentage, part London Huguenot French, part Irish. But ultimately it was his own personal, violent, reaction against the financial and social straits in which his father's well-meaning incompetence had landed the family that drove him forward. Apart from his father he was, after all, the only adult male member of the family when it was under siege in 1816. Once he found that, in charge himself, he could do the job, his thrusting ambition took off. And here it will not do to underestimate the powerful psychological role played by the family's awareness of its social position. It felt that it had come down in the world: a minor shift, no doubt, but in the intense preoccupation with social status which was (and still is) the peculiar prerogative of the English middle class this mattered. There was a good deal of cheeseparing to make ends meet; social calls had to be restricted; the girls helped in the mill, then had to go out as governesses. This caused Sophia II much heartache. In 1819 she told her brother, George II: 'I did at first feel rather awkward in "coming down", but now I do not mind it except in company, and that is still terrible.' Five years later: '. . . You will be glad to hear that I am spared all the mortifications that usually worry and depress those who are so unfortunate as to be compelled to undertake the situation of governess.'[1]

There is plenty more of this sort, and not only in Sophia's letters. Her father's emigration and his efforts to start a township in Ohio owed something to a yearning to repair lost status. He hoped that in such a township his own contributions would 'necessarily give me sufficient influence to be useful and respectable'.[2] It was all very well for him to warn his daughter, as she went out into the world, against adopting 'those horrible tenets known generally by the name of Calvinism',[3] but for creatures less idealistic than him, something else was needed. His long-suffering wife, Ruth, put it all in a neat nutshell of a groan when she said in 1819: 'Oh, did we but all know our proper stations and could we but be content with acting properly in them, what a world of pain it would save us.'[4] This is the background to those 'very high notions of appearance and respectability'[5] which George I complained of in Sam; to the view which Sam expressed to his brothers and sisters in 1821 when they joined their father in Ohio, 'I apprehend the well-intended settlement on the Hocking [River] will place our family vastly lower in the scale of society than their degree of cultivation merited; it remains to be seen how far this

---

[1] *C.F.L.*, vol. ii, p. 623; vol. iii, p. 1219.   [2] *C.F.L.*, vol. ii, p. 469.
[3] Ibid., vol. i, p. 237.   [4] Ibid., vol. ii, p. 561.
[5] Ibid., vol. i, p. 368.

cultivation of mind and taste can render very humble situations rationally pleasing'[1]. It was this sense of inadequate social status that motivated the allowances which Sam, as soon as he was really successful, began to make to his favourite sister so that she would no longer have to be a governess; and exalted, almost to a mission, his urge to repair and sustain the family. The qualities which started him on the road to business success were his own ability and intelligence; his powerful psychological need for achievement exhibited in an ill-defined ambition to make some sort of a name for himself somewhere; and his urge to mend the sagging social and financial circumstances of a large family dependent on an impractical father. To all this Unitarianism as a doctrine made no unique positive contribution. It may be that the rationalizing activity and serious-mindedness which it encouraged stimulated his mental faculties. It may also be that his Unitarianism meant that he found an outlet for his driving ambition in business rather than in public service because of the legal disabilities still imposed on Dissenters in general.

This is not to say that the family Unitarianism had no effects. The fact that under William Taylor and George Courtauld I the two families had become both united and Unitarian went a long way to determine who were to be the later partners in the business which their sons started. As members of a Dissenting sect, they tended to be inward-looking and separated from other social communities. Consequently their family encounters at the chapels and congregations which they attended, or the meetings of such bodies as the British and Foreign Unitarian Society, or the Unitarian Fund dinner, or of the radical political gatherings in which they took part, were all more than usually important in the choice of their friends, their associates, their future partners in marriage and in business alike. But if it was the fact of their common Unitarianism that provided the links which brought the Warrens and Frederick Nettlefold into the family and then into the management of the business, there is, of course, no means of knowing whether the fate of the firm would have been any different if this had not been so.

What is certain, however, is that the wealth created by the firm could, in some measure at least, be channelled into causes favoured by its Unitarian owners. In the last analysis it was the profitability of mourning crape that enabled the Peter Alfred Taylors, father and son, to take such active part in the movements of economic, political, or social reform so dear to them. His stature as a businessman surely helped Sam Courtauld in his

[1] Courtauld MSS.: S.C. III to Eliza, Sophia II, George II, and John Minton, 24 July 1821.

fight against church rates. To wives and nephews, nieces and cousins, the money found its way, and thus helped indirectly to finance such activities as those of Mrs. P. A. Taylor II and the Mallesons. It went to a variety of charities, and it permitted the welfare schemes, typical of Unitarian employers, which the firm sponsored in north Essex. Political activity and welfare: the former is the concern of the remainder of this chapter; the latter belongs to the chapter which follows.

III

On George Courtauld I's political views and activities there is no need to dwell for long. He became an enthusiastic supporter of the American republic; had joined the fight for the ratification of the Federal Constitution during his stay in the State of New York;[1] and, in true eighteenth-century American style, saw monarchy and King George III as one identical evil. In a letter of 1793 to his brother-in-law, the Reverend Henry Taylor, he paid a characteristically warm and fulsome tribute to his old mentor Richard Price, who had died in 1791, continuing:

... It must have been a great satisfaction to him to perceive the cause of Liberty was in so flourishing a state before he died. . . . That he was eminently useful in bringing about the American Revolution—there is no doubt; and that the Rev[olution] has produced all the succeeding ones in favour of Liberty appears I think evidently. You ask whether we are all peaceable and united in America, or whether we wish to return to the former Government under your Sovereign Lord the King of Great Britain, in short you ask whether we are running mad. . . .
... The Americans hold Monarchy in sovereign contempt, and can hardly avoid looking down with pity upon those people who pay homage to the person or name of a King. The enlightened part of Europe have long been convinced that absolute monarchy is a great evil, I hope the time is near at hand, when they will become persuaded that all monarchy is evil. . . .[2]

Holding such opinions, he was hardly likely to be happy back in England. He was starry-eyed about America, and long continued to be. In 1794 he told Henry Taylor: 'It does not I believe admit of a doubt, but that America is at this day, the most desirable country in the world.' He added that just before he left New York, he had seen and talked with Dr. Priestley, who 'was received as you may imagine with every mark of respectful attention'.[3] Twenty-four years later, in 1818, he reaffirmed his

---

[1] *C.F.L.*, vol. i, pp. xxx–xxxi.   [2] Taylor, p. 647.   [3] Ibid., p. 649.

preference for America over Europe, politically and economically. He became a typically idealistic enthusiast for emigration and the foundation of self-supporting communities. He had only to read pro-emigration pamphlets such as that of Morris Birkbeck to be convinced. 'His [i.e. Birkbeck's] views of forming a respectable English colony . . . and the certainty of his accomplishing this—with all the advantages of genteel society supported by intellect and property—removes any apprehension of difficulty in my employing my small capital to advantage in forming for us a valuable establishment. . . .'[1] Ultimately, of course, disillusionment set in. When he at last got some of his family to join him, his 'association' broke up; and suffering and hardship was the lot of a group of people, totally unsuited, mentally and physically, for pioneering in the wilds of Ohio.[2] Work of that nature needed more than political radicalism, Unitarian sentiments, and a 'genteel society supported by intellect and property'.

Samuel III, being much more of a realist, did not take over his father's republicanism. Nevertheless, he was evidently charged with an urge to engage in radical political activity, for in 1820 he was taking a leading part in a local demonstration at Bocking about the preposterous business of Queen Caroline's divorce. In this affair, one of the more absurd scandals that ever surrounded the British monarchy, all the Whig and Radical sentiments were marshalled in support of the Queen and against King George IV, and popular demonstrations were mounted all over the country.[3] At Bocking a lively procession was organized by Sam and two other like-minded spirits, supported by the local Radical leaders. It all finished with toasts being drunk, and then, as Sam reported to his brother George, still in Ohio, 'to my utter dismay my own health was given in a speech from the chair complimenting my exertions and support as essentially contributing to the glorious triumph of the day'.[4] Although nothing has apparently survived to illuminate in detail the nature of his political activity during the decade which followed, it is certain that in these years he was gradually coming to the fore in local Liberal-Radical politics. Between 1831 and 1835 he was actively supporting the Liberal leader in Essex, Thomas (later Lord) Western, and promoting the Parliamentary

---

[1] C.F.L., vol. i, pp. 355–7.

[2] For an interesting treatment of the hopes and failures of similar immigrants to America in the early nineteenth century (including George Courtauld I), see Charlotte Erickson, 'Agrarian Myths of English Immigrants', in In the Trek of the Immigrants (ed. O. F. Ander, Illinois, 1964).

[3] Halévy, op. cit., vol. ii, pp. 80–106.

[4] Courtauld MSS.: S.C. III to G.C. II, 19 November 1820.

candidature for the northern of the two Essex county seats of another Whig, Thomas Barrett Lennard, who was then M.P. for the Essex borough of Maldon. From letters between Lennard, Sam Courtauld, and Western, it is clear that Sam was a leading figure in the local reform association along with Peter Alfred Taylor I, and the then owner of Gosfield Hall, E. G. Barnard.[1] In about 1832–3 attempts were made by his friends to get him on the magisterial bench; one example in many of the general tendency towards the appearance of more Liberals and Dissenters amongst the magistracy and, especially after the Municipal Corporations Act of 1835, in local councils.[2] These attempts were fruitless, however, and in October 1834 he wrote to ask Western what had happened. He would obviously have liked the position and was hurt by the preference given to his local Tory rivals.

> . . . you will not perhaps think it altogether unreasonable in me to feel some degree of personal mortification, when after the lapse of some years, I learn that Mr. George Nottidge, the Tory banker, has obtained the promise of Sir John Tyrell that his name shall be included, on the next augmentation of the Bench in this district, and that the Tory Dean is also looked to by that party as his colleague.
>
> I freely acknowledge a *personal feeling* in the matter. The appointment would have been agreeable to me—per se—and, under all the circumstances *to be passed by*, and my most active opponents in this neighbourhood, on all questions of public interest, selected in my stead, would certainly be rather mortifying.[3]

In the later 1830s reforming political activity grew more vigorous; and Samuel Courtauld & Co. grew more secure, thus enabling its owners further to participate in that political activity. Sam Courtauld and Peter Alfred Taylor I became clearly identified with the middle-class Liberal-Radical political group then developing. They were not old-fashioned republicans like George I, nor new-fashioned working-class Chartists. The two causes which Sam and Peter most strongly espoused are clear indicators of their political complexion.

The obligation upon Dissenters to pay rates levied by the local vestry for the upkeep of the Anglican parish church was a grievance emerging as a major local issue at this time. Distraint upon goods or imprisonment

---

[1] E.R.O., D/DL. C. 61. In fact Lennard decided not to contest the county seat and was again returned for Maldon in 1833 and 1835. His father, Sir Thomas Barrett Lennard, Bart., sat for the southern division of the county in 1833.

[2] G. Kitson Clark, *The Making of Victorian England* (London, 1962), p. 161 and n.

[3] Courtauld MSS.: S.C. III to Lord Western, 23 October 1834.

were sometimes meted out to those who refused to pay.[1] Organized opposition to church rates burst into legal actions in various places; and what came to be known as the Braintree Church Rate Case was certainly the most famous and ultimately decisive. In fact there were two cases. It all started in 1834 when an attempt was made to levy a rate for the repair of the church at Bocking. Sam Courtauld, supported by other Dissenters including Peter Taylor and S. W. Savill, circulated an address opposing it, and the issue was settled by securing a majority in the vestry against the rate. This matter of a majority in the vestry was of course crucial in an area such as that of Bocking–Braintree and Halstead where a majority of the population were Nonconformists. The Anglican church could not hope to win against a vestry packed with Dissenters; the Dissenters objected, on various principles, to paying. Late in 1836 the battle started in Braintree. A rate was proposed; Sam Courtauld, supported by the local Noncon-formist minister, Rev. E. T. Craig, put down an opposing amendment. In 1837, after a further meeting, and despite Sam's opposing amendment being carried by a substantial majority, the churchwardens nevertheless levied a rate. The first test case was then started, *Veley* v. *Burder*, the former being churchwarden suing for the rate, the latter a Braintree Dissenter who, summoned to pay the rate, refused to do so. A Committee of Man-agement, with Sam Courtauld as chairman, was organized to collect sub-scriptions to defend Burder. The case was heard first in the Consistory Court in November 1837, where the judge, Dr. Lushington, found in favour of the churchwardens. Burder, supported by the Committee, then pursued the matter to Queen's Bench, where in May 1840 Lord Denman reversed Lushington's judgement and issued a prohibition on the grounds that the churchwardens had no authority to levy a rate against a majority of the vestry. The churchwardens took it to the Court of Exchequer where, in the following year, Lord Chief Justice Tindal upheld Denman's judge-ment, though leaving open a loophole which allowed the possibility of a rate being levied on a minority vote.

[1] S. Maccoby, *English Radicalism, 1832–52* (London, 1935), pp. 112–13, 216. This account of the Braintree Church Rates Case and Sam Courtauld's part therein is derived from: Maccoby, op. cit.; J. Irving, *Annals of Our Time* (London, 1890), esp. pp. 8, 65, 107, 290, 388; C. W. Johnson, *Judgements in the Braintree Church Rate Case* (1843); J. C. Evans, *Report of the Judgements pronounced in the Court of Exchequer . . . in Gosling* v. *Veley* (1852); W. W. Attree, *The Braintree Church Rate Case* (1853); *The Braintree Church Rate Case: Presentation of a Testi-monial to Samuel Courtauld, Esq., 1855* (1857); C.F.L., vol. v, p. 2287, vol. vi, pp. 2727–45; *B.P.P. 1851*, vol. ix (Select Committee on Church Rates); Halévy, op. cit., vol. iii, pp. 166–7, 206; J. Archer, *Gladstone and his Contemporaries* (London, 1886), vol. iv, pp. 13–16, 295.

Whilst these legal processes about the Braintree rate had been grinding their usual slow course, Sam Courtauld had been continuing to lead opposition to attempts to levy a similar rate in Halstead, where in November 1838 another large opposing majority was secured in a vestry meeting. In the spring of 1840 another attempt was made at Bocking. Again, Sam Courtauld and Craig, now able to quote the Queen's Bench judgement, secured an opposition majority.

In May 1841, seizing the possibilities opened up by Tindal's judgement, another vestry meeting was called at Braintree to see if there was still a majority against the rate. With Sam and Craig still active, there was. But in July, after a similar proposal and carried opposition amendment, the churchwardens again levied a rate, and the second test case, this time *Veley* v. *Gosling*, started. Again, the case was trundled slowly through various relevant courts. In May 1842, Dr. Lushington found against the churchwardens; they took it to the Canterbury Court of Arches where in March 1843 Lushington's decision was reversed; in February 1847 Queen's Bench upheld this reversal, and in January 1850 so did the Court of Exchequer. With so much legal backing behind them the churchwardens set about attempting to collect the rate in July 1850. They then found handbills—written by Sam Courtauld—widely distributed about Braintree. Headed by a preamble: 'To the rate-payers of Braintree, advocates of religious freedom and the sacred rights of consience', they summoned parishioners to 'boldly discharge their duty—and Heaven defend the right!' A further meeting again saw the opposition amendment carried by a majority, but a rate of 2s. was made by the minority. The contest continued, and finally the case reached the House of Lords, where in August 1853, the Queen's Bench and Exchequer judgements were reversed, their Lordships holding that a rate must be made by the majority and that no other rate was valid. This put an end to the business, at least in areas where Dissenters were in a majority. In parishes where they were in a minority, their invidious position remained. After various measures to abolish church rates had been defeated, finally in 1868 Gladstone, not without a further clash, secured their abolition.

There can be no doubt that Sam Courtauld's lead in the Braintree cases was a major cause of this final victory for the principle of religious freedom. His role was recognized first locally and then nationally by all sorts of ceremonies and presentations at various stages of the battle, in 1836, 1839, and finally in 1855. As *The Times* said in its obituary in 1881: 'Had the death of Mr. Courtauld happened some 30 or 40 years ago a popular hero would have passed away . . . the Braintree case . . . practically gave the law of Church rates in every shape its *coup de grace*.'[1]

The Times also observed that 'he had lived to be almost forgotten, reposing, as he had done for nearly 30 years, on his laurels'. This was true. What had happened to dam the apparently superabundant energy, in so far as it flowed in political channels? In the 1830s he may have been considering the possibility of standing for Parliament, for a letter to him from Lord Western in July 1836 observed: '. . . the expense of a contest I fear you have stated too low. I never got off under £5,000—a great deal of *previous treating* would be required'.[2] In the 1840s he joined Peter Taylor in London in his Anti-Corn Law activities; and found time to make a speech at Chelmsford in support of a Bill for the removal of Jewish civil disabilities.[3] After the early 1850s he seems to leave no political mark whatever. Why? A clue can be found in the minutes of the House of Commons Select Committee on Church Rates which sat in 1851. He gave evidence before that Committee, made some foolish allegations, and was roughly handled in cross-examination, particularly by Sir David Dundas, then Judge-Advocate General. In the course of the hearings he was referred to as being 'more distinguished . . . than anyone else in England by opposition to Church Rates, the leader in the greatest anti-church-rate battle that has ever been fought.'[4] Some members of the Committee may have found this description slightly at variance with his own admission that he possessed property in Gosfield and paid the church rate there, though objecting to paying it elsewhere. His answer was that he had been permitted to construct a family vault and mausoleum there, and therefore used the parish church of Gosfield on the death of any member of his family, becoming thereby 'a partaker of the advantages resulting from the Church of Gosfield'.[5] He explained that his objections to the church rates were based wholly on grounds of civil justice and religious freedom.

During his evidence he made the allegation that local tradesmen had been ruined and some cases of bankruptcy had arisen from the withdrawal by the church party of their custom from Dissenting tradesmen; and also that tenant farmers had been threatened by their landlords with dismissal from their holdings.[6] It was on this latter statement that he was taken up by Dundas, for he was forced to admit that he knew of only one case.

---

[1] *The Times*, 24 March 1881.
[2] Courtauld MSS.: Lord Western to S.C. III, 30 July 1836.
[3] C.F.L., vol. vii, pp. 3283–6; and see below, p. 224.
[4] B.P.P. 1851, vol. ix, p. 73. [5] Ibid., p. 59. [6] Ibid., p. 70.

What, then, did he mean by saying 'I know that tenant farmers have been threatened . . . etc.'? After a good deal of obviously bad-tempered wrangling, he asked to withdraw the plural. Dundas rubbed it in by pointing out that his statement had not been made in answer to a question but that he had volunteered it, and that a particular onus lay upon him to be accurate.[1] Sam went from bad to worse by saying: 'I talked of "they" as persons sometimes speak of "we" when they mean "I" using the plural instead of the singular.' The following unhappy exchange then took place:[2]

> *Chairman*: Did you mean to use the word impersonally, did you use it as necessarily expressing more than one, or merely as a form of expressing your belief that at least one such case had occurred?
> *Sam Courtauld*: That was undoubtedly my intention.
> *Dundas*: Who gave you any such authority to answer questions in that manner?
> *Sam Courtauld*: Nobody.
> *Dundas*: Is it not your duty as a witness to answer plainly to the truth?
> *Sam Courtauld*: Certainly, I wish I had been more verbally accurate.

This was neither the first nor the last occasion when Sam was badly rattled by hostile comment. Earlier he had said that at a meeting about the rate, attended by 300 persons, only seven were in favour of it. He was then asked what proportion of the 300 were ratepayers, admitted he did not know, and got the tart rejoinder: 'Then, without knowing that, of course all this statement that you have been making is perfect moonshine.'[3] There were complaints of vagueness in his evidence, and towards the end he got confused when cross-examined on the principles of his own objection or consent to the rate.

Sam Courtauld did not cut an impressive figure in front of this Committee. He was making the nasty discovery that what could be done in north Essex as the autocratic Dissenting boss of a highly successful business in a Dissenting area could not so easily be done before a Select Committee of the Commons, with more hostile than friendly members. There is no doubt that he felt it deeply, for he was soon in one of those phases of depression which we have earlier noted. In June 1851 came another of those unhappy letters to his wife:

Your letter is comforting—and yet I cannot feel that I am so undamaged in general public opinion as you may think from the 2 or 3 of your own personal

---

[1] *B.P.P.* 1851, vol. ix., pp. 122–9.   [2] Ibid., p. 130.   [3] Ibid., p. 113.

friends whom you may see. . . . altogether I feel quite stranded and done for—a fish out of water—a lost life—an existence out of joint—everybody else working out their particular place and position and function according to qualities and qualifications. . . . I am all wrong and every day getting worse.[1]

It was probably wise of him not to have exercised further his political energies. He had the qualities which made for a successful businessman— though they were not unique to businessmen—but not for a public political figure. Rather stiff and domineering, and yet sensitive to injury, he lacked the resilience necessary for the continuous battle of politics. By the 1850s, moreover, he suffered from the added handicap of increasing deafness. He had acquired the massive Gosfield Hall, a yacht on the coast, boats on the lake at Gosfield; he was still active in business; he and his wife were increasingly busy with local welfare matters; he attended Unitarian functions—though his faith, in common with the Unitarian trend, seemed to be growing dimmer and more secular than specifically Christian[2]—as well as the meetings of such bodies as the Association for the Promotion of Social Science.[3] He had his final triumph, in his one great essay in political activity, with the Lords' decision of 1853. With this he had to rest content—if contentedness was a quality which he ever really experienced.

The Peter Alfred Taylors, father and son, made their political splash in quite a different way. The step from the radicalism of the type in which the Courtaulds and Taylors were brought up to Free Trade economics was one often and readily made. The intellectual support of Adam Smith's ideas and the popularization of alleged economic truths jointly provided a passage to views about economic policy which did not have to depend

---

[1] Courtauld MSS.: S.C. III to Ellen C., 26 June 1851.

[2] 'I find my heart sinking about the Halstead Chapel; already it is assuming a far more *onerous* and burdensome aspect than at first ever thought of . . . and you are looked for to attend and uphold' (Courtauld MSS.: S.C. III to Ellen C., 25 August 1857).

'Robertson has given me a stupid Psalm to read . . . I get very tired of this scrap-reading . . . I have been 2 hours looking through all the old Bible for something to read, and can find nothing that can be read. To be sure that Book as a worship is the most monstrous thing in all history of mankind; it is a huge mass of rubbish, trash and abomination, with some truly venerable writings collated with it; and also here and there some good true beautiful things that you cannot get at for common use, they are so tangled up with what is unfit . . .' (Courtauld MSS.: S.C. III to Ellen C., 9 October (?) 1858).

[3] His attendance at a meeting held at Bradford in October 1859 produced a brief description, in letters to his wife, of Titus Salt's famous factory at Saltaire, which some of the delegates to the conference visited. He remarked, *inter alia*, that it was 'truly wonderful, compared with which our factories are all nothingness' (Courtauld MSS.: S.C. III to Ellen C., 11 and 12 October 1859).

upon immediate self-interest. So it is fair to suppose that Peter Alfred
Taylor I's enthusiastic embrace of that bouncy lady of economic liberalism,
the Anti-Corn Law League, was informed as much by a sincere admiration of her intrinsic charms as by an urge to lay hands on her money.
Unlike many firms in the silk industry Samuel Courtauld & Co. did not
lobby for protection. The Select Committee of 1832, the 1885 Royal
Commission on the depression in industry, the Tariff Commission of
1905: to none of these did the firm give any evidence whatever, though
other silk firms proved only too anxious to testify to the evils of international competition.[1] That this should have been so was partly due to the
personal radical-liberal views of the founding families, and partly to the
special competitive position of crape. By 1839, which is the first date we
have for Peter Alfred Taylor I's active sponsoring of the Free Trade cause,
the firm had clearly decided to concentrate on crape, which, as shown
earlier, enjoyed advantages in export markets denied to other products. So
self-interest was now joined to virtuous economic intent in the vigorous
wooing which followed.

The organized Anti-Corn Law movement got its initial push with the
successful founding of the Manchester Anti-Corn Law Association
in 1838. This was soon followed by a delegate meeting in London in
February 1839 out of which emerged the Anti-Corn Law League, operating on a national basis and co-ordinating the activities of local associations.
At this 1839 meeting, the delegates from London were Peter Alfred
Taylor I and Colonel Perronet Thompson, well-known Radical spokesman and formerly owner and editor of the *Westminster Review*. Peter
Taylor continued to appear as a London delegate at further meetings in
1839-41 in Manchester and London.[2] At the time of Peel's compromise
measures on the Corn Laws in 1842, a large meeting was held in London
beginning 8 February 1842 to press for no compromise on repeal. Amongst
the delegates Sam Courtauld appeared as the Braintree representative.[3]
On the 9th, after Peel had put forward his plans in the Commons, a meeting of Anti-Corn Law League delegates took place at Brown's Hotel, with
Peter Taylor as chairman.[4] Resolutions were passed condemning Peel's
proposed measures, which, however, passed into law in April 1842. The

---

[1] Some of the Manchester firms—in the authentic Free Trade tradition—were notable
exceptions to this, though after 1860 even they began to lose their faith: A. Redford,
Manchester Merchants and Foreign Trade, vol. ii, 1850–1939 (Manchester, 1956), pp. 6–8, 102.

[2] A. Prentice, *History of the Anti-Corn Law League* (London, 1853), vol. i, pp. 107, 120,
144, 272.

[3] Ibid., vol. i, p. 304.   [4] Ibid., vol. i, p. 313; *C.F.L.*, vol. vii, p. 2947.

League's pressure for full repeal continued, and Peter Taylor was again Chairman at a mass meeting in London in July of the associations comprising the Anti-Corn Law League and of the branches of the Metropolitan Anti-Corn Law Association. There was much vigorous speech-making, including speeches by John Bright and Peter Taylor, whose reported words in opening the proceedings on 5 July seem to carry the true ring of contemporary Radical demagogy:

> The Chairman, the same as at the former London conference, Mr. P. A. Taylor, . . . said—'The cry of suffering and distress would make itself heard, and if that distress were not speedily relieved, he believed that that distress would make itself heard in a *voice of thunder* (cheers) which would *frighten the government and the legislature from its propriety* (continued cheering)'.[1]

On 24 July he headed a deputation which waited upon Sir Robert Peel at Downing Street to acquaint him of the widespread suffering and deprivation in the country which was held to be due to the operation of the Corn Laws.[2] Although Peter Taylor appeared again as Chairman of the Metropolitan Anti-Corn Law Association in October of the same year,[3] he no longer acted as Chairman of the League. He addressed a meeting of the League at the newly opened Free Trade Hall in Manchester in January 1843, but not as Chairman.[4] Although he continued to attend meetings, and was described as 'a noted Leaguer', his role seems to have been of declining significance. The increasingly dominant figures were John Bright, Richard Cobden, and W. J. Fox. Four years after his attendance at the final meeting of the League in July 1846,[5] when the Corn Laws had at last been repealed, he was dead.

Peter Alfred Taylor I had evidently been an important figure in the Anti-Corn Law movement, though not in the front rank of speakers and leaders. The company contributed to the League's funds,[6] and unquestionably the policy of its leaders was identified with the Free Trade cause. Peter Taylor's speech at the famous dinner of 1846, as noted earlier, soon turned into an energetic Free Trade harangue.[7] But as an instance of the fervour which he brought to his Radical views, here is a sample of his feelings when faced with Peel's income-tax in 1842. It is from a letter to

---

[1] *Quarterly Review*, vol. lxxi, p. 280. I am grateful to Mr. Rhodes Boyson for giving me this reference.

[2] Prentice, op. cit., vol. i, pp. 337–8, 346–9, 362; Halévy, op. cit., vol. iv, pp. 28–32.

[3] Prentice, op. cit., vol. i, p. 411.   [4] Ibid., vol. ii, pp. 16, 20–22.

[5] Ibid., vol. ii, pp. 335, 442.   [6] *C.F.L.*, vol. vii, p. 3289.

[7] Above, p. 115.

his fellow partner George Courtauld II considering how the firm could best avoid paying much tax.

> . . . I don't know whether you and Sam feel justified in paying as little as possible to our ruling tyrants—But looking upon them as an unprincipled set of scoundrels—who have neither honor—honesty—or truth—who plunder us for their own sordid advantage by violating every constitutional safeguard—and every political right—who unblushingly purchase their power in the Legislature by the most corrupt and demoralizing means—who deserve trial for treason against the People—ten times more than if they were plotting against the crown —I consider them as having morally broken the political compact between themselves and the People—it is their own election to make necessary this oppressive law—because to preserve their own rents they have refused to liberate Trade by abolishing the [Corn Laws] and Provision Laws—and I hold no faith with them.[1]

Brought up by a father vigorously engaged in publicly propounding these views, Peter Alfred Taylor II quickly took to similar activity. In June 1841, when still only 22 years old, he was being congratulated by his grandfather on 'the fame you have acquired by your lectures on the Corn Laws'.[2] His early political practice was indeed as an Anti-Corn Law lecturer—a tough training. Peter Alfred Taylor II, like his father, was always at the London end of Samuel Courtauld & Co.; he lived in London; and he moved in London circles of Radical politics and Radical thought. The Taylors' political activities thus appeared on a more sophisticated, national plane than did those of Sam Courtauld, who, even in his greatest triumph, operated at an essentially local level.

The period between Peter Alfred Taylor II's early experience as an Anti-Corn Law lecturer and his election to the Commons as M.P. for Leicester in 1862 also covered most of his years as a partner in Samuel Courtauld & Co., i.e. from 1850 to 1865. During these years he made many of the Radical connexions which were important in his subsequent career. He met the Italian revolutionary leader Giuseppi Mazzini in the late 1840s, and he and his father were founding members in 1847 of the People's International League, an organization representing ideals of international radical democracy dear to Mazzini's heart. For all its title, it was in fact a body heavily loaded with middle-class intellectuals and had little appeal to the English working-class, revolutionary Chartists of the

---

[1] *C.F.L.*, vol. vii, pp. 2930–1.
[2] Taylor, p. 620.

PLATE 18

PETER ALFRED TAYLOR II (1819–91)

day.[1] As a friend of Mazzini and a sympathizer with movements for political freedom, Peter Alfred Taylor II was soon associated with such bodies as the Society of the Friends of Italy (of which he was Treasurer in 1851) and the Garibaldi Italian Unity Committee.[2] He unsuccessfully contested Newcastle in 1859 and Leicester in 1860. Three years after getting in for Leicester in 1862 he withdrew his capital, now approximately £72,000, from Samuel Courtauld & Co. For the previous ten years his average drawings from the company had been nearly £5,000 per annum. He was now free, and financially equipped, to concentrate on politics.

During the twenty-two years of his Parliamentary life he was a regular and frequent speaker in the House of Commons.[3] He was a consistent champion of personal and political freedom, and spoke against harshness and cruelty in the administration of justice. Though no republican, he often criticized extravagance in the royal household and grants in excess of the Civil List. In general, he represented, in a variety of ways, and in an advanced degree, that particular blend of English nineteenth-century political and social thought which combined economic liberalism and political radicalism. Many of the reforms which he supported have long since passed into law, but in his day stood little chance of success. He advocated, for example, an extension of the franchise, the redistribution of seats, and the abolition of the rate-paying qualifications. He revived an old Chartist cause in 1870 by demanding the payment of M.P.s; it was defeated by 211 votes to 24. He attacked the practice of flogging in the Army and Navy, of harsh sentences imposed by magistrates for minor offences against property, and was particularly fierce against game laws.

---

[1] A.R. Schoyen, *The Chartist Challenge* (London, 1958), pp. 152–3; J.L. and B. Hammond, *James Stansfield* (London, 1932), pp. 22–23.

[2] J. L. and B. Hammond, op. cit., p. 28. James (later Sir James Stansfield), another Unitarian Liberal M.P., hoping in 1862 that Garibaldi could then visit England, suggested Peter Taylor as a likely host as he possessed 'the only house in our set with accommodation enough ... for the rush of deputations and visitors'. In fact Garibaldi did not then come to England; and Stansfield and Peter Taylor later fell out.

In 1864 Peter Taylor described himself, in the House of Commons, as having for years been an intimate friend of Mazzini—*Hansard*, vol. 174, pp. 266–7.

[3] His frequent, sometimes lengthy, sometimes amusing speeches will be found in *Hansard*, vols. 165–288, *passim*. Peter Alfred Taylor II was sufficiently important to have merited inclusion in the *Dictionary of National Biography*, upon which entry I have also drawn for this brief account of his activities; also J. Ewing Ritchie, *British Senators* (London, 1869); R. J. Hinton, *English Radical Leaders* (New York, 1875); and *The Times* obituary, 21 December 1891.

He, and the group of Radical-Liberals to which he belonged, merit further study than they have yet received.

He wanted to see compulsory, secular education supported by taxation, to have less Sabbatarianism and more museums opened on Sundays. He attacked the Postmaster General for interference with Mazzini's correspondence in 1864; he pressed for freedom of meetings in Hyde Park and for disestablishment of the Church. He was the first member of the Commons openly to champion the cause of North against the South in the American Civil War. In the mid 1860s he was an active member of a group of political intellectuals and M.P.s of advanced Radical views such as John Stuart Mill, Professor Henry Fawcett, and W. E. Forster.[1] Their effective political power was trifling; their influence over the years left a real mark. Peter Taylor supported the activities of the Reform League in the later sixties;[2] and became proprietor of the old Radical newspaper *The Examiner* from 1873 to 1878. He and his wife—sometime treasurer and secretary of the London National Society for Women's Suffrage, a pioneer body in that cause[3]—maintained a household in London which was one of the social centres of radical Liberalism. As an M.P., despite his very radical views, he was generally respected and popular.[4] After his retirement from the Commons in 1884 the Taylors moved to Hove where Peter died, aged 72, in 1891. In his later years his more radical views underwent the customary mellowing and after 1886 he became a Liberal-Unionist.[5] His support for Liberal causes, Radical and humanitarian schemes, workingmen's clubs, and so forth was financial as well as vocal. He acquired a reputation not only as a Radical but as a philanthropist. It is perhaps an apt tribute to this, basically made possible by the profits of mourning

[1] M. St. John Packe, op. cit., pp. 457 et seq.; Leslie Stephen, *Life of Henry Fawcett* (London, 1886), p. 288.

[2] On the Reform League, see Hanham, op. cit., esp. Chapter 15. It is not perhaps surprising that the Reform League had a particularly effective 'branch' at Braintree (Hanham, p. 327).

[3] R. Strachey, op. cit., pp. 106, 118, and *passim*; Packe, op cit., pp. 493, 497–8; H. S. R. Elliot (ed.), *The Letters of John Stuart Mill* (London, 1910), vol. ii, pp. 218–19. One of the striking facts about the group to which Peter Taylor belonged is that both husbands and wives were active in these typically Radical-Liberal causes. As such they appreciably antedate the much more famous partnership of Sydney and Beatrice Webb.

[4] George Courtauld III recorded of his cousin: 'Now, *he*, tho' a great radical, and constantly an advocate of (in the House) the unpopular side of a question, was respected, and (in so far as he at all encouraged intimacy) liked by all parties; at least I have never heard a word said against him, and many for him.'—G.C.B., pp. 360–1.

[5] It seems very improbable, however, that he ever became a Tory, as alleged by the Owenite, working-class Radical, G. J. Holyoake—J. L. and B. Hammond, op. cit., p. 50 n. Holyoake seems to have made a practice of labelling as Tory those he came to disagree with —see Schoyen, op. cit., p. 269 and n.

crape, that at his death he left far less money than any of his former partners.

With George Courtauld III the pendulum of the families' political attitudes completed its swing. In 1877 George III accepted an invitation to stand as Liberal candidate for the Essex borough of Maldon. Although his friendly disposition towards the Established Church did not commend itself to the Dissenters who provided most of the Liberal support in Maldon, his expressed political views were otherwise agreeable to them. So in December 1878 he was duly elected with a majority of 141 over his Tory opponent. In 1880 he got in again, after the dissolution of Parliament, but this time with a majority of only 18. Five years later, on the rearrangement of the constituency, he decided not to contest it, despite confidence that the new constituency would be to his advantage.[1] Thus ended George III's eight years of membership of the Commons. During that time he 'but very rarely spoke there';[2] *Hansard* records a total of six brief and unimportant utterances in his name.[3] Though he started as a moderate Liberal he became increasingly out of sympathy with the progress of more radical reform; and before the century was out had become a moderate Conservative and Unionist. He did not, however, readily conform to any party political line.[4] In truth he never possessed the type of zeal which had informed his politically active relatives and forebears. He was pleased with the idea of becoming a Member of Parliament for much the same reasons as he became first a Justice of the Peace and later Sheriff of Essex: all were part of the social position of a country gentleman, which is what he had become, and had long wished to become. Three generations and a fortune made out of mourning crape separated George I's republicanism in New York from George III's conservatism in Essex.

---

[1] G.C.B., pp. 257, 279, 294, 364–5, 368. [2] Ibid., p. 558.
[3] *Hansard*, vols. 253, 259, 265, 278, 284. [4] G.C.B., pp. 419, 477, 557–8.

CHAPTER XI

Work, Wages, and Welfare

I

SAMUEL COURTAULD & CO. became, in the course of the nineteenth century, by far the largest industrial employers in north Essex. In 1820 Sam reported that his hands were 'now 72, excluding machinists'. Thereafter the firm's total labour force rose to about 1,000 in 1838, over 2,000 in 1850, and to 3,214 at its high point of expansion in 1886.[1] It must have been unquestionably one of the biggest firms in the silk industry. Within these totals perhaps the most notable change in the nature of employment was the rise and decline of outworking. In the early days the latter covered some silk winding as well as the ubiquitous hand-loom weaving. Sam reported to his brother in 1821 that he was adding the throwing of long-reeled silks to his business and that these were 'wound in the village'.[2] Winding was brought into the factories to join power-throwing and then the power-weaving of crapes. So hand-loom weaving, both of crape and of soft silk, remained, as indicated in Chapter VI, a marginal activity for the firm. But the numbers were substantial; as the hand-weaving of crapes declined, that of soft silks was maintained and expanded in the 1840s and 1850s. The 411 hand-loom weavers employed by the firm in 1838 may well have been over 500 at the mid century after Braintree mill had been taken over.[3] So at this stage, perhaps about 25 per cent. of Samuel Courtauld & Co.'s total labour force was still made up of out-working hand-loom weavers. In a decade or so most of them had gone, though a few hand-looms were long maintained and it was not until 1884 that they were finally abandoned.[4] The 3,214 employees of 1886 were wholly a factory force. Its approximate distribution was:[5]

Halstead	Earls Colne	Chelmsford	Bocking and Braintree	
1,571	130	c. 150	1,363	= 3,214

[1] Courtauld MSS.: S.C. III to G.C. II, 19 November 1872; *B.P.P.* 1834, vol. xx, p. 370; 1839, vol. xlii; 1840, vol. xxiii, p. 127; 1850, vol. xlii, p. 462; 1851, vol. ix (Sam Courtauld said that the firm employed 2,000–3,000); E.R.O., D/F 3/3/24, p. 85.

[2] *C.F.L.*, vol. ii, p. 851; Courtauld MSS.: S.C. III to G.C. I, 8 August 1821.

[3] See above, p. 81. [4] E.R.O., D/F 3/2/39, 17 October 1884; D/F 3/1/12.

[5] E.R.O., D/F 3/3/24, p. 85; D/F 3/2/67, p. 174.

The depression years brought a sharp decline. It is illustrated in these figures for total employment at Halstead:[1]

1857	1,089	1892	1,177
1878	1,229	1895	851
1886	1,571	1899	1,061

In recovery, what was lost in employment because of improved productivity in weaving was balanced by increased work in other branches. So 3,000 remained about the total force at the end of the period covered by this volume. It was supplemented by about 220 at Leigh and some 50 in the London office.

Chapter VI has already shown how strikingly dependent were silk throwsters upon female labour and especially that of girls and children. That was in the 1830s, and at that time nearly all soft-silk weaving was done by male hand-loom weavers. But in the crape trade, with its simple gauze weaving, female labour again predominated. At Panfield Lane in the 1820s the gauze was woven by girls; two-thirds of the hand-loom weavers employed by the firm in 1838 were women; and the power-loom crape weavers at Halstead were all women and girls.[2] So it was, too, with Grout & Co., who at the same time, in their factory and outside it, employed a total of 386 female and 24 male weavers in Norwich.[3] The following figures for Samuel Courtauld & Co.'s Bocking and Halstead mills in 1838 illustrate both the adult female employment at power-weaving (Halstead) and the child employment in winding and throwing (Halstead and Bocking):[4]

TABLE 28

Employment at Bocking and Halstead, 1838

	Males				Females				Total males and females
	13 and under	14–18	19 and above	Total	13 and under	14–18	19 and above	Total	
Bocking	9	6	..	15	24	93	91	208	223
Halstead	28	17	20	65	15	98	212	325	390
Total	37	23	20	80	39	191	303	533	613

[1] E.R.O., D/F 3/3/24, pp. 60, 85–86, 88, 90; *B.P.P.* 1857, vol. xiv, p. 182.
[2] E.R.O., D/F 3/3/22, 24; D/F 3/3/29; *B.P.P.* 1840, vol. xxiii, p. 127; above, p. 72.
[3] *B.P.P.* 1840, vol. xxiii, p. 157.
[4] *B.P.P.* 1839, vol. xlii.

The persistence of this general pattern, modified by the operation of the Factory Acts restricting child labour, can be seen from the following analyses of Halstead employment, by sex, age, and job, in 1886 and 1899.[1]

TABLE 29

Employment at Halstead 1886 and 1899

1886	Job		1899	Age	
Males	Loom attendants and cleaners	32	Males	18 and over	112
	Mill cleaners	24		Young persons under 18—full-time	35
	Overseers and assistants	18			
	Others	40			
	Total	114		Total	147
Females	Weavers	854	Females	18 and over	571
	Mill hands and drawers	108		Young persons under 18—full-time	338
	Warpers, twisters, and plug-winders	154		Children—half-time	5
	Winders (young persons and children half-time)	277			
	Others	64			
	Total	1,457		Total	914
Total	Male and female	1,571	Total	Male and female	1,061

In percentages, Halstead's labour force was 83 per cent. female in 1838, 92 per cent. in 1886, 86 per cent. in 1899. At Earls Colne in 1899, 96 per cent. of the employees were female.[2] At Braintree the situation was similar; only at Bocking, with its dyers, crimpers, and mechanics, was the proportion substantially different. Even at Bocking, however, finishing, as in the early days, used a large proportion of women and girls: about 60 per cent. of the finishing department's labour force was female in 1886; in 1883 there were over 150 women and girls working at the Bocking throwing mills.[3] All told, in the later nineteenth century, probably about 70 to 80 per cent. of the firm's entire labour force was female.

Until 1836 the firm of Samuel Courtauld & Co., in common with other silk-mill owners, was able to recruit its men, women, and children wholly as it liked, without State intervention of any sort. George I had been recruiting his workhouse girls in 1813–16; Samuel III in the early 1830s

[1] E.R.O., D/F 3/3/24, pp. 85–86, 90.   [2] E.R.O., D/F 3/3/30.
[3] E.R.O., D/F 3/2/68, p. 151; D/F 3/2/34, p. 148.

was employing his double shifts of children and adults alike 12 hours by day, 10½ by night.[1] In 1836, when the Factory Act of 1833 came into operation, regulations which applied to other textile mills were extended, with certain important exceptions, to silk mills. When the Commissioners appointed to inquire into child employment in factories began their work,[2] representations were soon made, as they had been earlier, to the effect that the silk industry was exceptional. Sam Courtauld's own observations in 1833 combined this argument with some general statements which bore the authentic hallmark of *laissez-faire*. 'Legislative interference in the arrangement and conduct of business', he remarked, 'is always injurious, tending to check improvement and to increase the cost of production.' It could be justified only where a strong case of hardship and wrong could be shown to exist. This was not true of children in silk mills, for their labour was so light, the mills of necessity so clean, dry, and airy, that to limit their labour to ten hours per day was wholly unnecessary. 'No children among the poor in this neighbourhood are more healthy than those employed in factories' (he was probably right: the operative word is 'poor'). As for the work which they did, 'their employment cannot be called labour'. Night work was 'perfectly voluntary'. Although maintaining that 'any interference must be mischievous both to master and servant', he conceded the possibility that because of 'popular excitement, delusion, or otherwise', something might have to be done. He suggested *inter alia* that no children under ten should be employed; and that none under seventeen should work more than twelve hours out of the twenty-four or work at night.[3] In fact the Act (3 & 4 Wm. IV, c. 103) prohibited children under nine from working in any mill, except silk; prohibited children under thirteen from working more than nine hours per day or forty-eight per week in any mill, except silk, where ten hours was the permitted maximum. It included silk mills in its prohibition of persons under eighteen working at nights or working more than a twelve-hour day. As the clauses of the Act relating to education for factory children applied only to those whose labour was restricted to forty-eight hours, children in silk mills were excluded. The effect of the Act was in some ways to make the position of children in silk mills complicated and obscure. One thing at least seems to have been clear: as a contemporary observed,

---

[1] Above, p. 98.

[2] B.P.P. 1834, vols. xix, xx.

[3] B.P.P. 1834, vol. xx, pp. 371–2 (Answers of Manufacturers to Queries sent by the Central Board of Commissioners).

'it was never intended [that] children employed in silk mills should be educated'.[1]

The Act of 1833, with its creation of a salaried factory inspectorate, was the first positive intervention of the legislature in the silk industry. It came, it is worth remembering, within a few years of the negative intervention of repealing the Spitalfields Act and cutting down the protective duties. Despite the protests of outraged non-interventionists on the one hand or of outraged protectionists on the other (sometimes they were the same persons), the industry, as we have seen, did not suffer calamity. Nor did the industry in general, or Samuel Courtauld & Co. in particular, suffer as a result of successive Acts extending the area of Government regulation of silk and other factories. In 1844 other existing factory regulations were extended to cover silk mills; women and young persons were grouped together for regulative purposes and their work had to end at 4.30 p.m. on Saturdays; the half-time system was established for children; various requirements were made concerning the fencing of machinery. After the Ten Hours Act of 1847, a sixty-hour week, with work ending at 2.00 p.m. on Saturdays, was decreed for women and young persons in 1850. The regulations were extended to dye-works in 1860. In 1874, the working week was reduced to fifty-six hours, and the Education Act of 1872 had already put an effective end to the labour of very young children. As the permitted hours were reduced by law for one group, so they were in practice for others; as a variety of regulations came into being, so were consolidating Factory Acts, such as that of 1878, necessary.[2]

This process of regulation did, of course, have the effect of limiting the potential labour force on which employers might otherwise have drawn and the hours of work which they might otherwise have induced it to work. There is no serious indication that in fact it tended 'to check improvement and to increase the cost of production'. It could indeed be argued that it might have helped, marginally, to stimulate improvements tending to lower the cost of production. The reduction of hours, the advent of compulsory primary education, and the onset of an economic boom, all in the early 1870s, may well have been a combined reason for the speeding up of mills and looms which went on at that time.[3] There is no evidence that the process of limitation by regulation caused any serious

[1] B.P.P. 1834, vol. xliii, p. 481, quoted in M. W. Thomas, Early Factory Legislation (Leigh-on-Sea, 1948), p. 161, n. 3.

[2] Clapham, op. cit., vol. i, ch. xiv; vol. ii, pp. 411–18.

[3] E.R.O., D/F 3/3/22, pp. 17–18, 20, etc.

difficulty to Samuel Courtauld & Co. in their recruitment of a labour force appropriate for their productive activities. In the earlier years, at least, there was, in north Essex, too much poverty and too little alternative employment for a firm which could establish itself to have any difficulty in recruitment. Sam Courtauld was surely right when he said, in 1833:

... the real hardship of the labouring poor here is rather the want of adequate employment than its severity; and the really painful task of a master manufacturer is the daily necessity of refusing employment to numbers of famishing applicants.

He added to it the Free Traders' cry:

... factory hours are comparatively few, and the factory employment is light; but the hand-weavers at their own homes sit in a confined posture for many more hours, their appearance is pallid and overwrought, and they are really entitled to the most benevolent consideration, and their cry and just demand is for cheap bread. May the wisdom of the legislature grant them relief.[1]

In the last decade of the century, however, the situation was looking very different. The need to increase productivity was made urgent by the crisis of the depression years and by a notable slackening of population growth in north Essex which began to make recruitment less easy.

TABLE 30

Population of Braintree, Bocking, and Halstead, 1801–1901[2]

	1801	1821	1841	1861	1881	1901
Braintree	2,821	2,983	3,670	4,620	5,182	5,330
Bocking	2,680	2,786	3,437	3,555	3,458	3,347
Halstead	3,380	3,858	5,710	6,917	6,701	6,900
Totals	8,881	9,627	12,817	15,092	15,341	15,577

Even allowing for recruitment from neighbouring rural parishes, and for the small outposts at Earls Colne and Chelmsford, it was obviously less easy to maintain a labour force of 3,000 (of which perhaps 75 per cent. were women) in the eighties and nineties than one of 1,000 or so in the thirties. Poverty was less pressing, the pool of underemployed hand-loom

[1] B.P.P. 1834, vol. xx, p. 371.
[2] From census returns, assembled in *Victoria County History: Essex*, vol. ii, pp. 342–54.

weavers had gone, travel to London was easier, and whilst north Essex was stagnating, the London fringe of south Essex was growing at a great rate.[1]

Not surprisingly these problems began to show during the great boom of the early 1870s. The weavers at Halstead came mainly from within the town and the immediately adjoining parishes; some, however, came from outlying areas, and the firm paid boarding money of 1s. per week to help them to lodge in the town, often in the company's own cottages.[2] There was a markedly more seasonal and casual element in the recruitment of these 'out-town' weavers, and turnover was quite high. But, as the following figures show, the proportion of 'out-town' weavers was increasing, at least in 1872-3:[3]

TABLE 31

Halstead weavers: turnover, 1872–3

Month	Total	Out-town	In-town	Taken each month		Left each month	
				Out-town	In-town	Out-town	In-town
1872 Sept.	711	57	654	..	..	..	..
Oct.	719	70	649	14	11	1	16
Nov.	720	72	647	7	8	4	10
Dec.	715	76	639	..	2	3	10
1873 Jan.	739	102	637	36	8	10	10
Feb.	759	120	639	22	10	4	8
Mar.	752	111	641	4	8	13	6
Apr.	749	107	642	..	7	4	6
May	744	101	643	..	6	6	5
June	728	91	637	..	4	10	10
July	720	88	632	..	6	3	11
Aug.	713	83	630	..	3	5	5

From 8·7 per cent. in September 1872, the proportion of 'out-town' weavers rose to 18·7 per cent. in February 1873, finishing at 13·2 per cent. in August 1873.

This was one aspect of the problem. Two years later the Halstead mill-manager was warning the company of the attractions of domestic service as a lure, actual or potential, to the weaving girls. 'A great many of our

[1] e.g. East Ham grew from 1,165 in 1801 to 69,758 in 1901 and Ilford from 85 to 26,241 in the same period.
[2] See below, p. 256 and Plate 20.
[3] E.R.O., D/F 3/3/22, pp. 30–31. 'Town' hands included all girls living within the parishes of Halstead, Grinstead Green, and Great and Little Maplestead; these workers went home every night 'except in the very depth of winter'.

younger weavers leave after they have been here from about eight to twelve months, and lately most of these have gone to service there being a large demand just now for domestic servants. . . . Some have left for London. . . .' These, he reported, were only 'middling weavers'; but sometimes, and much worse, they lost good weavers to domestic service.[1] Domestic service and marriage together accounted for about a quarter of the total number of weavers who each year left the company's service at Halstead.

TABLE 32

Halstead weavers: reasons for leaving, 1882–1903[2]

Date	Total left	Marriage	Increase of family	Domestic service	Bad health	Transferred, discharged, or other reasons
1882–3 (June–June)	87	15	5	11	7	49
1885–6 (June–June)	122	21	7	10	21	63
1896	129	16	9	18	21	65
1898	134	10	16	13	34	61
1902–3 (June–June)	123	7	13	15	30	58

Aggregating the first three periods in this table, marriage took away an average of 15 per cent. and domestic service 12 per cent. Very similar figures appear from analyses of the reasons for leaving in a sample of female hands in the finishing department at Bocking. Over the period 1860–95, marriage was the stated reason in 18 per cent. of the leavers, and domestic service 9 per cent.[3] In the last two periods in Table 32 the increase in the stated reason of 'bad health', taken in conjunction with that of 'increase of family' and the fall in 'marriage', suggests an older and more generally married labour force: a circumstance reconcilable with a stagnant or not rapidly increasing population from which a fair amount of emigration was taking place. For these two years marriage and domestic service together took away only 17 per cent. instead of 27 per cent. But the vague phrase 'bad health' may well also have covered sundry options which in earlier years were recorded under such observations as 'to suit her own purposes'. In short, the recruitment and maintenance of this predominantly female labour force were demanding attentions unnecessary in earlier years.

In 1884 when expansion was progressing to the extent of an extra 100 looms at Halstead, the manager there expressed a cautious hope that he

[1] E.R.O., D/F 3/3/22, pp. 82–83.   [2] E.R.O., D/F 3/3/28.   [3] E.R.O., D/F 3/2/22.

would be able to find the necessary weavers by drawing them in from 'out-of-town' and providing lodgings.[1] During the depression years which followed, the lack of work encouraged migration, and when recovery came again the firm was particularly concerned about the supply of potential weavers. In September 1895 Samuel Augustine Courtauld noted with satisfaction that Halstead was now beginning to get more weavers, for, as he said: '. . . it is most important that we should have new weavers coming forward. At present we have too few on our books.' Neither Bocking nor Braintree seem to have presented such problems of recruitment. The former demanded, on the whole, more specialized male labour; the latter with its smaller demand—there were 470 at work there in 1897—was expected to produce all that was needed. At Halstead, however, although the new extensions to the weaving sheds went forward in 1895 and 1903, they were surrounded with hesitancy about the labour supply. In 1900: 'Were Halstead a very promising weaving place affording abundance of skilled labour it might then be wise to put in hand more radical alteration.' Three years later the outlook looked rosier: 'Until comparatively recently the supply of hands at Halstead seemed so inadequate and the output from the looms so unpromising that we hesitated to recommend any large expenditure upon the place. But recently the conditions there have improved in both these respects, and we believe it worth while to take the place in hand without further delay. . . .'

In the last resort, once the labour market had ceased to be a buyers' market, as it had been for the company in the Bocking–Braintree–Halstead area in the 1830s and 1840s, then only by improvements in wages, earnings, or working conditions could the labour supply be maintained. What, then, did Samuel Courtauld & Co. pay their workers?

II

That question is much more readily posed than answered. With a very few exceptions, virtually nothing has survived to permit pay comparisons for comparable jobs over long periods. The miscellany of scattered figures of wages or earnings which have survived is fraught with all the usual hazards of comparative work in this field: differences of job, age, or training, piece-rates and time-rates, bonuses, fines, payments in kind, rewards, changes in hours. To these are added difficulties arising from the very specialized nature of some of the firm's operations. With what other

[1] E.R.O., D/F 3/3/22, p. 329.

pay is that of a crimper to be compared? What exactly does one do with an assembly of piece-rates for 'B. 5 rollers'?

From what has survived certain conclusions may be drawn more tentatively than certainly. It is clear that the lower-than-average level of wages found in East Anglia in the early decades of the century continued for a long time. The low wages paid to the mass of underemployed, irregularly occupied hand-loom weavers in the Essex–Suffolk border area meant, in turn, that employers, such as Sam Courtauld, installing the new power-loom for crape weaving had to offer only a very small amount more to attract labour to regular factory employment. Moreover, the job could be done by the cheaper female labour. So the new firms, of which Courtauld & Co. was the shining example, which were efficient enough to overcome the difficult days of the 1830s after the deceptive boom of the early 1820s were in a strong position. Whoever could survive in this barely industrialized area could depend, until the relative isolation was broken down, upon a cheap labour force.

In 1816, the average weekly wage of adult women attending George I's mills at Braintree was about 7s.; this amount was also paid in the boom years of 1824 when silk seemed a promised industrial land and every employer was clamouring for labour.[1] In 1833, with trading slump, Free Trade, and the struggle for efficiency, comparable wages in East Anglian silk factories had dropped, as already shown in Chapter VI, to an average of about 5s. per week for young adult women 21 to 31 years of age. These were also the approximate average earnings of women working in the Finishing Factory at Bocking in the mid 1830s; it was based upon a wage rate of 1s. to 1s. 2d. per day.[2] Virtually identical was the figure of 5s. 1d. given as the average earnings of female hand-loom crape weavers employed by the firm in 1837–8.[3] So a weekly wage of 5s. to 6s., which Sam Courtauld was said at the same time to be offering young women to become power-loom weavers at Halstead, seems a not unlikely figure.[4] About forty years later the Halstead manager dispatched to the demanding Sam a detailed account of women's earnings (see Table 33).[5] The figures relate to women of 17 years of age and over; the weavers' earnings are based on piece-rates per packet woven.

Any attempt to compare the scanty data from the 1830s with 1875 is obviously hazardous. But the evidence suggests a rate of increase which

[1] Courtauld MSS.: G.C. I to R. W. Oldham, 8 February 1816; *C.F.L.*, vol. ii, pp. 1215–16.
[2] E.R.O., D/F 3/2/19.   [3] *B.P.P.* 1840, vol. xxiii, p. 127.
[4] Ibid., p. 133.   [5] E.R.O., D/F 3/3/22, pp. 97–103.

was probably much the same as the average increase in industrial wages in the country as a whole. Wages generally stagnated between 1830 and 1850; between 1850 and 1875 the national average rose about 48 per cent.[1] For weavers and mill hands, who made up the majority of Samuel Courtauld & Co.'s female employees, the increase over the whole period looks as though it were about 40 to 50 per cent. Most of this occurred

TABLE 33

Halstead: women's average weekly earnings, week ending 10 April–week ending 22 May 1875

	*Inc. loss of time**			*Actual working time*		
Department	*Married*	*Single*	*Unmarried mothers*	*Married*	*Single*	*Unmarried mothers*
	s. d.	*s. d.*	*s. d.*	*s. d.*	*s. d.*	*s. d.*
Warpers	11 11¼	13 7	..	13 7	13 7½	..
Twisters	9 0½	12 3	6 11†	10 6	12 3	6 11
Weavers	7 5¼	7 3¼	6 10	8 6½	7 9¾	8 7¼
Gauze examiners	11 3	9 6	..	12 2	11 11	..
Plug winders	6 11	6 11¼	7 6½	7 6¾	7 8	7 6½
Mill hands	7 7½	7 8	..		not available	
Drawers	6 9¾	6 4½	8 2‡		,, ,,	

* i.e. 2½ days' holiday, absence through illness, etc.

† Crippled, unable to earn much. The firm employed a small number of unmarried mothers, but made a point of dismissing them after their second illegitimate child.

‡ Two first-class hands, mostly on doubling.

after 1850: between 1853 and 1875 weavers' average actual earnings per week rose from 6*s.* 0½*d.* to 8*s.* 2½*d.*, i.e. 36 per cent.; from 1853 to 1873 drawers' and doublers' rose from 5*s.* to 7*s.*, i.e. 40 per cent.[2] So there was nothing here to narrow the gap between East Anglian silk wages and the rest of the country. Indeed, for some industries it may even have widened. In Lancashire cotton mills, already in the 1830s, as noted in Chapter VI, paying substantially more than East Anglian silk mills, women's wages probably rose by over 60 per cent.[3] To take a quite different example: women linen weavers employed by Marshall's of Leeds were making average earnings of about 10*s.* per week in the 1860s which rose to 12*s.* in 1875.[4] Thus in 1875, according to how the comparisons are made,

[1] Clapham, op. cit., vol. ii, pp. 450–3.

[2] E.R.O., D/F 3/3/27.

[3] Clapham, op. cit., vol. ii, pp. 450–3.

[4] W. G. Rimmer, *Marshall's of Leeds, Flax Spinners, 1788–1886* (Cambridge, 1960), p. 318.

PLATE 19

Women workers in the Finishing Department at Bocking, 1859

their earnings were about 44 per cent. or about 60 per cent. above the Courtauld crape weavers at the same date. In both places, indeed in all the examples, the working week had been shortened by factory legislation, to sixty hours after 1850 and fifty-six after the Act of 1874.

Towards the end of the century, in the phase of recovery, the earnings of these women weavers at Halstead moved up appreciably. In 1896 they averaged 9s. 2d. per week, in 1897, 11s. 4d., and they continued to rise. This suggests an increase since 1875—which was a boom year for the company—of around 26 per cent. to 36 per cent., which was more than the national average for this period. By 1901 hours were down to 55½. Even with this increase, however, the crape-weaving women remained some of the poorest paid of industrial workers. In 1886—when the wages at Halstead cannot have been significantly different from what they had been in 1875—'everywhere the mass of full-time women workers made from 10s. to 14s. a week . . . the Government paid 12s. to the charwomen of Whitehall . . .'.[1] The earnings of women employed in the Finishing Factory approximated to this in 1886, when fifty-five women there made average earnings of 11s. 8d. and twenty-five reached 13s. 11d. per week.[2] But the crape weavers were barely making these figures in the later 1890s. So it is not surprising that in 1873 the Halstead mill hands told the manager that 8s. per week was not sufficient to keep them 'respectable';[3] that two years later he reported that promises of £14 to £18 a year to start at domestic service had attracted weavers to London;[4] or that the drain of weavers to domestic service continued right through to the end of the century. Moreover, the firm ensured that, when recovery came in the late 1890s, those on piece-rates in the finishing department should not earn too much. In 1897, 'in anticipation of next year's demand averaging at least as high and probably higher than this year's the wages of [two of the dressers] are reduced from 6d. per doz. to 5d. per doz.' In 1899, it was decided to cut the piece-rates of twenty of the hands in the finishing department as 'their wage has been excessive lately owing to increased facilities and greater pressure. On maximum finish this will effect an economy of £200 a year.' The extent to which labour was permitted to share in the gains of capital was limited. Before considering how, nevertheless, the firm kept its working force, or what these earnings meant in real terms, it is necessary first to look at the other end of the pay scale: the skilled male employees.

---

[1] Clapham, op. cit., vol. ii, pp. 465-6. [2] E.R.O., D/F 3/2/34, p. 148.
[3] E.R.O., D/F 3/3/22, p. 20. [4] Ibid., pp. 82-83.

At the top of the scale the salaried staff of mill managers and the like were well paid, and many of them shared in the firm's prosperity by receiving a percentage bonus based on profits. In the 1870s the manager of Steam Factory was drawing 3 per cent. on profits, over and above a guaranteed minimum of £1,000 per annum; in the very profitable years of 1870–5, his aggregate salary averaged over £3,500 per annum. The engineer was getting £825 per annum in 1855 with a bonus ranging from 4 per cent. to 6 per cent. according to the level of profits; the Finishing Factory manager was drawing £1,100 per annum in 1888, plus 2 per cent. on profits; the chief engraver, at the same period, was paid £500 a year.

The 'labour aristocracy' of the firm consisted of the crimpers and, perhaps slightly less elevated in status, the lathemen and chief mechanics of Steam Factory, with whom their wages were on a par. From the beginning the rates paid to these men were not only, as would be expected, far higher than those of the many female workers of the firm but compared very favourably with skilled wages outside. Here the relative pay situation of the firm was quite different. In the mid 1830s the two senior crimpers' earnings averaged about 20s. per week. In the 1860s, for a 70-hour week, the top men in the crimping room were making from 34s. 5d. to 39s. 8d. a week; in the 1870s, for a 58-hour week, the beginning wage in the crimping room was 27s. 6d., rising after three years to 33s. 10d.; the more experienced men got more, and the overseers 40s. to 45s. per week.[1] In addition, various rewards and bonuses were paid. A fitter's daily rates in the mechanical department of Steam Factory rose from 4s. in 1870 (62¼-hour week) to 5s. 4d. (58-hour week) in 1873 and 5s. 8d. in 1876; a mechanic and latheman on 6s. per day in 1870 moved up to 7s. 6d. when he went to work in one of the 'secret rooms' in 1873; his successor got 6s. 9d. as a starting rate there in 1887; a carpenter, with responsibility for looking after the throwing mills, was paid at 6s. 3d. per day in 1882.[2] Ordinary male hands started in the dye-house at 14s. per week (70-hour week) in the 1850's and moved up to 16s. 6d. in their third year; in 1883 (58-hour week) the comparable rates were 17s. and 19s. 10d.; the dye-house overseer moved up similarly from 23s. to 28s. The finishing department employed 44 men in 1886; their earnings averaged 25s. 10d. per week, and ranged from 18s. to 35s.[3] In 1878 (56-hour week) male loom attendants at Halstead were earning 19s. 4½d. per week, and loom and spindle cleaners 17s. 3½d.[4] In some ways it was true that the further away from the

[1] E.R.O., D/F 3/2/19.   [2] E.R.O., D/F 3/2/20.
[3] E.R.O., D/F 3/2/34, p. 148.   [4] E.R.O., D/F 3/3/22, pp. 149–50.

central mysteries of crimping and finishing the lower the rate of pay. Only with the crisis of the 1890s did this begin to change. Then it started with the foreman grade and particularly with loom overlookers as new men from the north were brought in with the higher rates of pay necessary to entice them southwards. A new loom overlooker from Bradford, for instance, arrived in 1892 and started at 35s. per week.[1] More were to come, once Tetley had taken over, and not always with happy results (see below, pp. 258-9).

In men's rates, as in women's, significant increases took place after 1850. Loom attendants' earnings, for instance, rose by 49 per cent. between 1852 and 1878 (apart from the reduction in hours).[2] When comparison is made with outside rates, the men's wages show up better. At Marshall's of Leeds, again, whereas the women weavers' wages were higher than at Courtaulds, the men's rates seem much the same: in 1851 mechanics and cleaners there received average weekly wages of 19s. 3½d.; overlookers' rates were 22s. 4d. in 1851 and 30s. in 1880.[3] In the Lancashire cotton industry between 1850 and 1886 mill mechanics' wages rose from 27s. to 32s.; carding overlookers in Manchester, from 27s. to 39s. 10d.[4] To make, finally, a rough general comparison, it is worth considering these scattered Courtauld wages, male and female, in the light of the following data for the country as a whole.[5]

TABLE 34

Average weekly adult earnings: England and Wales, 1886 and 1906

	Men			Women		
	1886	1906	Per cent. increase	1886	1906	Per cent. increase
	s. d.	s. d.		s. d.	s. d.	
Cotton	23 7	28 10	22	15 0	18 8	24
Woollen and worsted	23 3	26 10	15	12 7	13 10	10
Linen	19 9	22 4	13	8 11	10 9	21
Jute	19 4	21 7	12	9 7	13 5	40
Silk	23 0	25 5	11	10 4	11 6	11

At the earlier date the women's wages paid at Samuel Courtauld & Co. seem in the main to have been definitely below the average silk figure,

[1] E.R.O., D/F 3/2/81, p. 52.
[2] E.R.O., D/F 3/3/22, 27.
[3] Rimmer, op. cit., p. 318.
[4] Clapham, op. cit., vol. ii, p. 453.
[5] G. R. Porter, *The Progress of the Nation* (rev. ed. by F. W. Hirst, London, 1912), p. 53.

the men's wages probably about the same or rather above it. By 1906, the trend in north Essex seems to have been upwards and probably the women's wages had caught up with the average; the men's wages were almost certainly better than the average. But, as Table 34 shows, silk, as a whole, made one of the smallest increases of all the textile industries. Samuel Courtauld & Co. was an expanding unit in an industry which was not clamouring for more labour.

III

The recruitment and retention of the firm's labour force was made possible by a peculiar collection of circumstances.

The first circumstance was its near-monopoly of local industrial employment. It exercised this monopoly in an area initially suffering from the protracted decay of the old woollen cloth manufacture and then from the failure of the new silk industry—or indeed any other industry—to establish itself on any really substantial scale. By the mid decades of the nineteenth century Samuel Courtauld & Co. was an island empire of industrial employment, established in three small neighbouring market towns and set in a sea of agriculture; and, moreover, that agriculture paid some of the lowest wages in the whole country. This fact, and its significance for the move of the silk industry into the area in the early years of the century, has already been indicated in Chapter V (above, pp. 61–63). It remained true throughout the nineteenth century. Table 35 (below p. 245) compares the weekly cash wages of agricultural labourers in East Anglia with those in six other regions of England, for various periods from 1867 to 1907.

The East Anglian wages, starting as only slightly above the lowest and remotest region—the south-west of England (F in the Table)—end as by far the lowest of all. For it was the grain-growing areas of East Anglia and the marginal clays of Essex which were hardest hit by the great agricultural depression. Falling prices, as grain flowed in from across the Atlantic, were matched by falling agricultural wages—in the grain-growing areas. The livestock and dairy farmers were far less affected. So wages in western areas moved up substantially by the end of the century, far more than those in the agricultural sea surrounding the efficient crape makers of Bocking, Braintree, and Halstead. Compared with what local agricultural workers could earn, the men at Courtauld & Co. were well off indeed. Very few other comparable outlets existed. The other silk firms which survived were small and did not offer anything like the opportunities for male employment held out by Samuel Courtauld & Co. Only at the very end of the century did a major local alternative appear with the growth of the metal-working firm of Crittall & Co. It is a measure of the

TABLE 35

Average weekly wages of agricultural labourers:
East Anglia and regions of England, 1867–1907

Date	Essex, Suffolk, and Norfolk	Other regions					
		A	B	C	D	E	F
	s. d.	s. d.	s. d.	s. d.	s. d.	s. d.	s. d.
1867–71	11 0	15 1	13 4	11 8	11 7	11 4	10 6
1879–81	12 6	16 2	14 5	13 10	13 0	13 4	12 4
1892–3	11 10	16 5	15 2	12 10	12 4	12 6	11 8
1898	11 11	16 10	16 2	14 10	13 0	13 10	12 7
1902	12 11	18 0	16 9	15 4	13 7	14 8	13 3
1907	12 10	17 3	16 3	15 9	13 11	15 3	13 8

Adapted from W. Ashworth, *An Economic History of England, 1870–1939* (London, 1960), p. 63. The regions were:

A. Cumberland, Westmorland, Northumberland, Durham, Yorks., Lancs., Cheshire.
B. Derby, Notts., Lincs., Rutland, Leics.
C. Hants, Sussex, Kent, Surrey, Middx., Berks.
D. Cambs., Beds., Hunts., Northants., Herts., Bucks., Oxon.
E. Warwicks., Worcs., Staffs., Salop., Herefordshire, Gloucs.
F. Somerset, Devon, Cornwall, Dorset, Wilts.

beginning of change that in 1902 the Bocking manager made an arrangement with the Crittall company that they should consult each other before employing ex-employees from their respective factories.

The second of the special factors favouring the company as employers was the fact of its coming to demand, on the scale that it did and in the local circumstances outlined above, a labour force of a particular sex and pay structure. A central core of well-paid men, skilled and semi-skilled, topped by a crown of mechanics and crimpers, was surrounded by a mass of lower-paid, semi-skilled and unskilled women, girls, and—earlier—children. Here was what must have seemed the ideal structure for family employment. It arose directly from the technical needs of the firm's product. For crape demanded not merely some skilled men but also—because of all the secrecy and mumbo-jumbo of the crimping and engraving rooms and even some of the finishing rooms—well-paid skilled men who would not defect to Grouts or Hindes or another of the few rival crape firms. So from the beginning these men had to be well paid; here alone was there competition to respect. The influence of their pay made itself felt amongst near-comparable grades. The pay and position of the crimpers—with all the status and aura of responsibility which went with swearing-in before a Justice of the Peace—provided ambition and goals of achievement for the firm's male workers. Moreover, many of these men—crimpers, mechanics, dyers, overseers—were husbands or fathers, uncles or brothers of the girls and women who worked elsewhere in Bocking, Braintree, and Halstead, at the mills or the looms, at winding, warping, or weaving. So just as at the top Courtaulds, Taylors, Warrens, and their relations recur, so at a humbler level the same names constantly reappear throughout the nineteenth century amongst men and women employees alike—Rayner, Usher, Bearman, Gentry, Richardson, Butcher, Potter, Amey, and more besides.

This particular mixture of location, economic environment, and familiar pay structure meant that in the nineteenth century the financial position of many, though not all, Courtauld employees was rather better than might at first be supposed simply from comparing the money wages or earnings of the female employees with those of their counterparts elsewhere. In so far as the company provided something approaching family employment, then in terms of family earnings the firm's employees were probably in a better position than were their counterparts in the iron, steel, and mining communities, which offered little female or child employment, especially after 1842,[1] or in some textile districts where there were relatively fewer well-paid jobs for men. In comparison with cotton, the best paid of the textile industries, it was merely a narrowing of the gap; it certainly did not close it. Is it possible that in real terms the remuneration of the firm's workers was better or at least not significantly worse than those in the higher money-wage areas of the industrial Midlands and north? Real wages in general were certainly rising significantly from the 1850s onwards; for those not heavily affected by the unemployment of the depression years the continued fall in food prices probably more than counterbalanced wage cuts or short-time working. Courtauld's employees may perhaps have been relatively better off in real terms, for two reasons. First, it must be remembered that they worked in towns which were very different entities from many of the urban centres of industrialization.

---

[1] Women and children were then forbidden by legislation to work underground in mining (5 & 6 Vic., c. 99).

Halstead's population did not top 7,000 in the nineteenth century; Braintree and Bocking together never reached 9,000; many employees came from neighbouring villages of a few hundred people. For many of these employees it was surely likely that they or their families would have been able to grow some vegetables or fruit, keep some pigs or chickens, or at least obtain access to farm produce. That likelihood must have been very much greater than for their counterparts in towns like Leeds or Bradford, Sheffield or Salford, with populations, even in the 1860s, of over 100,000, like Birmingham with over 250,000, not to speak of London with its near 3,000,000 inhabitants at that time. Moreover, despite the proximity to London which may have kept up retail food prices, house rents were admittedly lower.[1] In general it seems likely that for the Courtauld employees the cost of living was lower than for the better-paid workers of the big urban centres of industrialization. Second, whilst food prices were falling sharply after 1872, Samuel Courtauld & Co. was enjoying a boom period which, except for 1877–8, lasted until 1886. So for a period in which unemployment and short-time were appearing in various parts of the economy, for the firm's employees both money and real wages were rising and employment was high. During the firm's depression period, 1886–96, though employment certainly did fall, and much short-time was worked, wage rates were not significantly reduced, and retail prices continued to drop. So, again, it seems possible that the impact of the 'Great Depression' in terms of real earnings for the Courtauld employees may have been shorter and less severe than it was at least for some firms in some industries.

This complex of circumstances, which helped the firm to recruit and retain its labour force in lowly paid north Essex, was undoubtedly itself aided by the policy of labour relations which the company developed. In the course of the nineteenth century Samuel Courtauld & Co. acquired a reputation as enlightened employers.

IV

It would be easy to characterize the firm's labour relations policy as one of benevolent despotism, kindly autocracy, or the like. Such phrases, however, say little of the motives and attitudes of mind of the men who created this policy. The policy was revealed in action; the attitudes of mind in the private utterances and public phraseology of the partners. In

---

[1] *B.P.P.* 1840, vol. xxiii, pp. 125, 127. If they were lower in 1838 it is unlikely that the gap narrowed later.

this context the partners or directors who mattered were all Courtaulds: Sam, George II, George III, to a lesser extent Sydney, and, at the very end of the period of this volume, Samuel Augustine, who was just beginning to reveal his inheritance of these attitudes. The Taylors, Warrens, Nettlefold, and the rest played virtually no part here; there was nothing in it for Tetley. It began with Sam and his brother George, themselves influenced by their father's idealistic concern with the improvement of man by rational processes and benevolent action. In Sam the rational processes came to mean the masterful implementation of free enterprise and free trade, tempered by his own concern for social justice and his wife's compassion for the poor.[1] In George II the need for benevolent action was transmuted into strong views about the social responsibility, the stewardship which the firm should possess as the biggest employer of industrial labour in north Essex. Both had also grown up with another attitude of mind which was a commonplace assumption of their father's day: that the working-classes, the 'labouring poor', were a sort of sub-species of mankind, congenitally idle, prone to depravity, born to irresponsibility. This long-enduring attitude was an essential, though not always revealed, assumption of the reformers of the day; it lies behind their seemingly contradictory beliefs in welfare and *laissez-faire*, in self-help and a self-governing economy, behind that fascinating paradox of the great Victorian century of free enterprise being also the great Victorian century of Factory Acts.

George II's attitudes were exhibited clearly in a letter of 1846.[2] Feeling, he said, that 'we have not done all which our position has placed it in our power to do', he went on to sketch the welfare problems of the company's work people as he saw them:

There are two grand miseries among our work people—among the men grown up from boys in our service receiving probably higher wages than might suffice for their respectable maintenance—the surplus has gone too often in ministering to a selfish personal indulgence of a more or less pernicious character rather than to furnish the means of self-culture or to provide for this respectability and comfort of his home—And among the girls and young women the various evils of ignorance are not only much aggravated by their being brought together in large numbers and to some extent compelled to associate—but the nature of their employment takes from them even the poor preparation they might have received at their *homes* for the duties of wives and mothers.

[1] For an account, scarcely dispassionate, of the welfare activities at Halstead of 'these noble-hearted employers, and more particularly the wife of the senior partner', see Mary Merryweather, *Experiences of Factory Life* (London, 1862).

[2] C.F.L., vol. vii, pp. 3193-5.

He looked to reform in the founding of various educational provisions. Were there other means, he asked, 'of turning our stewardship to account'? He saw the mutual relation in business of employers and employed as potentially productive of 'the greatest good' and this relation as 'one of the most important in our social economy'. But, he insisted, the duties of the relation must be understood:

... it should be known and felt that the duties of the employer and the employed tended to something other than a mere heartless strife of selfish interests; that the aim of the master need not be confined to the procuring of the greatest service for the least money—nor that of the workman to obtaining the greatest amount of compensation for the least service.

What of the poor? Though a score of years later his cousin was vigorously denouncing Sabbatarianism in the House of Commons, in 1849 George II was writing to his son George III to stress how important was a Sabbath to all, 'but more especially [to] the poorer and less instructed classes':[1]

... Just consider the state of the young people of the poor, who do not take advantage of this (i.e. Public Worship) their only mode of mental improvement—ignorant, loutish, animal; their holiday but leaves them at liberty to indulge their low and often depraved inclinations without restraint; and separated thus from that part of their own class whom either principle or mere force of habit and association induces, or compels, to an observance of the established decencies and proprieties of Society, they are left, in this their holiday, to such gratifications as they only are alive to, the gratification of sensualism in its worst form. ...

Of Sam's attitudes we have already seen something in his willingness to 'discipline' the habits of the hand-loom weavers, his indignation at State intervention, his persistence in fighting for personal rights on the issue of church rates.[2] There is no doubt that he knew well the poverty and misery of the many unemployed and underemployed in the area in which he had himself worked to set up his business. He saw, rightly, that only by the creation of sustained industrial employment was that poverty likely to be relieved. He was probably justified in claiming as he did in 1833 that 'the orderly and industrious habits introduced with our manufacture into this neighbourhood, and the better food and clothing obtained by its means, have been gradually improving the health of the class employed'.[3] 'Orderly and industrious habits' of 'the class employed': these are the meaningful

[1] G.C.B., pp. 37–38. [2] Above, pp. 103–4, 218–21, 233.
[3] B.P.P. 1834, vol. xx, p. 370.

phrases of Sam's claim. Merit only came by hard work; the employed classes could acquire this merit only by learning to change their habits in the school of industry.

> . . . all my sympathies, and all my feelings of fellowship, are with those who honestly and nobly earn the bread they eat by work, strenuous work, who in whatever situation of life they may be placed, are still ever up and doing with all their heart and with all their strength the work, whatever that work may be, which God has given them to do. . . .[1]

In this peroration, of 1846, God may have provided the work. But in a notice of 1839 about the recruitment of soft-silk, hand-loom weavers, it was made wholly clear that what Sam Courtauld could give, Sam Courtauld could take away. Announcing that the firm intended to make some high quality soft-silk goods, it went on to warn:

> . . . None therefore but QUITE THE VERY BEST HANDS can be employed by us. . . . After this notice it would be *the greatest folly* for any person to apply for our work who do not themselves know that they are really first rate weavers. Let no one calculate upon our unwillingness to discharge a weaver once engaged by us; in the market for which we design these goods NO IMPERFECTIONS WILL PASS, therefore if by mistake any second-rate weaver be engaged, it will be absolutely necessary to discharge him, and after this notice and warning he cannot complain of our strictness when we do so.[2]

In George II and Sam were the essential attitudes of mind which informed the firm's labour relations policies. They were combined and continued in George III. How did they exhibit themselves in practice?

Sam's views on work being what they were, it is hardly surprising to discover that an amplitude of fines and forfeits balanced by rewards and bonuses appeared from the earliest days. There was nothing very original about this[3]—and Sam was doubtless aware of the simple incentive system run by his father at Braintree in 1814[4]—but in the literature of the Industrial Revolution more tends to be heard of fines than of rewards. To the questions posed by the Children's Employment Commissioners in

---

[1] *Report of the Proceedings . . .*, p. 12.

[2] Notice dated 23 August 1839. I am grateful to Mrs. R. Hirst for kindly supplying a copy.

[3] For a fascinating list of the reasons for fines in an early cotton mill see R. S. Fitton and A. P. Wadsworth, *The Strutts and the Arkwrights, 1758–1830* (Manchester, 1958), pp. 232–8. In general, see S. Pollard, 'Factory Discipline in the Industrial Revolution', *Econ. Hist. Rev.*, 2nd series, vol. xvi, No. 2, December 1963, pp. 254–71.

[4] Above, p. 44.

1833 about the methods of securing the obedience of child employees, he answered that it was all done by 'a regular system of forfeits and rewards, the stimulus of piece-work, and dismissal in the last resort'. He confessed, in answer to a question about corporal punishment, that 'formerly something like a system of slight chastisement, connected with a system of task-work, was adopted'; but for several years this method had been superseded by piece-work, forfeits, and rewards.[1] The girls weaving gauze at Panfield Lane in 1827–8 got overtime payments, allowances of beer, and 'rewards for industry'; in the 1830s there were beer and rewards for crimpers and dressers and finishers.[2] Arrangements of this sort continued: in 1868, for example, in order to encourage careful crimping, a bonus of 3d. per packet was paid on every packet of crape the figure of which was deemed by the London office to reach a certain standard of excellence; in the 1880s a different scheme to the same end was adopted. The other side of the coin was a strict factory discipline in which mistakes were quickly penalized. 'Nov. 1872—very bad dressing work—fined and cautioned':[3] this is merely one of many entries of this sort, relating, in this case, to a woman hand in the finishing department, but applicable, *mutatis mutandis*, to many others. In 1889 the firm took counsels' opinion on the legality of certain sorts of fines, and heard that these were considered to be illegal. Fines for being late were then abolished, but those who arrived late were not admitted until after the next meal break, or the next day, thus missing earnings which may well have amounted to more than the fines. Rewards were then introduced for those of punctual attendance.[4]

Surviving records provide frequent examples of workers taking their pay grievances to managers, and often securing small advantages of pay.[5] In periods of bad trade, the discharge of hands was avoided as long as possible by the device of short-time working. The mechanics, for instance, were put on 60 hours instead of 70 from October 1857 to February 1858, on $51\frac{1}{4}$ instead of 58 in 1877–8.[6] This latter slump pressed hard upon some of the workers and the Halstead manager put the grievances of the loom attendants to the company in March 1878. The looms had last been working full-time at 56 hours in April 1877, at which time their earnings were 19s. $4\frac{1}{2}d.$ per week; the time had gradually been reduced to $42\frac{1}{4}$ in September 1877 which it still was in March 1878, thus reducing their earnings to

[1] B.P.P. 1840, vol. xx, p. 370.   [2] E.R.O., D/F 3/2/18, 19.
[3] E.R.O., D/F 3/2/22.   [4] E.R.O., D/F 3/2/35, pp. 191–3; D/F 3/3/22, p. 26.
[5] E.R.O., D/F 3/3/22, *passim*.   [6] E.R.O., D/F 3/2/75, p. 11.

14s. 8½d. 'The men', the manager reported, 'are quite aware that the firm were most unwilling to reduce the time to its present limits and that even these hours have been more than was desirable so far as the business was concerned.' In June 45 hours was resumed, 50 in July, and full-time in November.[1] During the long depression years after 1886 short-time was only gradually and reluctantly supplemented by dismissals. In the mechanical department of Steam Factory short-time started in November 1886, full-time was resumed in March 1890, and reduced again in October 1892. Meanwhile the staff had been reduced by some dismissals; for example, ten men were given a month's notice in October 1887.[2] At Halstead, only after hours had been reduced to 42½ in 1889[3] were the numbers cut down, and this was done as much as possible by allowing the normal wastage to take its course and not recruiting more weavers. In time, as the depression worsened, discharge of hands increased. The following figures[4] give some idea both of this procedure from 1889 to 1894, and of how readily the firm could recruit, when prosperity returned, temporarily, in 1890. The figures in brackets are the numbers in the total leaving who were discharged.

TABLE 36

Halstead weavers: turnover, 1889–94

Month	1889		1890		1891		1892		1893		1894	
	Left	Taken	Left	Taken	Left	Taken	Left	Taken	Left	Taken	Left	Taken
Jan.	7	..	8	..	3	6	4	..	14	..	7	2
Feb.	4	1	8	..	8	4	5	24	9	..	5	..
Mar.	5	3	3	7	9	3	3	1	17	..	7	..
Apr.	5	1	6	37	6	..	6	..	2	1	12(9)	14
May	15(8)	..	4	15	6	..	5	3	3	4	17(11)	4
June	29(9)	..	2	30	26(17)	..	5	..	6	2	27(19)	6
July	7	..	2	5	25(15)	1	9	..	4	..	19(11)	4
Aug.	9	..	4	10	2	12	8	..	6	4	19(10)	..
Sept.	10	..	6	34	9	..	6	..	7	7	11(2)	3
Oct.	9	..	6	15	16	2	11	..	11	1	9	7
Nov.	12	..	3	21	5	11	13	..	7(1)	3	5	5
Dec.	5	..	7	7	6	..	15	..	5	1	5(1)	6
Totals	83	5	59	181	121	39	90	28	91	23	143	51

[1] E.R.O., D/F 3/3/22, pp. 149–50; D/F 3/3/24, p. 50.
[2] E.R.O., D/F 3/2/69, pp. 81, 95; D/F 3/2/74, p. 141; D/F 3/2/75, pp. 11, 161, 180.
[3] E.R.O., D/F 3/2/24, p. 53.
[4] E.R.O., D/F 3/3/29. The figures include transfers to and from other departments: these fluctuated considerably, but did not normally form an appreciable proportion of the total.

When finishing orders were reduced in these bad periods, hands were sometimes transferred from one department to another rather than simply dismissed. In 1888, for instance, as the finishing orders were repeatedly cut down, hands in the finishing department who had earlier been transferred from the throwing mills found that they were earning less than if they had stayed at the mills. On being consulted by the Finishing Factory manager George Courtauld III ordered that they should be returned to the mills and compensated for their losses.[1] Crimpers were carefully conserved during these difficult years. When, for example, the crimping room was found to be over-staffed because of the decline of trade in 1889, two of the junior men were given jobs elsewhere at Bocking, one in the dye-house and one as a mechanic, paid for two months at crimpers' rates, and then offered these new jobs at the lower rates normally going with those jobs.[2]

If the company, in such ways as these, showed itself less ruthless than its position might have permitted, there was nevertheless no mistaking the authentic voice of Sam Courtauld in the reactions to an attempted strike by the power-loom weavers at Halstead in 1860. There had been some trouble about the pay for a particular sort of weaving. The weavers struck. Sam dispatched to their manager a letter which was then printed and posted as a notice to the weavers. It observed, *inter alia*, of the hands:[3]

They have, however, chosen to at once *strike* and have *by that hostile and injurious*, but at the same time in the present case *most wanton and unfitting*, and certainly as they will find MOST VAIN ATTEMPT AT INTIMIDATION, made it impossible for us to confer with them in the friendly spirit in which they must know in their hearts we have always acted towards them.

This note of injured and righteous indignation being thus tortuously sounded, the manager was ordered to get up steam on Monday morning so that the hands could resume work if they pleased. Then came the true expression of power:

... if they come in, well and good, and let me have the names of the first 50 who do so come in. If by the breakfast hour they do not come in, close all the Factories for the whole week. And if by the end of that week they still chose to be idle, we shall then take instant and vigorous measures to get a large portion of our goods at all events, permanently made in other parts of England. ...
... Meanwhile, report to me the names of the 20 to 50 of those who have been foremost in this shameful disorder, for immediate and absolute discharge.

[1] E.R.O., D/F 3/2/35, pp. 114–15.
[2] E.R.O., D/F 3/2/36, pp. 57–59; D/F 3/2/49, pp. 152–3.   [3] E.R.O., D/F 3/2/103.

What happened on this particular occasion remains obscure, though it is hard to believe that the weavers won. Of organized trade union activity in the firm at that time no trace survives. At the end of the century it had certainly made its appearance; there was more labour unrest at Halstead and a serious lock-out occurred there in 1898. But before examining these episodes—belonging as they do to the post-depression years, and which were closely related to the introduction of men from the north of England —it is time to take cognizance of an earlier episode which reflects very creditably upon the workers' regard for their employers, as well as of various welfare activities promoted by members of the Courtauld family.

In June 1846 the workers of the firm gave a much-publicized dinner and entertainment for their employers.[1] It seems to have been a spontaneous gesture—there are other examples in the industrial history of the day,[2] though this one must surely have been unique in Essex—and to have been organized by a committee of the senior workers. Processions of hands, with appropriate displays of banners, from Braintree, Bocking, and Halstead, converged on a field in front of Sam Courtauld's house at High Garrett (this was before his Gosfield Hall days), and there some 1,500 persons sat down to a meal in a vast marquee, after which there was much speech-making, mainly by the assembled guests. These included not merely Courtaulds and Taylors, but local Dissenting notables and that redoubtable orator of Unitarianism and Free Trade, W. J. Fox. As indicated earlier,[3] it was an occasion for much Free Trade tub-thumping. It is, incidentally, hard to believe that the timing of the dinner—26 June 1846—was unrelated to the fact that the Bill to repeal the Corn Laws had finally been passed by the Lords on the 15th. As the *Daily News* archly observed, 'Mr. S. Courtauld and Mr. P. A Taylor, with other members of their firm, are well-known as champions of the late legislative change, and of whatever is connected with the cause of civil and religious liberty'.[4] As a gesture by the workers of the firm it was in part a tribute to the sympathetic attitudes of their employers; in larger part it was a tribute to the fact that in this area which had, in the lives of the men and women there, known so much poverty and violent swings of fortune, here was a growing and prospering firm which provided jobs for something approaching

[1] *Report of the Proceedings....* This was printed by the firm and consists mainly of a reprinted account from the *Essex Herald* of 30 June 1846 and the *Daily News* of 2 July 1846, together with some additions, revisions, and an introduction. See also *C.F.L.*, vol. vii, pp. 3144–92.

[2] Pollard, op. cit., in *Econ. Hist. Rev.*, December 1963, p. 257.

[3] Above, pp. 115, 225.   [4] *Report of the Proceedings . . .*, p. 41.

2,000 men, women, and children. And this was more important to the suffering poor of Bocking, Braintree, and Halstead than anything else.

The welfare activities exhibited themselves in various ways. Schools were built and opened at High Garrett and Gosfield. Sam Courtauld, in a speech at the opening of the High Garrett school, addressed himself to his 'neighbours and friends of the working classes', and emphasized its non-denominational character, its co-educational arrangements, and its avoidance of corporal punishment.[1] As might have been expected, donations were made in the 1840s to the strongly Nonconformist-supported British and Foreign Schools Society.[2] In 1852 George II set up in Church Street, Bocking, a reading-room with a small library in the hope of attracting some employees from 'the beer shop and public house with their physical and mental excitements of drinking and a low and depraved literature'.[3] A new reading-room was inaugurated there in 1885 for use in conjunction with a free library then recently set up by Mrs. Sydney Courtauld. Meanwhile, also in Church Street, Bocking, a workmen's club, with George III as president, had been started in 1873—the firm defraying working expenses after subscriptions had been used up. In 1885 the firm built a large new workmen's hall in the same street.[4] In his will George II left money for the benefit of the Braintree and Bocking Literary and Mechanics Institute—the presence at which of *The Nonconformist* he defended in his lifetime against the stricture of his son George III, for, as he said, the paper represented the views of 'the more advanced and liberal section of Dissenters who are very strong in our county'.[5] He also endowed an existing school at Braintree and left money for future school building there, at the opening of which in 1862 stress was again put, this time by George III, on the non-doctrinal character of the school.[6] Mrs. Sam Courtauld was always particularly active in charitable works amongst the poor of the neighbourhood. She and Sam were responsible for the building of reading- and coffee-rooms and the like at Gosfield and High Garrett, for the maintenance of which, and the schools, there, Sam left money in his will.[7] An evening school was started at Halstead for the

---

[1] *C.F.L.*, vol. vii, pp. 3419–23.

[2] Ibid., vol. vii, p. 3289.

[3] *G.C.B.*, p. 48. This reading-room later formed part of the Mechanics' Institute.

[4] E.R.O., D/F 3/2/59, p. 15; D/F 3/2/72, p. 78; D/F 3/2/73, p. 22.

[5] *G.C.B.*, p. 108.

[6] Ibid., pp. 118–26.

[7] *Report of the Proceedings . . .*, p. 31; Courtauld MSS.: 'The Gosfield People' to Ellen Courtauld, 11 March 1862; Ellen C. to (?) the Gosfield Tenants (?) 1871.

factory girls; in the 1870s it was receiving a Government grant and its pupils were being annually examined by school inspectors.[1]

In the course of the nineteenth century the firm, or its partners, built a substantial number of cottages to house the company's workers. They survive today, at Gosfield, Bocking, Halstead, many bearing the date of building and the initials of S.C. or G.C. (III). Some of those in Bocking and Gosfield were built in a characteristically Victorian style which seems to hover between neo-Gothic and neo-Tudor. In them lived the more senior and skilled workers, including many of the crimpers. Sixteen 'mechanics dwellings' at Halstead and ten at Bocking cost £7,000 in 1872, i.e. about £270 apiece.[2] As well as this housing, mainly for the skilled men and their families, the firm provided at Halstead in the 1840s a hostel or 'Home' for the factory girls there, together with a soup kitchen.[3] (The problems of soup making, incidentally, seem to have been referred, as were so many other matters, to the engineer James Finney, who, in conjunction with Sydney Courtauld, an equally unlikely authority, was in January 1872 making elaborate inquiries into the reasons why the hands at Braintree mill did not like the firm's soup.)[4]

George III continued the tradition of welfare begun by his father and uncle. He, and his first wife, started the cottage hospital at Bocking; he built sundry cottages for the firm's employees, including those situated along the causeway at Halstead. In the course of his life he gave money to various wholly local causes—for a recreation ground and public baths at Halstead, for the Mechanics' Institute and public gardens at Braintree.[5] Within the firm he was a regular contributor to and attender at sundry activities designed to promote good staff relations: cricket matches; fêtes at his house for the factory employees; dinners and soirées at the Workmen's Hall; in 1890 he invited to dinner all those who had been in the business when he started in 1847; a tea in 1896 to celebrate the opening of the new weaving shed at Halstead, duly noted as being fifty years after the 1846 dinner.[6] Sydney Courtauld was also active in arranging festivals of this sort.[7]

Pensions were sometimes paid to long-service workers. In 1857, for example, the principal power-loom overseer, who had been with the

[1] E.R.O., D/F 3/3/22, pp. 134, 146, 154, 339.   [2] E.R.O., D/F 3/2/56, p. 159.

[3] E.R.O., D/F 3/1/8, p. 21; C.F.L., vol vii, pp. 3426–8; Merryweather, op. cit. pp. 43–9.

[4] E.R.O., D/F 3/2/56, pp. 94–95.   [5] G.C.B., pp. 161, 334–5, 560.

[6] Ibid., p. 339; E.R.O., D/F 3/2/59, p. 15; D/F 3/2/73, p. 92; D/F 3/2/77, pp. 188–90; D/F 3/2/78, pp. 78–79.

[7] E.R.O., D/F 3/2/65, pp. 24–25; D/F 3/2/68, p. 141; D/F 3/2/72, p. 78; D/F 3/2/77, p. 23.

PLATE 20

COTTAGES BUILT BY THE COMPANY AT BOCKING, as they stand today

Each of the five pairs in the row bears the legend: S.C. & Co. A.D. 1872. The company's highest profits in the whole of the nineteenth century were earned in 1872 and 1873

firm since 1825, retired with a pension of 10s. a week.[1] Skilled men, long
in service, or their widows were the usual recipients of acts of generosity.
In 1881, meeting the widow of an old employee, George III sent an order
to the mill manager: 'please allow Mrs. Arnold, widow of John Arnold,
5s. weekly—and charge it to my private account.'[2] But George III also
put ordinary hands upon his list of beneficiaries. On the closing of the
Chelmsford mill, he insisted that the fifty hands discharged should be
given bonuses of £1 apiece. John Warren—the then chairman—and the
other directors were rather shocked. 'I should suppose no firm but ourselves', he wrote to George III, 'would give any bonus at all—but we are
all quite prepared to do something. . . . This it should be most clearly
understood is not to be a precedent if more extensive reductions may be
needed in other places.' In fact, however, when old hands were discharged
in 1894, £250 was distributed amongst them, and a further £200 when
further dismissals were made in the following year. In 1897 sundry small
weekly allowances were being paid to forty-six former hands. In the 1870s
and 1880s George III and Sydney shared the cost of sending twenty-three
of the senior skilled men on paid holidays to Paris.[3] By the 1890s paid
holidays ranging from ten days to three weeks were granted to the salaried
staff at the mills. At Aldermanbury all the employees had holidays with
pay; these privileges were yet to come for the manual workers at the
factories.[4] George III's whole attitude to labour relations in the factory
was, in some ways, summed up in an answer he gave when asked if certain

---

[1] E.R.O., D/F 3/3/27.   [2] Arnold, a mechanic, had joined the firm in 1825.
[3] To which exotic destination they were guided by the hands of Messrs. Cook. E.R.O.,
D/F 3/2/72, pp. 138–9; D/F 3/2/72, p. 128 give details. A typical cost was:

				£	s.	d.
1 Cook's ticket	.	.	.	3	19	0
1 week's wages	.	.	.	1	8	0½
Railway ticket	.	.			7	8
Pocket money	.	.			7	0
				6	1	8½

[4] E.R.O., D/F 3/3/24, p. 77; D/F 3/2/37, p. 129. In 1866 the holidays allowed to the
factory hands were Easter Monday, Braintree New Fair (8 May), Whit Monday, Bocking
Fair (July, half-day), Braintree Old Fair (2 October), Christmas Day and the day following:
total 6½ days. After the Bank Holiday legislation, the factory no longer closed for Braintree
New Fair or for Bocking Fair but closed instead for August Bank Holiday—E.R.O.,
D/F 3/2/, p. 593. These arrangements were not dissimilar to the general run of holidays in
the nineteenth century, though the paid holiday for all employees, including the porters, at
Aldermanbury in 1891 was probably unusual. For general practice, see J. A. R. Pimlott,
The Englishman's Holiday (London, 1947).

welfare activites were to be ended. 'I do not wish', he said, 'to relieve the firm of one fraction of their assistance to the poor.' And by 'the poor', as the mill manager, to whom the remark was addressed, duly noted, he meant 'the Factory people'.[1]

Here, in brief, was a continuing flow of charitable activity, of measures large and small. It is easy to sneer at it; to point out that whilst wages rose perhaps 50 per cent. from the 1830s to the 1880s, the average level of profits rose by about 1,400 per cent.; that this sluggishness of wages was a potent contribution to those profits; that the weak position of labour and the strong position of capital made benevolence easy. But in the circumstances of industry in nineteenth-century England this building up of a tradition of good labour relations, of sympathetic personal attitudes, did much for the firm's reputation and eased the task of the recruitment and retention of its labour force. It is not without significance that there was a dinner in 1881 at which some 2,000 of the firm's workers again entertained their bosses.[2] In aggregate this welfare activity was surely a potent force in limiting very markedly the outflow of workers from this low-wage area. It stood Samuel Courtauld & Co. in good stead when, in the 1890s, much was changed in the factories, new men and new ideas appeared, organized labour grew stronger, and the seemingly comfortable isolation of north Essex was broken down.

The modernization of weaving brought, as we have seen, much deliberate recruitment of men from the northern textile centres.[3] They were mainly foremen and loom workers. In order to induce them southwards they were paid substantially higher rates than their Essex counterparts received: 30s. to 35s. instead of 25s. per week. They brought, too, different, less compliant, attitudes of mind; they were used to a different working atmosphere; not all were tactful. A 'slight disturbance . . . amongst the weavers at Halstead' in 1894 (a year of many dismissals) was followed by a strike in February 1897. It lasted from Friday till Monday when work was resumed after talk between the strikers and Tetley together with Sydney and Samuel Augustine Courtauld. The trouble was slight, but it arose from the behaviour of some of the Bradford loom attendants. One was sacked, two were cautioned. The mill manager threatened to resign, but reconsidered his decision.

This was small stuff compared with the disturbance of June 1898. Though resentment at the better pay of the men from Yorkshire had been building up, the northerners also brought with them something which

---

[1] E.R.O., D/F 3/3/26.   [2] G.C.B., p. 312.   [3] Above, pp. 191, 243.

held out the promise of a stronger bargaining position: the trade union. Shortly after the dispute of 1897 a branch of the East Riding of Yorkshire Weavers and Textile Workers' Association was formed; membership rose to about 350. All went smoothly until early in June 1898 when an order was given that the weavers should clean their own looms after a warp was finished and before starting a new one. This they refused to do. The mill manager, instructed by Tetley, offered a small additional payment, but to no avail. The weavers alleged that it was not women's work, that it had always been done by men and boys, and that the sum offered was inadequate. The management retorted that the new order was asking the weavers to do no more than was elsewhere done normally and without protest or extra payment—an observation which suggests Tetley rather than the Courtaulds as its source. The weavers still refusing to clean the looms, the directors decided on a lock-out and closed the Halstead factory on Saturday the 11th. There followed a series of employees' meetings in the town and public gatherings, at which the principal speaker was Mrs. M. Brodie, of the Lancashire Weavers' and Spinners' Association and Women's Trade Union League. In an action perhaps even more ironic than she knew, she addressed the assembled weavers, who no longer devoted their energies wholly to crape, from the fountain in Market Hill which had been erected by George Courtauld III to commemorate Queen Victoria's Jubilee. During the first week of the lock-out there were meetings between the Bocking directors and a committee of the weavers. On the 18th the weavers were obliged to accept the management's terms. But to rub in the lesson it was then decided to keep the factory closed for a second week, and it was not until 27 June that, as Samuel Augustine put it, 'work was quietly resumed'. To everyone in the company's employment a notice was then given that conforming to the company's rules must be an express condition of employment. 'Work is proceeding quietly', reported Samuel Augustine in July, 'although the woman agitator is remaining in the town to make what mischief she can.'[1]

---

[1] Relations between the London and Bocking directors do not seem to have been very cordial, to judge, at least, by the tone of a letter of 14 June 1898 from John Warren to Samuel Courtauld & Co., Bocking: 'Dear Sirs, We this morning received letter from Mr. Sydney Courtauld (which we may remark was quite unaddressed to any one except on the envelope) as to the Halstead "lock-out" and as therein requested we at once telegraphed to you "*Yes*" on the question of consulting Counsel in the matter as to the effect of our having closed the factory without notice. . . . We would venture to suggest that much time and probably some expense would have been saved had we here gone to Counsel directly, indeed Mr. S. A. Courtauld might have come up and gone with us, but we had no desire to interfere with your plans.'

The company won, without much difficulty, at the cost of a two-week stoppage. But the whole episode was symptomatic of the changes in the affairs of Samuel Courtauld & Co. Ltd. as the firm was pushed into the twentieth century. The paternalistic attitude, with its expectation of obedience and exercise of benevolence, was far from dead; it still had time to run, but it was being subjected to unwonted shocks. Like a good many other firms, the company did not take kindly to trade unions; but they had arrived and, sometimes without being indiscreetly overt, they stayed. During the first decade of this century a branch of the National Association of Power-Loom Overlookers was started; in time the gap between the pay of the Essex men and of those from the north was narrowed. So for the workers, as in management and in production techniques, improvement came by a tempering of their Essex isolation. It came to them, they did not go to secure it. The reduction in differentials was not secured, as the free movement of economic factors would theoretically demand, by an outflow from the low-wage area to high-wage areas. On the contrary, it was induced by the deliberate importation of better-paid expertise, at directorial, management, and foreman levels. This helped to instigate recovery, push up productivity, increase workers' earnings, and later, and more reluctantly accepted by the directors, to force up wage rates. But throughout there survived, and endured in the twentieth century, an attitude towards labour relations which had been fashioned in, and belonged to, an earlier era.

CHAPTER XII

Comparisons and Conclusions

THE experience of one firm or of one business family should not too readily be cited to prove or refute any of the numerous generalizations which have been made about the course of English industrial history in the nineteenth century. Faced with so seemingly curious a commodity as mourning crape, it is reasonable to feel doubts about presenting Samuel Courtauld & Co. as a 'typical firm' —whatever that may mean—in manufacturing generally, in the textile industry in particular, or even within the silk industry itself. But the nature of its product, faintly bizarre to mid-twentieth-century ideas, should not deceive us. In fact, the firm had many experiences in common with concerns making more conventional wares; its output was, as we have seen, sensitive to the fluctuations of the business cycle as revealed through other media; and in certain rather specialized ways it faithfully mirrored the Victorian social and economic scene. To consider every aspect of the business experience of firm and family in the light of more general knowledge might perhaps be virtuous but would inescapably be tedious. Selection must suffice.

The start of the path along which Samuel Courtauld trod to become what Victorians were pleased to call 'a captain of industry' was probably odd, in its suggestion of the reluctant entrepreneur coming into his own in consequence of an idealistic father's incompetence. But there was nothing odd in the exploitation of a patent; nor were the social yearnings of the Unitarian Courtaulds in any way unique. Indeed, in these words of guidance for social improvement which the Unitarian cotton spinner, Jedediah Strutt, sent to his son William in 1774, there is a striking echo of that homily about 'the kindly benignant *Bend*'[1] which George Courtauld I dispatched to his son Samuel in 1815:

> . . . I need not tell you that you are not to be a Nobleman nor prime minister, but you may possibly be a Tradesman of some emminence & as such you will necessarily have connections with Mankind & the World, and that will make

---

[1] Above, pp. 47–48.

it absolutely necessary to know them both; & you may be assured if you add
to the little learning & improvement you have hitherto had, the Manners, the
Air, the genteel address, & polite behaviour of a gentleman, you will abundantly find your acct in it in all and every transaction of your future life—when
you come to do business in the World.[1]

Though the practical and realistic Jedediah Strutt and the impractical and
idealistic George Courtauld I were utterly different sorts of men, they had
in common Unitarianism and a nice regard for social position.

When searching for the driving forces of ambition which projected the
business tycoons of the Industrial Revolution it is well to remember the
powerful social tensions of a world in which not merely most private
wealth but virtually all social and political prestige rested with the landowning gentry and aristocracy. The exceptionally able Dissenter, the
thrusting and gifted outsider, had little to lose and everything to gain.
Trade, industry, and finance had long given him his chance; the break-
through to the industrialized society offered a profusion of opportunities
in which the goals were far from the mere making of money. The journey
to the coveted social esteem which wealth could buy—if not always in one
generation then, with a little luck, in the next—needed unusual combinations of ability, energy, and dominance. The cost to the individual was the
not unusual one of a sense of isolation and insecurity, of achievement
counter-balanced by depression; and the tensions thus engendered may
well have been acute in the exceedingly unequal society of the day. In
presenting just such a combination Samuel Courtauld was not alone.
An earlier and much richer counterpart was John Marshall, founder of
what ranked in its day as the greatest flax-spinning firm in the world.
Here was a man who seems to have yearned for riches, fame, and social
prestige from his earliest youth. He got them. He died reputedly worth
some £2,000,000 in 1845, at the age of 80. The customary landmarks soon
loom up: Unitarianism, Utilitarianism, and reflections on his own achievements which strike a very familiar note:

It is true that I have gone through an uncommon share of labour and pain,
but it has not been altogether unattended with pleasure; and I had an active
mind which would have been miserable in idleness, and which courted difficulties for the pleasure of overcoming them.[2]

Marshall, Dr. Rimmer tells us, was 'temperamentally too reserved to enjoy

[1] R. S. Fitton and A. P. Wadsworth, op. cit., p. 145.
[2] Rimmer, op. cit., pp. 20–21.

the company of others and his domineering manner daunted them'; he confessed to having suffered as a youth from acute loneliness and 'deep dejection of spirits'; he married a Unitarian wife who was of a related family; he promoted educational schemes; he was, of course, immensely energetic; and he supported Free Trade.[1]

If John Marshall and Samuel Courtauld had such socio-psychological traits in common, the firms which they built also shared certain characteristics of capital structure. After the purchase or construction of a mill and the furnishing of it with machinery had been completed, so that the enterprise was initially under way, the value of stocks held accounted for a very substantial part of the total assets of the business.[2] This was far from being confined to these firms. Just as at Courtauld & Co. the value of stocks was consistently well above that of fixed assets from the 1830s to 1869,[3] so at Foster's Black Dyke Mills the most important single item of the firm's assets until 1862 consisted of 'stocks of raw materials, materials in process of manufacture and stocks of yarn and piece goods awaiting sale'.[4] A similar situation sometimes prevailed even in mining and metal firms, often regarded as especial examples of heavy fixed capital investment. Nor was this the only financial characteristic which Courtauld & Co. shared with other firms in their early years. The importance of family deposits and of trade credit—revealed in the high negative figures for net indebtedness and the low cash and security reserves in the 1830s and 1840s[5]—was exactly paralleled at Black Dyke Mills, and has been commented upon in other businesses of the age, in copper and cotton, in glass and pottery.[6] And the perils and difficulties of short-term credit accommodation were making themselves felt to William Balston, trying to set up and run his new paper mill at Maidstone, at about the same time as they were to Samuel Courtauld at Bocking.[7]

These features of finance, in Courtauld & Co. as in other firms, cannot fail to remind the historian of the procedures of an earlier community, of Tudor or Stuart industry for example. It is easy to move to the generalization that it was the existence of a credit system, of merchants and middlemen, friends and bankers, suppliers of materials and buyers of products,

---

[1] Rimmer, op. cit., pp. 15–22, 68 and n. 1, 102–10, and *passim*.   [2] Ibid., p. 313.

[3] Above, pp. 108–9, 135–7.   [4] E. M. Sigsworth, *Black Dyke Mills* (Liverpool, 1958), p. 223.

[5] Above, Table 12, p. 108.

[6] Sigsworth, op. cit., p. 227; S. Pollard, 'Fixed Capital in the Industrial Revolution in Britain', *Journal of Economic History*, vol. xxiv, No. 3 (September 1964), pp. 305–7.

[7] D. C. Coleman, *The British Paper Industry, 1495–1860* (Oxford, 1958), pp. 252–3; T. Balston, *William Balston—Paper Maker, 1759–1848* (London, 1954), pp. 53–54, 67–83, etc.

that allowed the smaller firm to enter the industry 'with only a small fraction of the capital it ultimately used and in this way to accumulate enough to enlarge the base of its operations, until perhaps in due course it had sufficient to become, in turn, a net lender'.[1] But we have, first, to ask why the new entrants were so readily granted credit; and, second, to consider how, as tiny firms, they managed so to succeed as to be able to accumulate further capital in industries in which larger units were continually appearing by this very process and, apparently, making the smaller units uneconomical.

The answer to the former question lies in the possession of previous experience somewhere in the industry, or in some related trade, and of personal connexions with responsible figures within its ranks. It was in such credit-giving that the network of personal acquaintance engendered by membership of the same church or chapel or meeting-house was of such importance. The local Unitarian church may well have covertly added not only marriage market but also credit market to its overtly spiritual functions. Samuel Courtauld got experience, business contacts, and money from his throwster father; so did John Marshall from his flax-spinning father; Jedediah Strutt got backing for his hosiery knitting machine from his fellow Dissenter, the wealthy Nottingham hosier, Samuel Need; William Balston had been apprenticed to the greatest paper-maker of his day, James Whatman, and got some of his finance from Whatman's widow and brother; John Dickinson set up his paper mills in the nineteenth century with money made in his stationery business into which he had been helped by a loan from his former master, the printer Andrew Strachan; and William Lever learnt about soap from working in his father's grocery business.[2]

The answer to the second question lies in the very heterogeneity of what we regard as an industry. Far more industries than today must then have contained units with varying cost-structures. That this could be so was a consequence sometimes of the legislated protection of tariffs which sheltered them from foreign competition, sometimes of the natural protection of poor communication and imperfect markets which meant in effect that even within the same country different firms in different regions were almost in different economies. Although in the long focus of

[1] Pollard, 'Fixed Capital . . .', op. cit., p. 309.
[2] Rimmer, op. cit., pp. 22–23; Fitton and Wadsworth, op. cit., pp. 38–39; Balston, op. cit., pp. 53–118; Coleman, op. cit., pp. 235–6, 244; Charles Wilson, *The History of Unilever* (2 vols., London, 1954), vol. i, pp. 22–24.

history the Industrial Revolution in Britain was a rapid economic transformation, in the shorter focus of the period it was a slow process for one industry to be totally transformed. Thus at any one time, certainly before the railways had really begun to integrate England into one economy—a task hardly completed by the mid nineteenth century—an industry could readily contain large and small units, old and new techniques, high-cost firms and low-cost firms, all in varying degrees able to make a living. So long as small units with relatively inexpensive technical plant offered an opportunity for entry, so could new men, the able along with the incompetent, the brightly ambitious future tycoon side by side with the dullard, make their start in manufacturing business; gain their experience with their small capitals, and, with fortune prevailing, accumulate savings and secure the confidence of the credit-givers. It was precisely by this procedure, rather than by the mere existence of a credit network, that Samuel Courtauld, in a firm which had protection both natural and artificial, could start up in Panfield Lane with two old men and a boy turning his throwing mills, almost a hundred years after water-powered throwing had come to this country.

Thereafter, he could move ahead with the aid, and again like John Marshall, of the money released by his father's death. Later, in 1828, he drew in the vitally necessary capital for the crucial stage of expansion from outside, from what probably was an essentially mercantile source, Andrew Taylor. In this sequence, Samuel Courtauld was following very well-worn trails of early English industrial finance. In renting, rather than buying, Savill's mill at Bocking, he was only doing what generations of entrepreneurs in mill-using industries had been doing for centuries. As ancient corn mills or fulling mills were turned to new uses—the slitting mills and water-powered forges and furnaces of the early iron industry, paper mills, the new power-driven cotton spinning mills, silk-throwing mills, and more besides—so was the initial renting of premises commonly followed, as it was in Courtauld & Co., by purchase, by expansion with the help of mortgages, loans, trade credit, and by ploughing-back from what was frequently a high rate of profit. It was the ability to finance this secondary stage of development which was crucial in an age of changing technology. Without a continuing flow of effective modernization survival was impossible. Getting in was easy, staying in much harder. Not only did Samuel Courtauld & Co. stay in and move to the top of their particular tree, but they did it in an area quite remote from the coal and iron resources of industrializing England.

Here, then, is an element of the seemingly untypical. Samuel Courtauld & Co. in north Essex were one of a small number of firms which survived or were developed successfully in the non-industrialized areas of England. The textile industry in general provides a number of examples, such as the Heathcotes in Devon, or J. & T. Clark at Trowbridge in Wiltshire. The gradual process of industrial concentration which in the course of the nineteenth century saw the disappearance of many small manufacturing firms—makers of woollens and worsteds, silk throwsters, weavers, tiny iron works or paper mills in remote valleys—left a few firms high and dry but remote from the great industrial centres on the coalfields of the Midlands and north. The explanation of these survivals must vary widely: partly it lay in unusual entrepreneurial skill, which Samuel Courtauld certainly exemplified; partly in the *comparative* slowness of technical change, so that Clarks at Trowbridge, for example, did not install power-looms for their woollen cloth until 1861,[1] nor, similarly, did the hand-loom weaving side of Courtauld & Co.'s business become insignificant to them until the 1860s; partly it lay in the development of special products; and partly in that variety of cost-structures permitted by the absence of national economic homogeneity—against higher transport costs, higher fuel costs, and various possible disadvantages of inaccessibility could be set lower wages, lower rents and site values, and perhaps a more docile and malleable labour force. For Courtaulds as for other silk firms, the light power demands of their machinery meant that coal was not a major item in production costs, whereas their techniques made labour and raw silk costs the dominating factors. All the crape firms which survived to the end of the century were in low-wage areas—Hindes, Grouts, and the Norwich Crape Co. in Norfolk, Courtaulds in Essex, Le Gros, Thompson in Somerset. The one which survived best was the nearest to London: the commercial centre of raw material supplies and the greatest mart for a commodity whose sales depended on the fashions of the Court and the upper and middle classes, and on exports.

If in the first half of the nineteenth century the establishment, early finance, and growth of the Courtauld enterprise shows some familiar patterns, its experience in the second half of the century again conforms in some ways, though certainly not in all, to the familiar outlines of English industrial change in this period. The high prosperity of the 1850s

[1] R. P. Beckinsale (ed.), *The Trowbridge Woollen Industry as Illustrated by the Stock Books of John and Thomas Clark* (Wiltshire Archaeological and Natural History Society, vol. vi, Devizes, 1951), p. xix.

to the 1870s, the 'Great Depression', changes in production and markets in the course of recovery, the coming of the joint-stock company, rising wages, and the appearance of trade unions: here they all are. Timing and details were often different. The experience of falling sales and prices comes in the eighties rather than the usual seventies; within the silk industry the firm is exceptional in expanding whilst many fall by the wayside. If in general its history at this time suggests no radical reorientation of accepted patterns, does the nature of its experience shed light on the character or causation of those patterns?

The fall in crape prices after 1885 was something dictated by the market. There is no evidence of any cost-reducing innovations significantly to reduce prices in the crape trade at that time. Although Hindes seemed to be underselling Courtaulds in certain lines in 1889, competition was primarily in finish, quality, and design of figure. Imports were virtually non-existent. Though some of the drop in Courtauld's sales may have been losses to rivals, the company must still have been the dominant firm. Though there was in the eighties some change in fashion away from crape, the company was still able to sell a record amount in 1899—at lower prices. Some of those record sales must have been gains from rivals. But there was evidently still a substantial aggregate demand for crape; not until after 1900 was this markedly declining. So the falling prices and, to some extent at least, the falling sales represented real consumer resistance to mourning crape at prevailing prices. Why had this developed? Changing trends in fashion were only part of the answer. A marginal expenditure by, mainly, the middle and upper classes, hitherto fairly inelastic to both income and price, was now acquiring an unexpected elasticity of demand. This accords with what has been said in general terms, e.g. by Rostow, in considering the forces making for lower prices: '. . . demand curves for particular firms and British industries became more elastic'.[1] But the nature of the product—a consumer good for a fashionable ritual—and the timing of the fall in prices—some ten years after the main break in prices—combine strongly to suggest a secondary spread of price resistance, following earlier examples in more important goods and operating partly through reductions in income and partly through a sort of inverse 'demonstration-effect'. Lowered incomes resulting from falling rents and profits may well have induced some members of the crape-buying classes to be more economical in their mourning. Moreover, having seen the prices of other fabrics fall, for example, soft silks affected by the flow of imports

[1] W. W. Rostow, *British Economy of the Nineteenth Century* (Oxford, 1948), p. 70.

after 1860, consumers began to regard the prevailing crape prices as excessive. Purchases were reduced, and then sharper competition, in prices as
well as in quality or design, began among the few producers.

It may well have been by some such process as this that the price fall made
itself felt over such an extraordinarily wide range of goods. The lead was
given, for various familiar reasons, by grains, iron and steel, cotton; so
curious and marginal a commodity as mourning crape must presumably
have been somewhere near the end of a chain of reactions, working
through reduced incomes and expectations of falling prices, and affecting
a widening range of consumer goods. It is well known that the physical
volume of sales or output of many goods did not fall as did prices, indeed
it often rose throughout the period of the 'Great Depression'. For goods
which entered into wide, general consumption, price-elasticity or income-
elasticity, working through higher real wages, soon brought renewed and
increased consumption after an initial brief stagnation in the late 1870s.
For goods selling on markets sharply limited by social distinctions, however, this took much longer to operate. It needed improved sales methods
as well as cost-reducing innovations to get Courtauld's sales of crape
expanding in the 1890s.

The shocks administered by the market, to Courtauld & Co. as to many
other British firms, hit profits and prices founded upon the country's
near monopoly of world business in manufacturing industry. Although
numerous general remarks bemoaned the fall in profits, very little was
heard of the rate of profits prevailing before this seeming catastrophe.
Nor indeed has much been subsequently dredged from surviving business
records, so there is little with which to compare the Courtauld figures.
Where comparison is possible, some remarkable similarities, as well as
certain dissimilarities, of rate and sequence emerge, as shown in Table 37.

The two firms could hardly have been more different: Scottish iron-
founders and Essex crape makers. If these figures were taken as representative of the general position in British manufacturing industry, they
would seem to confirm both the seriousness of the shock and the prosperity before the fall. It would, however, be dangerous to accept such rates
as necessarily typical. The products of both firms possessed certain special
characteristics; neither firm was in a branch of industry in which easy entry
permitted continuous and effective competition. In cotton spinning—a
much more competitive industry, comprising a large number of firms—
average profits in the later 1860s were said to be about $12\frac{1}{2}$ per cent.; the
accounts of the well-known cotton spinner, Henry Ashworth, offer

approximate confirmation for they show an average of about 14 per cent. (including interest) at this time.[1] It is hard to know what the representative rate may have been. But it is equally hard to believe that this famous period of Victorian prosperity owed little or nothing to relatively high rates of industrial earnings. In so far as a significant share of the British business community was content in a situation in which comfortable and acceptable rates could readily be earned then the urge to innovate was blunted.

TABLE 37

Percentage profits: Samuel Courtauld & Co. and Carron Company,
1868–1902

Five-year period	Carron Company[2] Average annual profits as percentage of nominal capital	Samuel Courtauld & Co. Average annual profits and interest as percentage of capital
1868–72	38·3	35·0
1873–7	38·9	37·8
1878–82	25·9	27·2
1883–7	10·6	27·1
1888–92	9·9	10·7
1893–7	33·3	1·5
1898–1902	35·1	9·1

With little competition from overseas the wish to cut costs, reduce prices, and seek wider markets did not present itself as urgent. It may well have been this very prosperity in the high noon of Britain's economic dominance that obstructed the coming of the mass market. Certainly in Courtauld & Co. and in Carron Company there was room for cuts in both profits and prices. Only in the timing of change and the extent of recovery do the two firms' profits records show marked divergence. The reasons for the late impact of the depression on Courtauld & Co. have already been considered. The Carron Company's recovery reflected technical improvements and the arrival of new men in control earlier than in Courtaulds, as well as the more advantageous position of iron than silk in the British economy.[3] Courtauld & Co.'s real recovery, and far more than that, its transformation, had to wait for rayon in the twentieth century. Even

[1] J. Watts, *The Facts of the Cotton Famine* (London, 1866), p. 342; for the information on Henry Ashworth's profits I am grateful to Mr. Rhodes Boyson.

[2] R. H. Campbell, *Carron Company* (Edinburgh, 1961), pp. 334–6.

[3] Ibid., pp. 240 et seq.

the Carron recovery in 1893–1902 did not produce the profit rates of 1868–77.

If so much in these crucial decades of crisis was a product of a peculiar economic conjuncture, not readily apparent to contemporary business-men, grappling as they necessarily were with immediate problems, how much are they to be blamed? We are back to the problem of responsibility already considered in Chapter VIII. Here, certainly, the experience of Samuel Courtauld & Co. seems to have been shared by many a firm. The British entrepreneur in the second half of the nineteenth century has come in for some hard knocks. For all sorts of industries—iron and steel, rail-ways or cotton, tinplate, chemicals, or shipping—evidence has been amassed of failure to keep up to date in techniques, of a conservatism in business practice often engendered or aided by the insidiously cramping influence of the family firm, of a take-it-or-leave-it attitude in commerce, of a powerfully seductive lure to interests outside those of business.[1] Already in 1879 the U.S. Consul in so busy an industrial centre as Brad-ford was reporting thus:

The channel of commerce is changing . . . instead of changing with the stream, English manufacturers continue to sit upon the bank of the old water-course and argue from plausible but unprofitable scientific and commercial premises that it had no right to alter . . .

By reason of England's intelligence and capital and by reason of the condition of foreign industries, Great Britain for a long time held the monopoly of manu-factures, so long in fact that she came to consider herself invulnerable in that direction; but in manufacture, as in science, the pupil not infrequently surpasses his master, and we now see America, France and Germany emulating their instructor in the world's markets. . . .[2]

Whether we look at the total failure of John Marshall's sons to run the business created by their father, and the final ignominious end of the once great mills under the auctioneer's hammer in 1886;[3] or the 'un-willingness to accept innovation either in the design of ships or in the well-tried methods of commercial procedure' which bedevilled Holt's Ocean Steam Ship Company in the 1870s and 1880s;[4] or at George

---

[1] See the evidence summarized in D. H. Aldcroft, 'The Entrepreneur and the British Economy, 1870–1914', *Econ. Hist. Rev.*, 2nd series, vol. xvii, No. 1, August 1964, pp. 113–34.

[2] Quoted in J. Potter, 'The British Trade in Timber since 1850' (unpublished M.A. thesis, Manchester University, 1949), p. 108 n. I am grateful to my colleague for drawing my attention to this quotation in his thesis. [3] Rimmer, op. cit., pp. 296–7.

[4] F. E. Hyde, *Blue Funnel: a History of Alfred Holt & Company of Liverpool from 1865 to 1914* (Liverpool University Press, 1956), p. 55.

Courtauld III's ultimately satisfied longing to get out of business and become a country gentleman: these and similar examples seem to lay a heavy burden of blame on a certain generation of British businessmen. Was this generation so peculiarly full of entrepreneurially guilty men? And if so, why?

It is not the business of this book to answer these questions. But before we accept too readily a thoroughgoing theory of entrepreneurial deficiency certain explanatory suggestions may be worth making. It is perhaps worth noting at the outset that exceptions to the picture of feebleness do exist. In the glass industry, for example, the second generation of Pilkingtons amply continued the vigorous entrepreneurial ability of their fathers, and in an industry similarly marked by falling prices, their firm not merely survived but expanded whilst 'all their long-established rivals succumbed'.[1] It is also worth emphasizing that the removal of businessmen to other pursuits was so very far from being unique to a particular generation as in fact to have been common form for centuries. So if one castigates successful mid-Victorian businessmen for quitting their offices and factories, one is only blaming them for following a long-established English custom. Perhaps the real trouble lay in a particular, and unfortunate, socio-economic conjuncture. The high hey-day of our Victorian industrial and commercial supremacy, with its massive 'monopoly' profits, facilitating rapid accumulations of wealth, happened largely to coincide with the last great period of prestige for the English landowning classes. Furthermore, apart from railways and overseas investment (itself largely in foreign Government bonds and still more railways) there were very few accessible outlets for industrial savings because of the near-absence of public joint-stock companies in British industry. Some profits were ploughed back in order to maintain them at their currently comfortable level, and naturally they went into well-tried and proven plant and methods. Courtauld & Co.'s investment habits in their prosperous years must have had many counterparts. And there were still ample margins over for—what? The monetary yield of land was derisory compared with that of successful business. But its social and political prestige was as immense as ever and its economic safety still seemed assured. 'A wealthy millowner would well be content with such a bargain, giving him the status of country gentleman, a seat on the bench, sport for his sons when home from Eton and Cambridge, "the sherrifalty, a squeeze of the hand from the Lord Lieutenant, the county balls for his wife and daughters, and perhaps an opening to the

[1] T. C. Barker, *Pilkington Brothers and the Glass Industry* (London, 1960), p. 165.

House of Commons".'¹ Whatever the precise motives, social or psychological, of Samuel Courtauld's investment in Gosfield Hall and its acres or of George III's in Cut Hedge and its surrounding lands, the resemblance to the phenomenon so described in *The Economist* in 1867 is obvious enough. A different example on a larger scale comes from the Fosters of Black Dyke Mills. By 1867 the firm's fixed assets were of small significance compared with nearly £700,000 of investments, mainly in railways and foreign securities; and between 1860 and 1873 five partner members of the family firm bought estates to a total value of nearly £710,000.² The 'Great Depression' brought change, in this field, as in so many others. In a din of falling rents and reform of the franchise the great days of prestige and power for the landed interest waned. At the same time the use of joint-stock in manufacturing increased; more investment and more entrepreneurial energy were needed in a world of competition and new techniques; new managers and directors came in, as did Tetley and Latham to Courtaulds. Though the drift into landed dignity continued, it was no longer so formidable a trap; land's seeming safety had been nastily shaken; there were other ways to political power. Though some industrial barons built up substantial estates in the 1880s and 1890s—Samuel Cunliffe-Lister, Lord Masham, and Edward Guinness, Lord Iveagh, for example—the acquisition of land 'was no longer the obligatory step towards a peerage which it had once been'.³ Business was still not quite respectable, but it was nearer to it than when Britain was the 'workshop of the world'. If we seek to blame the British entrepreneur—and throw in some examples from Samuel Courtauld & Co. to add to the evidential weight—for myopia and complacency in the decades before the depression, we must recall again those social tensions of what Bagehot called the 'deferential community', the very tensions which had helped to give an edge to economic ambitions and bring monetary rewards to business skills. The entrepreneur is not a peculiar animal to be judged by abstract criteria of economic efficiency; he is moral man, *moyen sensuel*, a creature of his environment.

Yet, however we choose to regard the men of Samuel Courtauld & Co.'s last partnership before the joint-stock company of 1891, however we ponder their actions in the light of the contemporary situation, it is instructive to take a final look at the firm's long-term curve of output

---

¹ F. M. L. Thompson, *English Landed Society in the Nineteenth Century* (London, 1963), p. 254, quoting *The Economist* of 1867. See also H. J. Habakkuk, *American and British Technology in the Nineteenth Century* (Cambridge, 1962), pp. 177–8.

² Sigsworth, op. cit., pp. 223–5 n.   ³ Thompson, op. cit., pp. 297–8.

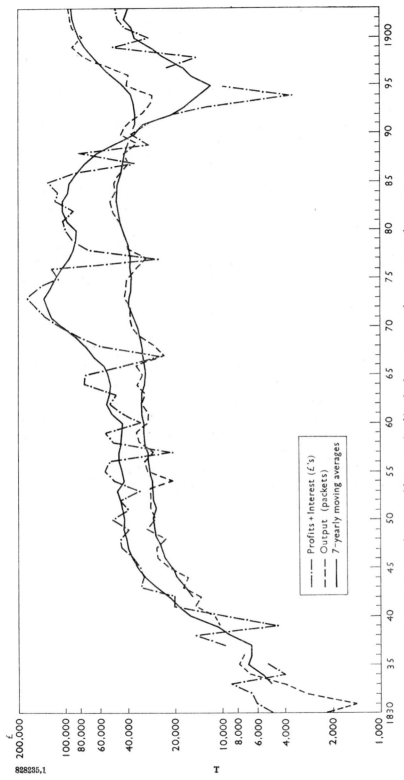

£

200,000

100,000
80,000

60,000

40,000

20,000

10,000
8,000

6,000

4,000

2,000

1,000

1830   35   40   45   50   55   60   65   70   75   80   85   90   95   1900

- · - · Profits + Interest (£'s)
- - - - Output (packets)
——— 7-yearly moving averages

FIG. 26. Samuel Courtauld & Co. (Ltd.): the long-term trend—earnings and output, 1830–1903

T

and profits. Fig. 26 presents the record of nearly three-quarters of a century. The very rapid rate of initial growth is a common enough phenomenon, as is the phase of consolidation thereafter. More remarkable, however, is the slow growth in output in the prosperous quarter-century from 1860 to 1885. Between 1861–5 and 1881–5, output (as measured by numbers of packets finished) rose by only 41 per cent., but average profits rose by 87 per cent. As we have seen, much of this windfall was attributable to the sharp drop in raw silk prices. Just as it was one market which broke crape prices after 1885 so it was another which had done much to present the firm with the high profits of the lush years. With such a gift what was the point of expanding output? If the profits had not been so high we cannot be sure that the financial resources of the firm would have been strong enough to carry on through the bleak decade 1886–96. On the other hand, had the profits been lower, complacency might have been less evident and a search for reduced costs and wider markets more urgently prosecuted. We cannot know.

In another twenty years, from 1881–5 to 1901–5, the volume of total output rose by 105 per cent. This increase in the growth rate, across the hazardous negotiation of the depression years, was achieved almost wholly by the new business in colours. Crape output increased by a mere 14 per cent.: the boom year of 1899 was a final flash in the crape pan. But if new men and new fabrics seemed the recipe of success, it is salutory finally to note that between 1881–5 and 1901–5 profits *fell* by 60 per cent. For all the strength of the recovery, for all the work of the new men, *crêpe* as a substitute for crape was only a very partial success. This was the harsh prelude to the search for artificial silk.

Index

Courtauld (*cont.*):

— Catherine I, 101; marries, 34, 208; bears fourteen children, 34.

— (Taylor), Catherine II, 115; supervises girls' labour, 43–4; marries Peter Alfred Taylor I, 51; joins father in Ohio, 51, 114; returns from U.S.A., 70–1; in Ostend, 54; as widow and sleeping partner, 144; as Unitarian, 204.

— Christophe, *marinier*, and origins of the family, 2; as Huguenot, 2.

— Eliza, supervises girls' labour, 43–4; joins father in U.S.A., 51; marries, and returns to England, 70.

— (Taylor), Ellen, marries Samuel Courtauld III, 56; and husband, 123–4, 128; trip to Europe, 104; and welfare, 205, 255–6; her death, 123.

— George I, 21, 56–7, 174; his education, 33, 213; and Peter Merzeau, 8, 33–6; his character, 33, 47, 214.

debut in silk industry, 8, 12, 21, 32; return to England, 36; in paper industry, 37; established in silk industry at Pebmarsh, 37–8, 208; and crape in East Anglia, 21, 37; in business with Joseph Wilson, as Wilson & Courtauld, 38–44, 49–50, 70; legal action and dissolution of partnership, 40, 50.

inept at business, 40 ff., 51, 262; his technical ability, 39, 121, 213; spindle patent, 39, 64–5, 78–9, 117.

and labour, 42–3, 91, 100, 232.

his politics: republicanism, 33, 37, 216–18, 229; sympathy with French revolution, 37, and with American revolution, 37, 216–17; and Unitarianism, 33, 204–5, 215.

journeys to U.S.A., 34, 51, 216–17; as farmer, 36, 51, 214, 217.

and wife Ruth, 34–6, 44; union with Taylor family, 34; discord in the family, 44–7, 50–2, 56; and daughters: Catherine, 43, Eliza, 43, 51, Louisa, 43, Sophia, 43, 50–1; and Samuel Courtauld III, 44–8, 65, 124, 214, 261, 264; finances Samuel Courtauld III, 56–60, 64–5, 110; and George Courtauld II, 51; and Nouaille, 36–7, 70; and P. A. Taylor, 113; and Witts & Co., 37; and John Minton, 51; and Beuzeville, 204.

his death, 52–3, 64, 70.

— George II, 53, 55, 112, 116; goes with father to U.S.A., 51, and returns, 70–1; on parents, 204; and mother, 53; his five children, 116; and his sons, 207; his character, 116–20, 204, 213; technical

aptitude, 65, 76, 92, 116–17; and Steam Factory, 71, 78, 90, 142; at Bocking, 70, 92; and Samuel Courtauld III, 55, 64–5, 70–1, 117, 119, 121–3, 217; capital in Samuel Courtauld & Co., 73; and P. A. Taylor, 112–16, 226; and James Finney, 142.

and labour, 205, 248 ff., 255.

death in 1861, 116, 120, 144.

— George III, 150; his education, 207, 209; enters business, 116; as partner, 146; in control of firm, 149–50; tries new techniques, 167, 171–2; directorate at Bocking, 180; and 'outsider' Tetley, 181; his income in 1871–90, 176–7; his shares in 1891, 178; and expansion, 200; and father, 126, 249; and Samuel Courtauld III, 126–7, 175–6; and P. A. Taylor, 116; and Samuel Augustine Courtauld II, 182; on employment at Samuel Courtauld & Co., 143; on labour, 250, 253, 255–9; 'reluctant businessman', 174–6, 182–3, 201, 213; plans to retire, 182–3, 201.

his political activity and in Parliament, 205, 209, 229; holds public offices, 209; as 'country gentleman', 176, at Cut Hedge estate, 272.

wealth at death, 213.

— John Minton, 51, 71, 110, 207–8; considered as partner, 144; his marriages, 207–8; and son, 148; his personality, 148; his death, 148.

— Julien, as chemist, 148; his premature death, 148.

— Louis, 149 n., 207.

— Louisa Perina, 208; daughter of silk weaver, 7; with Cowles as goldsmith, 5; in partnership with son Samuel II, 5, 8; and son George Courtauld I, 8; her death, 5.

— Louisa Perina II, supervises girls' labour, 43–4; discord with father, 45; governess in Edinburgh, 51; as Unitarian, 204.

— Peter, as goldsmith, 3–5; his death, 5.

— Pierre, 2.

— Ruth, 56, 113; marries George Courtauld I, 34; and eight children, 34; separation from husband contemplated, 44; discord in family, 51–2, 214; and Samuel Courtauld III, 53, 126.

— Samuel I, as goldsmith, 3–5; freeman of Goldsmiths Company, 5; as Huguenot, 7; his death, 5.

— Samuel II, 34; as goldsmith in partnership with mother, 5, 8; sells business and emigrates to U.S.A., and dies there, 5, 8.

— Samuel III, 1, 120, 135; his birth, 45.

PRINTED IN GREAT BRITAIN
AT THE UNIVERSITY PRESS, OXFORD
BY VIVIAN RIDLER
PRINTER TO THE UNIVERSITY